Keep 2/09 ED

THE GILBERT AND SULLIVAN BOOK

ALSO BY LESLIE BAILY

BOOKS

The BBC Scrapbooks
The Yorkshire Radio Book
Travellers' Tales

RADIO SCRIPTS

*Gilbert & Sullivan, the Scrapbooks, As It Might Have Been, Star-Gazing,
The Story Behind The Show, There's A Song About It, South With Shackleton,
Elgar and Land of Hope and Glory, Three Tales From Tibet,
The Trial of William Penn, The Schubert Discoveries,
The Life of Leslie Stuart, The Wonderful Year 1851,
Leslie Baily's Log Book, etc.*

TELEVISION

First Time Ever

CINEMA

Scrapbook for 1922 (with Peter Baylis)
Scrapbook for 1933 (with Peter Baylis and Jack Howells)
The Story of Gilbert and Sullivan (with Sidney Gilliat)

THE
GILBERT AND SULLIVAN
BOOK

LESLIE BAILY

SPRING BOOKS · LONDON

Originally published 1952 by Cassell and Company Limited
Copyright 1952 Leslie Baily
Revised edition 1956
This edition published 1966 by Spring Books
Drury House · Russell Street · London WC2

Printed in Great Britain by Fletcher & Son Ltd, Norwich
and bound by
Richard Clay (The Chaucer Press) Ltd, Bungay, Suffolk.

DEDICATION

To the memory of the greatest partnership in the history of entertainment:

GILBERT – SULLIVAN – CARTE

JACK POINT: *For, look you, there is humour in all things, and the truest philosophy is that which teaches us to find it and to make the most of it.*

W. S. Gilbert,
THE YEOMEN OF THE GUARD.

There are so many things I want to do for Music, if God will give me two days for every one in which to do them.

Arthur Sullivan,
in a letter to his mother.

The starting of English comic opera in a theatre devoted to that alone was the scheme of my life.

Richard D'Oyly Carte.

Woodcut by Gilbert

PREFACE TO THE 1966 EDITION

by Leslie Baily

The worst that the Gilbert and Sullivan Traditionalists feared has now happened. All restrictions on productions of these classics have gone; "modernising" has begun. When in 1956 I wrote the ensuing chapter *Jazzed-up Gilbert and Syncopated Sullivan* I questioned what would happen after the expiry of copyright, and reported loud alarms that vandals would desecrate the holy temple. What, in fact, has happened? On 1 January 1962, the first day after copyright's end, the Sadler's Wells Opera Company presented its version of *Iolanthe*, since seen in Stuttgart, Hamburg, West Berlin, Frankfurt, Munich, Amsterdam, Vienna, and Prague. Producer Frank Hauser had never seen a Savoy Opera, so tradition counted for little, but changes were in style of presentation, not in Gilbert's words and Sullivan's music. The general effect was refreshing. A Sadler's Wells *Mikado* (producer Douglas Craig) followed. Sir Tyrone Guthrie showed London his Canadian versions of *HMS Pinafore* and *The Pirates of Penzance*.

New minds have brought out afresh the sterling merits of Messrs Gilbert and Sullivan, though these new versions tended occasionally to press the comedy over-hard. The D'Oyly Carte Company has itself been re-styling some of the operas, and has obviously lost nothing by the new competition of (say) a British film *The Cool Mikado* in which (to quote its producers) "Gangsters, sexy girls, art students, and twist sessions transform the staid traditional presentation". Another film is a cartoon version of *Ruddigore* made by the witty Halas and Batchelor, with sound-track by the D'Oyly Carte Company and the London Philharmonic Orchestra.

Whatever may yet come, Guthrie summed the whole matter up on television when he said there will always be wild and woolly interpretations, but—"If they are the stuff of which classics are made the Savoy Operas will stand up to a bit of mauling. Shakespeare and Verdi, Heaven knows, have been plenty mauled about. They emerge stronger from the tussle, more admirable not less. I think that it is much better for works of art to be re-interpreted in all manner of ways, some of them possibly very silly and in very bad taste, than for them to be preserved in the aspic of a carefully maintained routine."

CONTENTS

vii

CONTENTS

COLOUR PLATES

(Between pages 246–247)

Sullivan – Carte – Gilbert. Cartoons by Ape and Spy.

Princess Ida re-dressed in 1954: James Wade's costume design
for King Hildebrand

Playbill of Sullivan's first comic opera, *Contrabandista*. Twenty years later:
the D'Oyly Carte Opera Company tours Germany

Illustrations from the programme of the Children's Company production of
The Pirates of Penzance

Designs for *Patience* by George Sheringham, 1929. An original design by
Wilhelm for *Ruddigore*, 1887, and Peter Goffin's new costumes, 1948

The cover and an inside page of the programme for *The Mikado* in 1885

Drop curtain for *The Yeomen of the Guard* designed by Peter Goffin in 1939;
One of Percy Anderson's sketches for the re-dressing of this opera in 1919

Cover of the souvenir programme for *Ivanhoe*

Special programme for the Royal Command performance of *The Gondoliers*,
before Queen Victoria

George Sheringham's designs for *The Pirates of Penzance*, 1929;
Percy Anderson's sketches for a revival of *Utopia* in the 1920's

Charles Ricketts' original designs for the new presentation of *The Mikado* in 1926

ix

An innovation by Miss Bridget D'Oyly Carte in 1954: She and her Director of Productions, Mr Robert Gibson, discuss the complete redesigning of 'Princess Ida' with the artist, Mr James Wade

And, below, an innovation by Miss D'Oyly Carte's grandfather 70 years earlier: electric light at the Savoy

THE TIMES, FRIDAY, AUGUST 31, 1883.

SAVOY THEATRE.--Proprietor and Manager, Mr. D'Oyly Carte.—Every night, at 8.40, the original Fairy Opera, in two acts, the words by W. S. Gilbert, the music by Arthur Sullivan, IOLANTHE ; or, the Peer and the Peri. Produced under the personal direction of the author and composer. PRIVATE WIRE, at 8. Doors open at 7.30.

IOLANTHE—278th performance, THIS EVENING. —Electric Star Lights in the Hair are worn by the principals and the whole of the chorus ladies in the last scene.

IOLANTHE. — MORNING PERFORMANCE every Saturday, at 2.30.—SAVOY.

SAVOY.—The only theatre lighted entirely by electric light, securing perfectly PURE and COOL AIR. The highest points touched by Hick's registering thermometers during the performance on Wednesday evening were :—Stalls, 73½deg. ; pit, 74½deg. ; balcony, 74deg. ; circle, 74deg. ; gallery, 74deg., the highest point in the street during the 24 hours being 75deg. in the shade.

FOREWORD

THE DEATH of Gilbert and Sullivan (meaning their comic operas) is much exaggerated. It has been pronounced and prophesied by many people for a good many years—in fact, ever since the ending more than half a century ago of a most brilliant collaboration. Yet Lytton Strachey's rather startling prophecy that the most permanent and enduring achievement of the Victorian Age would prove to be these genial satires looks like coming true as we enter the second half of the twentieth century. So much else that seemed important or significant in Queen Victoria's reign has crumbled and faded. Nothing in the whole range of popular entertainment has been enjoyed by so many people for so long. As I write, seventy-six years after Richard D'Oyly Carte sent his first opera company to New York, a D'Oyly Carte company is touring in America—the only British theatrical company playing British works which regularly visits the U.S.A. The traffic in entertainment nowadays is usually in the opposite direction.

On both sides of the Atlantic there is every sign of enduring vitality, and on the English side there is every reason to expect an increase in public interest in the Gilbert and Sullivan operas with the expiry of their copyright in 1961, for reasons discussed later in this book.

After the first publication of *The Gilbert and Sullivan Book* in 1952 I received letters from readers all over the world, itself a mark of widespread interest and enthusiasm. The magic spell of the works of Gilbert and Sullivan is not only world-wide: it cuts clean across class divisions. Some of the letters were on coronet-headed notepaper; many came from humble folk like this:

Deal, Kent.

Dear Sir,

This may seem a strange letter to you, but please accept it all in good faith as it is written and please forgive scribble and grammar, it's from an old coal-miner who loves music. My wife and I have heard your Gilbert and Sullivan life story on the BBC. Since then, sir, we have spent a few pounds on records of the songs, we love them all; we went to the Savoy in London to see and hear *The Mikado* and *The Gondoliers*, also we have been to Folkestone on several occasions to hear various works of G. & S. Now sir, my favour I ask is this—I would like to know where I could buy a pair of small miniature busts of Gilbert and Sullivan. You know the kind one sees in music shops, of Bach and Chopin. I have tried all the shops here.

Before I close, sir, allow me to thank you for your *G. and S. Book*, it is one of my treasures.

May you be allowed to keep giving us pleasure.

Goodnight, sir,

C. WM. C.

xi

This letter alone was worth all the effort that went into the writing of *The Gilbert and Sullivan Book*. There were other readers who pointed out errors which had slipped through the sieve of the very extensive research that I had done. These are now corrected. There were letters offering me further historical matter. Mr Reginald Allen, Business Administrator of the Metropolitan Opera, New York, has been especially generous in giving access to his private collection of Gilbert and Sullivan documents. Then, after the book was published new developments occurred, among them a revival of *Princess Ida* breaking very considerably with the traditional presentation and pointing towards greater changes that will come in 1961. The idea of a new volume which should compass the additional information, bringing the whole story up to date and looking forward to 1961, now matures with this enlarged and completely revised edition. I ask the indulgence of those who sent corrections that I have not accepted; there are some details (such as the year of Sullivan's first meeting with Gilbert) on which available evidence is conflicting. In such cases I have drawn what appears to me the most likely conclusion.

The fabulous story of Gilbert, Sullivan, and D'Oyly Carte becomes more romantic and fabulous the more one looks into it. All three made large fortunes. In Sullivan's case wealth melted away almost as fast as he minted it. A page from his diary (reproduced in the chapter on *The Pirates of Penzance*) shows him earning £10,000 a year in 1880. Later he doubled this; but even £10,000 a year was El Dorado judged by modern values. Roland Bird, deputy editor of *The Economist*, draws my attention to the fact that in present-day money it would represent an income of £35,000 a year. Moreover, the buying power of this sum in 1880 was much greater than it would be now because income tax was then fivepence in the pound.

This is, however, no ordinary backstage success story, to be measured in £.s.d. As my work has continued with the preparation of this present volume, the characters and achievements of these remarkable men have filled out and some misconceptions have been cleared up. Previously, the published information about Richard D'Oyly Carte in particular had been sketchy. The powerful part he played can now be understood, and the sinister assumptions some earlier writers made about his part in the Carpet Quarrel can be dismissed. Documents indicating what really happened were found among the family papers when Miss Bridget D'Oyly Carte was clearing up her late father's estate in 1951; her telephone call inviting me to her office at the Savoy Hotel to see them was one of the dramatic moments in this research work.

If the man in the street knows nothing else about Sullivan and Gilbert he usually knows that they quarrelled over a carpet. But the remarkable thing is not that they quarrelled but that they worked together so well and so long, for they were opposites in temperament—and, oddly enough, that oppositeness was in a measure the secret of their success. If we look at their lives, as this book tries to do, against a background of the social history of their period, we shall see something other than financial riches in their fabulous success, and we shall see something more important than Gilbert and Sullivan opera: we shall recognize a revolution in the whole field of entertainment, a revolution of which they were the main energizing agency.

It was a revolution in the art of the Theatre, it infused a new quality of Humour now known the world over as 'Gilbertian', and it raised Popular Music to a new status. The effect of Britain's leading serious musician, Arthur Sullivan, conducting in the orchestra pit at the Opéra Comique was just as revolutionary as the barbs which Mr Gilbert hurled at Victorian Society. This revolution is not usually credited to the greatness of these men, because its consequences have become the ordinary stuff of our daily lives. We are apt to forget the extent to which Gilbert and Sullivan, with Richard D'Oyly Carte, saved the British and American musical theatre from the tawdriness and vulgarity of the mid-nineteenth century—from the 'vice and indecorum' described by Charles Dickens, who tells us that the respectable middle-classes did not like 'the strong smell of orange peel and lamp-oil, with an undercurrent of sawdust'. The Gilbert-Sullivan-Carte partnership invented a new kind of entertainment. Their sharpness of wit, their musicianship, their sense of satire, their high production standards, set the pace for the Jerome Kerns and Edward Germans, the Cowards and Cochrans and Hammersteins, their followers in this modern age.

I hope that this book will show the true proportions of the achievement. I have quoted extensively from original sources, newspaper reports, autobiographies, eye-witness accounts, diaries, letters, because I want the facts to speak for themselves, to inform the reader of what Sullivan and Gilbert and their contemporaries said and wrote and thought about the operas and about one another. I am deeply indebted to the late Mr Rupert D'Oyly Carte (son of the original impresario) and to his daughter Bridget for giving me free access to the 'bricks and mortar' of history; and likewise to Mrs Elena Bashford and the late Miss Nancy McIntosh, who inherited the personal treasures of Sullivan and Gilbert, to which I have had the privilege of unlimited access. A word of explanation should be given of how these ladies, having no blood relationship with Sullivan and Gilbert, came to inherit their estates.

Arthur Sullivan never married. When his actor-brother Fred died soon after creating the part of the Judge in the original production of *Trial by Jury*, Arthur adopted his child, Herbert, who grew up and married but had no family. When Sir Arthur Sullivan died he left most of his effects to this nephew, and in due course the estate passed to Herbert Sullivan's widow. She married again and is Mrs Elena Bashford. She owns many of the Sullivan letters and documents which are reproduced in this volume.

Like Sullivan, Gilbert had no family and Sir William and Lady Gilbert adopted as their daughter Nancy McIntosh, the leading lady of Gilbert's opera *Utopia Limited* (1893). She lived to a great old age in Kensington, surrounded by the priceless furniture and works of art collected by Sir William Gilbert; surrounded, too, by a host of personal memories of him. Many a time when I was gathering material for *The Gilbert and Sullivan Book* I called upon her, a frail little lady who seemed at first acquaintance like a pathetic, lonely echo drifting back from a statelier age that has gone, a soft note of an echoing voice mingling oddly with the feverish roar of London's traffic outside.

Her manners and dress were those of fifty years ago. She sat over the tea-tray, quiet and gentle; it was difficult to reconcile this lavender lady with one's knowledge that she had once been a lady of comic opera. All the great ones had gone from around her, those who came in their carriages to Grim's Dyke in the far-away time when the Gilberts held court at their mansion at Harrow Weald.

Now she sat here alone, and the soft echoing note of the past seemed infinitely sad until one reminded her of one's mission, then she would turn to a low table at her side—to a pile of Gilbert's diaries or plotbooks or letters that she had carried carefully from the cupboards. Her eyes would light up, and there was gladness in her voice, especially when she found some quotation or anecdote to defend Sir William's memory. Despite failing health and solitude she then seemed a happy woman—and as I looked around me I knew why.

On the shelves were Gilbert's books, his favourite Dickens, the collected editions of his own plays and *Bab Ballads*; on the walls his pictures, his Tintoretto, his Rubens. One day, out of tissue paper, she unfolded a photograph of Gilbert and she said: 'I know he would have liked you to have this.' Then she took me across to the massive desk at which Gilbert had written the operas, with the shining brass letter scales, the blotting pad and letter box kept by Miss McIntosh just as they were in those wonderfully creative days when the Lord Chancellor first popped out of the inkwell and Pooh Bah first oozed unctuously from the tip of Gilbert's quill pen, and Bunthorne and Jack Point and the Pirate King and all the other Gilbertian figures were born, to be immortals of the English stage.

Now Nancy McIntosh has gone, the Kensington flat has been sold up, Gilbert's possessions are distributed to relatives, museums, the sale rooms. The last direct link with the days of Gilbert and Sullivan is broken. Only history remains. But what a history it is!—so packed with drama, with comedy and tragedy, with the caperings of clowns and the dreams of poets. Let us get on with its telling.

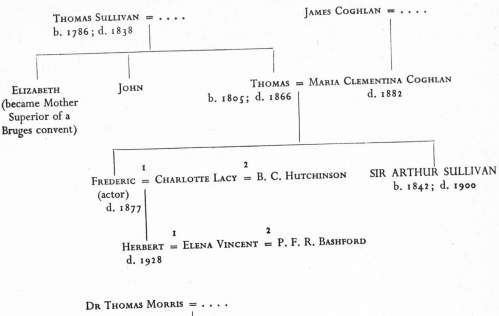

THOMAS SULLIVAN = ...
b. 1786; d. 1838

JAMES COGHLAN = ...

ELIZABETH
(became Mother
Superior of a
Bruges convent)

JOHN

THOMAS = MARIA CLEMENTINA COGHLAN
b. 1805; d. 1866   d. 1882

FREDERIC =¹ CHARLOTTE LACY =² B. C. HUTCHINSON
(actor)
d. 1877

SIR ARTHUR SULLIVAN
b. 1842; d. 1900

HERBERT =¹ ELENA VINCENT =² P. F. R. BASHFORD
d. 1928

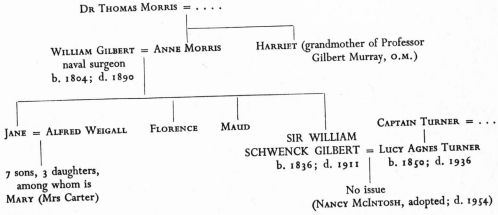

DR THOMAS MORRIS = ...

WILLIAM GILBERT = ANNE MORRIS
naval surgeon
b. 1804; d. 1890

HARRIET (grandmother of Professor
Gilbert Murray, O.M.)

JANE = ALFRED WEIGALL   FLORENCE   MAUD

CAPTAIN TURNER = . . .

7 sons, 3 daughters,
among whom is
MARY (Mrs Carter)

SIR WILLIAM
SCHWENCK GILBERT = LUCY AGNES TURNER
b. 1836; d. 1911   b. 1850; d. 1936

No issue
(NANCY McINTOSH, adopted; d. 1954)

XV

NEW YORK, Tuesday.

, like all right-minded ritons over forty, you e a Gilbert and Sulli- an you may be grati- learn of a remark- meback: three re now to be York.

just finished; a h film version

you might The Hot ed The part of able

Bill Robinson
The Mikado in a bowler hat.

Square, through which the parade marched without stopping befo it dispersed. The columns of fou went on passing the platform, w few gaps, from noon till nine p After dark, floodlighting torches were used.

EVERY nationality and was represented. Im children from twelve countries danced round maypole. A poodle, wea bow was one conting There was a squadr in uniform. A Neg band was led by wearing a busby, white breeches.
Slogans shouted an astonishing va ranged from Un-Americ tion of

'Life is a joke that's just begun'

'The Hot Mikado', 1939: While the headlines in the 'Daily Express' astonished London, audiences in New York heard the 'Three Little Maids from School' sung in swingtime to the bowler-hatted Mikado and Ko-Ko

1961

JAZZED-UP GILBERT
AND
SYNCOPATED SULLIVAN?

LET US BEGIN by looking into the future. You may think it Gilbertian that a
history of Gilbert and Sullivan and their operas should begin in the future, that
the telling of a tale which opened with the birth of Gilbert in 1836 and Sullivan
in 1842 should now be approached from 1961. So be it; we are dealing with Gilbertian
matters. The greatest test of the enduring merits of these astonishing operas will come
in and after 1961.

Since the partnership of Arthur Sullivan and W. S. Gilbert crumbled after their last
successful opera in 1889 (*The Gondoliers*) nothing in this history has happened so interesting in its possible effects, nothing so far-reaching, disturbing, liberating, healthy,
comical, or dreadful, according to your point-of-view, as will happen in 1961 when
the operas are fully released from copyright. It will then be open to anyone not only to
perform them free of charge but to adapt them, modernize them and mash them,
rehash them, plunder them, cut them up and serve them in hot pots, as trifles, in the
air, and doubtless on ice: *carte blanche* rather than *à la Carte*.

Stage and screen are likely to present Gilbert jazzed and Sullivan streamlined in
productions boosted with sex and speed to fit the temper of the age we live in. The
opportunity may also, one hopes, bring forward directors who will give us freshly
charming interpretations of these Old Masters.

Once the copyright is gone there is no limit to the artistry that will be possible, nor
to the vandalism. Advertising and commercial TV will find in Gilbert's immortal
verses a new source of 'plugs'. America has already shown us what entertaining
possibilities a copyright-free Gilbert holds out to the ad.-writer. An undertaker in
Portland, Connecticut, offers burials 'In a rapt ecstatic way' (*Patience*), while the First
Lord's song in *H.M.S. Pinafore* acquires a new significance:

> . . . I polished up the handle of the big front door.
> I polished up that handle so carefulee
> That now I am the ruler of the Queen's navee,
>   But I couldn't have polished it bright, I know,
>   If I had not used Sapolio.[1]

[1] *Gilbert and Sullivan Influence on American Tradecards*, from the collection of Bella C. Landauer; New
York Historical Society.

*A cartoon of 1885—year of 'The Mikado'.
D'Oyly Carte, Gilbert and Sullivan*

The copyright law which prevents this in the British Commonwealth does not run in the United States of America — and it will expire everywhere fifty years after Gilbert's death: in 1961.

I have called Gilbert and Sullivan's operas astonishing. They are astonishing because they are unique. There is nothing comparable in the whole field of entertainment. They are astonishing because, in spite of a loss of topicality here and there, and in spite of some outmoded stage techniques, their popular appeal seems to be ageless. I am writing eighty years after *Trial by Jury*, the first success, was produced. It is still going strong. In normal evolution each generation breeds its own distinctive style of entertainment: the coy and frilly musical comedies of hansom-cab days, or the ragtime revues just before the First World War, or the *No, No, Nanette* type of show in the nineteen-twenties, or the *Oklahoma!* spectacles in the nineteen-fifties—each fashion blossoms and wilts, then a new variety is bred and the old becomes a memory. The best of the Gilbert and Sullivan operas disregard this rule. In the sense that they continue to make their appeal to so many successive generations, they are classics. The fact that in the fifties I can speculate on what will happen to them in the sixties is itself astonishing, for how many of our contemporary stage and film shows will then have any life left? How many of the tunes of today shall we be whistling as we whistle the tunes written by Sullivan eighty years ago?

Some people say that when copyright protection is withdrawn and the operas are thrown into what lawyers call the public domain they will soon be killed off by exploitation. They forget that American law has never given copyright protection to any of the Gilbert and Sullivan operas that matter, yet they flourish in the U.S.A. like flowers that bloom in a perpetual spring, firmly rooted in a foreign shore that has by now become their own. They have not been killed off; but they have sometimes run wild. The famous English comedian, Charles Coborn, once told me that he had seen his music-hall song 'Two Lovely Black Eyes' interpolated into an American version of *The Mikado* 'to bring it up to date'. It is true that what has happened in America will not necessarily happen in Britain. I propose to put before the reader certain happenings and certain tendencies on both sides of the Atlantic which have a bearing on 1961. Since *The Gilbert and Sullivan Book* was first published in 1951, the situation has developed in an interesting way. I have acquired new information from both sides of the Atlantic, some of which I am presenting to the reader in this chapter and some later.

[2]

We must first look back to the early days of the partnership of Sullivan and Gilbert when the commercial management of their operas came into the hands of Richard D'Oyly Carte. Very soon in this three-cornered collaboration we find Carte's secretary (who later became his wife) writing this letter:

Dear Mr Sullivan

The proprietor of the South London Palace writes to us asking if he can introduce the Captain's first song (from 'Pinafore') into an Entertainment. As I don't know whether you like any 'Pinafore' songs sung at <u>Music Halls,</u> I should be much obliged if you would kindly advise me as to your wishes.

Yours sincerely,

HELEN LENOIR[1]

The South London, only a short distance from Sullivan's humble birthplace in Lambeth, was one of those rorty gin-and-joke palaces, half-pub, half-theatre, where the customers sat drinking while the chairman introduced with stentorian voice the buxom charmers and rough-and-tumble comics of Victorian vaudeville. Small wonder that Sullivan scribbled two words across the letter: 'Certainly not'. Having struck a fresh and golden vein of entertainment, he and Gilbert were naturally anxious that it should not be plundered by all and sundry. They rented to Mr Carte the exclusive British right to present the operas.

For close on a century the D'Oyly Carte family has enjoyed the monopoly, and has rigorously guarded these works from exploitation. Even today they seldom give the BBC permission to broadcast Gilbert and Sullivan songs; professional stage performances in Britain are limited to the D'Oyly Carte Company; amateur productions are only permitted on condition that the authorized words and music are strictly adhered to. This guardianship will continue until the copyright expires. After that any entertainer anywhere will be able to help himself to the Captain's song from *Pinafore* or anything else in the Savoy repertoire. Sullivan's 'Certainly not' in 1879 will carry no weight after 1961.

So far as his music *alone* is concerned, as distinct from its use with Gilbert's words, the rights have expired already. British law provides that (with certain exceptions which

[1] Letter hitherto unpublished, dated 15 July, 1879, in the archives of the D'Oyly Carte Opera Company.

David Blair in the ballet 'Pineapple Poll', staged at Sadler's Wells, London, in 1951, to music selected from Sullivan's operas after his copyright had expired

[3]

do not concern us now) for fifty years after the death of a writer or composer his works may be published and performed in public only by consent of his heirs or executors, or persons to whom he may have assigned the rights. That is the position throughout the British Commonwealth.

Sullivan died in 1900. The first effect of the expiry of his copyright in 1950 was that all sorts of new arrangements of his music appeared. One of the best was the score for *Pineapple Poll*, an exhilarating pot-pourri of tunes from the operas arranged and rescored by Charles Mackerras as the music for John Cranko's ballet at Sadler's Wells in 1951. Then the Ballet Russe de Monte Carlo presented in New York in 1955 a ballet version of *The Mikado* of which fuller details are given in my final chapter. The second effect of the ending of copyright was that various people had a shot at inventing new words to Sullivan's tunes. 'Three Little Maids in a Queue' appeared in a London pantomime. Frank Muir and Denis Norden, witty writers of the BBC comedy series *Take It From Here*, put into it a London bus scene *à la* Gilbert and Sullivan. 'Take a Pair of Sparkling Eyes' became

> Take a 6 to Kensal Rise
> Starting out from Hackney Wick,
> It's a one-and-threepenny fare,
> Miss the rush hour if you're wise,
> 'Cos the traffic's very thick,
> From St Paul's to Leicester Square . . .

The tune of 'Three Little Maids from School' introduced:

> One little lady bus-conductress,
> Leaping about like a gym-instructress,
> Half civil servant, half seductress . . .

and 'A Wandering Minstrel', appeared in modern guise as:

> A bus inspector, I,
> And wise to all the fiddles,
> The dodges, tricks and diddles,
> The nipping aboard on the sly . . .

and so on.[1]

Having gone thus far, the way might seem open for enterprising rewriters to bring entire Savoy operas up to date, cutting out the antiquated bits, retaining that part of Gilbert which remains fresh, and introducing topicalities and modernized situations in new lyrics and dialogue; but in fact the way is shut until fifty years after Gilbert's death, which occurred on 29 May 1911. Meanwhile anyone who attempts it may find himself in the law courts.

[1] Copyright Frank Muir and Denis Norden. Quoted by permission.

So British copyright and D'Oyly Carte's exclusive management are the twin reins which guide the performance of the Gilbert and Sullivan works along a straight and narrow path. This control has shielded them from pillage and wild exploitation, but it has also restricted to a narrow circle of producers and performers the range of artistic interpretation that might have been brought to bear upon them.

It would be unfair to say that the D'Oyly Carte Company has done nothing to save the operas from getting into a rut. I shall show that it has done more than it is generally given credit for. Nevertheless, very broadly speaking the performance laid down by W. S. Gilbert has become traditional. In fact, Savoyards call it The Tradition. Yet the technique of the theatre has advanced since his time, and we also have in cinema, radio, and television new and untraditional media for artistic expression in which the operas have yet to take their full measure. When Paramount filmed *The Mikado* in 1938, in association with the D'Oyly Carte Company, it was largely a traditional presentation of the opera and it proved, if proof was needed, that stage techniques do not easily translate to the screen's entirely different pace and viewpoint, especially when they are the highly stylized techniques of the Savoy Tradition. Again in 1953, when London Film Productions made *The Story of Gilbert and Sullivan*, the most successful of several excerpts from the operas was that from *Trial by Jury*, wherein the camera was used with a certain abandon and forgetfulness of The Tradition.

Some day an inspired stage, film, or television director will take wing with the Gilbert and Sullivan material and soar with it as Sir Laurence Olivier did in the cinema with Shakespeare's *Henry V*, possibly as the American producer of *Carmen Jones* did in reinterpreting Bizet's opera, but this cannot happen while the operas are held on a tight reign.

In foreign countries where they have escaped the protection of British copyright there have always been unorthodox stage versions of the operas, though they have not always been inspired. In Germany in 1927 a Berlin theatre which followed the tradition of the Folies Bergère rather than that of the Savoy presented *The Mikado* with Nanki-Poo, the wandering minstrel, as an American in Oxford bags, Katisha made her entry in a taxi-cab, and an astonished English visitor to the show reported: 'The Charleston is jogged by a troupe of semi-clad damsels as the first act curtain falls. It rises on the second to show an absolutely naked girl bathing. Clearly, she is meant to be Yum-Yum, and her conspicuous ablutions precede her adornment in bridal attire . . . Usually Sullivan's airs are used very much as we

Nanki-Poo in Oxford bags: Berlin, 1927

'The Mikado' à la *Folies Bergère: the German stage version which drew 5,000 people nightly to the Grosses Schauspielhaus, Berlin, in 1927*

know them until they reach the sound and fury of a kind of ultra-jazz "tail-piece". This sends the trumpets and saxophones and other tortuous instruments crashing. In fairness I must say that the orchestral playing, like much of the chorus work, was at times unusually good, and some numbers I have never heard made half so impressive (and artistically impressive) in England.'[1]

America followed with *The Swing Mikado* (1938) and *The Hot Mikado* (1939), both of them played by Negro casts. We may wonder how the British would react to such productions. It is worth paying some attention to the line American theatre critics took. Mr John Mason Brown (*New York Post*) complained not that *The Mikado* was swung but that it was not swung enough. He wrote that 'having recently retasted the all-too-familiar pleasures of the orthodox version as revived by such experts as the D'Oyly Carte Company' he went to the theatre in unorthodox mood, hoping that the jitter-bugs would take full possession of Titipu: 'The simple truth is that whenever *The*

[1] Mr A. H. Godwin, in *The Gilbert and Sullivan Journal*, London.

'*The Mikado*' à la *Pinewood: the English film version, 1938, director Victor Schertzinger, producer Geoffrey Toye. Here are Sydney Granville as Pooh-Bah and Martyn Green as Ko-Ko*

Swing Mikado is swung it is grand good fun. At such moments it literally leaps to life. It becomes gay, impudent, original, convulsing and decidedly worth seeing.' But between whiles there were long stretches, complained Mr Brown, when the piece was traditionally played, when the Negro singers and dancers who had been so exuberantly in their element in swing-time failed to do justice to Gilbert's satire and robbed it of its point. This critic's argument is that you can't have it both ways.

The *Hot Mikado* went more like the whole hog. Produced by the renowned Hassard Short at the Broadhurst Theatre, New York, it had Bill 'Bojangles' Robinson, a negro tap-dancing star, as the Mikado in a bowler hat. The *New York World Telegram* declared that 'It makes the Gilbert and Sullivan original seem as gentle as playing charades in a country parsonage . . . Everything is chucked overboard but the basic melodies, and these sometimes disappear in a welter of hot licks. Of its type it is magnificent—the loudest, craziest, hottest, and most brilliantly organized jam session of this cockeyed jazz age.'

[7]

The New York Sun: 'They have done amazing things with the lyrics in the hope of improving on Gilbert. They thus firmly reinforce the prevailing opinion that it is pretty hard to improve on Gilbert and also that it is no great improvement to leave large chunks of Gilbert out entirely. It's very entertaining, though, to have Katisha sung to torch rhythms and to see everybody so larky.'

'It has the great virtue of possessing the only Hot Katisha in history', wrote Richard Watts, Jnr, in the *New York Herald Tribune*. 'Katisha has always seemed to me the most boring and embarrassing character invented by Gilbert. Miss Rosa Brown makes her the life of the party, singing and playing with heat and gusto.' This critic entirely approved of hotting-up *The Mikado*. 'This now somewhat groggy classic', he called it. Not everyone agreed:

Some like it swing,
With a zing-zing-zing;
Some like it hot;
Others do not.
Some like it negroid;
Others, instead,
Incline toward red.
Some like it screened
When Martyn-Greened;
Some rate it duller,
Done in technicolor.

All in all, I find that I've
Remained a little conservative.

Yes, in spite of all temptations
To succumb to adaptation,
To the stunty and the arty,
I'm committed to the party
And the creed of D'Oyly-Cartey.

—Melville Cane in the *New York Herald Tribune*.

To keep things in perspective let us make it clear that these syncopated *Mikados* have been the exception rather than the rule. Plenty of Gilbert and Sullivan opera is played more or less 'straight' on stage and radio, and a great welcome is always accorded to the D'Oyly Carte Company from England. Nevertheless in 1939 these jittery transformations burst like bombshells on Broadway, and in London the explosive effect may well be even more sensational when it comes, if only because playing fast and loose with the Savoy Operas has been unthinkable over here.

After the initial impact I think it doubtful that the British public will be impressed by stunt productions. This is because we hold a tender place in our hearts for Gilbert and Sullivan, which is only natural when the institutions and people that Gilbert lampoons are so essentially English, and when the music of Sullivan springs from the very heart of this land in its style, sentiment, and sense of humour. Americans have always taken to Gilbert and Sullivan opera with zest (the orthodox as well as the jazzed) but they look at it from the outside; the British live it from the inside.

Dr Boyd Neel, the eminent conductor, voiced this when he wrote to *The Times* on

[8]

the eve of the expiry of Sullivan's copyright in 1950: 'Tunes which have become part of our national heritage deserve some sort of respect and the thought of "Mikado Boogie" is horrifying in the extreme. May we hope that good taste will prevail?'

This is a salutary reminder of the ethics of the matter. What would Arthur Sullivan himself think about it? I have been intrigued to find in American newspaper files an interview on travesties of his work which were appearing in his own lifetime. It was 1885: *The Mikado* was making its first appearance in New York in the authentic version played at the Fifth Avenue Theatre by a D'Oyly Carte Company from England. There

were also sundry pirated perversions, among them that presented by Mr Duff at the Standard Theatre. Later in this book I tell in detail the fantastic story of these piratical producers who put on the operas without payment of a dollar piece to Gilbert and Sullivan, and how the Englishmen did their best to protect their rights; for example, the music was not printed and Sullivan's original scores were kept in D'Oyly Carte's safe (they still are).[1] But the pirates found their own ways to filch the tunes, for which they made their own orchestrations. After a series of copyright law suits, Carte *v* Duff, the United States Supreme Court gave a verdict for Duff. The Judge's ruling was that a production 'with a different orchestration' was no violation of copyright. Evidently the Judge felt that the law was an ass, for he remarked in court that it was not his job to make the law, only to administer it. Sir Arthur Sullivan said to the Press:

'It is a misrepresentation of my work and should not be allowed. We were in hopes that the decision would be the same as in the cases of Gounod's *Redemption* and

AT LAST! HERE IT IS!
OPENING TUES. SEPT. 2
LIMITED ENGAGEMENT 3 WEEKS ONLY
THE 1947 VERSION OF
Gilbert and Sullivan's
SWING MIKADO

CONCEIVED AND DIRECTED BY HARRY MINTURN
CHOREOGRAPHY BY SAMMY DYER

OPERA HOUSE
WACKER DR. at MADISON

MAIL ORDERS NOW
BOX OFFICE OPEN
FROM 9:30 A.M. TO 9:30 P.M.
PRICES EVES. (Inc. Sunday)
$3.60, 3.00, 2.40, 1.80, 1.20. Mat. Sat. and Sun. Only, $3.00, 2.40, 1.80, 1.20 (tax inc.)
For Inf. Call Franklin 7800
Company of 80

"A CLASSIC GETS ITS PACE LIFTED."—Life Magazine
FOR THE ENTERTAINMENT THRILL OF A LIFETIME
DON'T MISS IT!
AIR CONDITIONED BY ELECTRICAL REFRIGERATION
MATINEES SATURDAY AND SUNDAY ONLY

[1] Except *The Yeomen of the Guard* now at the Royal College of Music, *The Mikado* (at the Royal Academy), *Ruddigore*, and *Utopia Limited*, the full scores are kept in close custody by the D'Oyly Carte Opera Company in London.

our *Iolanthe* in the Massachusetts circuit, which was directly opposite to that in this case. The judge held in that case that the work was not given as the composer wrote it, and therefore was not justifiable.'[1]

'It is a misrepresentation of my work and should not be allowed.' That is Sullivan's view.

Though smarting under the decision, Sullivan added that the authentic *Mikado* at the Fifth Avenue Theatre was taking 10,000 dollars a week, a lot more than the Duff version at the Standard. This was the real answer to the pirates.

Is it still going to be the answer after 1961, to 'Mikado Boogie' etc.—simply to present the pure, original, traditional versions of the operas? I believe it can be only part of the answer, because remarkable new techniques have been evolved in the style of dancing, décor, and presentation generally in musical productions, and also because time has changed the acceptable idiom of the theatre: that is, what we now regard as suitable music, an apt joke, or an appropriate action for a given situation. Some of Sullivan's churchier choruses are as dated as Gilbert's worst puns. There has been a revolution in the entire idiom and pace of life; it is reflected on the stage and to it a sensitive producer must be alert. This does not mean that he should chuck everything of his author's intentions overboard 'in a welter of hot licks', as the critic said of the *Hot Mikado*. That would be what Sullivan's interview above shows he resented: misrepresentation. But at the risk of maddening the Gilbert and Sullivan Traditionalists I say that the time has come for modification without misrepresentation.

If Gilbert were here now I believe that he would considerably restage his operas. He was a realistic person, and would wish to know why the general attitude of New York newspapermen at *The Hot Mikado* was to hail anything which saved them from the ennui of having to attend once more to these 'somewhat groggy classics'. Why 'somewhat groggy'? One must allow for the occupational disease of professional critics, a dyspeptic flatulence due to perpetual attendance at a banquet to which the ordinary man comes only occasionally when he is on the spree; nevertheless something more than wind motivates such harsh judgments. To some extent they are a sickened reaction away from the fanaticism of the fans: from those intoxicated people who regard Gilbert and Sullivan as holy writ, and from those audiences whose standards are so debauched by the ecstasy of their fetish-worship that they applaud and encore performances of a standard that would have made Gilbert himself livid. As the producer as well as the writer of his operas, Gilbert was a stickler for quality and a hater of gush. Once at a *Mikado* rehearsal he had to check Nanki-Poo for the vehemence he put into a single-word speech: 'Rapture!'

'Modified rapture', scolded Gilbert, from the stalls.

'Modified rapture!' cried the actor—and so the line has remained ever since. It is a commendable motto for fanatics.

[1] *New York Mirror*, 10th March 1885.

Unhappily, this fanatical attitude gives the operas a bad name—or one might say a bad smell, judging by the nose-in-the-air attitude of those, at the opposite extreme, who decry the Gilbert and Sullivan works as extravagantly as the idolaters ballyhoo them. 'No musical audience can be induced to go near them', said one such nose-in-the-air critic. 'They are operas for the unmusical.'

Richard Capell, the late music critic of the *Daily Telegraph*, wisely replied (1946): 'This is ingratitude. That some people have been overdone with Gilbert and Sullivan, that the famous pieces have been wearily performed by professional companies and botched by amateurs—all that is neither here nor there. It is ingratitude not to recognize the stroke of luck that gave to English music of the nineteenth century a series of little masterpieces, exquisitely good-natured, which surpass everything else of their order.'

The future vitality of these classics in the face of competition *à la* Harlem or the Folies Bergère, or whatever it may be, depends on relating them to our understanding in the present time through productions of the highest modern quality, recapturing the fresh and spirited approach of the unweary days when the operas were very young. That they are older now and that some things in them, once revolutionary, have become outmoded is no reason why this cannot be done. Shakespeare's plays are older still, and is it not true that the most revealing and enjoyable performances often come when a fresh and sensitive mind cuts through accumulated traditions and customs and sees Shakespeare new?

If 1961 brings a liberation from The Tradition I do not think Gilbert will turn in his grave, for he was never a traditionalist. He was a daring innovator. At rehearsals he drilled his Gilbertian mock-seriousness into the actions and inflections of his actors and actresses; this was the beginning of the traditional *style* of performance, and that is something to which all wise producers will pay attention, but Gilbert never intended it to be inflexible. This can be proved by many things he did and said. For example, Henry Lytton's interpretation of Jack Point was utterly different from that of George Grossmith: Gilbert approved of both.

Towards the end of his life Sir William Gilbert called at the Savoy Theatre while they were rehearsing a revival of one of the operas. He said he disliked a certain piece of business. The stage manager remarked that it was, in fact, the original way of doing it. Fixed by Gilbert's beetling eye, the stage manager turned to Rutland Barrington for support. The veteran actor said yes, this was how they had always done it. It was classic.

'Oh, it's classic, is it?' was Gilbert's dry retort, 'Well, we must not interfere with the classics.'

Gilbert even permitted gagging. This will surprise those people who imagine that not a comma in any Gilbert and Sullivan opera was ever altered after the first night. Not long ago an English newspaper told its readers that 'Since the very first days not a costume, not a hair style, not even the layout of the advertising posters has been

'THE TRADITION'

HOW IT COMES AND GOES

LEFT, *the costume of the Queen of the Fairies in 'Iolanthe' prior to World War I. The original Wagnerian burlesque has since been dropped*

BELOW, *the business with the disjointed toe. This began years ago when Henry Lytton accidentally tripped over and caused a roar of laughter. Here is the same joke—now traditional routine of 'The Mikado'—being played by Martyn Green while Derek Oldham and Sylvia Cecil look on*

changed.' This is a hoary old myth. The D'Oyly Cartes have closely cosseted the operas in Britain, but they have never been as conservative or as stupid as that. I am going to quote some Gilbert letters, hitherto unpublished,[1] which show his own attitude. But first here is the sort of thing that gave rise to the myth, a letter from Gilbert to Richard D'Oyly Carte during the original run of *The Gondoliers*:

> I hear great complaints of Barrington's 'gagging' . . . The piece is, I think, quite good enough without the extraneous embellishments suggested by Mr Barrington's brief fancy. Anyway it must be played *exactly as I wrote it*. I won't have an outside word introduced by anybody. If once a license in this direction is accorded it opens the door to any amount of tomfoolery. I wish you would ask the Stage Manager to send me a daily report of all divergences from the strict text. I am determined to stamp out the nuisance. It is not enough that the departures are unimportant—there should—and shall—be no departures of any kind whatever.

A typical outburst by Gilbert the disciplinarian. What he most resented was *not being consulted* about the 'embellishments'. There is much evidence that he recognized that good actors must be allowed to express their own individuality to some extent, i.e., to an extent that would not upset the overall style of his productions. He wrote to Mrs Carte in 1896:

> With regard to the gags I must decline, on principle, to formally sanction *any* gags that have not been submitted to me before introduction. At the same time, I have no desire to injure the prospects of the piece by doing anything that would give any actor an excuse for walking sulkily through his part—so I will leave it to you to do exactly as you think best.

A few years later when a great deal of gagging crept into *The Mikado* during tours in the provinces Mrs Carte posted to Gilbert a long list of them. It was returned with his brief comments:

> *Mrs Carte:* Ko-Ko says 'Pooh-Bah, I appoint you Lord High Substitute' instead of 'my substitute'. This appears to be unauthorized. I understand it is effective, but it is of course for Mr Gilbert to decide.
>
> *Gilbert:* Yes.
>
> *Mrs Carte:* Pooh-Bah, interrrupted while he is singing the word 'pedigree' by Pitti-Sing, says to her 'I'll give you such a Japanese smack in a minute'. This seems to have sprung out of some business between Miss Bond and Mr Barrington.
>
> *Mr Gilbert:* Omit. Utterly stupid. There is too much clowning in this scene.

And so on, for several pages. Inventions which had some wit about them, and which fitted the style of the opera, he approved. Improvisations without his sanction were an impertinence and might earn the offending actor a reprimand such as this:

> I have just seen a telegram from the Stage Manager to the effect that on his remonstrating with you as to your performance of Ko-Ko you defied his authority. I assure

[1] From the archives of the D'Oyly Carte Opera Company.

you, in your own interest, that such a course of action is most prejudicial to your advancement. The principle of subordination must be maintained in a theatre as in a regiment. If an unreasonable order is given it must be acted upon, and its unreasonableness represented to a higher authority. This is the rule of the Savoy Theatre and no one would be retained on its staff who hestitated to recognize it. I find on enquiry that Mr Carte's grievance does not refer to your altering the dialogue, but to the introduction of *inappropriate, exaggerated and unauthorized 'business'*.

Severe as this reads, there is no doubt that Gilbert intended the style of performance he laid down to be a guide, not a strait-jacket. What he objected to was the inappropriate. That being so, there is no doubt that were he here now he would be the first to blue-pencil worn-out one-time topicalities. Some of Gilbert's gags were far too topical to last. There is a rousing song in *Patience*:

> If you want a receipt for that popular mystery
> Known to the world as a Heavy Dragoon,
> Take all the remarkable people in history,
> Rattle them off to a popular tune.

—the verses of which are now almost incomprehensible because many of the allusions have gone stale: 'The pathos of Paddy, as rendered by Boucicault' refers to the acting of Dion Boucicault in Irish plays. 'A smack of Lord Waterford reckless and rollicky' commemorates a once famous sporting peer, now forgotten.

I am not suggesting that every line in the operas should be made plain. Obscurity itself is sometimes a good joke. But whatever can modern audiences make of 'The keen penetration of Paddington Pollaky'?—until reference to a glossary of Gilbertianisms (there are such things!) enlightens us that Ignatius Paul Pollaky was a detective attached to Paddington Police Office in the nineteenth century. Would there be anything un-Gilbertian in hiring an up-to-date wit to doctor such obscurities? Gilbert did some doctoring himself in the case of *The Mikado* when in the last years of his life he revised the song about people who 'never would be missed', to include the lovely suffragist and the red-hot Socialist.[1] Since then the D'Oyly Carte Company has cautiously modernized a line here and there in this and other operas, but not to any great extent.

Danny Kaye, the great American comedian, went much further when he recorded in America some songs from the operas. These Decca records cannot be bought in Britain because they would infringe the copyright. The Policeman's Song from *The Pirates of Penzance*, sung in broad Cockney, has a new verse, and so have songs from *Patience* and *Iolanthe*, all of them performed in clever but unorthodox style by the American comedian. Gilbert's old verses are helped out with new ones written by Sylvia Fine (Mrs Danny Kaye).

[1] *See* p. 424. Compare also modernized American lyric used in *The Hot Mikado*, p. 447.

I was curious to know why Sylvia Fine took this liberty. I wrote and asked her. Replying from her Hollywood home, she says that it all began when she was staging operettas at children's camps and found that many of Gilbert's once-topical references meant nothing to present-day Americans. Hearing the Nightmare Song in *Iolanthe*, for example, what can the young American of the atomic age make of the reference to the steamer from Harwich —'Which is something between a large bathing machine and a very small second-class carriage' — and which presently changes into 'a four-wheeler'?

'Much of Gilbert's humour was lost,' writes Sylvia Fine. 'In an effort to preserve Gilbert's original intent, when Danny made the records I substituted the new verses for that purpose only. The verses were written in all diffidence and humility with no thought that they would equal the quality of the original.'

Danny Kaye's record of the Nightmare Song starts with the first ten lines of Gilbert's lyric unaltered (as on page 223 of this book), then these lines by Sylvia Fine are substituted:

Ignatius Paul Pollaky whose 'keen penetration' was immortalized by Gilbert in 'Patience'. This is a rare cartoon of the detective, who died at Brighton in 1918

For you dream that you're ill, having swallowed a pill,
    that was made out of ossified onyx
And the doctor you've found, he is trav'ling around
    on a subway that's bound for the Bronnyx[1]
Oh, you must find him fast, as the hours go past
    you're convinced you are headed for tragedy
For you saw him on Sunday, felt much worse on Monday
    and here it's the following Sagedy.

[1] 'A borough of New York City spelled and pronounced Bronx except in the provincial tongue of those who live there, who pronounce it as I have used it.'—Sylvia Fine.

You're full of suspicion: that trav'ling physician,
    he fed you some stuff with a barb in it,
So you dash to the street while you frantically eat
    a soufflé made of sodium bicarbonate.
To a druggist you rush but he gives you the brush
    saying 'Who let this asthmatic gasper in?'
Though you plead with the villain you need penicillin,
    he won't even give you an aspirin.
Then a pill on the shelf it leaps down by itself
    and it lands on your head like a lead post,
You suddenly awake, and no wonder you ache,
    you've been hitting yourself with the bed post.

'With "The Policeman's Lot" from *The Pirates of Penzance*', adds Sylvia Fine, 'our problem was quite a different and unique one, and one that Gilbert never had to face; i.e. filling out a three-minute record side. The number of verses extant just didn't take up the necessary amount of time, and yet the piece was too long to allow two songs to go on one side of the disc. Therefore I added another verse in what I hoped was the spirit of the original.'

I had the opportunity of observing the effect of the Danny Kaye records on an English audience when an American visitor smuggled a set into this country at the time of my radio-biography of Gilbert and Sullivan. During a rehearsal interval in the BBC studio I played them to the cast which included a number of veteran and conservative Savoyards like Leo Sheffield as well as young singers of the post-war generation. The reaction varied from delight to petrified shock. If there was a consensus of opinion at all it was that some of the lines in the modernized lyrics were justified (not all), but never the liberties taken with Sullivan's music. When Danny Kaye sang 'The Moon and I', the joyous soprano aria from *The Mikado*, it sounded to me like a burlesque of the lugubrious style of a modern crooner. One remembered then, rather sadly, Sullivan's 'Certainly not' when asked if his songs might be sung on the music halls.

Sylvia Fine, on hearing that this was my reaction, wrote to me: 'It is unfortunate that "The Moon and I" sounded like a burlesque to you. It certainly was not meant to be interpreted that way. The song was done in modern ballad form at the request of the recording company. As you probably know, in America and, I think, in Europe as well, there has been extensive use of some of the most famous material of great symphonic composers, the most melodious arias from operas and the most engaging folk songs, by commercial music firms. At the time this record was made there was a definite trend in that direction, and it was Decca's hope that this lovely piece of Sullivan music would become a very popular ballad. You will note that the man who made the arrangement is one of our most noted composers—Mr Johnny Green, and it certainly was not done with tongue in cheek.'

I accept the assurance. But who is Johnny Green to improve on Arthur Sullivan?

Gilbert was a prince at his own game, so was Sullivan, and the moral of all attempts to modernize them, so far, is that it must be done superlatively well to come near the standard of the original. The art of lyric-writing for comic opera has not greatly advanced since Gilbert's day. What does wear thin is the heavy pun and the forgotten topicality. But the art, technique, and standard of theatrical *production* have advanced immensely. They did not stop with Gilbert. It is here that we find the most exciting opportunities for modification without misrepresentation.

Since the Victorian period the influence of the producer Diaghilev and of Bakst with the Russian ballet, and of such impresarios in the field of operetta and revue as Charles B. Cochran, and the general change of idiom which I have mentioned, have tended to make what is left of the antediluvian dancing, décor, and 'business' in the Gilbert and Sullivan operas very fusty indeed. The late Rupert D'Oyly Carte began to recognize this when in the twenties he commissioned a fine artist, Charles Ricketts, to

And apologetic statesmen of a compromising kind,
Such as—what d'ye call him—Thing'em-bob, and
likewise—Never-mind . . .

In 1949 the suggestion was discussed in the London Press that the Government should take over the copyright in the operas after its expiry, to safeguard the tradition of these works. 'Vicky' of the 'News Chronicle' gave his own version of the nationalization of Gilbert and Sullivan in this cartoon of the Socialist cabinet—Bevin, Attlee, Cripps, Morrison, Strachey, Dalton redesign the scenes and costumes of *The Mikado* and *The Gondoliers*. The action of these operas was left alone, but in 1939 Mr Carte ventured further by employing Peter Goffin not only to redesign *The Yeomen of the Guard* but to produce it as well—and Mr Goffin's ideas on stage presentation are such that this meant altering the fifty-years'-old movements and 'business', entirely re-presenting the opera within sets which were a radical innovation. A storm of controversy broke out.

'There will be devotees,' said *The Times*, 'who will resent not being shown a photographic representation of the White Tower flapping on the backcloth.'

Mr. Philip Page of the *Daily Mail* was one of the critics who bluntly preferred the traditional *Yeomen*: 'Frankly,' he wrote, 'the only adjective strong enough for this Tower of London is that which is traditionally associated with only one of its towers.'

THE YEOMEN OF THE GUARD: *Finale, Act 2*
The old setting, with 'the White Tower flapping on the backcloth.' Compare the new décor, opposite

The Tradition overthrown: Peter Goffin's restaging of 'The Yeomen of the Guard' for Rupert D'Oyly Carte, 1939

When Mr Goffin was reading through such Press notices with Mr Carte, the designer-producer expressed some concern at having provoked the storm. Mr Carte replied: 'I don't care what they say about the production. I should care if they said nothing.'

Public indifference could be the consequence of keeping these operas too long shut up in moth-balls at the Savoy. And yet Mr Carte did not open wide the cupboard doors to innovation, for he knew that Gilbert and Sullivan audiences are comprised of elderly Traditionalists in about equal parts with young enthusiasts, and while the latter are likely to welcome modern ideas of production their elders are as apt to be antagonistic. Mr Carte stepped cautiously—but he showed his faith in Peter Goffin by making him artistic adviser to the D'Oyly Carte Company.

Mr Carte's increasing years and the onset of the 1939–45 war retarded the further restaging of the operas but since Miss Bridget D'Oyly Carte took over control on her father's death there have been, as the London *Sunday Times* declared in a 1953 head-line—SIGNS OF A NEW SPIRIT.

The most spirited of these signs, so far, is the new production of *Princess Ida*, first seen in 1954; which is not to say that the revamping of this opera has in my opinion produced an entirely successful result, but it does give the following important indication of the direction towards which the operas are moving as 1961 approaches.

Princess Ida had suffered more from declining topicality than any piece in the repertoire. After two world wars and a suffragette campaign had given us WRAFS and WRENS, votes for women and 'equal rights', its satire about lady undergraduates and lady soldiers could no longer be taken as seriously as in 1884 when women's emancipation was something of a novelty. Miss D'Oyly Carte's response to time's marching on was to give the 1954 revival a fantastic dreamlike quality. This was felt to be the appropriate key to strike for a story which has now lost all association with ordinary life and has become a fairy tale. With its script pruned, its movements redevised by a new producer (Robert Gibson), and with décor by James Wade rather in the fantastic mode of modern ballet design, the new *Princess Ida* provoked another storm ('*Swan Lake* gone wrong', said one critic), but at any rate here was evidence of fresh young minds at work on the old operas.

The most interesting thing about it, if we are thinking of the future development of other Gilbert and Sullivan operas, is the stress on the fantastic. Visually—that is, in dresses, sets, movements, and 'business'—there are latent elements of delightful fantasy in several of the operas, and modern methods of production could surely bring them to life. Some of the traditional dancing is fossilized; a witty modern choreographer could replace it with fresher dances, yet retaining the Gilbertian spirit such as inspires, for example, the spry little dances of the Lord Chancellor in *Iolanthe*—

which are among Gilbert's unique inventions, and which should themselves, of course, be sacrosanct.

This element of fantasy in Gilbert and Sullivan has fascinating possibilities outside of opera—in ballet, for instance. A New York correspondent, commenting on the Ballet Russe de Monte Carlo's production of *The Mikado*, writes: 'What might an imaginative choreographer make of *Iolanthe* or *Ruddigore*?'[1]

Oddly enough (as it seems to us now) the scenery for the operas when originally produced in the nineteenth century had no element of fantasy whatsoever. It was flatly realistic. In this it accorded with the simple Victorian notion that a photographically-accurate picture of the place wherein the scene took place was all that was

[1] *See p. 454.*

Robert Gibson, director of productions, D'Oyly Carte Opera Company

[20]

Another break with tradition: James Wade's décor for Castle Adamant in the 1954 production of 'Princess Ida', designed to give 'a fantastic dream-like quality'

necessary. A twentieth-century designer such as Peter Goffin has quite a different conception of his job. It is not merely to paint a picture, it is to play a part (to quote Goffin's own words) 'in a symphonic composition with parts scored for sight as well as for sound, in which the chief instruments are the living players'. The stage designer must immerse himself in the mood and purpose of the whole 'symphony'. He must score his own part for sight in such a way as to harmonize with the sound and movement of the play.

What this amounts to is something almost unheard of in Gilbert's time: the designer has become an impressionist, and through the style and colour of scenery and costumes he tries to reflect the mood of the opera. In *The Yeomen*—primarily a romantic and even tragic operetta, rather than comic—Mr Goffin's décor was romantic and sombre. One can imagine where this impressionistic trend may lead the more humorous operas—what a delicious delirium such a master of fantasy as Emmett could make of the scenery for the ruined chapel by moonlight (*The Pirates of Penzance*), and what an atmosphere of crazed aestheticism he could work out for *Patience* whose two acts are at present set in the uninspiring 'Exterior of Castle Bunthorne' and in that unatmospheric piece of pretty-pretty pictorialism called 'Act 2—A Glade'.

There will be more of such fantasy, of dash and daring, I believe, in the presentation of the operas after 1961; perhaps there will be some of it before that date if Miss Bridget D'Oyly Carte takes her *Princess Ida* experiment further. Miss Carte belongs to

[21]

THE GILBERT & SULLIVAN BOOK

the generation that grew up between the two wars, a generation not awed by Victorian traditions, and it is clear that she is prepared to break with them, but Miss Carte *is* a Carte: she has inherited a respect for the general rightness of Sullivan's music and Gilbert's words—after all, it was her grandfather who first understood what these would add up to when put together. She is not likely to insert 'Two Lovely Black Eyes' (or whatever its modern equivalent may be) into any of the operas. In getting rid of what is old-fashioned, she will not throw away the baby with the bath-water.

And what about the future of Sullivan's music? There has lately developed a healthy move, largely through Sir Malcolm Sargent's example, for a more musicianly handling of it. During the 1955 season of Promenade Concerts at the Royal Albert Hall, London, Miss D'Oyly Carte agreed that excerpts from several Gilbert and Sullivan operas should be performed at a Saturday evening concert under Sir Malcolm Sargent's conductorship. With first-class concert singers and the BBC Symphony Orchestra, this innovation caused something of a sensation.[1]

One of our leading music critics, Mr Neville Cardus, wrote in *The Manchester Guardian*:

> It is possible that one or two highbrows in Saturday's audience—if highbrows are able to breathe at all in the honest air of a Promenade concert—shared my experience during the first half of the programme, which was devoted to pieces taken from the Gilbert and Sullivan operas. Several years ago I decided that I had outlived the music, and so I put it behind me, grateful for the pleasure it once had given me. The brilliant, refined, and sensitive performances on Saturday caused me to recapture the first delights. The main factor contributing to this renewal of interest and musical satisfaction—apart from the excellent singing and playing—was Sullivan's orchestration. Sir Malcolm Sargent, who conducted, saw to it that we were hearing Sullivan's scoring completely and precisely; and precision, being three parts of wit, is necessary in any presentation of much of Sullivan's music.

Another critic, Mr Arthur Jacobs, has urged that after 1961 the Gilbert and Sullivan operas should be included in the repertoire of such companies as Sadler's Wells and Carl Rosa. He writes:

> Many of the overtures, not being by Sullivan,[2] need cutting or rewriting. And, though it would be an error to exchange the discreet piquancy of Sullivan's own scoring for such glittering new orchestrations as Charles Mackerras has already

[1] Though it was an innovation at these particular Proms, there is, of course, the famous precedent of Sullivan himself conducting his *H.M.S. Pinafore* music at the Covent Garden Promenade Concert in 1878. *See* p. 160.

[2] Mr George Baker has done research into the much-disputed question of which overtures Sullivan composed throughout and which he left to such assistants as Alfred Cellier and Hamilton Clarke. In *Musical Opinion* (Feb. 1955) Mr Baker declares his belief that the pure Sullivan overtures are those of *The Yeomen of the Guard*, *Patience*, *Iolanthe*, possibly *The Pirates of Penzance* and *The Gondoliers*. In the others he probably called for help during his race to have things ready for the opening night.

provided for the ballet *Pineapple Poll*, some amplification of the orchestra will be necessary. A theatre's second and third trombones need not sit idle just because Sullivan was limited to one.[1]

The *Ruddigore* overture was rewritten by Geoffrey Toye in 1921, when certain songs were scrapped and other musical changes made. Sir Malcolm Sargent has altered *The Gondoliers* overture to bring it to a more brilliant close. Mr Toye and Sir Malcolm could be trusted to carry out these improvements without misrepresenting Sullivan. Such adjustments are like the desired changes in Gilbert's text and staging, they are the consequence of the forward march of taste and the change of idiom in the musical theatre. Some of the Sullivan sentimental passages which endeared him to our fore-fathers in the second half of the nineteenth century are not so appealing to us in the second half of the twentieth. But the marvellous thing about the major part of Sullivan's music is its enduring freshness. Writing to Mr Hesketh Pearson in the nineteen-thirties, Mr George Bernard Shaw declared: 'Sullivan has been gaining ground and Gilbert losing it since they died.' Mr Pearson commented, quite rightly: 'A comparison between the two men is worthless, because each was vitally necessary to the other.'[2]

The chief need is that we should hear all of the grace, wit and beauty that Sullivan wrote into his music. During the BBC's Gilbert and Sullivan life-story I was in the studio, listening to a rehearsal in company with an elderly Savoyard when he said, 'Whatever have you done to the music?' We had done nothing but put Sullivan's score on the desks of a full-scale BBC orchestra which always works as a team under a first-rate conductor. A touring company taking seven or eight musicians round the country and picking up augmentations as best it can in each town it visits cannot hope to get a comparable musicianly performance.

The Sadler's Wells Opera can tour a sizeable orchestra because it has an Arts Council (i.e. Government) subsidy: it is a non-profit-making enterprise. It may be that the future will bring some sort of collaboration between the D'Oyly Carte Company and the Arts Council so that these classic English operettas may be mounted in the best possible way.

I have discussed so far those modifications in the words, music, décor, acting and dancing of the operas which may come after 1961, for better or worse. But what about the plots? Mr Sidney Gilliat, the British film director who made *The Story of Gilbert and Sullivan*, has some strong views about this. He is a showman with a high reputation in the field of modern film comedy. We were discussing recently what chance there is of Gilbert and Sullivan opera being modernized as drastically as *Carmen Jones* modernized *Carmen*.

'The real difficulty,' he said, 'lies in Gilbert's plots. Most of them are period pieces.

[1] *The Sunday Times*, December 1954.
[2] *Gilbert and Sullivan*, by Hesketh Pearson (Hamish Hamilton), 1935.

'*Princess Ida*', 1954: Cyril (Leonard Osborn), Hilarion (Thomas Round), and Florian (Jeffrey Skitch)

The Yeomen of the Guard has a basic plot fairly typical of Victorian melodrama and so far as its plot is concerned has little to offer today. *Patience* and *Princess Ida* suffer plotwise from outmoded topicality. Indeed, if I had to make a guess I would say that I can only see a future for a really free adaptation where there is an opportunity to bring the plot, the story, the entire atmosphere, into keeping with modern public taste, and in this category I would put *Iolanthe*, *Ruddigore*, perhaps *The Gondoliers*, and possibly *The Pirates of Penzance*.

'My reason for this is that each of these is a fantasy and each could perhaps be given the necessary modern degree of sophistication because the plot could be made to have some satirical application to present-day institutions, or those of 1961. In each case I think the libretto would have to be largely rewritten, but with Gilbert as a departure-platform, e.g. I can see a modern political application of *Iolanthe*; for *Ruddigore* a social application—good and evil in relation to death-duties and the decline of old family estates, probably with the National Trust (or Coal Board!) coming in somewhere; *The Gondoliers* perhaps being applied to the U.S.A. and the Presidential office, and so on.

'What I am guessing is that just a handful of the operas may prove susceptible to an exceedingly free modern (1961) treatment in which their plots are brought up to date in whatever vein is then current, but still bearing some definite relationship to the original. I would also guess that these very few and much-changed operas will probably each include music taken from some of the other operas and that each will almost certainly include a ballet with music from other Sullivan works.'

This will certainly be a drastic new departure if it ever comes—'And kindly note that I am guessing, not advocating,' adds Mr Gilliat. It will need some very brilliant writers to bring off such a remodelling as wittily as Gilbert brought off the first models of all.

Many lovers of Gilbert and Sullivan are worried about the possible 'desecration' of the operas after 1961, and from time to time they make suggestions whereby to dodge the expiry of copyright. One idea widely discussed in the Press before Sullivan's copyright lapsed was to nationalize the operas. Then, in 1955, Miss Dorothy Alderley, of Oxford, collected eight thousand signatures to a petition asking the Government to perpetuate Gilbert's copyright in the words, and she said she hoped to get eight million before the copyright expires in 1961. Of Danny Kaye's records she said to a reporter: 'I'd like to smash them over his head.'

Like all lovers, G. & S. lovers are prone to speak from the heart rather than the head. Only a very full heart could bring support to so unrealistic and, I suggest, unnecessary a proposal as the special exemption of Gilbert from the law of copyright.

I asked Mr D. Graham Davis, editor of *The Gilbert and Sullivan Journal*, for the view of the Gilbert and Sullivan Society on this. He replied:

> The demand for special copyright consideration cannot be regarded seriously. No one could claim for the operas what is not vouchsafed to the works of Shakespeare, Sheridan, Wilde, Purcell, Arne, Handel and countless others of equal or greater stature to Gilbert and Sullivan. Public taste and opinion are the best protections.

They certainly are. The risk of abuse after 1961 is a necessary risk that will accompany the release of Gilbert and Sullivan opera from its leading strings, and its reinvigoration with the new life that fresh minds may bring to it. While sympathizing with Miss Alderley and her petitioners concerning the worst that may happen—and stunt productions there are certain to be—I believe that the expiry of copyright may provoke the best thing that could happen: the rising of the D'Oyly Carte Company to new heights through the stimulus of competition. It is a company which has given long service to a devoted public. It will continue to hold a special place in public favour, especially if it brings its musical standards to the highest possible point.

To sum up, it is unlikely that stunt productions in jazz or other idioms are likely to compete seriously for long, after the first flush, with the 'conventional' D'Oyly Carte Company. The more exciting and interesting prospect is that new producers of integrity, skill, and quality will enter the field as competitors. It is not generally known that Sir Malcolm Sargent put forward a proposal for the large-scale production of *The Yeomen of the Guard*, *The Mikado*, and *The Gondoliers* at Covent Garden Opera House during the Festival of Britain in 1951. His idea was that these operas should be presented on fairly conventional lines, but with the finest singers, a large chorus and orchestra, and scenery to match. The proposal had influential support in the operatic world, but it was not supported by the D'Oyly Carte Company, whose contention is that Gilbert and Sullivan opera is essentially 'intimate' and would suffer by translation into such a large scale. This is debatable; nevertheless, after 1961, when new producers seek to breathe new air into these old works, whether for opera house, for film or radio, they will be wise first to go back to the man Sullivan and the man Gilbert, to study what inspired them and what result they sought to inspire on the stage. That story is told in this book. Let producers instil the magic original essence into new productions enriched by modern techniques of lighting, dancing, and décor, equated to the idiom and understanding of modern audiences, and performed by singers and orchestras worthy of the classics, and these operas will last a long time yet.

Having written the foregoing chapter, and recognizing its controversial nature, I felt it right that the last word should be given to Miss Bridget D'Oyly Carte. I invited her comments. She writes:

So much of the speculation concerning the future of the Gilbert and Sullivan Operas appears to be based on the assumption that these works have become moribund in something called the 'Savoy Tradition', and that when they are released from copyright in 1961 they will be performed at last as they deserve to be.

I do not pretend to know what this may mean; but I do know that in spite of our 'traditional' limitations—or perhaps because we have come to understand them—the operas have enjoyed nearly eighty years of vigorous public life both here and abroad, and as yet their entertainment value shows no sign of depreciation.

We are essentially a travelling repertory company, and fully recognize the artistic, technical, and economic limitations of such an organization. Our productions have, of course, evolved quite a long way from their beginnings, and are doing so all the time. While preserving the essence, the forms must change and be freshly re-created. If this had not been understood in the past the operas would not have survived.

It remains to be seen, when anyone may perform the works anyhow, if more of the essential Gilbert and Sullivan will come to light.

B.D.C.

An illustration by W. S. Gilbert for 'The Algerian Monkey', 1864. Twenty-five years later he introduced the same hands-on-shoulders posture in 'The Gondoliers'

HOW THEY BEGAN

First you're born—and I'll be bound you
Find a dozen strangers round you.
'Hallo,' cries the new-born baby,
'Where's my parents? Which may they be?'
　　　　　　　　　　—Utopia Limited

THE YOUNG PRINCESS VICTORIA was living quietly at Kensington Palace, reading the poetry of Sir Walter Scott, singing to herself the arias of Italian opera, and hardly dreaming that within a year she would be called to the throne of Britain.

Charles Dickens was publishing a new serial story called *The Pickwick Papers*. Stage-coaches still rumbled in a properly romantic Dickensian manner along the Strand, when in a comfortably well-to-do household in a side-street off that famous London thoroughfare the natal squawk of William Schwenck Gilbert was heard.

'Where's my parents? Which may they be?' . . . The parents his eyes opened upon were William Gilbert, naval surgeon, lately retired from service in the wood-and-sail battleships of His Majesty King William IV, and his Scottish bride Anne, daughter of Dr Thomas Morris.

In later years Sir William S. Gilbert told an interviewer[1]: 'Date of birth, 18 November, 1836. Birthplace, 17, Southampton Street, Strand, in the house of my grandfather, who had known Dr Johnson, Garrick and Reynolds, and who was the last man in London, I believe, who wore Hessian boots and a pig-tail.'

In 1837, when Queen Victoria began her reign, the baby who was destined to be the Jester of the Victorian Age was seven months old. How Gilbertian it is that today, over a century later, of all the achievements and products of that Victorian era, which seemed in its own time so solid and permanent and rigidly right-side-up, one of the few which remain with us is the topsy-turvy art known as Gilbert and Sullivan Opera. For observe the judgment of posterity, delivered in a lecture by the late Maurice Baring, poet and author, in 1922:

Queen Victoria

[1] 'Illustrated Interviews', by Harry How, *Strand Magazine* 1893.

London in 1842, the year of Sullivan's birth: a view of Piccadilly Circus, looking down Lower Regent Street, drawn and lithographed by Thomas Shotter Boys (from the original in the Guildhall Library). At the Royal Gallery of Illustration (X) Gilbert first met Sullivan, and many of Gilbert's early works were produced there

'One night, during the recent revival of *Iolanthe*, I was sitting next to that celebrated modern author and extremely accomplished manipulator of words, Lytton Strachey. When the chorus sang:

> To say she is his mother is an utter bit of folly!
> Oh, fie! our Strephon is a rogue!
> Perhaps his brain is addled and it's very melancholy!
> Taradiddle, taradiddle, tol lol lay!

he said to me, "That's what I call poetry," and he added that he thought that the most permanent and enduring achievement of the Victorian Age would be neither that of Tennyson, Browning or Swinburne, nor of Gladstone, Disraeli and Parnell, nor of Darwin, Huxley and Ball, but the operas of Gilbert and Sullivan. I am inclined to agree with him; and I should not be in the least surprised if, in ages to come, people will talk of the age of Gilbert and Sullivan as they talk of the age of Pericles. Perhaps they will confuse fact with fiction, and the children of the future will think that trials by jury in that amusing age were conducted to music; that pirates and police hobnobbed at Penzance; that Strephon, the Arcadian Shepherd, brought about the reform of the House of Lords; that the Bolshevist Revolution took place in Barataria; and the Suffragist movement happened at Castle Adamant.'[1]

[1] *Lost Lectures* by Maurice Baring (Peter Davies), 1932, quoted by permission of Messrs Heinemann.

Gilbert's impish whim of viewing the world upside down through his legs was inherited from his father, ex-Surgeon William Gilbert, who wrote in his *Memoirs of a Cynic*: 'From my earliest childhood the ridiculous has thrust itself into every action of my life. I have been haunted through my whole existence by the absurd.'

When this old gentleman took up authorship in later life he lived at Salisbury, where there was a long-established Gilbert family home, and where indeed a branch of the Gilbert family may still be found today. The Gilberts were a south-of-England family. Ancient manuscripts in Winchester Cathedral, dating back to 1500, mention them as yeomen in Hampshire. There they lived, according to C. R. Everett, F.S.G. (the *Genealogists' Magazine*, March 1937), until some of them migrated to Middlesex and Surrey in the eighteenth century and Mr Everett says their graves are to be seen in many village churchyards of Wiltshire and Hampshire, but he finds no confirmation for the old story that they were descended from Sir Humphrey Gilbert, the Elizabethan sea-dog who annexed Newfoundland for Britain in 1583. Nevertheless, Sir W. S. Gilbert was a bit of a sea-dog himself and when in his heyday he built a house in Harrington Gardens, Kensington, he had a stone model of Sir Humphrey's ship mounted on the gable. One day a visitor innocently asked whether the ship was H.M.S. *Pinafore*. 'Sir,' replied Gilbert, 'I don't put my trade mark on my house.'

To return to Gilbert as a baby. If his father had been 'haunted through his whole existence by the absurd', history soon repeated itself with W.S.G. At two years of age Baby Gilbert—they called him 'Bab'—was absurdly stolen by two very charming brigands in Naples, where the holiday-making Gilberts had left him to be pushed out by Nurse. Stopping his pram, the brigands declared that 'the Engleesh papa' had sent them for 'dis lofly bambino'. Nurse handed Bab over.

W. S. Gilbert never wasted anything. The idea of the stolen baby was used years later in the plot of *The Pirates of Penzance*, and again in *The Gondoliers*:

> I stole the Prince, and brought him here,
> And left him, gaily prattling,
> With a highly respectable gondolier,
> Who promised the Royal babe to rear . . .

Of course, Bab was not reared by a gondolier: his irate father redeemed him from the Neopolitan brigands for £25. From the point of view of posterity it was a bargain.

He went to Great Ealing School. According to Miss Edith Browne, a biographer who had the advantage of getting her information direct from Sir W. S. Gilbert before he died, he told her that 'he speedily won the reputation of being a clever, bright boy, who was extremely lazy.

Sketch by Gilbert

It was soon discovered, however, that he could work so quickly that this natural tendency to idleness was no handicap to his abilities.'[1] Out of school hours his hobbies were drawing and reading, and he was especially fascinated by the theatre. 'Under the influence of social intercourse with many literary and theatrical friends who frequented his father's house, his bias for the stage naturally entered largely into his ambitions.' He played the part of Guy Fawkes in a melodrama at school, and then, at fifteen, fired by having seen Charles Kean in *The Corsican Brothers*, he packed his bag, went to the theatre and asked for a job on the stage. Mr Kean sent him packing, back to his books at Ealing.

In 1851, the year of the Great Exhibition, schoolboy Gilbert, on his way home from Ealing must often have passed the wonderful glass Crystal Palace the engineers had erected in Hyde Park. It had another visitor, a small boy six years Gilbert's junior: 'I remember going by coach from York Town to London to see the Great Exhibition of 1851 and returning in the same manner. There was no railway near us.' So said Sir Arthur Sullivan half a century later.[2] York Town is near Bagshot in Surrey.

Gilbert was fifteen and Sullivan nine at the time of the Great Exhibition. In that year the only reputable musical entertainments to be seen in the theatres of London were foreign operas like Donizetti's *L'Elisir d'Amore* and Meyerbeer's *Robert the Devil*. The Queen went to see *The Magic Flute* at Covent Garden (then called the Royal Italian Opera). There was no English musical theatre. The nearest approach to it in 1851 was *The Far West, or the Emigrant's Progress from the Old World to the New*, by Henry Russell (father of Sir Landon Ronald): this was a sequence of scenes depicting life in the Canadian wilds, tricked out with Russell's tuneful songs, among them 'Cheer, Boys, Cheer' and 'A Life on the Ocean Wave'. There was, of course, plenty of erotic and bucolic song to be heard in London's midnight supper rooms, such as the Coal Hole in the Strand, and the masses found light musical entertainment in the open air at the Cremorne and Vauxhall Gardens, or in the taprooms of such elaborate gin-palaces as the Eagle Tavern and Grecian Saloon in the City Road, immortalized by the jingle:

> Up and down the City Road,
> In and out the Eagle,
> That's the way the money goes—
> POP goes the weasel!

In these more enterprising taverns ballad-singers and comedians were hired to lead the company in such ditties as 'Villikins and his Dinah' and 'The Ratcatcher's Daughter' (and thus began the English music-hall).

There were even American musical shows in London a century ago: Hector Berlioz, who came from France to see the Great Exhibition, wrote of how fascinated he was to hear in London the nigger minstrel troupes from the U.S.A. They brought with them the ballads of Stephen Foster, who published 'The Old Folks at Home' in 1851.

[1] *W. S. Gilbert* by Edith A. Browne (John Lane), 1907.
[2] *Sir Arthur Sullivan* by Arthur Lawrence (Bowden), 1899.

Arthur Sullivan's birthplace (X) in Bolwell Terrace, Lambeth

Thus, apart from the lusty songs of the taverns, the British had little of contemporary native music to put into the international shop-window during the Great Exhibition of the Industry of All Nations; when little Sullivan went to the Crystal Palace the music he was most likely to hear on its several mighty organs was that of Handel's *Messiah*.

It is romantic that the Crystal Palace should be among Sullivan's earliest memories, for this fantastic building seems to have been destined to haunt him: some of the greatest moments of his later life, and some of his closest friends, were intimately connected with it. One of the engineers who built it, John Scott Russell, was the father of Rachel, a girl whom Sullivan nearly married. At the Crystal Palace—when it had been removed some years later to the heights of Sydenham—Sullivan made his sensational London début as composer and conductor; he frequently conducted there during his lifetime, and the Secretary of the Palace for many years was Sullivan's bosom friend, Sir George Grove (1820 – 1900). It was a fabulous house of glass for the nine-years'-old Sullivan to see in 1851; the shadows which it cast across his path as he walked round its iron-pillared aisles, and the glittering sunlight that flashed down from a thousand windows, were to return upon Arthur Sullivan again and again in his life-time. Sullivan was always haunted by the romantic in life, just as Gilbert was haunted by the ridiculous.

There was an equally sharp contrast between the homes of the two boys. If you took a cab from the comfortably middle-class Gilbert home in Southampton Street, Strand, crossed Westminster Bridge and turned along the unfashionable south bank of the river into Lambeth, you would come to Bolwell Terrace; here, at number eight, an ugly little house with iron railings round the front area and a prim parlour with a piano, Arthur Seymour Sullivan had been born on 13 May, 1842 (in the same year Mendels-

Sullivan's mother

sohn wrote his 'Spring Song'). Across the end of Bolwell Terrace runs Lambeth Walk, and beyond that is the Thames with its fascinating ebb and flow of tugs and barges. Here, in the full stream of Cockney London, Sullivan had played in the street, and in the little parlour had made his first acquaintance with music: 'When I was not more than four or five years old', he writes, 'it became perfectly evident that my career in life must be music and nothing else. When I was barely five I used to go to the piano and make discoveries for myself.'[1] He was a likeable boy. His father's family were Irish, his mother's part-Italian. He inherited from both races some endearing young charms. He was warm-hearted and romantic—and prodigiously musical. When he was eight he had already written his first anthem, 'By the Waters of Babylon'. He inherited his music and his gay love of life from both sides of the family, for his mother, Maria Clementina Coghlan, came of an artistic Italian family (the Righis), and his father, Thomas Sullivan, was Irish, and a military bandmaster. Thomas's father had also served in the British Army. In fact, when Sir Arthur Sullivan dictated his autobiographical notes to Arthur Lawrence in 1899 he took great delight in relating the story of this hard-living Irish grandfather who was born in 1786 at Kerryshane, County Cork:

He was an impoverished young squire, much given to steeple-chasing. One day he won a noteworthy steeplechase, and riding homewards he stopped at a little village inn to celebrate the event. This he did, as was the wine-bibbing custom in those days, somewhat too freely. At that time every able-bodied man was being pressed into the Queen's[2] service. There happened to be a recruiting-sergeant in the inn, who pressed the Queen's shilling into my grandfather's hand. The next morning when he awoke from his heavy sleep he discovered that he had enlisted. There was no help for it. Unfortunately, he had just married the handsome daughter of a well-to-do farmer, but the farmer absolutely declined to buy his discharge, and having no money him-self, there was nothing to be done but to submit to the inevitable. He was immedi-

[1] Article by Sir Arthur Sullivan in *M.A.P.*, 1899.
[2] A slip of the tongue. This happened in the reign of King George III.

ately ordered off for foreign service, and took part in the Peninsular campaign, and behaved with distinction at Vittoria, Salamanca, and Badajos . . . After the battle of Waterloo my grandfather was ordered with a detachment of his regiment to St Helena, and his wife accompanied him. At first they lived in the regimental quarters close to Longwood, where Napoleon lived, and, whilst there, a child was born to my grandmother. During her confinement one of the soldiers was sentenced to receive twenty-five lashes for being drunk on duty, but the doctor declared that his cries would make my grandmother very ill, so he was taken down from the triangle, let off, and was eternally grateful to my grandmother.

My grandfather—who was a man of superior education for those days—became, I believe, paymaster of Napoleon's household. The children were brought up together, and when the little ones were old enough to toddle about Napoleon would make them the companions of his daily walks, taking one child by each hand, giving them cakes, sweets, etc, and became very much attached to them both . . . Napoleon complained of both the quantity and quality of the food supplied, but his complaints were in vain. By way of remedy, he conceived the notion of breaking off the gold and silver eagles from his covers and plates, which my grandfather, who was devoted to him, used to sell for him, in order to furnish necessaries for the table. When this device was discovered it would seem to have had some effect, for better treatment followed.

When Napoleon died on 5 May, 1821, his body was opened for embalming, and his heart taken out and placed in a wash-basin in an adjacent room, with a lamp on the table beside it. Longwood was infested with rats, and fearing the result of an incursion of these voracious creatures, my grandfather volunteered to sit in the room all through the night with an old 'Brown Bess' in his hand, and shot the rats when they came too near.[1]

The Sullivans of Lambeth were a lowly family; they lived in a small house, they had no servants, when they went out they did not go horse-back or spinning along in fine carriages—they walked, or caught the horse-bus; and all around them was the squalor of early-Victorian industrialism: 'Working-class life a hundred years ago,' says Professor G. M. Trevelyan, 'divided between the gloom of dreary quarters and the harsh discipline of the workshop, was uncheered by the many interests that now relieve the lot of the town-dweller. Few of the workmen or their wives could read; holiday excursions and popular entertainments were rare, except some sporting events of a low type, such as setting on men, women, or animals to fight. In the vacant misery of such a life, two rival sources of consolation, drink and religion, strove for the souls of men.'[2] But Mr and Mrs Sullivan made No. 8 Bolwell Terrace an oasis of high-spirits and music. Their Irish-Italian blood would not be subdued. For their sons, Frederic and Arthur, they dreamed and schemed. Thomas Sullivan played first clarinet in the orchestra at the Surrey Theatre, and augmented a modest income by working as a

---

[1] Grandfather Sullivan returned to England and became a Chelsea pensioner. He died at the Royal Hospital, 1838.

[2] *British History in the Nineteenth Century and After* by G. M. Trevelyan (Longmans, Green).

copyist and music teacher. After a few years he got a job as bandmaster at the Royal Military College, and they all moved to Sandhurst. This was a stroke of fortune for Arthur, for his father allowed him not only to attend the daily band practices but to play in them! Thus the boy picked up a working knowledge of every instrument in the military band, and as he said later, 'I learnt in the best possible way how to write for an orchestra.' But when Arthur was eight his parents sent him to a boarding school back in London, in Bayswater.

Sullivan (aged ten) to his mother:

I say, I want to speak to you. One of our boys, Higham, has taken a great fancy to my knife. He has a little gold pencil-case which I have taken a great fancy to. He asked me whether, if he gives me the pencil and a two-bladed knife, I will give him mine. I have submitted this to your discretion . . .

It happened that there was in this Bayswater house a lodger—'Miss Matthews, who has a nice piano and I often go up to her room to play'. There was no laziness about this schoolboy, as with young Gilbert; Arthur Sullivan did his lessons, then he played the piano and he sang and already he had a burning ambition to be a chorister. 'It means everything to me,' he wrote home.

Letter to the Rev. Thomas Helmore, Master of Her Majesty's Chapel Royal, from the Rev. Percy Smith:

My dear Sir,

I am requested by a parishioner of mine, Mr Sullivan, Band Master to the Royal Military College, to write you a line with reference to the possibility of getting his son into the Chapel Royal. The boy is very desirous of becoming a chorister. His name is Arthur and he is a few months more than ten years of age. My reason in writing is to bear testimony to his abilities and character on the supposition that there may be a chance of his succeeding in other respects . . . Independently of his remarkable abilities (for he is very quick in every subject) I am fully convinced of his being a most highly principled boy. He is very amiable and obedient and gentle in his manner . . .

*   *   *   *

6 Cheyne Walk, Chelsea

My dear Sir,

Little Sullivan has called here this evening and this reminds me that you are still unanswered. I like Arthur Sullivan's appearance and manner; his voice is good, and if arrangements can be made to obviate the difficulty of his age being greater than that of our probation in general I shall be glad to give him a trial. Your testimonial of character, ability, and sweetness of disposition is most satisfactory and weighs very much in my desire to procure his admission to the Chapel Royal.

Yours very truly,
THOMAS HELMORE

The choristers of Her Majesty's Chapel Royal were (and are) a small and exclusive clan of boys who sang regularly at services in the royal palaces, wearing a scarlet-and-gold uniform; they also formed the nucleus of great choirs on State occasions; they had their own private boarding school at 6 Cheyne Walk, under the stern patriarch, Helmore, who soon recognized he had acquired a star pupil.

Mr Helmore to Mrs Sullivan:

Arthur sang a very elaborate solo in Church today. His expression was beautiful, it brought the tears very near my eyes (although the music itself was rubbish), but as I was immediately to enter the pulpit I was obliged to restrain myself.

Sullivan, writing home:

M. was caned today because he did not know the meaning of fortissimo.

Sullivan had a first-rate musical and educational grounding. Helmore kept his nose to the grindstone: 'Arthur should try to get on in his Latin and other lessons, so that he may take rank in the school more proportionate to his excellence in music.'

In 1854 the Crystal Palace, having been removed from Hyde Park to Sydenham, was reopened with what must have been ear-shattering effect by a mammoth chorus, an orchestra of two hundred and fifty, and the bands of the Grenadier Guards and Coldstream Guards, in the presence of the Queen and the Prince Consort—seventeen hundred performers in all, among whom sang Arthur Sullivan, together with the other choristers of the Chapel Royal. The twelve-year-old boy was greatly impressed:

Cheyne Walk,
16 June, 1854.

My dear Father,

Tomorrow is a half holiday with us and I could meet you in the afternoon at Frith Street if we are not kept in for anything. Our holidays begin about the end of July. I shall be glad when they do begin. I can't tell you by letter the grandeur of the scene on Saturday . . . Give my love to dear Mother and tell her I hope she will soon be coming up here as I want to see her very much. My poor old desk wants mending most awfully. Good bye. God bless you.

Your affectionate and dutiful son,

ARTHUR

By 1856 Arthur had become 'first boy'. Helmore frequently picked him out to sing solo parts at the royal palaces, and so Sullivan caught his first glimpses of the circle of Society around the Throne. He also sang before the Bishop of London at Fulham Palace; the Bishop was 'much pleased', patted him on the head and gave him half a crown. When Queen Victoria's eighth child, the Duke of Albany, was christened, Sullivan was chosen to sing a solo at the ceremony. This time the Prince Consort congratulated him and gave him half a sovereign.

The Rev. Thomas Helmore

It was at a rehearsal of this ceremony that the conductor, Michael Costa, a native of Italy, pulled Sullivan up over his diction. The boy had sung the solo in Costa's anthem 'Suffer little children to come unto Me', when the composer said: 'Vell done, Soolivan; very vell done. But you must put your accent as clear as your words, like this: Soofer leetle cheeldren to cume after Me, and forbeed them not, for of sooch is the Kingdom of Heaven.'[1] It made a good joke among the choristers, but Costa was a power in the musical world, a power not to be under-estimated, and no doubt Arthur Sullivan, like a sensible boy, kept a straight face.

Sullivan enjoyed his life at 6 Cheyne Walk, despite the hard work. The nine other 'Children of the Chapel Royal' in Mr Helmore's charge included Alfred Cellier, afterwards composer of *Dorothy*, and his brother François, afterwards conductor of Gilbert and Sullivan operas at the Savoy. In their schooldays it was always Arthur who came out top.

Sullivan, writing home, 1855:

When I had composed my anthem I showed it to Sir George Smart, who told me it did me great credit, and also told me to get the parts copied out, and he would see what he could do with it. So I copied them out and he desired the Sub-Dean to have it sung, and it *was* sung. The Dean was there in the evening and he called me up to him in the vestry and said it was very clever, and said that perhaps I should be writing an oratorio some day. But he said there was Something Higher to attend to, and then Mr Helmore said that I was a very good boy indeed. Whereupon he shook hands with me, with half a sovereign.

This was the first fee he ever received for the public performance of one of his own works. He was not quite thirteen. A few months later the music shops displayed in their windows a sacred song, 'O Israel', published by Mr Novello, composed by Arthur S. Sullivan—his first published music.

At this time Gilbert had not earned a penny, though he was nineteen. As an infant prodigy Sullivan had easily outpaced his future partner, who was nothing sensational of that sort. W. S. Gilbert had been merely Head Boy at Ealing School; had then passed in unspectacular fashion into King's College, London. He was never tipped half a sovereign by Royalty. He had no obvious ready-made career before him. Sullivan, on

[1] Article by a fellow pupil, C. V. Bridgman, the *Musical Times*, 1 March, 1901.

the other hand, has said: 'I was always composing in those days. Every spare moment I could get I utilized for it. A short time ago I came across a four-part madrigal in an old manuscript book perfectly complete, and scribbled across it is *Written on my bed at night in deadly fear lest Helmore should come in and catch me.*'[1]

Sullivan, then, was all set for a musical career by the early 1850's. Gilbert was studying for his B.A. at King's College. Friends of the Gilbert family assumed that W.S.G., as the son of an upper-middle-class household, would enter the law, the church, or the army, if he did not follow his father into the navy and medicine. The first sign of a deviation towards satirical verse came when he was about sixteen. This piece of verse has never been published, until now.

THE FIRST COMIC VERSE OF W. S. GILBERT

Sleeping in the sunshine of the Cathedral Close at Salisbury there is the old English house which was the Gilbert family home for many years. Here the ex-naval surgeon, William Gilbert, lived during the height of his son's career, and here he died in 1890, and was carried across the Green and buried in the Cloisters. Nearly sixty years later when the BBC was broadcasting its *Gilbert and Sullivan* programmes Mrs Francis Carter, grand-daughter of old William Gilbert, and niece of the dramatist, was still living at Salisbury, a tall, forthright old lady, a thorough chip off the Gilbertian block.

'I was born in the house in The Close,' she said, 'and of course I remember Grand-father Gilbert very clearly, and also his famous son, known to us in the family as Uncle Schwenck—he often came down from London to stay. Grandfather had one son (W. S. Gilbert), and three daughters, Jane, Maud, and Florence, all brilliant and attractive women, but only one of the girls married—my mother, Jane. Grandfather was tall, with blue eyes, very good-looking: that's him—' (the old lady pointed to an oil-painting on the wall, rather resembling Charles Dickens). 'He was a Liberal, and ran his hobby-horses to death. He was a tempestuous old gentleman, but very kind to us children . . . couldn't get on with his Scottish wife, so she lived in London, while he wrote books in Salisbury. Oh yes, he was a writer, too, but he began writing his novels comparatively late in life, when his son already had a considerable literary reputation. Grandfather was a sort of literary Don Quixote, always tilting at windmills. Uncle Schwenck inherited this trait, but otherwise I don't think he was much influenced, at least professionally, by his father.'

Another relative who remembers the Gilberts, both father and son, is Professor Gilbert Murray, O.M., of Oxford University: 'W. S. Gilbert was my mother's first cousin. We knew all the Gilbert family quite intimately: Schwenck himself, his sisters, and his very interesting and handsome old father, after whom I was called.'[2]

[1] *Sir Arthur Sullivan* by Arthur Lawrence (Bowden), 1899.
[2] In a letter to the author. *See* Family tree, p. xv.

William Gilbert
father of the dramatist

W. S. Gilbert
the earliest portrait

Uncle Schwenck—W. S. Gilbert—was in appearance very much like his father, but without the beard—a handsome six-footer with mutton-chop whiskers, a military bearing, and an incisive, assertive, manner of speech. The earliest-known portrait, a painting in oils of a youth in his teens, hangs in Mrs Carter's house at Salisbury alongside old Grandfather Gilbert. 'One of my earliest recollections of the two of them,' she says, 'is of Grandfather coming down to breakfast one morning brandishing a newspaper and crying "Well, the boy has made a success this time".' Then he read out a review of the first performance of *The Mikado*. He was immensely proud of his son.

'All of us who lived in the old home in The Close knew a verse which was, I believe, the first literary effort of my Uncle Schwenck. This is the story of it. When he was still a schoolboy at Ealing my Uncle caught typhoid fever; he had it so badly that he became emaciated, and his head was shaved. The family took him to France to recuperate, and one day they were waiting in the streets to see the Emperor Napoleon and the Empress Eugénie go past. Afterwards they noticed the youth writing in an exercise book, and this is what he had written—or so it has been passed down to us, from mouth to mouth.'

And then the old lady recited:

> When the horses, white with foam,
>   Drew the Empress to her home
> From the place whence she did roam,
>   The Empress she did see
>   The Gilbert Familee.
> To the Emperor she said:
>   'How beautiful the head

Of that youth of gallant mien,
Cropped so neat and close and clean—
    Though I own he's rather lean.'
Said the Emperor: 'It is!
And I never saw a phiz
More wonderful than 'is.'

Napoleon III, nephew of Napoleon Bonaparte, reigned in France from 1852 (the probable date of this verse) until the Revolution of 1870, when he and the Empress Eugénie found refuge in England. Gilbert, when he grew up, was not an admirer of the French monarchy. He was the artist who drew a savage caricature (reproduced here) to illustrate an attack in verse on Napoleon and Eugénie in the magazine *Fun*.[1] In contrast, Sullivan as an adult basked in the personal friendship of these exiled French royalty . . . which was characteristic of him.

Today, more than a century later, if we try to analyse the cause of the perennial success of the Gilbert and Sullivan operas, we may quite reasonably trace some of it right back to the early environment of these two men. Sullivan, in the lowly but musical home in Lambeth, began life with his feet firmly on the ground. He was never ashamed of this when success lifted his head into the clouds, nor yet when it rubbed his shoulders with royalty. He had an ability always to tune his songs to the hearts of the common people. His occasional tendency to sentimentality in the comic operas was

counterbalanced by the astringency of Gilbert, a quality the dramatist inherited from that tempestuous tilter at windmills, William Gilbert, ex-R.N. Although W. S. Gilbert came from the upper middle class he was to experience hard apprentice years in journalism and the law before he met Sullivan; this ensured that he, like Sullivan, had his feet firmly on the ground even when his head soared into endless clouds of Gilbertian fantasy. Sullivan and Gilbert were the very different sides of a penny. It was a penny which was to bring the English-speaking people a unique peepshow.

[1] Several books, including *W. S. Gilbert* by Sidney Dark and Rowland Grey (Methuen), have stated that the verses were written by W. S. Gilbert, but Mr Reginald Allen, of New York, has in his collection (now in the Pierpont Morgan Library) a letter from Gilbert to a journalist named Hindle in which W.S.G. writes 'The absurd verses on Napoleon III were not written by me.' It appears that he only perpetrated the cartoons.

[39]

Royal Academy of Music, Midsummer Concert,
Tuesday, July 14, 1857.

M S S with soprani chorus--(Op. 1)--"It was a lover
and his lass" (Sullivan).

S ince now the first fruit of your genius sees the light,
U nworthy tho' I feel myself its praise to write,
L et me the event proclaim, and stamp on mem'rys page--
L ong there to live--your debut on the world's great stage.
I n fortune's golden paths henceforth may you proceed,
V ictorious at each step, no enemies to heed.
A nd when the sand of fleeting life has run its course,
N ew life in Heaven be yours, and joys of endless source.

J. G. T.

A prophetic tribute to Arthur Sullivan (aged 15) by a fellow student at the Academy, **J. G. T.**

BELOW. Nearly a century later Sir Malcolm Sargent bows to the audience before conducting the opening performance of the Festival of Britain season of Gilbert and Sullivan operas at the Savoy Theatre, 1951

1855-60

BOOTS ARE THROWN AT GILBERT
BOUQUETS FOR SULLIVAN

See how the fates their gifts allot,
For A is happy—B is not.
                    —*The Mikado*

AT KING'S COLLEGE, in London, they still possess the minute books of the King's College Scientific Society for 1855, in the untidy handwriting of the hon. secretary, W. S. Gilbert. If you read these minutes you may observe an autocratic note about them which smacks of the Gilbert-to-come. Here is young Gilbert, a newcomer to the learned debates of the Scientific Society; in next to no time he is its secretary; soon we find him encouraging a dissenting faction who prefer literature to science. He backs up a proposal to dissolve the Scientific Society and to appropriate its funds to literature's pursuit, but when the proposer suggests a Shakespearean Reading Society, Gilbert jibs. He moves 'that it be called a Dramatic as well as a Shakespearean Reading Society'. This is carried, and at its meetings thereafter Gilbert leads the Society along the path of his own theatrical enthusiasms. (But as soon as he left College it reverted to its old name, the Scientific Society!)[1]

Gilbert was never a fanatic for Shakespeare. When he had become a famous dramatist he said to George Grossmith: 'If you promise me faithfully not to mention this to a single person, not even to your dearest friend, I don't think Shakespeare rollicking.' And once when his patience was tried by the ecstatic remarks of a Shakespearean rhapsodist, Gilbert said: 'I think Shakespeare is a very obscure writer. What do you make of this passage?—"I would as lief be thrust through a quicket hedge as cry Pooh to a callow throstle".'

[1] Mr J. T. Combridge, Registrar of the University of London King's College, writes to the author: 'Gilbert took his B.A. degree in the University of London after spending four years, 1853-7, in the Department of General Literature and Science (as it was then called) in this university. With the departure of Gilbert in 1857, the Engineering (or Scientific) Society was re-established with its original objects and except for an interruption of one year in 1866, has continued to the present time, being now the oldest Society of its kind in the country.'

[41]

'That is perfectly plain,' replied the pedant. 'A great lover of feathered songsters, rather than disturb the little warbler, would prefer to go through a thorny hedge . . . But I can't for the moment recall the quotation. In which play does it occur?'

'I have just invented it,' said Gilbert, 'and jolly good Shakespeare too!'

As the nineteen-year-old secretary of the King's College Dramatic and Shakespearean Reading Society, Gilbert was definitely the boss of his own little circle, but outside of it he was unknown. Sullivan was the first of the two to get his name into public print.

The *Illustrated London News*, 10 March, 1855:

A series of Vocal Concerts, selected entirely from the numerous works of Sir Henry Bishop, has been commenced at the Hanover Square Rooms. The first concert consisted of a selection of glees and concerted pieces, chiefly taken from Bishop's theatrical works; they were sung by Masters Sullivan, Cooke, and Malsch . . . All the music was admirably sung and warmly applauded, many familiar faces of our most distinguished musicians and lovers of music being visible in all parts of the room.

To perform at the Hanover Square Rooms gave one a cachet, for this was London's chief centre for serious music. Here had performed J. C. Bach, Haydn, Liszt, Mendelssohn, Joachim, and in this very year 1855 Wagner made his first public appearance in England, conducting the Philharmonic Society's symphony concerts, and angrily denouncing the mediocrity of the performance: 'You are the famous Philharmonic Orchestra,' he thundered throwing up his arms. 'Raise yourselves, gentlemen, be *artists!*' English orchestral playing was extremely bad at this period.

One can imagine Sullivan, still a choirboy of the Chapel Royal, singing in his clear, unbroken voice to the crowded lamp-lit room—but what happened to his young colleagues Cooke and Malsch? No doubt they were equally pleasing to the audience, and equally excited, and had similar dreams of fame when they saw their names mentioned in the *Illustrated London News*, but what do the names of Cooke and Malsch mean today? . . . no more than those of the 'distinguished musicians' which are appended to the above report, as being 'among those present'. Music in the fifties was at a low ebb. Mendelssohn had died in 1847, and no one had yet risen to take his place at the head of English music; certainly, no one in the Hanover Square Rooms that night was likely to guess that his successor was among them.

Music was at a low ebb, but that was not the only reason why this paragraph was tucked away in an insignificant corner of the magazine. It was overshadowed by lurid engravings of the field of Balaclava covered with cannon balls and dead bodies. Hostilities had broken out between Britain and Russia, and the papers were full of war news. The campaign was not going well; in the Crimea Florence Nightingale was tackling the terrible plight of the wounded; in London one of the many young men who answered the call for volunteers was W. S. Gilbert. He began studying to take an examination for a commission in the Royal Artillery.

Thus in 1856 both our young men were hard at their exams. While Gilbert (aged twenty) was studying for his commission, Sullivan (aged fourteen), still at the Chapel Royal, was trying for the first great prize of his career, the Mendelssohn Scholarship, tenable at the Royal Academy of Music. The result of these endeavours was (as usual) success in the case of Sullivan, frustration in the case of Gilbert. In Gilbert's own words: 'The war came to a rather abrupt and unexpected end, and no more officers being required the examination was indefinitely postponed. Among the blessings of peace may be reckoned certain comedies, operas, farces and extravaganzas which, if the war had lasted another six weeks, would in all probability never have been written.'[1]

In Sullivan's case the result of the examination was thus announced in the *Illustrated London News:*

MENDELSSOHN SCHOLARSHIP. — The successful candidate for the above scholarship, instituted this year at the Royal Academy of Music, Hanover-square, London, in memory of the late much lamented composer, Felix Mendelssohn Bartholdy, is Arthur Seymour Sullivan, chorister in Her Majesty's Chapels Royal; he is 14 years of age, and was the junior candidate. Master Sullivan is the youngest son of Mr. Thomas Sullivan, master of the band at the Royal Military College, Sandhurst.

The celebrated singer Jenny Lind (Madame Lind-Goldschmidt) and her husband were chiefly responsible for the founding of this scholarship in memory of the composer whose music was revered throughout the land, the more so because it was known that the Queen admired his works before all others. Sullivan took a very active interest in the Mendelssohn Scholarship to the end of his days; now, in 1856, while still a chorister, he became its first scholar.

To Mr and Mrs Sullivan, who had struggled and denied themselves to give their son his chance, this was a triumph beyond their wildest dreams. Arthur was the youngest of seventeen competitors. Old Tom Sullivan, the bandmaster, wrote: 'I could not suppress the tears that accompanied my prayer to the Almighty for his goodness.' Ever since Arthur was a toddler and had shown a quickness at his father's knee for learning the various instruments of the military band, Tom had encouraged him and dreamed dreams for him; now he realized that his son was in fact quite outstanding. What a sensation the boy was causing we may gather at first hand from another choirboy, who became in due course Bishop of Korea, Dr Corfe:

On the Feast of St Michael and All Angels in 1856 I was one of the senior choristers at St Michael's College, which had just been built in Tenbury by Sir Frederick Ouseley. For the opening services the small school choir was augmented from various sources. I have never forgotten the prodigious sensation caused amongst us

[1] From a brief autobiographical article he contributed to Clement Scott's magazine the *Theatre*, 2 April, 1883.

[43]

youngsters by the singing of young Sullivan (then of the Chapel Royal). We found him very sociable and free from 'uppishness' of any kind. To entertain his numerous musical friends Sir Frederick asked them to his house in the evening. We boys had to go to provide the soprano parts for the concerted music. Whether Sullivan sang that evening or not I cannot remember. We knew, of course, that he was a Mendelssohn Scholar, and that he could play the piano; but I do not think anyone present was prepared for what happened. Suddenly Ouseley said, 'Sullivan, I will challenge you to play an extempore duet with me.' This savoured of the impossible, considering one was a chorister and the other Professor of Music at Oxford. But Sullivan said very modestly and quietly, 'Very good, Sir Frederick.' The room was pretty still by this time, and everyone looked on. 'You take the treble, Sullivan, because it will be easier, and I will take the bass.' Forthwith they sat down at the piano, agreed upon the key and the rhythm and fell to. I do not suppose that as music it was very remarkable, but they played on without stopping until the piece came to a natural end.[1]

With Arthur Sullivan launched into the Royal Academy of Music, his father wrote a letter of thanks to Mr Helmore, and prophesied that 'Should the Almighty spare him I think he will at no distant day achieve much greater things.'[2]

From 'The Bab Ballads'

It was in the same year, 1856, that W. S. Gilbert, B.A., obtained an insignificant and uncongenial job as a clerk in the Education Department of the Privy Council, at £120 a year. 'I was one of the worst bargains any government ever made,' he said.

His life cannot have been happy at this period. At home his father and mother were quarrelling. He had three young sisters, no brothers. He hated his office work. He was beginning to have the reputation of being difficult to get on with, because his mind was sharply unconventional and his tongue had a whip in it. He was not tactful. But he had a great sense of humour. With these characteristics, and with his commanding presence (he was now over six feet tall), W. S. Gilbert was the sort of person who stood out in a crowd. But what had he yet to show for it?

His first appearance in print was a thrill he never forgot. A singer named Mlle Parepa asked Gilbert to do a translation of the laughing song from *Manon Lescaut*, to be printed in the programme of the Promenade Concerts: 'I remember that I went night after night to those concerts to enjoy the intense gratification of standing at the elbow of any promenader who might be reading my translation, and wondering to myself what that promenader would say if he knew that the gifted creature who had written the

[1] From article by Dr Corfe in the *Musical Times*, 12 November, 1901.
[2] Quoted in *Arthur Seymour Sullivan*, by H. Saxe Wyndham (Kegan Paul), 1926.

very words he was reading was at that moment standing within a yard of him? The secret satisfaction of knowing that I possessed the power to thrill him with this information was enough, and I preserved my incognito.'

Sullivan (20 May, 1857, writing home):

I enjoyed the Philharmonic Concert very much last Monday, all except Rubinstein.[1] He has wonderful strength in the wrists, and particularly so in octave passages, but there is a good deal of clap-trap about him.

As for his composition, it was a disgrace to the Philharmonic. I never heard such wretched, nonsensical rubbish; not two bars of melody or harmony together throughout, and yet Mr E. thinks him wonderful.

Every day at the Royal Academy of Music Sullivan's professors were delighted by his prodigious musicianship, yet he never appeared a prig in the eyes of his fellow students, for he had high spirits and friendly charm, and tact, qualities which were to smooth his social course all through his life. 'He was as merry and as mischievous a boy as can well be imagined,' says a fellow student. 'Although a huge favourite among the students, he was a sad thorn in the side of some of the professors, and to none more than Charles Lucas, the director of the Academy Orchestra. It was no unusual thing at the rehearsals to hear at times the most unearthly noise proceed from one instrument and then the other, and the reason therefor was usually summed up in Lucas's exclamation, "Now, Sullivan, you are at it again", which might possibly have been further from the truth. Sullivan's mastery over orchestral instruments even then, at fourteen years of age, was marvellous. He played them all with apparent ease . . .'[2]

By now Sullivan's father had obtained a post as professor of the clarinet at the Kneller Hall School of Music, the training school for British military bands, and had moved with Mrs Sullivan to a house made by throwing a couple of cottages into one, at York Town. Thirty years later, by a strange coincidence, Sir Arthur Sullivan was to write his oratorio *The Golden Legend* in the same house: 'In 1886 when I wrote to some friends living in that part, asking them to find me some quiet country lodgings, so that I might peacefully write *The Golden Legend*, they took rooms for me in the very house at York Town where I had lived as a child.'[3] Back in 1857, he wrote to this home of his, from the Royal Academy of Music:

Dearest Mother and Father,—Every time I have made up my mind to sit down and write to you some fellow or other is sure to turn me away from it by asking me to come and lead our band, which, by the by, consists of two French 'squeakers' which produce a twangy sound like an oboe, two combs, a cover of a book for a drum. By the bye, I have sold 22s. worth of songs to different gentlemen.

[1] Anton Rubinstein, famous Russian pianist, 1830–94.
[2] *Sir Arthur Sullivan*, by Arthur Lawrence (Bowden), 1899.
[3] *Ibid.*

There was another youth in London who was trying to make some money. Perched on his office stool, he often had a jingle in his mind as he scratched at a blot; he now ventured to post one of these verses, called 'Satisfied Isaiah Jones', to Fleet Street. It came back: 'The Editor of *Once a Week* regrets that he cannot use the enclosed clever and amusing poem owing to its length.'

As an escape from his desk, W. S. Gilbert now joined the volunteers. He was gazetted Ensign in the 5th West Yorkshire Militia, with headquarters at Knaresborough. For nearly twenty years he was to retain this connection with the army, later transferring to the Royal Aberdeenshire Militia and attaining the rank of captain and the splendour of kilt and sporran.

After 'four uncomfortable years' in the Privy Council Offices, W.S.G. met with a turn of fortune. He came into a legacy of £300. Straightaway he sent in his resignation. In later days he always looked back on this as 'the happiest day of my life'. He said: 'With £100 I paid my call to the bar (I had previously entered myself as a student at the Middle Temple), with another £100 I obtained access to a conveyancer's chambers, and with the third £100 I furnished a set of chambers of my own, and began life afresh as a barrister-at-law.'[1]

In two years at the Bar he earned just £25; but his work as a lawyer earned him a great deal in experience which he put to good use later in his operas and other writings.

> When I, good friends, was called to the Bar,
> I'd an appetite fresh and hearty,
> But I was, as many young barristers are,
> An impecunious party.
> I'd a swallow-tail coat of a beautiful blue,
> A brief which I bought of a booby,
> A couple of shirts and a collar or two,
> And a ring that looked like a ruby.
> —*Trial by Jury*

The ridiculous still haunted him, even in court. One day when an old woman was accused of picking pockets Gilbert made an impassioned speech for her defence, whereupon she rather illogically hurled a heavy boot at him. Gilbert was not the man to waste such an experience; it appeared soon after in a short story in the *Cornhill Magazine*: 'No sooner had the learned judge pronounced sentence than the poor soul stooped down and, taking off a heavy boot, flung it at my head as a reward for my eloquence on her behalf. The boot missed me, but hit a reporter on the head, and to this fact I am disposed to attribute the unfavourable light in which my speech for the defence was placed in two or three of the leading papers next morning.'

While Gilbert was dodging boots, Sullivan was receiving bouquets. Towards the end of his second year at the Academy of Music he proudly showed his father and mother

[1] The *Theatre*, 2 April, 1883.

a letter from the Secretary of the Mendelssohn Committee: 'You have been re-elected a Mendelssohn scholar for another year in order to enable you to pursue your studies in the Conservatoire at Leipzig . . .'

Leipzig!—this was Mecca. The musical centre of Europe. The Conservatoire that had been founded by Mendelssohn. This meant that Arthur would be taught by old Moscheles, who had taught Mendelssohn harmony . . . Moscheles, who once upon a time actually walked and talked with Beethoven.

On the first day of his studies in Germany the boy began keeping a diary.

    *   *   *   *

Extract from an interview with Sir Arthur Sullivan in the *Strand Musical Magazine*, 1895:

'Did you work very hard in Leipzig?'

'Sometimes,' replied Sir Arthur with a smile, 'but you know what a student's life means; loafing as well as working.'

'Who were your ideal composers in the early days of your career?'

'Mendelssohn, Schumann and Schubert appealed most strongly to my feelings, and *Tannhäuser* and *Lohengrin* of Wagner were especial favourites of mine; but I am very eclectic in my tastes.'

    *   *   *   *

To Sullivan his visit to Germany was more than an education. It was a pilgrimage. He was always highly sensitive to atmosphere; now he sensed near him the great composers of the Past. 'I took lessons in counterpoint in the very room where Bach wrote all his great works when in Leipzig, so you can imagine the atmosphere of that room as being impregnated with counterpoint and fugue.'

He also met the great composers of the Present. Spohr, the German composer who was then thought by many musicians to be greater than Beethoven, heard a Sullivan quartet and said to him 'So young and yet so advanced in art.' And Arthur wrote home:

I have formed the acquaintance of Liszt. Mr David[1] gave a grand musical matinée to which he invited me. Liszt, Von Bülow (Prussian court pianist) and many other German celebrities, musical and non-musical, were there. In the evening when

[1] Ferdinand David, famous violinist and conductor at the Conservatoire.

nearly everyone was gone, Liszt, David, Bronsart and I had a quiet game of whist together, and I walked home with Liszt in the evening . . . The next evening a grand concert in the theatre, Liszt conducting . . . Liszt is a very amiable man, despite his eccentricities, which are many. What a wonderful player he is! Such power and at the same time such delicacy and lightness.

And he met at least one of the great composers of the Future, a fellow student named Grieg, who was a year his junior.

I have a very nice room with a little sleeping apartment for five thalers a month. I mean to be very careful, and not spend a groschen more than I can help. I began fires today for the first time. I did without them for as long as I could, but it is so cold now I thought it right to have one, for I cannot work in the cold, and I am working very hard now.

His scholarship was extended for another year at Leipzig:

My great hobby is still conducting. I have been told by many of the masters here that I was born to be a conductor, and consequently have been educating myself to a high degree in that branch of the art. If I can only once obtain an opportunity to show what I can do in that way I feel confident of my success afterwards. Do not mistake this for conceit . . . but I am getting of an age now when I shall be obliged to have confidence in myself and in my resources. I often try to think what would have become of me had I never come to Germany. In England there was very little more for me to learn. I had heard and knew well almost all the small stock of music which is ever performed in London (and it is very little compared to what one hears here).

A third year brought the most exciting triumphs: he wrote and conducted an Overture to Moore's poem 'The Feast of Roses' from *Lalla Rookh*:

It was such fun standing up there and conducting that large orchestra! I can fancy Mother saying 'Bless his little heart! How it must have beaten!'

It was such fun at Leipzig. Sullivan had grown into a charming high-spirited young man. The girls fell in love with him. The men admired and envied him. He was 'received' everywhere, and made his entry into German musical Society graciously.

'It was Sullivan's very nature to ingratiate himself with everyone that crossed his path. He always wanted to make an impression, and what is more always succeeded in doing so. He was a natural courtier: which did not prevent him from being a very lovable person.' So he is summed up by Clara Rogers, *née* Barnett, a fellow student. She describes him as 'a smiling youth with an oval, olive-tinted face, dark eyes, a large generous mouth and a thick crop of dark curly hair, which overhung his low forehead . . . The sight of him excited in me a strange emotion never before experienced!' But she adds sadly that Arthur Sullivan 'showed a distinct inclination to flirt with Rosamund' —her sister, who was also studying music at Leipzig.[1]

[1] *Memories of a Musical Career*, by Clara Rogers (Boston), 1919.

While Sullivan was there he wrote a great quantity of music which has disappeared. One item, a love song, has lately come to light again. It is worth our special attention not only because it reveals the talent of this youth of seventeen, but also for the romantic little story which goes with it.

Dedicated by Sullivan to Rosamund Barnett

Composed by Arthur S. Sullivan at Leipzig, 3 December, 1859

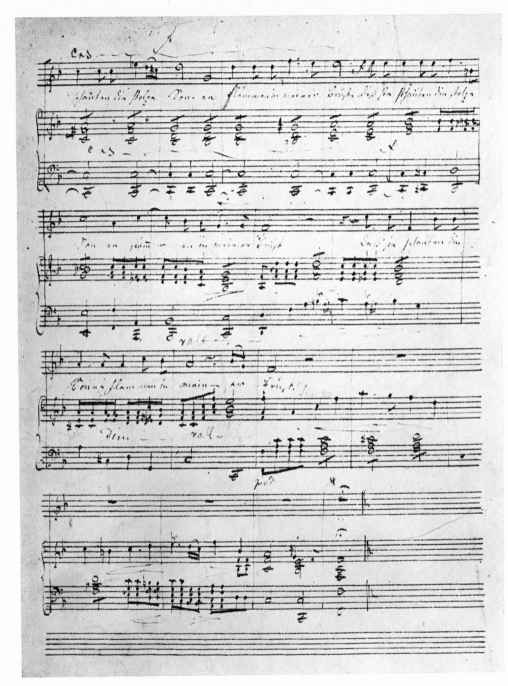

Continuation of Song for Contralto Voice dedicated to Rosamund Barnett

Rosamund Barnett

In the mail which reached the BBC in 1947 after the radiobiography *Gilbert and Sullivan* there came this song of 1859, unpublished and hitherto unknown, scored in the neat hand of Arthur Sullivan, together with some letters written to him by Clara and Rosamund Barnett.

The Barnett sisters were aunts of the radio listener who sent Sullivan's lost ballad to the BBC. He wrote: 'Rosamund married my Uncle, R. E. Francillon, who was a well-known novelist in Victorian times.'

The writer of this letter, Mr F. Edward Francillon, of Dursley, Gloucestershire, told how he had come across the song while clearing out a cupboard. It had been hidden and forgotten there for many years. It does not figure in any of the official lists of Sullivan's compositions. The music is charming and melodious, and has more than a trace of Schubertian influence.

The words are in German, freely translated:

I want to go out and shout with joy,
Out into the warm summer's night,
To confide to the dreaming flowers
What has made me so wonderfully happy.

Two years after composing this song, on the eve of his final departure from Leipzig for London, Sullivan wrote a letter of farewell to Rosamund Barnett who was in Berlin:

I have treated you badly, very badly, my dear Miss Rosamund, inasmuch as three months have elapsed and I have written to you once, but I know your kind and forgiving disposition . . . I intend staying about three days in Berlin and going straight to London from there . . . My *Tempest* is done (except one duet) and I suffer three hours headaches every day from correcting the parts.

His musical apprenticeship was over. He said good-bye to his friends in Leipzig. He returned to London, to an England musically asleep, with a bombshell in his bag: the music he had been writing for Shakespeare's *The Tempest*. Sullivan at nineteen was determined to make the old folk at home sit up, not only by his own music, but by his revolutionary ideas. He came back from Germany singing the praises of the unrecognized Schumann and the neglected Schubert. Another unusual idea of his was that there should be *English* orchestras. He had been impressed in Germany by the efficiency of German orchestras; he knew that in England there were only about two orchestras worth the name, and that all were manned heavily by foreign players, and he had the daring idea that this could be altered. He did in fact alter it during his lifetime.

His music for *The Tempest* was not particularly revolutionary in style; but it had a polished maturity and at the same time a youthful exuberance (it still bubbles up wonderfully fresh when it is played today); it had melody and at the same time musicianship. It followed the path of Schubert and Mendelssohn. It was bound to be popular.

There may seem to be no connection whatsoever between the return of this amiable but pushing young musician and the fact that in the very same year (1861) an unsuccessful twenty-five-year-old barrister posted a humorous article to a new comic paper, *Fun*. But see how the Fates conspire: the letter to *Fun* led Gilbert into writing *The Bab Ballads*, and in turn *The Bab Ballads* led directly to the Gilbert and Sullivan Operas. So we may say that in 1861 the fuse was started which presently ignited the dazzling blaze of fireworks engineered jointly by those masters of pyrotechnics, Messrs Gilbert and Sullivan. Yet when Sullivan arrived home from Leipzig, comic opera was the most remote of his dreams and ambitions. He wrote to Clara Barnett:

my "Tempest" Music is progressing & going to take the world by "Storm"

—And meanwhile Gilbert was busy with his pencil.

CAPTAIN REECE.

OF all the ships upon the
blue,
No ship contained a
better crew
Than that of worthy
CAPTAIN REECE,
Commanding of *The
Mantelpiece.*

He was adored by all
his men,
For worthy CAPTAIN
REECE, R.N.,
Did all that lay within
him to
Promote the comfort
of his crew.

'THE ROOTS OF THE GILBERT AND
SULLIVAN OPERAS ARE IN THE
BAB BALLADS . . .'

*Sir Joseph Porter, K.C.B., First Lord
of the Admiralty in 'H.M.S. Pinafore' (here played by Martyn
Green), with 'his sisters, and his
cousins, and his aunts'—direct
descendants of—*

*—the sisters, cousins, aunts, and niece,
And widowed ma of Captain Reece*

1861-6

A CERTAIN WILD MAGIC

SIR MAX BEERBOHM has written:
The Bab Ballads—how shall I ever express my love of them? A decade ago Clement's Inn was not the huddle of gaudy skyscrapers that it is now; and in the centre of it was a sombre little quadrangle, one of whose windows was pointed out to me as the window of the room in which Gilbert had written those poems, and had cut the wood blocks that immortally illustrate them. And thereafter I never passed that window without the desire to make some sort of obeisance, or to erect some sort of tablet. Surely the Muse still hovers sometimes, affectionately, there where 'Bab's' room once was. Literature has many a solemn masterpiece that one would without a qualm barter for that absurd and riotous one. Nor is the polished absurdity of the Savoy lyrics so dear as the riotous absurdity of those earlier ballads wherein you may find all the notions that informed the plots of the operas, together with a thousand and one other notions, and with a certain wild magic never quite recaptured. I know nothing comparable, for extravagance, with *The Bab Ballads*. None but Mr Gilbert could have written them.[1]

In 1861 Britain was in mourning for the death of the Prince Consort. In America the Civil War had just broken out. As a diversion from these disasters the polite society of the Victorian drawing-room was laughing at the jokes in the new humorous journal *Fun*, edited by H. J. Byron. How W. S. Gilbert became one of the funsters he has himself related:

> With much labour I turned out an article three-quarters of a column long, and sent it to the editor, together with a half-page drawing on wood. A day or two later the printer of the paper called upon me, with Mr Byron's compliments, and staggered me with a request to contribute a column of 'copy' and a half-page drawing every week for the term of my natural life. I hardly knew how to treat the offer, for it seemed to me that into that short article I had poured all I knew. I was empty. I had exhausted myself: I didn't know any more. However, the printer encouraged me (with Mr Byron's compliments), and I said I would try. I did try, and I found to my surprise that there *was* a little left, and enough indeed to enable me to contribute some hundreds of columns to the periodical throughout his editorship, and that of his successor, poor Tom Hood. And here I may mention, for the information

[1] The *Saturday Review*, 14 May, 1904.

and encouragement of disheartened beginners, that I never remember having completed any drama, comedy, or operatic libretto, without feeling that into that drama, comedy, or operatic libretto I had poured all that I had, and that there was nothing left. This is a bogey which invariably haunts me, and probably others of my kind, on the completion of every work involving sustained effort. At first it used to scare me; but I have long learnt to recognize it as a mere bogey, and to treat it with the contempt it deserves.[1]

Gilbert made such a hit with *The Bab Ballads*, plus journalism and dramatic criticisms in a variety of papers, that he was able to give up the law and settle down as a writer. In four years at the Bar he had averaged five clients a year. During these threadbare years he lodged at a boarding house at Pimlico where a fellow-boarder was the father of C. B. Fry, the cricketer. Now *The Bab Ballads* brought him into prominence.

There was something revolutionary in his absurdities:

> Strike the concertina's melancholy string!
> Blow the spirit-stirring harp like anything!
>   Let the piano's martial blast
>   Rouse the echoes of the past,
> For of Agib, Prince of Tartary I sing!

> Of Agib, who, amid Tartaric scenes
> Wrote a lot of ballet-music in his teens:
>   His gentle spirit rolls
>   In the melody of souls—
> Which is pretty, but I don't know what it means!

'This,' said G. K. Chesterton in later years, 'this is the pure and holy spirit of Nonsense; that divine lunacy that God has given to men as a holiday of the intellect . . . and rather especially to Englishmen.'

[1] The *Theatre*, 2 April, 1883.

Bab could also be rather shocking. He submitted to *Punch* a piece called 'The Yarn of the Nancy Bell', the story of a ship's crew wrecked on a desert island, as told by 'an elderly naval man' . . .

> For a month we'd neither vittles nor drink,
> Till a-hungry we did feel,
> So we drawed a lot, and accordin' shot
> The captain for our meal . . .

but it was so cannibalistic a joke . . .

> The next lot fell to the Nancy's mate,
> And a delicate dish he made;
> Then our appetite with the midshipmate,
> We seven survivors stayed . . .

that Mr Punch declined the contribution for fear of offending his readers . . .

> Oh, I am a cook and a captain bold,
> And the mate of the Nancy brig,
> And a bo'sun tight, and a midshipmite
> And the crew of the captain's gig.

Gilbert also poked fun at the House of Peers, he made faces at Bishops, and leg-pulled the Navy. The roots of several of the Gilbert and Sullivan operas are in *The Bab Ballads*. The original idea for *H.M.S. Pinafore*, for example, may be found here. The Victorians laughed—a little uneasily. They were never quite sure whether Bab was being serious, underneath his nonsense. At any rate the *Ballads* clearly established his style of humour, and in one of them Gilbert gives the key to his entire career:

> The other night, from cares exempt,
> I slept—and what do you think I dreamt?
> I dreamt that somehow I had come
> To dwell in topsyturveydom—
> Where vice is virtue—virtue vice:
> Where nice is nasty—nasty nice:
> Where right is wrong and wrong is right:
> Where white is black, and black is white.

In contrast to this, the world of Arthur Sullivan was a harmonious one where the white notes were definitely white notes and the black notes were always black notes:

The *Musical World*, 11 May, 1861:

Mr Arthur Sullivan begs to inform his friends that he has returned from Germany. All communications respecting pupils, etc, to be addressed to his residence, 6, Ponsonby Street, Pimlico.

Mr George Grove (later Sir George Grove, editor of *Grove's Dictionary of Music*) was at this time a great power in the musical world and Secretary of the Crystal

Sir George Grove

Palace. 'Sitting one day in the gallery at a concert in St James's Hall, Sir George espied someone peering through the glass panel of the gallery door. "Who is that engaging-looking young man?" he enquired. "Oh, that's Sullivan," was the reply. "He's just come back from Leipzig." A friendship between the two men was quickly formed and soon became steadfast.'[1]

On 5 April, 1862, Sullivan's music for *The Tempest* was performed for the first time in England at the Crystal Palace.

This music sounded the Sullivan keynote of gaiety and romance. While Sullivan was composing it at Leipzig his father had written to him:

'Make up your mind to be cut to pieces by the knowing ones when you produce anything in London. If you escape you will be lucky indeed.'

But the critics were kind. They 'made' Arthur Sullivan overnight. In his own words: 'It is no exaggeration to say that I woke up the next morning and found myself famous. All musical London went down to the Crystal Palace to hear the second performance. Charles Dickens met me there. He seized my hand with his iron grip and said, "I don't pretend to know much about music, but I do know I've been listening to a very great work." '

The Tempest shot the twenty-year-old composer straight into Society. London fawned upon him—and he enjoyed it.

When Sullivan died nearly forty years later Sir Alexander Mackenzie wrote that his **return** from Leipzig had happened just at a favourable moment, when there was an 'opening' for a new young composer: 'Wallace and Balfe, almost at the end of their careers, were writing their last operas. Sterndale Bennett (never a prolific composer) wrote at rare intervals. The popular John Hatton and George Macfarren were probably the most active producers at that moment. Taking into consideration the musical tendencies in England at that time, the newcomer's success need not cause great wonder. For, although Schumann's music was beginning to pierce its way slowly, in spite of considerable opposition, Mendelssohn still reigned supreme, his clear-cut and melodious style was the fashion, and his was the most popular music with the large majority of musicians and amateurs. Now this music of Sullivan's, wearing (as most of it does) a smile on its face, carried with it no elements of discordant discussion, no

[1] *Life of Sir George Grove*, by Charles L. Graves (Macmillan).

temptations for controversy. Clear in its design, bright in its instrumentation, it was precisely in the style which admirers of Mendelssohn, Schubert and Bennett expected, hoped for, and wished to see perpetuated. It had, moreover, a distinctly English flavour of its own, the natural outcome of the early training its composer had received.'[1]

After his Crystal Palace début Sullivan wrote to Grove:

> April 25, 1862.
>
> . . . I must tell you how grateful I am for all your kindness during the C.P. affair, and I know how much I am indebted to you with regard to the success of *The Tempest*, for suppose this great man, the Secretary C.P., had been cold in the matter or had taken no interest whatever in the work, do you imagine the thing would have gone off as it did?
>
> No!
>
> I left an umbrella at the C.P. on the last Tempest day, in the washing room I think. Is there any chance of recovering it?—and did my letter to the Directors do?
>
> > Believe me, dear Mr Grove,
> > Ever yours sincerely,
> > ARTHUR S. SULLIVAN.

P.S. Have you seen Blondin?[2]

In the same year Sullivan went to Paris with a party of friends, including Dickens and Grove; he saw the sights, and met old Rossini. The composer of *The Barber of Seville*, seventy years old, white and rheumatic, crept from his armchair, sat at the piano with the young man, and they improvised duets from *The Tempest*. Sullivan says: 'I think that Rossini first inspired me with a love for the stage and things operatic, and this led to my undertaking the duties of organist at the Royal Italian Opera (London) under the conductorship of my friend Sir (then Signor) Michael Costa. At his request I wrote a ballet entitled *L'Ile Enchantée*, and my necessary interviews with the stage employees, dancers, and others gave me much insight into the blending of music and stage management, which became very valuable to me as time progressed.'[3]

At Covent Garden Sullivan received his first lessons in tailoring music for the stage, sometimes being called on to run up 'a few bars of tiddle-iddle-um' (as he would say in later years) to suit some last-minute change in the ballet. He also played the organ behind the scenes for such operas as *Faust*.

Now the careers of Sullivan and Gilbert began to converge. At the very moment when Sullivan was receiving his initiation into the theatre at the Royal Opera, Gilbert was getting in by another door. It was opened for him by T. W. Robertson, who is best remembered today as author of the 1867 play, *Caste*. Gilbert said of him:

---

[1] *The Lifework of Arthur Sullivan*, by Sir Alexander C. Mackenzie (1900).

[2] Blondin, the tight-rope walker, who had crossed Niagara three years previously, was making appearances at the Crystal Palace. The above letter is kindly supplied by Mrs C. Garrett Smith.

[3] Interview in the *Strand Magazine*, 1895.

'Of the many good and staunch friends I made on my introduction into journalism, one of the best and staunchest was poor Tom Robertson, and it is entirely to him that I owe my introduction to stage work. He had been asked by Miss Herbert, the then lessee of St James's Theatre, if he knew anyone who could write a Christmas piece in a fortnight. Robertson, who had often expressed to me his belief that I should succeed as a writer for the stage, advised Miss Herbert to entrust me with the work, and the introduction resulted in my first piece, a burlesque on *L'Elisir d'Amore*, called *Dulcamara; or, The Little Duck and The Great Quack*.'[1]

This was produced on 29 December, 1866, at the Theatre Royal, St James's, London.

How much Gilbert owed, as stage producer as well as author, to Tom Robertson's example may be gathered from a conversation Gilbert had many years later with the celebrated critic, William Archer:

ARCHER: Robertson was a great stage-manager, was he not?

GILBERT: A great stage-manager! Why, he invented stage-management. It was an unknown art before his time. Formerly, in a conversation scene for instance, you simply brought down two or three chairs from the flat and placed them in a row in the middle of the stage, and people sat down and talked, and when the conversation was ended the chairs were replaced. Robertson showed how to give life and variety and nature to the scene, by breaking it up with all sorts of little incidents and delicate by-play. I have been at many of his rehearsals and learnt a great deal from them.[2]

Thus Gilbert's contact with Robertson was worth a great deal more to him than the meagre £30 he received for writing *Dulcamara*.

Sullivan was also selling cheap at this period: 'I was ready to undertake everything that came my way. Symphonies, overtures, ballets, anthems, hymn-tunes, songs, part-songs, a concerto for the violoncello, and eventually comic and light operas, nothing came amiss to me, and I gladly accepted what the publishers offered me, so long as I could get the things published. I composed six Shakespearean songs for Messrs Metzler and Co, and got five guineas apiece for them. "Orpheus with his Lute", "The Willow Song", "O Mistress Mine", were amongst them, the first having been since then a steady income to the publisher. Then I did "If Doughty Deeds" and "A Weary Lot is Thine, Fair Maid", for Messrs Chappell. These were sold outright for ten guineas each.'[3]

Once established as a popular song composer, Sullivan insisted on payment by royalties: 'And oh! the difference to me!' He became organist at the fashionable church of St. Michael, Chester Square, and made his choir the best in the West End: 'We were well off for soprani and contralti but at first I was at my wits' end for tenors and basses. However, close by St. Michael's Church was Cottage Row Police Station, and here I

1 The *Theatre*, 2 April, 1883.

2 *Real Conversations*, by William Archer (Heinemann), 1904.

3 *Sir Arthur Sullivan*, by Arthur Lawrence (Bowden), 1899.

CAPTAIN GILBERT OF THE ROYAL ABERDEENSHIRE MILITIA

When I first put this uniform on,
I said as I looked in the glass,
*   'It's one to a million*
*   That any civilian*
My figure and form will surpass'—'Patience'

completed my choir. The Chief Superintendent threw himself heartily into my scheme, and from the police I gathered six tenors and six basses, with a small reserve. And capital fellows they were. However tired they might be when they came off duty, they never missed a practice. I used to think of them sometimes when I was composing the music for *The Pirates of Penzance*.'[1]

There's a Sullivanesque sparkle about such reminiscences, as there is in the boyishly racy description he wrote to a friend when he went to Manchester to attend the first performance there of *The Tempest* music by the Hallé Orchestra. On the previous evening he was 'taken to a ball and shown about like a stuffed gorilla . . . I stood about the room in easy and graceful postures conscious of being gazed upon; walked languidly through the lancers & then talked a good deal to Mrs Gaskell the authoress, & at half-past 2 was in bed. The next day we went down to rehearsal, where I met with a most enthusiastic reception from the band on being introduced by Mr Hallé. They played through the whole thing with goodwill & took no end of pains about it. Then I went & got shaved (!) had an Eccles cake, a glass of sherry & a cigar . . . home to dinner, & then to the concert. I sat with the Hallés in the two front rows (I on only one, of course). A splendid hall & well filled—nearly 3,000, I am told:

'Overture, Egmont . . . . Beethoven
'Song . . . . Miss Banks
'Music to the Tempest . . . . A.S.S.!

'I felt calm & collected & smiled blandly at the few people I knew.'

At the end of a superb performance: 'It is all over & loud applause follows. The band applauds at me. The audience see that something is up, & continue. At last Hallé beckons to me to come up. I wink, I nod, I interrogate with my eyebrows, & at last rush madly from my seat, & up the platform. When I show myself my breath is literally taken from me by the noise. It is gratifying though. I bow six times, twice to the orchestra (who throughout have been so kind & friendly) & shake hands with Hallé; then down again & all is over. I stay behind during the 15 minutes interval & am overwhelmed with—not reproaches—from critics, artists, rich merchants with hooked noses, &c. One gentleman sitting near Mrs Hallé seeing me rush away said "What! Is *that* Sullivan, that boy!" (Oh that I had a dagger!).'[2]

[1] Quoted in *Sir Arthur Sullivan*, by Herbert Sullivan and Newman Flower (Cassell), 1927.
[2] Letter to Mrs Lehmann, quoted in *Memories of Half a Century*, by R. C. Lehmann (John Murray), 1908.

This young man had a sense of humour. Invited one day to play the organ
at the consecration of a church by the
Bishop of London, he had to fill-in with
impromptu playing, for owing to a misunderstanding the Bishop was an hour
late: 'First I played "I Waited for the
Lord" and then went on with a song of
mine "Will He Come"?'[1]

Sullivan's ballads were now the rage
of the upper classes. When the Scan-
dinavian Princess Alexandra came to
Britain in 1863 he hailed her with a
song, 'Bride from the North', and when
she married the Prince of Wales (later
King Edward VII) Sullivan's 'Wedding
March' was played through the length of

the land. There was no radio to flash a reputation overnight from London to the ends of
the earth, but Sullivan's songs were lavishly displayed in the music shops, and he was
rapidly gaining a reputation as a conductor of orchestral and choral concerts: these
engagements took him up and down the country, where provincial audiences were
coming to know the impeccable and genial little figure on the conductor's rostrum.

In 1863 he went to Ireland, the land of his fathers, for a holiday. He lazed and
dreamed dreams of his future.

Sullivan to his Mother:

Already I feel my ideas assuming a newer and fresher colour. I shall be able to
work like a horse on my return. Why, the other night as I was jolting home through
the wind and rain on an open jaunting car, the whole first movement of a symphony
came into my head.

This was his first symphony, in E flat; Sullivan believed, and his friends encouraged
him in the belief, that it would be the first of many Sullivan symphonies. At twenty-one
years of age, it appeared that his place was to be in the concert hall rather than the
theatre. His job at the Royal Italian Opera had lapsed; no further orders for ballet
music had come his way. He had already composed his first opera, *The Sapphire Necklace*,
but the libretto by H. F. Chorley, music critic of *The Athenaeum*, was so bad it was never
performed.

His Destiny seemed to be Serious Music. In 1864 he received from Birmingham a
commission to compose a work for production at the next Festival there. As he took
the railway train to the greatest and richest of provincial cities Arthur Sullivan felt

[1] *Sir Arthur Sullivan*, by Arthur Lawrence (Bowden), 1899.

something more than ordinary satisfaction. It was in fact a Mission to which he felt called, a duty to spread good music through the dark, smoke-bound industrial cities of Britain. He was a sensitive and imaginative young man, and as he looked out of the carriage window he must have reflected upon the low state into which Music had lapsed in this nation, and perhaps he dreamed of how Arthur Sullivan would lift it up again.

Artistically, the Victorian era (1837–1901) can hardly be mentioned in the same breath with the reign of Queen Elizabeth (1558–1603), when the literary giants, Shakespeare, Marlowe, Ben Jonson, were matched by the musical giants, Thomas Tallis, William Byrd, Orlando Gibbons.

Since the Elizabethan Golden Age there had been only two giants of music. Henry Purcell had died in 1695 and George Frideric Handel in 1759. There had been smaller fry, English composers of talent especially in the lighter fields, men a century before Sullivan like Thomas Arne with his ballad opera *Love in a Village*, and John Gay who had arranged with Dr Pepusch *The Beggar's Opera* in 1728, but since Handel no great figure had come to raise up our music—if you except Mendelssohn, who was even more of a German than Handel. Mid-Victorian England was known on the continent of Europe as 'the Land without Music'. During his student days at Leipzig, Sullivan had written thus about the popular English attitude to new music:

If something does not please them the first time they hear it they will throw it aside and will not have anything more to do with it, forgetting that really good music is seldom appreciated the first time of hearing . . . Take Beethoven, for instance. His fifth symphony was pooh-pooh'd and laughed at when it was first tried at the Philharmonic . . . It is my opinion that music as an art in England will go to the devil very soon if some enthusiastic, practical, and

Purcell

Handel

Mendelssohn

[64]

Arthur Sullivan about 1864

capable educated musicians do not take it in hand. I get so savage sometimes when in company here, and talking to great artists who have been to England, at the sneering way in which they talk of 'England's art'!

Sullivan returned from Germany very conscious of the musical poverty of Britain. For the present, he thought of this mediocrity in terms of the concert platform—of symphony and oratorio. It probably never occurred to him that the same blight had fallen upon English stage music. Since *Love in a Village* and *The Beggar's Opera* there had been a relapse to rubbishy 'burlesque' and pantomimes and shoddy operettas imported from the Continent. Sullivan felt no Mission to reform this.

He would have been perplexed if he could have looked into the future, to read the judgment of a modern critic, Dr T. F. Dunhill, who points out that of all music in the mid-Victorian period, Sullivan's comic operas, practically alone, 'have survived to mirror the period for succeeding generations. This fact by itself is almost sufficient to justify the contention that, despite his limitations, Sullivan was the most completely national composer that England had produced since Henry Purcell. Like all men of

[65]

genius, he possessed the faculty of saying the memorable things unconsciously and without apparent effort.'[1]

We recall him in the 1860's and the 1870's, this genial missionary, travelling about England and Scotland, to the industrial cities of the Midlands and the North, where musical festivals were set amid the 'dark satanic mills', and the inhabitants of the deadly rows of working-class houses thrown up by the Industrial Revolution gathered together to sing with gladsome voice at their festivals under the guttering gas-lamps of Town Halls. At Birmingham, Norwich, Glasgow, and later at Leeds, Arthur Sullivan became the musical idol of these people, their conductor, their Leader who carried the key to the Promised Land where music should transcend all the grime and ugliness of their daily lives. There was no one else in the field who combined the musicianship and the magnetic personality for such a role, though others contributed to the great upsurge of choralism, notably Hullah, Costa, Hallé, Benedict, and especially Joseph Barnby, who had been Sullivan's runner-up in the competition for the Mendelssohn Scholarship in 1856.

The invitation to compose a work for Birmingham was not entirely unsolicited: typically, the pushful Sullivan had written to ask a celebrity to put in a word for him with the Festival authorities.

Sullivan to Sir Michael Costa:

I need scarcely say how grateful I should be, if, through your instrumentality, my name were to come before the public under such honourable circumstances, and I would try and write my very best, in order to bring no discredit upon your recommendation.[2]

And so, on 8 September, 1864, Sullivan is on the conductor's dais at Birmingham, bowing as the audience acclaims his masque of *Kenilworth*, the words adapted from Sir Walter Scott by Chorley: a bad libretto again, but Sullivan has somehow overcome its crudities in the white heat of long hours of composition.

Only the *Musical Times* sounds a note of caution, suggesting that *Kenilworth* is premature, even puerile, and warning the composer's friends 'not to aid and encourage him to imperil his reputation by risking comparison with the great men at an age when he should be simply guiding himself by their example'. His age is twenty-two.

But on 10 March, 1866, he stands before the orchestra under the vast glass roof of the Crystal Palace, his arms raised for silence—and for the first bars of his first Symphony in E flat ('the Irish'). Behind him an audience of 3,000 people. All the critics are there. And John Goss, Sullivan's old teacher at the Royal Academy. And George Grove. On the platform is Jenny Lind (Madame Goldschmidt), the greatest singer of the day. It is a Sullivan Concert, including examples of his other works, with the new symphony as the plum. It is his greatest opportunity yet. The symphony begins . . .

---

[1] *Sullivan's Comic Operas*, by Thomas F. Dunhill (Arnold), 1928.
[2] Letter now in the collection of Mr Reginald Allen, of New York.

Is this the key to a great academic musical career? The critics are wondering . . .

Once again the light flashes down from a thousand panes in the great glass roof, upon Arthur Sullivan. Then come wave upon wave of applause. Sullivan bows and bows again, scuttles off the platform, bobs back again, beaming all over his face. How he loves it . . .

Goss to Sullivan:

> I rejoice that I was at your concert and that I can heartily congratulate you on all points. It was a great triumph, and that Madame Goldschmidt should have given her help crowned it to perfection! Her you can never repay, except in the way she, the greatest of artists, would heartily desire! I mean, by going on—on—on—on—on until (as I hope) you may prove a worthy peer of the greatest symphonists. Enough now that I congratulate you and I enjoy with you—for you have attained a great success. Go on, my dear boy, and prosper.

Six months later Sullivan was offered the professorship of composition at the Royal Academy of Music, alongside his old teacher.

While Sullivan always loved the applause of a first night audience, Gilbert was not that sort of showman.

'My first piece gave me no sort of anxiety,' he says. 'I had nothing in the matter of dramatic reputation to lose, and I entered the box on my first night of *Dulcamara* with a *coeur léger*. It never entered my mind that the piece would fail, and I even had the audacity to pre-invite a dozen friends to supper after the performance. The piece succeeded (as it happened), and the supper party finished the evening appropriately enough, but I have since learnt something about the risks inseparable from every first night, and I would as soon invite friends to supper after a forthcoming amputation at the hip-joint.'[1]

Meanwhile, *Fun* continued to publish Gilbert's comic verses and drawings. At first they had been anonymous; now he signed them with the pet name of his childhood; and when he published a book of them as *The Bab Ballads*, he put this on the title-page:

[1] The *Theatre*, 2 April, 1883.

Mr and Mrs Gilbert, newly married, 1867

PRIVATE LIVES IN THE 1860's

1. BAB AND KITTEN

COMPARATIVELY LITTLE has been known of the private life of W. S. Gilbert. Among the sources from which we may fill out the hitherto sketchy outlines are his sketch books, diaries, and letters made available for our inspection by the late Miss Nancy McIntosh. His diary entries (unlike Sullivan's) are brief, unemotional, little more as a rule than a record of business engagements and the weather. The only autobiography Gilbert ever wrote was the scrappy fourteen-page article in the *Theatre* from which we have already quoted; but he carried a sketch book in his pocket and he was for ever doodling on odd bits of paper. Doodles, drawn in absent-minded moments, may perhaps reveal depths of a man's sub-conscious. It is a fit subject for psychologists. What would they make of this surrealist doodle by Gilbert?

—and what do they deduce from the fact that his own face is sketched so frequently in his notebooks?

Gilbert's drawings fall into two distinct categories. There is the 'wild magic' of the *Bab Ballad* creatures: grotesque, gnome-like caricatures of humanity . . . satirical, and even savagely satirical. And then, almost as though by another artist, there is the dainty charm of the girls and fairies he drew in his private notebooks and used, occasionally, for book illustrations. These seductive sylphs even creep into *The Bab Ballads*. Here is a chorus girl whose daring dress must have raised many a Victorian eyebrow; in fact, Gilbert, conscious that it would do so, rebuffs the so-called moralists who would denounce 'this tawdry, tinselled thing' of the theatre:

. . . And stately dames that bring
　Their daughters there to see
Pronounce the 'dancing thing'
　No better than she should be,
　With her skirt at her shameful knee,
And her painted, tainted phiz:
Ah, matron, which of us is?
(And, in sooth, it oft occurs
　That while these matrons sigh,
Their dresses are lower than hers,
　And sometimes half as high;
　And their hair is hair they buy,
And they use their glasses, too,
In a way she'd blush to do).

Under the clown, the moralist. Behind the satirist, the sentimentalist. Even in the most savage of the *Bab Ballad* sketches, if a young woman is introduced she is inevitably a comely young woman (elderly women are another thing). Here is Annie Protheroe, who 'loved a skilled mechanic, who was famous in his day, a gentle executioner whose name was Gilbert Clay'...

Annie Protheroe is a charming girl in a brutal ballad. (Incidentally, this idea of the last minute reprieve from the axe pops up again in *The Yeomen of the Guard*).

Even when Gilbert rhymed about that 'man-eating African swell', King Borria Bungalee Boo, he illustrated the harsh cannibalistic joke ('We have come for our dinners, my dears') with a dusky beauty chorus . . .

And the Amazons simpered and sighed,
  And they ogled, and giggled, and flushed,
And they opened their pretty eyes wide,
  And they chuckled, and flirted, and blushed.
  (At least, if they could, they'd have blushed.)
                              —*The Bab Ballads.*

It is the same in Gilbert's private sketch books. Pencil drawings of all sorts of grotesque figures rub shoulders with dainty feminine creatures. And, when you come to think of it, it is the same in the Comic Operas. The *young* women are all beautiful (elderly women are another thing).

Occasionally a sketch from his notebook is elaborated into such an exquisite pen-and-ink drawing as this, on the right. The low neckline, narrow waist, and flowing skirt of contemporary Victorian fashion is exploited to the full degree of sex-appeal by an artist who clearly had an eye for feminine beauty.

When he was thirty-one the eye of that artist came to rest on Lucy Agnes Turner, aged seventeen, daughter of an officer in the Indian Army. On 6 August, 1867, they were married at St Mary Abbot's, Kensington. Miss Turner was a dainty little creature, fair-haired, with blue eyes. Mr Gilbert was—in the modern phrase—high, wide, and handsome. They made a splendid-looking pair as they walked abroad in Kensington, where they lived first in Eldon Road and later at Essex Villas.

The wedding came within a few weeks of Gilbert's second stage production, *La*

Vivandière; or True to the Corps, first produced at St James's Hall, Liverpool, in which Gilbert introduced that bogey-woman type which was to haunt his work all his life, the ageing female who in *Trial by Jury* could 'very well pass for forty-three, in the dusk, with a light behind her', who became Katisha in *The Mikado*, and Lady Jane in *Patience*:

> Stouter than I used to be
> Still more corpulent grow I—
> There will be too much of me
> In the coming by-and-by!

In *La Vivandière* she was an elderly Marchioness. Puns were dragged into almost every line, as was then the fashion, for though Gilbert was a brilliant innovator in *The Bab Ballads* he was content to go slow and follow the fashion in his early stage work. Thus in *La Vivandière*, which Londoners saw at the Queen's Theatre in 1868:

MARCHIONESS: Some people say and tell me as a duty
My cheeks are much too *ruddy* for a beauty.

LD. MAR: The wretch who said so is with falsehood tainted,
They're nothing like so ruddy as they're *painted*.

MARCHIONESS: That I should use more powder!

LD. MAR: *Powder?* Puff!

MARCHIONESS: And that my figure's padded!

LD. MAR: *Padded?* Stuff!

MARCHIONESS: My hair's a wig, that's rudeness pretty blunt.

LD. MAR: Rudeness? I stigmatize it as *affront*.

MARCHIONESS: That it's stained yellow—things which I denied at first.

LD. MAR: *You* stain your tresses yellow? You'd have *died* first!

La Vivandière ran 120 performances. If the reader is astonished that W. S. Gilbert chose to enter the theatrical business at this lowest common denominator of taste, let him read what a master of the English theatre, Harley Granville-Barker, has written about it.[1] After remarking upon the 'wave of vulgar foolery that had rolled in upon the theatre' Mr Granville-Barker says of Gilbert's early pieces:

'The interesting thing is that they are cut quite to conventional pattern, that the jingling dialogue is as poor, the puns as execrable as—and often worse than—was usual; and that there are even passages in sufficiently bad taste. The authentic Gilbert is there, nevertheless. There are two ways of developing original genius in an art. The one, and doubtless nobler, is to absorb its principles in

[1] 'Exit Planché—enter Gilbert', article by Harley Granville-Barker, the *London Mercury*, 1932.

secret and deny all expression to them till genius is full fledged. For some reason or other, however, this seldom works out well. The other plan is to serve your apprenticeship as you would to carpentering or house painting, carrying out your orders with quickness and despatch, and making the momentary best of them, such as they are. Then, when you are master of your trade, write masterpieces—if you can! This was Shakespeare's dramatic plan, and (comparisons apart) it was Gilbert's too.'

And soon, within a play or two, Gilbert the apprentice was showing his masters their trade. His next play was billed at the Royalty Theatre as *The Merry Zingara, or the Tipsy Gipsy and the Pipsy Wipsy*, 'a whimsical parody on *The Bohemian Girl* by W. S. Gilbert,

Gilbert's pencil sketch of his wife at the time of their marriage

member of the Dramatic Authors' Club'. A critic in the *Illustrated London News*, after remarking that 'It is remarkable, even among punning extravaganzas, for the abundance of its puns which came down among the audience like a sparkling shower', added that 'The music is admirable, it having been found possible to get through the piece without resorting to a music-hall tune'. The lyrics in these punning parodies of mid-Victorian England (or 'burlesques') were commonly fitted to popular music-hall tunes, but now Gilbert went one better than his fellow writers by marrying his words to tunes of higher pedigree. For his opening chorus he selected the air of 'Sound now the trumpet fearlessly' from *Puritani*, an opera by Bellini; the words went thus:

Brown now the crumpet fearlessly!
Circulate the muffins and the brown bread!
Toast now the tea-cake peerlessly!
Sally Lunn, the Sally Lunn, Sally Lunn, Sally Lunn!

(this Sally Lunn idea was to be rehashed later in *The Sorcerer*).

Just after Gilbert's marriage he was commissioned to write the pantomime for the Lyceum Theatre, London, the following Christmas. As 'Kitten' (as he nicknamed his wife) looked over his shoulder what may she have thought of the prospects of the young writer who sketched out titles like this?[1]

LYCEUM PANTOMIME, 1867-8

HARLEQUIN COCK-ROBIN & JENNY WREN

or

FORTUNATUS and THE WATER OF LIFE

THE THREE BEARS
THE THREE GIFTS
THE THREE WISHES

and

THE LITTLE MAN WHO WOO'D THE LITTLE MAID

By W. S. Gilbert

Then comes a 'characteristic cast of cachinatory characters', and even in the cast-list Gilbert cannot forbear to pun: 'Great Bear, Middle-sized Bear, and Little Bear (afterwards changed into three baser Bar-bear-ians)'.

One suspects that it was all written with tongue-in-cheek. The pantomime has everything scenic, including 'The Demon Miasma's Dismal Swamp', 'A Resplendent Transformation', and 'The Fairy Aquarium', and concluding with 'St James's Park after a snowstorm, cold comfort and a warm reconciliation . . .' an inconsequential Gilbertian touch which may well have earned a peal of laughter from Kitten, for she was a woman with a sense of fun that matched her husband's.

In one scene of this pantomime the Fairy Fresh Air sings, and the tongue comes out of Gilbert's cheek. He writes the tenderly amusing kind of lyric that is going to earn him fame and fortune in years to come (but it wasn't fame and fortune yet—the Lyceum pantomime earned him £60). The first two verses he adapted from an old English nursery rhyme :

[1] A copy of this rare libretto is in the British Museum.

There was a little man,
And he woo'd a little maid
And he said 'Little Maid, will you wed, wed, wed?
I have little more to say,
Than, will you?—yea or nay?
For the least said is soonest mended-ed-ed'.

The little maid replied,
And some say, a little sighed,
'But what shall we have for to eat, eat, eat?
Will the love that you're so rich in
Light the fire in the kitchen,
And the little god of love turn the spit, spit, spit?'

The little man replied,
And, I'm told a little cried
For his little heart was full of sorrow, sorrow, sorrow,
'We will manage as we can',
Said this foolish little man
'And what we haven't got we can borrow, borrow, borrow'.

The high dramatic scene of the pantomime arrives when the Little Maid goes to the House of the Three Bears, who catch her and decide to make a meal of her, and here once again we get that dramatic switch-over from tenderness to an almost savage humour, which was so peculiar to W. S. Gilbert:

LITTLE MAID: Oh, dear me!
Oh, hear me!
You couldn't come for to go for to cook such a particularly
Nice little girl as I?
Oh, spare me!
Don't tear me!
You mustn't come for to go, if you please, sir, for to take and put me in a pie!
Oh, sir, please spare me
Don't in pie prepare me!
Don't come for to go, sir, for to put me in a pie.
(Bears seize her and put her in pie)

This Gilbertian pie was far superior to the usual theatrical tripe of the time. Most stage scripts were so bad that (says Granville-Barker) 'the scene-painter came to the fore and it was all an attempt at spectacle'. The producer of the Lyceum pantomime did not know, of course, that he had a budding genius as a script-writer, so, in accordance with habit, Gilbert's story was interrupted for the Fairy Aquarium (with

Espinosa's Grand Ballet), or for St James's Park After a Snowstorm, not to mention the Electric Light and Magic Fountain patented by M. Delaporte of Paris. As a beginner Gilbert had to hold his peace. But in *Fun* the following January he let himself go. He printed the plot of *Harlequin Wilkinson, or The Fairy Pewopener and the Vicar of Pendleton-cum-Turnuptop*, in which at the very height of the drama, when 'the lovers are embracing more than ever':

> Scenes 5, 6, 7, 8, 9, 10, 11, 12, 13, 14, 15, 16, 17, 18, 19, 20 and 21:
> These scenes are introduced to allow time to set a Magic Drinking Fountain, or an Ethereal Wash-hand Basin, or a Chromatic Pump, or a Lime-lit Tub, or any other elaborate 'property' which the Management may think fit to introduce into the story at the last moment.
> Scenes 22, 23, 24, 25, 26, 27, 28, 29 and 30:
> Have no reference to the plot, but allow time to 'strike' elaborate property aforesaid.

Now Gilbert's work began to attract attention. The tall figure of the new dramatist was seen about Town; but not in the circles where that mercurial young fellow Sullivan was so prominent. Gilbert's haunts were theatres rather than concert halls, men's clubs rather than Society salons. His bluffness got him talked about. His manner was astringent, where Sullivan's would have been urbane.

CLUBMAN: I beg your pardon, Mr Gilbert, but do you happen to have seen a member of this club with one eye called Matthews?
GILBERT: H'm, don't know that I have. What's his other eye called?

Such quips became classics of London wit. Today they are chestnuts, especially the famous story of Gilbert leaving the Haymarket Theatre after a play and a stranger mistaking him for an attendant.

STRANGER: Hey, you. You!
GILBERT: Eh? You talking to me, sir?
STRANGER: Yes, you. Call me a cab.
GILBERT: H'm. Certainly. You're a four-wheeler.
STRANGER: How dare you, sir. What d'you mean?
GILBERT: Well, you asked me to call you a cab—and I couldn't call you 'hansom'.

Less hackneyed is his remark about someone who entertained him to a bad dinner. 'Never mind,' said Gilbert. 'I'll pay him out by asking him to dinner. I have an avenging sherry at one and nine which I think will astonish his digestion.'

Every summer Gilbert went to camp with the militia, and in 1868 the experience earned him a few guineas with a cartoon in *Fun*. To his dying day he carried himself like an officer, and the meticulous accuracy of military uniforms in the comic operas is a mark of this interest.

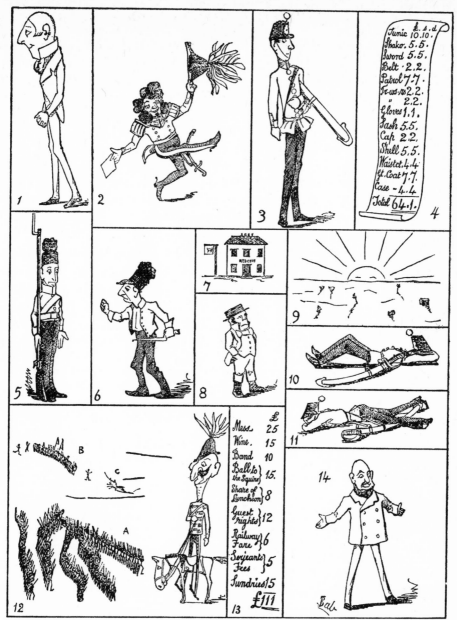

OUT WITH THE MILITIA, *by W. S. Gilbert*

1. *I apply for a subaltern's Commission*
2. *The Lord Lieutenant, his joy*
3. *The lovely uniform*
4. *The bill for it*
5. *The army, on its peaceful parade*
6. *The army, in its warlike billet*
7. *Our headquarters*
8. *The squire*
9. *Principal objects of interest in our neighbourhood*
10. *Morning Parade*
11. *Afternoon Parade*
12. *Our Inspection:* A. *The regiment, going right*
    B. *My company, going wrong*
    C. *The adjutant, his frenzy*
13. *Expenses of three weeks' training*
14. *Military M.P. wanting to know why the deuce* **we can't**
    get any militia subalterns

His love of the sea was a bond between W. S. Gilbert and his ex-naval father. Another was authorship. When old William Gilbert published his first novel, *Shirley Hall Asylum*, in 1863, his son provided the illustrations. Literature can show few such family collaborations. Later the elder Gilbert wrote a cleaned-up life of Lucrezia Borgia, and another novel, *King George's Middy*, with 150 illustrations by W.S.G. This is a story of a midshipman's adventures at sea, and of his being wrecked in Africa.

W. S. Gilbert used to say, with characteristic frankness, that he had inspired old William Gilbert to be a writer: 'I think the little success which had attended my humble efforts certainly influenced my father. You see, my father never had an exaggerated idea of my abilities; he thought if I could write, anybody could, and forthwith he began to do so.'[1]

W.S.G. illustrates his father's book

Among Gilbert's papers when he died was found a pencil sketch of his wife as she was when they married, inscribed 'Kitten'. They lived together forty-three years, and were happy. Lucy Gilbert was the complete mistress of his household, holding the reins firmly as they became affluent, as the staff increased, and the dinner parties became more imposing; but she kept apart from his professional affairs and never sought to 'influence' him. In this she differed from the women in Sullivan's life.

[1] *W. S. Gilbert*, by Edith A. Browne (John Lane), 1907.

'Go to the maintop gallant-masthead, sir, and let it serve as a lesson to you!'

2. O, FAIR DOVE! O, FOND DOVE!

Un poco piu lento.
very tenderly.

O fair dove! O fond dove! And dove with the white breast!

In the middle-sixties, when Bab was courting Kitten, Arthur Sullivan met the Scott Russell sisters, Rachel and Louise, and a romantic and almost daily correspondence began. His emotions always directly affected Sullivan's music. One of his love songs, 'O, Fair Dove! O, Fond Dove!' bears the inscription 'Dedicated to Rachel Scott Russell'. It became a best seller and was sung in drawing-rooms throughout the land, and thereafter Rachel signed her letters to him 'Fond Dove'.

In 1866 an emotional crisis came from another direction to wring music of a different kind from the depths of Arthur Sullivan's despair, the death of his father. A fortnight previously this devoted son had written:

> Birmingham
> Sept. 7th, 1866.

Dear Father,

I wish so much that I could persuade you to run down tomorrow by the 2.45 . . . You see, 1st: You will never have another opportunity of hearing the work performed in such a magnificent style again; 2nd: It is a great event in my career, and one which I should like you to witness. Do come (with Fred), there's a dear.

> Yr. affec. son,
>
> ARTHUR

This was the *Kenilworth* at Birmingham Festival. How Bandmaster Tom's heart filled with pride; and after *Kenilworth* came the first Symphony at Crystal Palace; and then an invitation to write a work for the Norwich Festival of 1866. Arthur was rising swiftly . . . but he was over-working. One day Thomas Sullivan found his son sitting at his desk with a litter of scoring-paper before him: rejected sketches, bars of music scribbled, scratched out, torn up.

'I can't do it, father. I'm worked out. I shall have to give up the Norwich job.'

'Nonsense! You mark my words, Arthur. You're tired now. Something will occur which will put new vigour and fresh thought into you.'

[79]

The young man threw down his pen. New vigour he needed, yes . . . a rest . . . Another inspiration-finding holiday in Ireland? No time for that with the Norwich Festival only a month away. Perhaps some rowing on the river, or a trip down into Surrey, some tennis . . . it was good to feel the wise support of the old man.

But only three days later George Grove wrote to Arthur Sullivan:

> It's little I can say to comfort you. Only I have been thinking of you all through the day . . . It was a great thing for him to have lived to see your triumph. If he had died last year, or even in January of this year, before your symphony was done it would have been quite a different thing to him and he could not have felt such a satisfaction in the thought of your success as he did . . . God help you, my dear fellow. . . .

When Arthur Sullivan read this letter he turned it over and wrote on the back the words 'In Memoriam' and some bars of music; a week after his father's death he was hard at work, day and night, and the overture *In Memoriam* was ready in time for the Norwich Festival.

'Something will occur to put new vigour into you . . .'

(Compare with first sketch of the melody, opposite)

This overture of loving remembrance is one of the few works of the Serious Sullivan which have survived. 'His more serious music has not become as popular, perhaps rightly, as his light music,' says Sir Malcolm Sargent, 'but when we come to an overture like *In Memoriam* we have first-class music.'

Writing to his friend Mrs Lehmann a few days after his father's death, Sullivan described the agony of that night when his brother Fred knocked him up: 'He tried to tell me quietly but broke down at once. I got up & dressed, & then went out in the pitch-dark night, & together we drove home in a hansom which was waiting at the gate, and gave out a little faint glimmering light in the midst of the terrible darkness . . . Oh, it's so hard—it is terribly hard—to think that I shall never see his dear face again, or hear his cheery voice say "God bless you, my boy".'[1]

Rachel Scott Russell comforted Sullivan at this first great sorrow of his life. Grove had brought him into touch with the Scott Russells and introduced him into the comfortable and well-ordered but somewhat restrained family life of intellectual Sydenham. This suburb of London was dominated by the Crystal Palace, where George Grove and John Scott Russell were notabilities. In the evening Arthur Sullivan often dined quietly

[1] Quoted in *Memories of Half a Century*, by R. C. Lehmann (John Murray), 1908.

On George Grove's letter of condolence for the death of Sullivan's father, Arthur Sullivan sketches the first idea for his Overture 'In Memoriam'

with the Scott Russells, played their piano after dinner, and walked in the hushed and scented garden with their daughters.

Here too he made friends with the painter John Everett Millais, R.A., then in his thirties, successfully riding out the storm of opposition which had greeted his Pre-Raphaelite pictures. Says Sullivan: 'I made his acquaintance in 1863, shortly after I began to make a name for myself, and from that day to his death I held him in the greatest affection, and I know that he returned my feeling towards him. He came frequently to the Saturday afternoon concerts at the Crystal Palace and afterwards we would dine and spend the evening at the Scott Russells'. The girls of the family were brilliantly gifted and highly educated and (frequently joined by Henry Phillip, the painter, George Grove, Frank Burnand, Fred Clay, and distinguished artists and literary men) we would discuss music, painting, poetry, literature, *and even science* until the clock told us that the last train back to London was nearly due . . . Those evenings were amongst the happiest of my life.'[1]

There was plenty for them to gossip about. Swinburne's *Poems and Ballads* had been withdrawn by the publisher; Browning, Matthew Arnold, the Rossettis, Tennyson, Ruskin were in full spate; Marx had just written *Das Kapital;* Wagner's *Mastersingers* was the latest operatic innovation. And then there was science—the first Atlantic cable, Lister's revolutions in antiseptic surgery—'even science' . . . the slightly condescending tone of Sullivan's afterthought is as revealing as his omission from the above memory of any mention of his host, Rachel's father; the two did not get on well.

Mr John Scott Russell was a prominent engineer and a Fellow of the Royal Society. He had had a lot to do with the Great Exhibition of 1851, as Secretary of the Society of Arts, and in his shipyards on the Thames he 'had developed the waveline system of construction of ships'.[2] A founder of the Institute of Naval Architects, he was associated with Brunel in building the fabulous liner *Great Eastern*. He was a man of eminence, and expected his daughters to make good matrimonial matches. This young fellow Sullivan was clever and charming—but what about his bank balance? Again and again in her letters to Sullivan, Rachel urges him to put his affairs in order, so that Papa's blessing may be won. 'What are your prospects, young man?' was the proper demand of a Victorian Papa. But to Sullivan at this period might well be applied Gilbert's latter-day lines in *The Mikado*:

> A wandering minstrel I—
> A thing of shreds and patches,
> Of ballads, songs, and snatches,
> And dreamy lullaby!

---

[1] *The Life and Letters of John Everett Millais*, by J. G. Millais (Methuen), 1899.
[2] *Dictionary of National Biography*. John Scott Russell (b. Glasgow, 1808) and Sir Stafford Henry Northcote were Joint Secretaries to the Great Exhibition Commissioners. Scott Russell died 'in somewhat reduced circumstances' at Ventnor in 1882.

Rachel

'*Sorry her lot who loves too well,*
Heavy the heart that hopes but vainly'
'*H.M.S. Pinafore*'

From the letters of the Scott Russell girls to Sullivan[1] we may gather that Rachel and her elder sister Louise were both in love with him, though Louise's attitude was perhaps more flirtatious. As the affair of her sister met opposition Louise shows a genuine desire that it be brought to a happy conclusion: 'My own most precious ones, you have been through a great deal but I am sure God will make it up to you' . . . and when Rachel and Arthur have one of their tiffs it is Louise who does the 'explaining'.

Louise to Sullivan, April, 1868:

You see, she is so very peculiar. I do not think she can love evenly. Passionate outbursts and then coolings down—that will always be her way, but then I think that suits you. You would tire of anybody who loved you always the same . . . It makes me sick to think of you going through this cheerless time . . .

Most of the letters are from Rachel. The correspondence extends from 1863 to 1869. Rachel was a passionate girl, with intellectual and musical talents, and a temperament as erratic as Sullivan's. One day she writes in the heights of ecstasy, the next from the depths of despair. In one and the same letter she can switch from expressing her love in a frank and unrestrained manner, to sentiments as straight-laced as one conventionally expects from the daughter of an upper-middle-class Victorian family: 'How fortunate it is that I trust you quite implicitly otherwise I should be inclined to think you have deceived me, for you were seen in Bond Street on Saturday in a hansom with Lady Katherine.'

Though the restraints of the Victorian code were holding her back, her heart was for ever breaking its bonds: 'There are fireworks on Friday and we shall see them from our old corner. Mind, I don't make an appointment. But Oh my darling, I do so long to see you and why should you not be there?'

When he goes to Paris she reads him a lecture on the evils of the Gay City at one end of the letter, and is dashingly frivolous at the other: 'I want you to get me three pairs of cool cotton stockings—coloured—which will wash well. Are you answered? Blue I like best.'

[1] Now owned by Mrs Bashford.

[83]

She is continually spurring him on in his work: 'Is the Symph in D getting on? Do write it, my bird. It is the language in which you talk to me. I also want you to write an octet. Mendelssohn's is splendid, and I am sure you could do a glorious thing. Will you?'

Sullivan wrote neither a Symphony in D nor an octet, but it was this girl who first set in Sullivan's mind the ambition to write grand opera which was to have so disturbing an influence throughout his life.

Rachel to Sullivan:

I want you to write an opera. Such an opera—a grand, vigorous, great work. Oh, strain every nerve for my sake. Women love to be proud of their friends, and I don't think you know how ambitious I am. I want you to write something for which all the world must acknowledge your talent—only your libretto must be well chosen. It must be nothing tame, petty—it must be grand, noble, stirring! Have you ever seen Byron's translation of Silvio Pellico's Francesca da Rimini? Do get it and see if nothing can be done with it. It is such a splendid subject and there is so much scope for you. There is first of all the pageant of the lovers' entrance into Florence, wonderfully bright, vivid, intense and southern—and then there is that touching beautiful story which we all know. That libretto wins half your battle for you, and as for the catastrophe at the end, almost all operas end badly—and it is much nicer and more life-like . . .

I have said so often that you could and will be the first musician of the times. Will you let Gounod carry off the palm? You have the tools all ready—you have the prizes before you—will you mould a beautiful form with all your soul and your strength—the best—and win for yourself a name and a place among the great men who have gone before? I wish I had you here and that I could talk to you. There is nothing you cannot do if you will only *will* it. No man ever had such a chance— you have a name already, and scarcely any rivals—you dislike Gounod, and yet you cannot beat him. Why don't you *force*, *wring* the acknowledgment of better, higher music out of men by showing them here, living, what it is?

Nothing came of this idea, but among the Sullivan papers is a sketch-plot of a grand opera in five acts, *Guinevere*, the Arthurian story, based on Tennyson, and with it a note from Rachel:

Darling, I am so interested in Guinevere. I feel as though it were *the* thing. I care dreadfully that it should be a splendid work, and a success. Do it with your whole soul and your strength—work at it intensely and religiously, as the old masters worked—like dear old Bach—and it *must* be a great work, for you have the power in you. It is such a gorgeous book that it almost makes me feel as if I could write the music myself. Ahem! The only thing I fear for are Guinevere's and Launcelot's love songs. They must not be too pure or they won't be in keeping with their characters.

Sullivan never wrote this opera, possibly because he heard that Hubert Parry was contemplating the same theme. (Parry's *Guinevere*, written in 1885–6, has never been

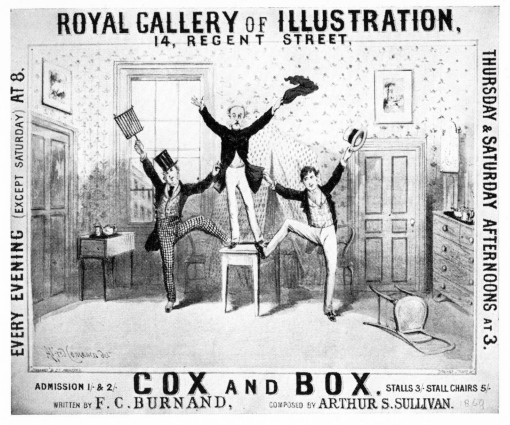

Sullivan's first playbill, now in the collection of Miss Bridget D'Oyly Carte

produced). But he fell in with a scheme of George Grove's that Sullivan (music), Tennyson (poetry), and Millais (painting) should join forces in a work of art. Grove persuaded Tennyson to write some verses called 'The Window, or the Songs of the Wrens' and took Sullivan to see Mr and Mrs Tennyson at their house in the Isle of Wight: 'In the evening,' says Grove, 'we had as much music as we could on a very tinkly piano, very much out of tune, and then retired to his (Tennyson's) room at the top of the house where he read us the three songs, a long ballad, and several other things, and talked till two o'clock in a very fine way about the things which I always get round to sooner or later—death and the next world.'[1]

Sullivan composed the music and Millais made some of the pencil sketches, but Tennyson became doubtful about the songs: 'He thinks they are too light and will damage his reputation,' Sullivan confided to his mother. So the idea lapsed for some

[1] Letter to Miss Olga von Glehn quoted in *Arthur Seymour Sullivan*, by H. Saxe Wyndham (Kegan Paul), 1926.

[85]

time, Millais dropped out, and eventually the song-cycle was published in 1871 with an apologetic preface by Tennyson.

When Mr Scott Russell's engineering projects took him to the continent of Europe Rachel often travelled with him. She sends Sullivan her photograph from Constanz; she makes love from St Petersburg; she implores him to send her copies of his latest-published songs ('I must hear your music, all of it, as soon as other people'); she writes from Zürich:

> If you are ready to marry me next year then well and good. I will tell Mama[1] and Papa when you see the project clear before you without a doubt—clear of debt— and then there will be no reasonable objection . . . I will try and not fret, and keep up my courage. My father *doats* so on me that I think it will be a fearful blow to him.

That was in 1867 . . . and Sullivan was very much preoccupied in 1867. He, too, made a Continental journey, with Grove, in search of lost manuscripts by Schubert; the romantic story of how they brought back five symphonies hitherto unknown in England, and discovered Schubert's *Rosamunde* music in the dusty depths of a cupboard in Vienna has been told by Sir Newman Flower.[2] During the same journey Sullivan took a party of English glee-singers to Paris, where he had an appointment to help with the music at the 1867 Exhibition, and on the boat he met Johann Strauss (the Elder), the waltz king, who had been visiting England: 'We fraternized and sat on the deck to-gether, and suffered agonies in company, so that it was quite jolly.'[3] Strauss's son, Johann the 2nd, had just that year composed 'The Blue Danube'. Sullivan and Grove went on to Munich and Salzburg, and trod in the footsteps of Mozart; they visited Madame Schumann at Baden-Baden; at Leipzig they drank an 'excellent Bohle', the recipe for which was duly noted in Sullivan's diary; and in Vienna they encountered a lame old clerk who had sold music to Beethoven and had been present at Schubert's christening! Would all this affect Sullivan's career? Would it inspire him? All

Bohle. or Bole

Three bottles of Moselwein,
One — — Champagne.
½ — — Rothwein.
¼ pound of Sugar
Six to Ten peaches cut in quarters.
Ice ad lib.

[1] Mrs Scott Russell was a grand-daughter of the 1st Earl of Clancarty.
[2] *Sir Arthur Sullivan*, by Herbert Sullivan and Newman Flower (Cassell). See also George Grove's appendix to *The Life of Franz Schubert*, by von Hellborn (1869); and *Arthur Seymour Sullivan*, by H. Saxe Wyndham (Kegan Paul), 1926.
[3] Letter quoted in *Sir Arthur Sullivan*, by Arthur Lawrence (Bowden), 1899.

this refreshment at the founts of classical music was approved by Rachel. When his *Marmion* Overture was first performed by the Philharmonic Society, 3 June, 1867, she wrote:

> I am so pleased about your Overture, especially as I was a little afraid the great hurry might have affected it. Now, my darling is not to rest upon the laurels which may accrue to him from this but is to go on and do even better. You are to be prolific, darling, like the great men before you, and to try your hand at all things. I want you now at once to re-write your violoncello concerto, there are beautiful things in it but it is incomplete and unequal. I insist.

Sullivan did write a large number of ballads, hymns and anthems (including 'O Hush Thee, My Babie') in 1867, but his only large-scale works this year were a comic frolic called *Cox and Box* and his first comic opera, *The Contrabandista*. That the Great Hope of English Music should turn to this sort of thing shocked the pundits; it was saddening that the young man whom they had believed to hold a golden key that would open the door to great and solemn music should consort with theatrical comics.

Sullivan held a golden key all right, but it was to open a different door. His contemporaries could not see what a modern critic, in the clear retrospect of history, has said of this sudden and unexpected twist in his career: 'It showed that success in the wildest kind of musical farce was not inconsistent with musical scholarship.'[1]

A real musician had entered a field which had been for a century the bawdy hunting ground of hacks and mediocrities. It is worth noting that Sullivan's entrance into the comedy theatre occurred in the year of his European tour. This mission was in aid of 'serious' music but its by-products were as frivolous as Rachel's blue cotton stockings. While Sullivan was worthily attending to his duties at the Paris Exhibition, Offenbach's comic opera *The Grand Duchess* was the talk of that city, and Sullivan would not have been Sullivan had he ignored its gaiety and musicianship—or the ravishing beauty of its leading lady, Hortense Schneider. Offenbach was writing comic opera in the idiom of France, he was making the people laugh and sing, and earning a fortune himself. Then on to Vienna: while Sullivan was earnestly searching there for the lost manuscripts of Schubert, he heard the cafés and ballrooms thrumming to the waltzes of Johann Strauss the Second. This genial composer was soon to move on from ballroom to theatre, to waltz-operas such as *Die Fledermaus*; he too was writing in the idiom of his people, the Viennese, with an emphasis on the gaiety rather than the earnestness of life. Offenbach . . . Strauss . . . Why not Sullivan? The thought must have occurred to him. But his first steps into the comedy theatre were not taken deliberately.

It was a casual meeting in Bond Street with F. C. Burnand, the dramatist, later Editor of *Punch*, that produced *Cox and Box*. Burnand declares in his reminiscences[2] that he was getting up a musical supper party at his home and had the idea of

---

[1] *Sullivan's Comic Operas*, by T. F. Dunhill (Arnold), 1928.
[2] In a letter to the *Spectator*, quoted in *Souvenir of Arthur Sullivan*, by Walter J. Wells (Newnes), 1901.

entertaining his friends with Maddison Morton's farce *Box and Cox* turned into comic opera. Sullivan agreed on the street corner to write the music, the title was reversed, and within a few days the party was held at midnight, attended by many of Burnand's actor friends who had come on from their theatres. The part of Box was played by George du Maurier.[1] Such musical supper parties in the homes of the artistic set were a feature of Bohemian London. There has been some discrepancy among biographers of Sullivan as to which home should have the credit of being the birthplace of his first operetta, but Burnand insists that it was under his roof that this event occurred. Certainly, there was a presentation of *Cox and Box* at Arthur Lewis's house, Moray Lodge, Kensington, on 27 April, 1867, and this is usually quoted as the première performance, but it seems likely to have been the second. At any rate, the night at Moray Lodge was to prove a fateful one for Arthur Sullivan.

Moray Lodge was the exquisite artistic home of Arthur Lewis, head of a Regent Street millinery firm, who had married into the Terry family and was himself a talented painter. His wife was Kate Terry, sister of the great Ellen; his grandsons are Sir John Gielgud and Val Gielgud, chief of BBC drama. Through their mother, Kate Terry Gielgud,[2] the present biographer has been able to see the printed programme of the 27 April, 1867, when the 'Moray Minstrels' met for madrigals, glees, and part-songs by Mendelssohn and Hatton, and for 'A new triumviretta entitled *Cox and Box*; or, *The Long Lost Brothers*, in one act and ten tableaux, adapted to the lyric stage by F. C. Burnand.' George du Maurier again played Box, the journeyman printer in whose humble lodging the action takes place, and the programme states that 'The Lodging, including the Little Second-Floor Back Room, has been furnished with Music by Arthur Sullivan.'

Who were the Moray Minstrels?

W. Holman Hunt, the Pre-Raphaelite painter, says: 'It was a strange mixture of company, for men of all classes were pleased to go into Bohemia for the night. There might be Thackeray, Anthony Trollope, Millais, Leighton, Arthur Sullivan, Canon Harford, John Leech, Dicky Doyle, Tom Taylor . . . Val Princep, Poole the tailor who helped to found the renewed French Empire by lending £10,000 to Louis Napoleon, and Tattersall the horse dealer.'[3]

We can imagine young Sullivan thoroughly enjoying himself at the Moray Minstrels, pounding out an accompaniment at the piano, relishing the applause of such Bohemian big-wigs, and little realizing what he had started, for shortly afterwards when a member of *Punch's* staff died and the Moray Minstrels put on a benefit concert at the Adelphi Theatre *Cox and Box* was suggested for the programme—and in the audience was Mr German Reed, of whom more anon. The Adelphi performance was planned with

[1] George du Maurier, 1834–96. Famous *Punch* artist, author of *Trilby*. Grandfather of the present-day novelist, Daphne du Maurier.
[2] *See also* p. 452.
[3] *Pre-Raphaelitism and the Pre-Raphaelite Brotherhood*, by W. Holman Hunt (Macmillan), 1905.

orchestra, which meant that Sullivan had to write a full score. 'The performance was to take place upon a Saturday,' says Burnand, 'and on the previous Monday Sullivan had not touched a note.' It was scored in the nick of time, and was presented at the Adelphi, 11 May, 1867—Sullivan's first public appearance as a musical comedian. The critics received it warmly.

F. C. Burnand

Ninety years later *Cox and Box* is still in the repertory of the D'Oyly Carte Opera Company.

Later in 1867 another benefit performance of *Cox and Box* was presented. It is intriguing to find that the magazine *Fun* sent as its reporter a journalist named W. S. Gilbert. In his review Gilbert declared that: 'Mr Sullivan's music is, in many places, of too high a class for the grotesquely absurd plot to which it is wedded. It is very funny, here and there, and grand or graceful where it is not funny; but the grand and the graceful have, we think, too large a share of the honours to themselves.' This criticism is astonishingly similar to that which later became Gilbert's favourite bone of contention against Sullivan during their own partnership (the 'grand' music in *Ruddigore* was 'out of place in a comic opera' he was to say in 1887).[1]

In 1867, exactly at the same time as Sullivan was throwing off *Cox and Box* as a sort of jocular 'aside' to the main flow of his music, Gilbert was writing *Harlequin Cock Robin* for the Lyceum pantomime, to supplement his earnings in journalism. In the very year when Sullivan was enjoying his Bohemian evenings with the Moray Minstrels in Kensington 'consuming vast quantities of oysters until the small hours of the morning', Gilbert was getting married and quietly settling down, also in Kensington.

There was to be no marriage for Sullivan. *Cox and Box* was not likely to impress Mr Scott Russell with Sullivan's earnest dedication to Music, nor did a young man who was frequently in debt and who vacillated between symphony and comic operetta appear to have the assured financial future that he expected of a suitor for his daughter's hand. And Rachel herself had qualms about Arthur's weakness for late nights and smoking concerts. There were unhappy scenes in the Scott Russell home at Norwood, and the young people were forbidden to meet. Letters and meetings after this were clandestine:

'If when you get this you want to see me dreadfully, I will go to the rockery at ½ past 3.'

Notes were sent via George Grove. Often the lovers met in his office at the Crystal Palace.

---

[1] Gilbert's review of *Cox and Box* (in *Fun*, 1 June, 1867), hitherto unrecorded, has been discovered by Mr Reginald Allen, of New York. It is unsigned, but Mr Allen writes: 'I had access to the proprietor's copies of *Fun* which were so marked as to indicate who wrote each item'.

Rachel to Sullivan:

> If only I could see you openly it would be quite different, but it is useless to think of that. Something must be done soon. I cannot go on living like this. The misery is too great and I see no way out of it . . . I think the *Contrabandista* music too lovely all through—especially *my* pieces.

The Contrabandista was produced by Mr German Reed at the St George's Opera House in Langham Place, London, on 18 December, 1867. As a showman Mr German Reed was unique. He had not floated on the theatrical wave of vulgarity. He was the first man to realize that the time had come for the tide to set in the opposite direction. Having seen the charity performance of *Cox and Box* at the Adelphi, he had acquired the little piece for his Royal Gallery of Illustration in Lower Regent Street, a place of entertainment for that substantial class of the respectable Victorian public who would never on any account visit a 'theatre': hence its camouflaged name. Here Papa could safely take Mama and the children to see 'illustrations' (playlets) which were clean and amusing, and discreet operettas which were modestly accompanied by a piano and a harmonium. Here *Cox and Box* ran 300 performances. Reed saw how the tide was running and decided to widen his audience. St George's Hall had just been built; he took a lease, renamed it St George's Opera House, and invited Burnand and Sullivan to collaborate again, offering them an orchestra of forty and the best singers in London. Such was the genesis of *The Contrabandista*.

We may laugh nowadays at the priggishness which would accept a musical comedy if it were called an Illustration, but the English theatre—and particularly the musical theatre—had got itself a thoroughly bad name in respectable family circles, and with some reason. The vulgarities of pantomime and 'burlesque', in which we have observed Mr Gilbert to be serving his apprenticeship, were equalled and exceeded in the field of comic opera, or what the French called *opéra bouffe*, to which Mr Sullivan was now going to attach his illustrious name. There had been such a dearth of English composers that most *opéra bouffe* was imported from France, where Jacques Offenbach (1819–80) was its king, but in 'adapting' these works for the English stage the Gallic naughtinesses were cut out and replaced by all the shoddy stock-in-hand of the English stage: puns, clumsy innuendos, men dressed as women, women as men, feeble singing, slatternly acting. Naughtiness was merely converted into grossness. Any delicate Gallic spice which remained seemed to weather badly its transportation into the strange foreign atmosphere of an England where prudishness and vulgarity flourished side by side. Thus when Mlle Schneider, the idol of Paris, appeared in Offenbach's *La Grande Duchesse* and *La Belle Hélène* in London in the season of 1868 *Punch* declared that 'Schneider was far more vulgar in London than in Paris, though on her native heath her performance was witnessed chiefly by ladies of the faster set'.

The *Tomahawk*, a magazine similar to *Punch* but more blood-thirstily pugnacious, had been busy during the previous year tomahawking these foreign operettas and performers,

St George's Opera House, 1867, the scene of the failure of Sullivan's first comic opera, 'The Contrabandista'. In later years St George's Hall became the home of Maskelyne's 'magic' show, and later still was the BBC's chief variety studio in London, until blitzed in the second World War

and the benighted London managers who foisted them on the public: 'Nothing more pitiable can be imagined than these abject attempts to transplant in England that which flourishes in France,' said the *Tomahawk*, and pounced on the production of *La Grande Duchesse* at Covent Garden as 'so rare a piece of folly as can ever have been in the serious contemplation of anybody—even a London manager. The absurdity of the idea lies in the fact that Covent Garden is no theatre for comedy of any kind; and if *opéra bouffe* is to find a home in England, a residence must be selected, if possible, not larger than the Adelphi Theatre.' The writer in the *Tomahawk* might well have been crystal-gazing into the future, for his article[1] goes on in a most astonishingly prescient way to outline the main requirements for English comic opera, which in fact came eventually into being in the Gilbert-Sullivan-D'Oyly Carte collaboration: (1) a smallish, intimate theatre; (2) an English author and composer, because 'French taste is not

[1] The *Tomahawk*, 24 August, 1867.

English taste'; (3) a permanent company of players. 'It must be borne in mind,' slashed the *Tomahawk*, 'that in Paris a piece of this sort is written for the resources of a particular theatre and the vocal infirmities of each member of the troupe are consulted. How much more necessary, then, that our actors, who have not half the intelligence of the French, should receive similar consideration. Let us hope that somebody, with a head on his shoulders, may soon be found to take this matter seriously in hand. It is by no means so difficult as might be supposed; and we feel satisfied, if a fitting-sized theatre were opened tomorrow for the performance of light opera in a worthy manner, that the enterprise would meet with ready and lasting support on the part of the public.'

A few months later the same magazine announced: 'We are informed that Mr German Reed is about to become the lessee of St George's Hall, for the purpose of placing before the public light musical works from the pens of native, as well as of foreign, composers. We speak advisedly in saying that the fate of English *opéra bouffe* could scarcely be entrusted to better hands . . .'

But when German Reed invited Sullivan to set *The Contrabandista* to music he could hardly have chosen a less favourable moment, for since *Cox and Box* Sullivan's thoughts had been back on serious music. When in Germany looking for the Schubert manuscripts he had found something else: at Leipzig the theme came to him for an oratorio, the parable of the Prodigal Son. It appealed to the religious instincts of the ex-choirboy of the Chapel Royal. 'Its lesson is so thoroughly Christian,' he wrote.[1] And he knew that Oratorio was what Musical England expected of him; a Mendelssohn scholar to follow in the footsteps of Mendelssohn. So now he was spending much time and thought on *The Prodigal Son*, while turning out hymns and ballads as pot-boilers. Why, then, did he take the fateful side-turning to *The Contrabandista*? He certainly needed the money; and he was only twenty-five, and with his mercurial spirit he could readily turn from oratorio to a merry bit of nonsense like *The Contrabandista*, which took only sixteen

[1] Preface to oratorio *The Prodigal Son*.

W. S. Gilbert could have made a living as an artist had he never been a writer: two of his sketches for his father's novel, 'King George's Middy'

days of his time to write and rehearse. And after all why shouldn't a serious musician write comic opera? What about Mozart? Why not Sullivan?

Rachel to Sullivan:

Shall I never spend a long summer's day with you again? Will you let me come and forget everything for six bright hours with you? Will you not let me? Let us wander again hand in hand under the shadow of green trees, and cast away all this bitter pain. I have never been happy for an hour since we parted in that little room, and I ache for a little happiness. My whole nature revolts against all this pain . . .

I went to *Cox and Box* the other day and enjoyed it greatly, only it all made me sad, because I remembered when every note of it was written, and our discussions as to the pros and cons of certain changes over the little white piano which then stood in the dining-room . . . There is always the sad yawning chasm, and it gets bigger rather than smaller . . . George Grove has just been here and has told me about *The Prodigal Son*. It will be the first thing of yours of which I shall not hear the first performance.

The yawning chasm was not due only to parental opposition. Two such temperaments as Sullivan's and hers, easy-hot and easy-cold, were almost sure to clash. Rachel was jealous of Sullivan's women friends. She was apt to chide and scold him for 'going out to miserable, sickly London parties, smoking half the night through . . .'

And yet: 'I am so anxious about yr. operetta. I heard it was expected to be weak on account of the hurry. But I know better, darling mine!'

She helped him with the scoring: 'Mine own true love. I am so very happy and sweet today. So sweet that it is perhaps as well you cannot see me for you would be so hopelessly in love . . . Freddie and I have been through the whole of *The Contrabandista* tonight, checking over all the passages, and more and more charmed with the whole.'

A few days later she sends him a news cutting headed SOMETHING THAT DESERVES PUFFING. It is a review of Burnand-and-Sullivan's *The Contrabandista* in which the critic trusts that his praise 'will stimulate and encourage the young composer whilst he is journeying on the thorny road which leads to true art'.

The *Tomahawk* whooped with delight: 'We are glad to see that Mr Sullivan understands what musical comedy should be, and although his music is gay, tripping, and humorous, he has in no single instance allowed it to degenerate into burlesque; from first to last his work is that of a musician, and we are all the more pleased with it, inasmuch as he has contrived to steer clear of the modern French school—which, however attractive in itself, will scarcely bear imitation. The piece was completely successful: there were musical *encores*, and both composer and author were called to the footlights at the conclusion of the performance.'[1]

But the critic who spoke of a thorny road to true art spoke true. A thorny road it certainly was. Thus says Mr Ganz, conductor at the St George's Opera House: 'The performances were artistically successful, but Mr German Reed did not receive enough

[1] The *Tomahawk*, 28 December, 1867.

support from the public to continue them, and therefore gave up the speculation as a bad job.' [1]

After a very short run Reed found that takings would not cover so expensive a production. An orchestra of forty! . . . it was back to piano and harmonium for German Reed. For Sullivan it was back to *The Prodigal Son*. He had had enough of comic opera. Rachel's belief in his star runs like a golden thread through this period:

'You have others to work for, and your beautiful genius to live for, and neither I nor any other woman on God's earth is worth wasting one's life for. With all my heart I thank you for the past which has given colour to my life.'

The storms have gone out of the letters. Rachel sends Sullivan flowers on his birthday and drops a sentimental tear to smudge the ink of her letter. Sullivan asks Rachel to copy his score of the new oratorio. She replies:

'The *Prodigal* is too beautiful and it made me weep to read it. I rejoice to do the copying, and I want you to conduct from my copy—will you, I should so like it, and I will try to do it beautifully and make as few mistakes as possible.'

She went to the first performance after all. It was the greatest day in Sullivan's life so far, for oratorio was then the most highly respected form of music in England, and this young man was challenging comparison with Handel and Mendelssohn. The scene was the Three Choirs Festival, 1869, in the Cathedral of the city of Worcester, where a small boy named Edward Elgar, aged twelve, was living. The gods were to choose Elgar, not Sullivan, to raise the standard of English oratorio to new and enduring heights. [2] But in 1869 . . .

Rachel to Sullivan, from Norwood:

I am far prouder of *The Prodigal Son* than of anything. The *divinity* of your gift of God breathes through the whole work and it is a glory to have written a thing which will stir men's souls to their depths, as it does, and make them feel better and nobler, even if it is transient. You know now what your gift is—and you will use it. That hour in the Cathedral yesterday was perfect happiness and everyone is talking even here of your success.

*   *   *   *

In 1872, three years after her engagement to Sullivan was broken off, Rachel Scott Russell married William Henn Holmes, of the Indian Civil Service, by whom she had two daughters. Ten years later Rachel died of cholera in India, when she was but thirty-seven years of age. Her sister Louise never married. Mr Holmes returned to England with the two daughters, Madeline Rachel, and Beatrix. Madeline, who married Douglas Wells, a London architect, is a painter of distinction; she can just

---

[1] *Memories of a Musician*, by William Ganz (John Murray).

[2] Elgar's setting of Newman's *The Dream of Gerontius* was first performed in 1900. In 1888 Sullivan himself considered this poem, 'but the difficulty in condensing it appeared to me its great obstacle in setting it,' he wrote in a letter now in the collection of Mr Reginald Allen, of New York. 'As soon, however, as I get a little leisure I shall reconsider it.'

remember her mother as 'a very beautiful woman'. The old family home at Norwood
has long since vanished; so has the Crystal Palace. All that remains of the romance of
Rachel Scott Russell and Arthur Sullivan are the songs he wrote for her, and a bundle
of the letters she wrote to him. Sullivan kept them all his life.

The photograph shows a house party on the croquet lawn at Norwood. Sullivan, extreme
left, is sitting next to Mr Scott Russell, in tall hat. Third from the right is George Grove.

And Gilbert? He also was interested in croquet. He had just published in the *Broadway
Annual* of 1868 an article on this Victorian sport: 'It is an outdoor game, and differs
from leapfrog in being one of the very few in which both sexes can join with propriety.
It is allied to many pleasant associations—a fine day, a smooth lawn, pretty boots,
bewildering petticoats, and agreeable interludes.' He discloses that he once played
croquet far into the night with the aid of candles, but he admits he doesn't know the
rules, and he objects to—

THE PEOPLE WHO GO IN FOR SCIENCE.

The genesis of a Gilbert and Sullivan Opera:

LEFT: The ancestral portrait comes to life in a modern production of Ruddigore (the actor is Darrell Fancourt)

BELOW: The same picture gallery idea in Gilbert's early play 'Ages Ago': an engraving from the 'Illustrated London News', 1870

1869

MR GILBERT MEETS MR SULLIVAN
THERE'S A REVOLUTION CLOSE BEHIND US

> *Mrs and Mr German Reed have commenced a new winter season at the Gallery of Illustration in Regent Street. Their entertainment consists of a new operette entitled 'Ages Ago' written with much skill and cleverness by Mr W. S. Gilbert, accompanied with music by Mr Frederic Clay, which for elegance, lightness and sparkle cannot be easily excelled.*
>
> —*Illustrated London News*,
> 27 November, 1869.

ONE MORNING IN 1869 a cab drew up at the Royal Gallery of Illustration and Mr Sullivan stepped out with Mr Frederic Clay. Sullivan at this period was a short, rather squat young man, beautifully dressed in frock coat and tall hat, with glossy black hair and sidewhiskers, an eyeglass, and a jaunty manner. Two years had passed since the failure of his comic opera *The Contrabandista*; Mr German Reed had retreated from St George's Hall back to his simple family favourites at the Gallery of Illustration, while Sullivan had advanced with *The Prodigal Son* to a recognized position as England's master musician, so there was no particular reason why the composer of oratorio should call at this little theatre except out of friendship for Clay, his colleague.

Frederic Clay is known to posterity mainly for his ballad 'I'll Sing Thee Songs of Araby', but he was a frequent composer for the German Reed entertainment, and on this particular day in 1869[1] he invited Sullivan to come in and watch a rehearsal of his latest piece, *Ages Ago*. The score of this work carries the line 'Dedicated to Arthur

---

[1] The date has been variously given as 1869, 1870, and 1871. The evidence seems to me to point to 1869.—L.B.

Sullivan'. The author was W. S. Gilbert, who had been contributing short dramatic pieces to the German Reed entertainment for some time.

In the empty theatre Clay introduced Gilbert to Sullivan. Gazing up at the towering figure of W.S.G., Sullivan made some polite remark, only to have his breath taken away by this unexpected broadside:

'I am very pleased to meet you, Mr Sullivan, because you will be able to settle a question which has just arisen between Mr Clay and myself. My contention is that when a musician, who is master of many instruments, has a musical theme to express, he can express it as perfectly upon the simple tetrachord of Mercury (in which there are, as we all know, no diatonic intervals whatever) as upon the more elaborate dis-diapason (with the familiar four tetrachords and the redundant note) which, I need not remind you, embraces in its simple consonance all the single, double, and inverted chords.'

Many years later Gilbert said to an interviewer: 'Sullivan reflected for a moment, and asked me to oblige him by repeating my question. I did so, and he replied that it was a very nice point, and he would like to think it over before giving a definite reply. That took place about twenty years ago, and I believe he is still engaged in hammering it out.'[1]

Actually, there was no dispute with Clay at all; the above speech was from Gilbert's comedy *The Palace of Truth*. It was a passage which Gilbert had adapted into his play from an article on music in the *Encyclopaedia Britannica*, and which he now reeled off to Sullivan on the spur of the moment—'curious to know how it would pass muster with a musician'.

So their acquaintance began with a leg-pull. In 1869, however, there was no immediate sequel to their first meeting. The first idea of a partnership came in 1870:

German Reed to Sullivan:

Gilbert is doing a comic one-act entertainment for me—soprano, contralto, tenor, baritone and basso. Would you like to compose the music? If so on what terms? Reply at once as I want to set the piece going without loss of time.

Nothing came of this. Sullivan's thoughts were elsewhere. John Goss wrote to him:

All you have done (*The Prodigal Son*) is most masterly. Some day you will, I hope, try at another oratorio, putting out all your strength—not the strength of a few weeks or months. Show yourself the best man in Europe! Don't do anything so pretentious as an oratorio or even a symphony without *all your power*, which seldom comes in one fit.

Rachel to Sullivan:

I wish you would set to work on something big, another symphony or a concerto. Tell me of *Queen Isabel*. You will get it played if you will write it in Italian, and it is quite worth making a present sacrifice to show that an English composer can write opera.[2]

[1] 'Illustrated Interviews', by Harry How, *Strand Magazine*, 1893.
[2] Sullivan never completed *Queen Isabel*.

Sullivan to Dearest Mum:

I am coming home. I want quiet—and you. I want to work. The Overture last night was a great success; I was recalled, flowers, etc. But I am coming home to work. Better still, I am coming home for your birthday.

The Duke of Edinburgh

This 'great success' was the overture *Di Ballo*, first performed at the Birmingham Festival, 1870, a scintillating piece of orchestral gaiety. In the same year Sullivan was writing ballads, hymn tunes, a cantata for the International Exhibition, some carols—among them 'It came upon the midnight clear'. He was conducting up and down the country. Queen Victoria asked for a complete set of his works to be sent to Windsor. This was an honour which had not been accorded even to the Queen's late favourite, Mendelssohn. A strong friendship had been struck between Sullivan and the Queen's second son, Prince Alfred, Duke of Edinburgh, who was a genuine lover of music. The boy from Lambeth had gone far. Royal recognition meant that every mansion in Belgravia and Mayfair was open to him.

Sullivan himself gives us a glimpse of a fragrant Victorian world of well-to-do mansions where he was much in demand for private performances of his works: 'Once I conducted *The Prodigal Son* at a lady's house in Grosvenor Place. All the chorus were amateurs. The house was crowded. It was a hot night, and all the windows were open. Just as the tenor was singing the pathetic solo, "I will arise and go to my father, and will say unto him", he was overpowered by the linkman's voice, who bellowed: "Mrs Johnson's carriage stops the way". It came in so appositely that the interruption proved too much for our gravity.'[1]

At twenty-eight, Sullivan was England's foremost composer. His tunefulness was the first ingredient ripe and ready for the approaching collaboration with Gilbert. His talent was fully matured. And now Gilbert was ready to finish his apprenticeship on the pun-ridden stage of burlesque; he had been content to learn his theatre-craft at the 'house painter' level, as Granville-Barker puts it, carrying out his orders and making the best of it. Now that phase was ending. *The Pretty Druidess*, the last of Gilbert's conventional 'burlesques', ends with an apology to the audience:

Forgive our rhymes;
Forgive the jokes you've heard a thousand times;
Forgive each breakdown, cellar flap and clog,
Our low-bred songs, our slangy dialogue:
And—above all—oh, eye with double barrel,
Forgive the scantiness of our apparel.

[1] Quoted in *Sir Arthur Sullivan*, by Arthur Lawrence (Bowden), 1899.

'It could not be better, and it could not be more loyally done,' comments Granville-Barker, 'but evidently Gilbert had known from the beginning—how should he not?—what this burlesque game was worth, and now even more certainly he knows that the game is up. The history of his career from now on, in its consequence to the English theatre, is the history of his creating something of permanent value (though intensely individual and not to be further developed after him) out of the wreck and the rubbish of it: Savoy Opera, that is to say. His progress is instructive; from the throwing over of the pun, through the abandoning of the jingle for prose (in *Thespis*, his first work done with Sullivan), the insistence upon original music written to his lyrics, the rejection of the men playing women and the women playing men, the forbidding of "gags", and finally to the stern discipline of his stage management at the Savoy itself . . . For over twenty years he had taken pains with his own talent, till it could rank, in its kind, as genius. The old slapdash days had been jolly enough; he could always affectionately laugh at the memory of them. But now if anything was to be done with English dramatic art, discipline was needed. When its history in the nineteenth century comes to be written it will probably be seen that the informing change in the practice of it, upon which the later advance was based, was largely this disciplinary change. Macready had bitterly complained, Charles Kean and his wife had done their best, Phelps was an honest worker; but the 'fifties and 'sixties saw the English theatre in a state, on the whole, of slovenly chaos, redeemed, when it was redeemed, only by the sheer vitality of an individual figure or two. Then came its disciplining to a standard of all-round accomplishment undreamt of before, and to a standard of civilized behaviour, by Irving, the Bancrofts and the Kendals, by Hare and Wyndham, by Sydney Grundy and Henry Arthur Jones, and, most particularly, by Pinero and Gilbert. And Gilbert's task was, for obvious reasons, the hardest of all. But single-handed he succeeded . . . out of the debris of extravaganza and burlesque he made something consistent in form and sanely comic in spirit, worthy to rank as art.'[1]

When Gilbert first met Sullivan at the Royal Gallery of Illustration the scene in rehearsal on the stage was set in the picture gallery of an old manor house. The central idea of *Ages Ago*, by Gilbert and Clay, was that the family ancestors came to life and stepped down from their frames. Eighteen years later in the comic opera *Ruddigore*, by Gilbert and Sullivan, the big scene was a similar picture-gallery with similar ancestors-coming-to-life. Compare the two.

In *Ruddigore* (1887):

ROBIN: I recognize you now—you are the picture that hangs at the end of the gallery.

SIR RODERIC: In a bad light. I am.

ROBIN: Are you considered a good likeness?

[1] From 'Exit Planché—enter Gilbert', an article by Harley Granville-Barker, the *London Mercury*, 1932.

SIR RODERIC: Pretty well. Flattering.

ROBIN: Because as a work of art you are poor.

SIR RODERIC: I am crude in colour, but I have only been painted ten years. In a couple of centuries I shall be an Old Master, and then you will be sorry you spoke lightly of me.

In *Ages Ago* (1869):

SIR CECIL: I am indeed a painting, so are you.

LADY MAUD: How do you know that?

SIR CECIL: How do I know it? Why, didn't you hang up there during the ten years I occupied this castle?

LADY MAUD: But how do you know that I'm not the original of whom that picture is a portrait?

SIR CECIL: Because there's a limit to the beauties of Nature, there's no limit to the beauties of Art. In other words, you're a great deal too good to be true. Angels are not half as bright as they are painted, and the famous Leonardo da Vinci was a terrible flatterer.

Gilbert used the 'too good to be true' gag on another occasion when, at a convivial party, he was flirting with a circle of gay young ladies and one of them asked why he was so inconstant. 'Because,' he answered, 'I am too good to be true.' He liked to play the gallant in private society, but he rarely did so in the theatre. That was a place needing discipline.

In the period 1868–71 he was still writing and drawing for *Fun*; his magazine work is full of frivolity. Look at the comic strip he did after he and Mrs Gilbert had been to France for a holiday: 'Mr Peters takes a bath at Boulogne'. If W. S. Gilbert had never

written a comic opera, he would still have made his name as a comic artist. Tom Hood put the adventures of Mr Peters into *Tom Hood's Comic Annual* for 1871, and in the very same issue was a short story by Gilbert, 'The Wicked World', of which we shall hear more anon, for the scene of the story is Fairyland—'A land where no collars or boots are worn, a land where there is no love-making, but plenty of love ready-made'—and a land which is going to bewitch W. S. Gilbert on and off throughout this life.

Gradually the contributions to magazines become fewer, while Mr Gilbert's plays occur more frequently in the German Reed entertainment. He is trying out his ideas. *No Cards* (1869), with music by L. Elliott, contains a foretaste of *Patience*, for it has a

> . . . timid, and a bashful, and a shy young man,
> A nervous, and an awkward, and a shy young man . . .

and also

> A gentlemanly, sensible, urbane young man,
> A quick and unquestionably sane young man.

Again, in *Our Island Home* for which Thomas German Reed wrote the music in 1870, Gilbert presents us with a Pirate King who foreshadows not only *The Pirates of Penzance* . . .

> Oh, tremble! I'm a Pirate Chief;
> Who comes upon me comes to grief,
> For I'm a murderer and a thief;
> A Pirate Captain, I . . .

but also *H.M.S. Pinafore* . . .

> I'm a hardy sailor, too;
> I've a vessel and a crew
> When it doesn't blow a gale
> I can reef a little sail.
> I never go below
> And generally I know
> The weather from the 'lee'
> And I'm never sick at sea.

To quote an old pun, Gilbert and Sullivan opera was cradled among the Reeds.

At the same time Gilbert was beginning to reveal his stature as a writer of plays-without-music: 'I had determined for some time to try the experiment of a blank verse burlesque in which a picturesque story should be told in a strain of mock-heroic

Sketch by Gilbert

seriousness . . . The story of Mr Tennyson's *Princess* supplied the subject matter of the parody, and I endeavoured so to treat it as to absolve myself from a charge of wilful irreverence. The piece was produced with signal success . . .'[1]

A picturesque story, 'told in a strain of mock-heroic seriousness'. Here is the basic recipe for all Gilbertian opera . . . and in point of fact *The Princess* was duly transformed into a Gilbert and Sullivan opera in later years (*Princess Ida*).

[1] W.S.G. in the *Theatre*, 2 April, 1883.

In the same year as *The Princess* (1870) came the first of Gilbert's fairy plays, *The Palace of Truth* at the Haymarket Theatre. And now the Gilbertian pendulum swung right across, from the ridiculous, via the mock-heroic to the serious. He always wanted to be a 'serious' dramatist. In 1871 he dramatized Dickens's *Great Expectations*. 'It afforded,' says Gilbert, 'a curious example of the manner in which the Censorship of those days dealt with plays submitted to it for licence. It seems that it was the custom of the then Licenser of Plays to look through the MS of a new piece, and strike out all irreverent words, substituting for them words of an inoffensive character. In *Great Expectations* Magwitch the returned convict, had to say to Pip: "Here you are, in chambers fit for a Lord". The MS was returned to the theatre with the word "Lord" struck out, and "Heaven" substituted, in pencil!'[1]

In 1871, too, came *Pygmalion and Galatea*, in which a lovely and gifted actress, Mrs Kendal, charmed all London by her playing of Galatea, the statue that comes to life.

Miss Fortescue, a renowned Victorian beauty, as Galatea in Gilbert's play. Later she was the original Lady Ella in 'Patience', 1881

GALATEA: Sounds that had hummed round me, indistinct, vague, meaningless, seemed to resolve themselves into a language I could understand. I felt my frame pervaded, a glow that seemed to throw my marble into flesh—its cold hard substance throbbed with active life—my limbs grew supple and I moved, I lived, lived in the ecstasy of newborn life, lived in the love of him that fashioned me, lived in a thousand tangled thoughts of hope.

This again was the serious Gilbert. With its subsequent revivals, *Pygmalion and Galatea* earned him £40,000. There were some beautiful passages of speech in it, and the play was exquisitely staged. The loveliest ladies of the London and New York stages aspired to appear in it. It is a token of the change towards a more elegant style which was coming over the theatre, and even into English life in general. John Ruskin, at the height of his fame, Slade Professor at Oxford, was preaching the gospel of Beauty. The Pre-Raphaelite artists were painting

[1] The *Theatre*, 2 April, 1883.

Beauty as they saw it, meticulous paintings, 'true to Nature', often with a 'message'. Lewis Carroll was publishing *Alice Through the Looking Glass*, with its charming illustrations by Tenniel. A spirit of Change was in the air. The wind of rebellion blew across the Channel, that fierce wind of the 1870/1 revolution which made France a Republic and sent Napoleon III flying to England with his Empress Eugénie, but the wind moderated as it reached the cliffs of Dover—the British Queen sat squarely on her throne, around her a social system seemingly imperishable—yet even here a breeze of change was blowing the cobwebs away. Charles Darwin published in 1871 his *Descent of Man*. The Education Act of 1870 provided that all children must have an elementary education. Two refugees from the Franco-Prussian war and the French Revolution who came to London were Pissarro and Monet, members of that school of French painters who were soon to be known as Impressionists; and while Monet was here he painted the Thames, not 'true to Nature', not like a photograph, but as an unheard-of, moody, poetic impression of the dark river with Big Ben looming through an English fog.

W. S. Gilbert, observing all this, himself became the agent of Change, of a new spirit in the theatre. He was writing better stuff; he was determined to see it presented with taste and vigour, so he now began throwing his weight about as producer, as well as author. By autocratic, hard-hitting methods he set about his task—'to break up the turgid tradition of mid-Victorian drama and expose its theatricalities'.[1] Jessie Bond, one of the earliest and greatest stars of Gilbert and Sullivan Opera, recalls in her autobiography: 'Both actors and audiences needed educating in Gilbert's new theory of fun, which had thrown aside all the hoary traditions of the stage. He would have no horseplay, no practical joking, no make-up of the crude, red-nosed order or ridiculous travesties of dress and manner. All must be natural, well-behaved and pleasant, and the actors were trained to get their effects by doing and saying absurd things in a matter-of-fact way, without obvious burlesque of the characters they were representing.'[2]

At the same time John Hollingshead, a showman ahead of his time, was concerned about the state of the average London theatre as a building: 'Dirty, defective and scanty gas, hot stifling air, narrow passages, weak and unmelodious orchestras, delays that consume one-fourth of the acting hours, and refreshment-room-keepers who sell nothing but the original fire-water which exterminated the red man, are only some of the curious attractions provided for playgoers by miserly managers.' So wrote John Hollingshead in the *Broadway Magazine*, 1868. He built the new Gaiety Theatre[3] as an attempt towards drastic improvement. Then he invited Gilbert to write a play (*Robert le Diable*) for the opening night. This was, rather disappointingly, a more elaborate treatment of the pun-ridden early comedies, a mock-melodrama:

---

[1] *Studies in Literature—W. S. Gilbert*, by Sir Arthur Quiller-Couch (Cambridge University Press), 1929.
[2] *Life and Reminiscences of Jessie Bond* (John Lane).
[3] Not the Gaiety of recent times, on the corner of Aldwych, but its predecessor which stood in the Strand west of Wellington Street.

*This programme fan, sold to ladies in the audience at Mr Gilbert's 'Robert le Diable', is in the
Enthoven Theatre collection at the Victoria and Albert Museum, London*

Stand off!—the man who touches Aline dies,
She is my foster-sister—nothing less—
You see, I'm *forced to 'sist her* in distress

Nevertheless, John Hollingshead remarks in his memoirs:[1]

'Mr W. S. Gilbert as a dramatist was original from the top of his head to the sole of his
foot, though it is difficult to say at which end of his body we should place the head or
the feet.'

Robert le Diable opened on 21 December, 1868, but it was nearly three years before
Hollingshead took the next step. And what a step! It was then 1871. In that year we
find Sullivan addressing 'in a very happy manner' (according to a *Musical Times* reporter)
the successful examination candidates at the Royal College of Organists where he was
Professor of Theory; he was still composing hymns (including in 1871 'Onward,
Christian Soldiers'); he was conducting the Promenade Concerts at Covent Garden
(but only the 'classical and sacred performances'); and he made a brief appearance as
conductor of an ill-fated Royal National Opera at the St James's Theatre, where on

[1] *Gaiety Chronicles*, by John Hollingshead (Constable).

[105]

*John Hollingshead of the Gaiety—
a cartoon from his autobiography*

the opening night the impatient crowd broke down the gallery doors, and there was such a 'feeble orchestra and badly trained chorus' that Sullivan and his chief tenor, Sims Reeves, swiftly resigned . . . but this excursion into the theatre, together with the fact that Sullivan had just composed the incidental music for a production of *The Merchant of Venice* at the Prince's Theatre, Manchester, may have turned Hollingshead's mind towards a daring venture.

In 1871 Hollingshead startled London's theatreland by announcing that he was about to present a new comic opera by Mr Gilbert, entitled *Thespis*, with music by Mr Sullivan. How surprising the second name seemed on the bill of the Gaiety Theatre we may judge by comparison with this passage written by Rachel Scott Russell to Sullivan after hearing one of his choral works, at the end of a long concert programme:

Tired as the people were there was a great deal of applause. To me it was perfect bliss. Nothing except those gorgeous choruses at the Handel Festival ever gives me the same rapturous feeling as that great burst of rejoicing at the end. 'Faith conquering'—that great cry of victory—the triumph over death and the grave—the resurrection of the body—and the life everlasting. It is like a great blaze of light; before we saw through a glass darkly, but now face to face. I thought, sitting there, how curious it is to think of generations and generations who will sit there and be thrilled by that, knowing nothing and caring less for the emotions which called it forth—of the life of him who wrote it. They will have their stories and their lives, and the music will suit them, and we shall be 'dust to dust'—or perhaps in the 'blaze of light' which is as yet a mystery to us.

But the generations and generations who are thrilled by Sullivan's music know nothing and care less for his serious works such as inspired the above adoration. 'How curious it is . . .' said Rachel, but not in the way she expected.

All through his life there were two diverging ways before Arthur Sullivan, and he never solved the dilemma of which to follow: to aspire as Rachel's 'beautiful genius', the hope of the highbrow, the favourite of the Court, to be what Gounod was to France, what Verdi was to Italy, what Wagner was to Germany; or to write comic opera as no one else could write it in Europe or America. Fortunately for us all, there was a humorous streak in Sullivan's make-up, plus a romantic disposition which responded to anything theatrical. So he set to and provided the music for *Thespis*.

He had just been to Paris where he witnessed the Communist rising of 1871, writing home: 'After a series of thrilling adventures, not unaccompanied by danger, I just find time amidst the rattling of the shells and the thunder of the cannon, to write and say that hitherto I am safe and unwounded.'[1] (It was after this that he developed his warm friendship with the exiles Napoleon III and Eugénie). Back in London he found himself faced with new hazards in presenting comic opera at the Gaiety.

'Among the difficulties,' he says, 'was the fact that in those days there were comparatively few actors or actresses who could sing, and of those who pretended to, hardly any could be said to compass more than six notes. Naturally I found myself rather restricted as a composer in having to write vocal music for people without voices!'

It is astonishing that a composer of his standing should have bothered with the stage in these circumstances. But Sullivan did so, and the effect was ultimately felt far beyond the Gaiety Theatre, or indeed beyond the Gilbert and Sullivan operas; it was felt in an immense general improvement in the standards of English stage music, parallel to the improvement in the words, acting, production, and *décor* which Mr Gilbert was to insist upon. In 1871, as the new collaborators set to work on *Thespis*, they were both well fitted by training and disposition to play the part of revolutionaries.

[1] *Sir Arthur Sullivan*, by Arthur Lawrence (Bowden), 1899.

In his book 'Gaiety Chronicles' John Hollingshead describes this picture as a rehearsal of 'Thespis'. It is difficult to reconcile the costumes, which suggest a burlesque of St George and the Dragon, with the characters in the comic opera; but at all events we have here an interesting contemporary illustration of a rehearsal in the light of gas T-pieces (over the orchestra), with Gilbert top left.

W. S. Gilbert:

Thespis was put together in less than three weeks, and was produced at the Gaiety Theatre after a week's rehearsal. It ran 80 nights, but it was a crude and ineffective work, as might be expected, taking into consideration the circumstances of its rapid composition.

Arthur Sullivan, in a letter to his mother:

I have rarely seen anything so beautiful put upon the stage.

The Critic of the Times:

The piece, as a whole, deserves high praise. The music was animated and full of airs to be remembered.

Another Critic:

That the grotesque opera was sufficiently rehearsed cannot be allowed, and to this cause must be ascribed the frequent waits, the dragging effect, and the indisposition to take up points, which, recurring so frequently, marred the pleasant effect of Mr Sullivan's music and destroyed the pungency of Mr Gilbert's humour.

Self-portrait by W.S.G.

1871

'THESPIS, or THE GODS GROWN OLD'
A REVOLUTION MISFIRES

Lit..tle maid of Ar..ca..dee,   Sat by Cou..sin Ro..bin's   knee,

THIS IS THE OPERA that everybody has forgotten. So much so that *Trial by Jury* is frequently misquoted as the first collaboration of Sullivan and Gilbert. *Thespis* has never been seen since the first run in 1871–2, and it can never be seen again because all the music has disappeared, except one song, 'Little Maid of Arcadee', which was published as a separate ballad, and one chorus, 'Climbing over Rocky Mountain', which was served up again in *The Pirates of Penzance*.[1] Why was *Thespis* a failure? In the absence of living witnesses, the only evidence is the recorded comments of those who wrote, produced, and saw the opera in 1871 (see opposite). One guesses that Sullivan and Gilbert had not yet got into their combined stride; and the fact that the piece was under-rehearsed shows that they did not foresee what a hopeless task it would be to have their new kind of comic opera well performed. Sullivan mentions to his mother that on the first night the music went rather badly, with one singer half-a-tone sharp. There was also trouble because Gilbert insisted on an 'innovation'—that the chorus should play an active part.

'Until Gilbert took the matter in hand, choruses were dummy concerns and practically nothing more than a part of the stage setting,' says Sullivan. 'In consequence of this innovation, some of the incidents at the rehearsals were rather amusing. On one occasion one of the principals became quite indignant and said, "Really, Mr Gilbert, why should I stand here? I am not a chorus girl!" to which Gilbert replied: "No, madam, your voice isn't strong enough, or you would be." '[2]

The engraving of the *Thespis* rehearsal is a valuable piece of history. It is the first picture known to exist of a Gilbert and Sullivan opera, and it shows the conditions under which a play was rehearsed in 1871. Mr Gilbert and Mr Hollingshead are in the

[1] Search for the music of *Thespis* still continues. Mr D. Graham Davis, of the Gilbert and Sullivan Society, writes: 'The people who have tried to locate the lost music are legion, and they have taken the greatest pains—without success. My own view is that the score must have long since been destroyed.'

[2] *Sir Arthur Sullivan*, by Arthur Lawrence (Bowden), 1899.

top left-hand corner of the picture; the orchestra play in top-hats; the actresses are in their everyday dresses; illumination comes from naked gas-jets known as T-pieces. What Gilbert himself thought of these rehearsals may be gathered from a magazine article he wrote shortly afterwards:

'The piece flounders through rehearsal—the dingy theatre lighted by a T-piece in front of the stage, which has no perceptible effect at the back; the performers usually (at all events during the first two or three rehearsals) standing in a row with their backs to the auditorium that the light may fall on crabbed manuscripts they are trying to read from; the author endeavouring, but in vain, to arrange effective exits and entrances, because nobody can leave the T-piece; the stage manager or prompter calling a halt from time to time that he may correct an overlooked error in his manuscript or insert a stage direction.'[1]

The 'crabbed manuscripts' were at this date all hand-written, for a typewriter was a rare novelty in 1871; but Gilbert, characteristically, had the go-ahead idea of getting his plays set up in type. In the above article he advises authors to spend £5 out of their own pockets for type-setting, it is worth while because managers are more likely to read a printed play, and actors can follow it so much more easily at rehearsal. He concludes: 'Eventually the piece is ready for representation—three weeks' preparation is supposed to be a liberal allowance—and with one imperfect scene rehearsal, and no dress rehearsal at all, the piece is presented to the public.' And he concludes that until efficient, sufficient, and 'earnest' rehearsals may be had 'the English stage will never take the position to which the intelligence of its actors and actresses, the enterprise of its managers, and the talent of its authors would otherwise entitle it'. Gilbert's bitter experience with rehearsing *Thespis* was going to have a far-reaching sequel in the future, but for the time being he had to witness the first Gilbert and Sullivan opera get away to a lame start. It ran for several weeks at the Gaiety, then disappeared for ever.[2]

There was another party to the *Thespis* failure: the audience. We have seen what sort of stuff they were accustomed to:

> When a man sticks his hat at the back of his head
> Tell me, Oh, Editor, why do they roar?
> And then, when he pushes it forward instead,
> Why do they scream twice as loud as before?
> When an elderly gentleman rumples his hair
> Why do they all go delirious as well?
> When he uses a handkerchief out of repair,
> Why do they, why do they, why do they yell?
> —*Fun*, 1865.

[1] 'A Stage Play', by W. S. Gilbert, in *Tom Hood's Comic Annual*, 1873.
[2] Estimates made by modern researchers compute the run to have been sixty-four performances. Gilbert's eighty (*see* p. 108) may have been an exaggeration.

—this had been Gilbert's own pen-picture of a mid-Victorian audience. Imagine their bewilderment on the first-night of *Thespis*. They are accustomed to 'coarse men garbed as women'. It is near Christmas. They have come into the smoke-laden, gas-lit Gaiety expecting puns and pantomime. The curtain rises on what Gilbert calls, not a burlesque but 'a grotesque opera'. Something quite new: an excursion into the ridiculous. The scene is the summit of Mount Olympus, the ruins of the Temple of the Gods. Here are discovered the gods and goddesses of mythology. A bit intellectual for the Gaiety audience? Perhaps it is, but there is plenty of comedy. These gods are 'gods grown old'. They are tired of their jobs. Mercury is worn out. Jupiter is jaded. Mars wants a rest. Diana is an elderly goddess, wrapped in cloaks and shawls, with galoshes on her feet. Into this comic Twilight of the Gods there comes an intrusion of Mortals. A holiday-making theatrical troupe out on a picnic climb Mount Olympus and enter to this gay tune (later transplanted to *The Pirates of Penzance*):

Climb-ing o - ver rock-y moun-tain,

Skipping riv - u - let and fountain, Passing where the— wil - lows qui - - - ver,

The troupe are frankly disappointed to meet such a senile set of gods and goddesses: they offer to change jobs with Jupiter & Co. and put a bit of modern pep into mythology. To be effective, such a plot requires a particularly subtle and stylized kind of mock-serious acting; at the time of *Thespis* most actors knew nothing about it. One of the few who had the knack was Fred Sullivan, the composer's brother.[1] In *Thespis* he took the part of Apollo. He had recently changed his profession. One day he had to give evidence in the law courts. 'You are an architect, I believe?' asked the examining barrister (who later became Lord Chief Justice Russell, and used to tell this anecdote). 'I have been an architect,' said Fred Sullivan, 'but am now on the stage. You see, I am still drawing big houses.'

Nellie Farren, a popular Gaiety idol of the day, played Mercury in *Thespis*. This was the first—and the last—Gilbert and Sullivan opera in which popularly established stage stars were cast in the leading roles. Gilbert found them intractable: in future he would make and mould his own stars.

J. L. Toole had the best comic song in the show, the first of the many Gilbertian patter-songs, all about the Chairman of Directors of the North, South, East, West Diddlesex Junction Railway who was 'conspicuous exceeding, for his affable ways and easy breeding':

[1] Arthur and Fred Sullivan had previously appeared together in amateur dramatics; as far back as 1857, when Arthur was fifteen, they were members of the Pimlico Dramatic Society, Arthur conducting the band and Fred proving himself to be 'a very clever actor', according to an eye-witness, Mr E. Peacock (*Musical Times*, March, 1901).

Each Christmas Day he gave each stoker
A silver shovel and a golden poker,
He'd button-hole flowers for the ticket sorters,
And rich Bath-buns for the outside porters.

Behind the Gilbertian joke is the Gilbertian moral. Beware! says W.S.G., such over-ingratiating behaviour is out-of-place. People will take advantage of it. As the railway staff did in this case:

In course of time there spread a rumour
That he did all this from a sense of humour,
So instead of signalling and stoking
They gave themselves up to a course of joking . . .

If he wished to go to Perth or Stirling,
His train through several counties whirling,
Would set him down in a fit of larking,
At four a.m. in the wilds of Barking.
This pleased his whim and seemed to strike it,
But the general Public did not like it,
The receipts fell, after a few repeatings,
And he got it hot at the annual meetings.

He followed out his whim with vigour,
The shares went down to a nominal figure,
These are the sad results proceeding
From his affable way and his easy breeding!
The line, with its rails and guards and peelers,
Was sold for a song to marine store dealers,
The shareholders are all in the work'us,
And he sells pipe-lights in the Regent Circus.[1]

Gilbert had the 'book of words' of *Thespis* printed and sold in the Gaiety gallery and pit for sixpence, and elsewhere in the house for a shilling. This was to prove a money-making side-line throughout his career, but in 1871 the state of the American copyright law was such that anyone could take a copy of a libretto to the U.S.A. and perform it there without paying a penny to the English author. Gilbert tried to frighten them by printing a 'Caution to American Pirates' in the libretto of *Thespis*, but the law left the door wide open. In fact, Gilbert's *Ages Ago* had already been pirated in America.

After the partial success of *Thespis*, Mr Sullivan and Mr Gilbert separated pro-fessionally for three years, except for a couple of ballads they wrote and published in

[1] The Regent Circus is now Piccadilly Circus.

1874, 'Sweethearts' and 'The Distant Shore'. The English light opera revolution had fizzled out. Gilbert spent the four years writing and producing plays—an extraordinarily mixed bag, in fact a rag-bag of sentiment, seriousness, sententiousness, and satire—about which another Victorian-Edwardian playwright, Sir Arthur Pinero, has written:[1]

'*The Palace of Truth* was succeeded at the Haymarket in 1871 by *Pygmalion and Galatea*, and in 1873 by *The Wicked World*. These three plays are full of charm, notwithstanding their decided savour of cynicism, and possess a literary quality which, without any loss of theatrical effect, makes them eminently readable.' Pinero adds this anecdote about Gilbert's version of the Faust legend, *Gretchen*:

'*Gretchen* failed to attract. One evening at the Beefsteak Club, Gilbert was induced by a little group of admirers to explain in detail his treatment of the Faust story. A too-eager listener broke in with the question, "How did it end?"

' "Oh, it ended in a fortnight," said Gilbert, annoyed by the interruption'.

Meanwhile, during his three years apart from Sullivan, Gilbert's course was like that of a sailing vessel which fails to get the right wind into its sails. The ship went by fits and starts; at one time it was in the doldrums; at another it had a good deal of momentum and crashed into one obstacle after another. The austere *Charity* provoked the wrath of Mrs Grundy. This play at the Haymarket Theatre dealt quite seriously with the problem of 'the fallen woman'. Gilbert was ahead of the morality of his time.

'I believe in the morality of Almighty God and not in that of Mrs Grundy,' says a character in *Charity*.

Then Gilbert had a row with the *Pall Mall Gazette*. It arose, in truly Gilbertian manner, out of that earlier short story of fairyland, 'The Wicked World', which had appeared in *Tom Hood's Comic Annual*. Now Gilbert turned it into a stage play, and the *Pall Mall Gazette* condemned one or two lines as 'coarse and indecent'. A deeply indignant Gilbert sued them for libel—and lost the case. This hurt him, for Gilbert was in love with his fairies, and he didn't forget the snub: he waited thirty-six years, then served the same story up again as another stage piece, *Fallen Fairies* (1909)—by when manners and codes had changed and no one thought it anything but the mildest of fairy fantasies.

Back in that strangely uncertain period

She shook hands with Prince Paragon, but when she looked at Prince Snob she

gave a shriek and fell fainting into his arms. Prince Snob was the villain who had broken her heart when she was a mortal on earth!

The end of Gilbert's story of 'The Wicked World'

[1] In *T.P.'s Weekly*, April, 1929.

of his career immediately after *Thespis*, we find Gilbert being sentimental in *Sweethearts*, melodramatic in *On Bail*, and hilariously upside-down in *Topsy-Turveydom*, at the climax of which the young heroine enters carrying her grandfather who is dressed in swaddling clothes.

Out of the ragbag comes a three-act farce, *Tom Cobb*, at the St James's Theatre; and the *Ne'er Do Well*, 'an absolute failure at the Olympic' (to quote Gilbert's own words), and *Broken Hearts* at the Court. Gilbert sent an advance copy of the last to the editor of the *Theatre*.

Gilbert to Clement Scott:

I am delighted to think that you like the piece so much. I have been so often told that I am devoid of a mysterious quality called 'sympathy' that I determined in this piece to do my best to show that I could pump it up if necessary.[1]

But when the play was produced Scott tore it to bits, whereupon Gilbert wrote him an angry letter, for *Broken Hearts* was Gilbert's pet child. In later years, even when he had had time for reflection and had written the Savoy Operas, he said: 'There is more of the *real me* in *Broken Hearts* than in anything I have written.'

Here again is revealed the serious Gilbert, the man who thought his best libretto was *The Yeomen of the Guard*, the moralist who believed that of all his comical *Bab Ballads* about the best was one called *At a Pantomime* which pictures with a scathing Dickensian sense of social injustice the Christmas scene in the steaming slums of mid-Victorian Britain:

They've seen that ghastly pantomime
　　They've felt its blighting breath,
They know that rollicking Christmas-time
　　Meant cold and want and death—
Starvation—Poor Law Union fare,
　　And deadly cramp and chills,
And illness—illness everywhere—
　　And crime, and Christmas bills.

Gilbert's comment on this verse was: 'I can do something more than wear the cap and bells.'[2]

He said: 'I consider the two best plays I ever wrote were *Broken Hearts* and a version of the Faust legend called *Gretchen*. I took immense pains over my *Gretchen*, but it only ran a fortnight. I wrote it to please myself, and not the public.'[3]

He pleased the public with *The Wedding March* (1873), adapted from the French:

[1] Letter in collection of Townley Searle, author of *Sir William Schwenck Gilbert* (Alexander-Ouseley), 1931.
[2] To Miss Edith A. Browne, author of *W. S. Gilbert* (John Lane).
[3] 'Illustrated Interviews,' by Harry How, *Strand Magazine*, 1893. *Broken Hearts* was produced at the Court Theatre, 1875, and *Gretchen* at the Olympic, 1879.

Gilbert's house, No. 24, The Boltons

'I had only to reduce it from five acts to three,' he told William Archer. 'How long do you think it took me? Just a day and a half, and it brought me in £2,500.'

By now Mr Gilbert was a celebrity in London. He could afford to live in quite a substantial residence in a quiet backwater of Kensington, No. 24, The Boltons. Jenny Lind, Madame Albani, and F. C. Burnand lived in the same distinguished road. The hobbies of his private life were literature (with Dickens a favourite), and collecting antique furniture, ivories, and Old Masters in oils, for which he had a good taste, though oddly enough he had no taste for the Old Masters of music. 'I know only two tunes,' he said. 'One is "God Save the Queen" and the other isn't.' When Gilbert strode into

[115]

any public place he was pointed out, and people chuckled over his latest wisecrack. He was no respecter of persons. He sat at dinner next to the former Editor of *Punch* . . .

GILBERT: I suppose you often have funny things sent in by outsiders?

EX-EDITOR: Heaps.

GILBERT: Then why don't you put them in?

Mrs Kendal,[1] who starred in *The Wicked World*, has recalled that one night Gilbert made an unannounced appearance as an actor; one of the players had to make his entrance through a trap door, but instead up popped W. S. Gilbert. 'He had quarrelled with the actor and had come to fisticuffs with him, and I am bound to say he had the best of it. The public never knew that the right actor was not appearing . . . At dress rehearsals Gilbert was often in front when we did not know he was there, and he would suddenly shout out: "What on earth do you think you are doing?" '[2]

Thus, in these years of varied productions, Gilbert set his mark very forcibly on the English stage. Ellaline Terriss said in later years: 'He was a great stage manager and could show you what he meant by acting a scene for you. Sometimes having to impersonate a girl's part, being six feet in height and big in proportion, he seemed funny, but he wasn't really, for he conveyed even to the ladies the exact way his dialogue should be spoken.'[3]

Gilbert's reputation, the controversies over his plays, his collisions with persons and authorities—all these spread the name and fame of W. S. Gilbert. And then came a double sensation in the newspapers. A mysterious new writer, F. Tomline, had collaborated with Gilbert à Beckett in writing a play, *The Happy Land*, a parody on W. S. Gilbert's *The Wicked World*. Sensation 1: F. Tomline turned out to be W.S.G. himself. Sensation 2: The Lord Chamberlain banned *The Happy Land* because it contained impersonations of three leading statesmen. A few alterations to make-up, and hey presto!—the play got past the censor, and thanks to this notoriety, ran 200 nights at the Court. Mr Tomline looked in one night, and in the stalls, roaring with laughter, he saw one of the statesmen he had guyed—Mr Gladstone.

Gilbert even returned, during these four years, to the cradle—to Mr German Reed. He was not above earning an honest guinea at the Royal Gallery of Illustration with *A Sensation Novel* (music by Florian Reed) and with *Happy Arcadia* (music by Frederic Clay). When Mr Thomas German Reed retired his son Alfred took over, moved the enterprise back again to St George's Hall, and opened with a revival of Gilbert and Clay's *Ages Ago*. In the cast was a beginner, Leonora Braham, who was destined to become one of the stars of Savoy Opera. In another Reed production, *Eyes and No Eyes* (words by Gilbert, music by F. Pascal) the curtain rose unconventionally with nobody on the stage but a girl at a spinning-wheel, singing . . . the

[1] Dame Madge Kendal (1848–1935).
[2] Quoted in *W. S. Gilbert*, by Sidney Dark and Rowland Grey (Methuen), 1923.
[3] *Ellaline Terriss*, by Herself (Cassell).

same idea occurs years later in *The Yeomen of the Guard*. This was its first trial.

In the four years after *Thespis* Arthur Sullivan followed a smooth, swift, and un-swerving course. He was never becalmed. He collided with no one. He fought no law-suits. He made the music that England wanted. The music made him the bard of the people and the friend of princes. When the Prince of Wales (the future King Edward VII) contracted typhoid fever through the bad drains of a Yorkshire mansion where he had been staying, it was Sullivan who, on the Prince's recovery, was called upon to write a *Te Deum* for a mammoth public rejoicing at the Crystal Palace, with an orchestra of 2,000, a gigantic chorus, and Royalty in the audience.

Mr Arthur Jacobs, in his penetrating analysis of the Gilbert and Sullivan operas,[1] refers to Sullivan's way of occasionally dropping apt and scholarly quotations from other composers into his own works (in *The Mikado*, for example, the reference to fugues by Bach in the song 'My Object All Sublime' is underlined in the orchestration by a quotation from Bach's organ fugue in G minor), and Mr Jacobs draws attention to a part of the *Festival Te Deum* where a passage beginning 'Vouchsafe O Lord' is set to the hymn-tune 'O God, Our Help in Ages Past', and later when the chorus are busy with a fugue on another subject the hymn returns as a counterpoint on the trumpet. 'To Sullivan', says Mr Jacobs, 'musical quotation was not necessarily a comic device.' It reflected his wide musical knowledge and sympathy.

When in 1873 his second oratorio *The Light of the World* was first performed at Birmingham that royal patron of the arts, the Duke of Edinburgh, acclaimed it as 'a triumph'. His mother, Queen Victoria, went even further: '*The Light of the World* is destined to uplift British music,' she said. This work, 'dedicated by special permission to H.R.H. the Duchess of Edinburgh', was received with the most widespread interest and enthusiasm in 1873. Thirty years later the *Westminster Gazette* was declaring that '*The Light of the World* is the dullest and flattest oratorio in existence'; today it is almost completely forgotten. But in the seventies it helped to make Sullivan the Bard of the People.

In Birmingham one day, Manchester the next, travelling, conducting, always com-posing, we see Sullivan huddled in his greatcoat on the night train, paper on his knee, writing yet another of his popular ballads . . . 'The Sailor's Grave' . . . 'Golden Days' . . . 'Guinevere' . . . he composed twenty-four of them in these four years, and they stood on the parlour piano in a million homes. In the churches the people sang his tunes . . .

> Onward Christian Soldiers,
> Marching as to war . . .

and the Society for Propagating Christian Knowledge made Sullivan editor of their Hymnal.

---

[1] *Gilbert and Sullivan*, by Arthur Jacobs (Max Parish), 1951.

Queen Victoria's Private Secretary to Sullivan:

I have had the honour of submitting your letter to the Queen. Her Majesty has no objection at all to your using the two tunes called 'Coburg' and 'Father' in your new hymnal, but wishes you to obtain them from Mr Cusins, the Master of the Private Band, in order that they may be correct. The Queen is not aware of there being any other hymn tunes of the Prince's.

Sullivan could hardly have pleased the Queen more than to ask her for the hymn tunes written by the late Prince Consort.

Sullivan, writing home, 1874:

If you are bothered again by newspaper reporters, just say that so far as I am concerned I know nothing about the proposed knighthood beyond what I have seen in the papers.

It is said that the inspiration to write *The Light of the World* came from a woman in Ireland with whom Sullivan was now in love.[1] When this work was first performed at Birmingham, the *Musical Times* noted the adulation of Sullivan's highly-placed friends and uttered this warning: 'If he can reconsider and calmly analyse the merits and demerits of his oratorio when removed from the flattery of his friends . . . he is truly on the right road to attain that eminence which he covets, and which with his exceptional talent he has a right to aspire to.'

The same eminent journal said of Sullivan's *Te Deum*: 'With much of the breadth of Handel, some of the grace of Mozart, and an orchestral colouring almost unique in its masterly handling, this *Te Deum* ought to serve as a gratifying promise that English music is blossoming into a Spring to be succeeded by a Summer such as this land has not experienced since the death of Purcell.'

It was a wonderful prospect . . .

Sullivan threw himself constantly into new and sometimes rather curious activities. When the Royal Westminster Aquarium was opened (opposite Westminster Abbey) to offer Londoners a combination of live fish and lively music, Sullivan was a co-director along with Whiteley of Westbourne Grove, Henry Labouchère, and Bassano the photographer; but the concerts could not be disassociated from a somewhat chilly atmosphere, and before long Sullivan resigned.

He was frequently in the company of the Duke of Edinburgh. Typical letter to his mother, from Eastwell Park, Kent:

I had a lot of musical letters to write for H.R.H. today, so missed the post for you. This morning we were to have gone out shooting, but it was wet. The Duchess and I played some duets after dinner—Schubert's marches. She plays extremely well. Princess Christian asked me to try and help a *protégé* of hers at Windsor. I wish I had a quarter the influence that folks think I have.[2]

[1] See *Sir Arthur Sullivan*, by Herbert Sullivan and Newman Flower (Cassell), 1927.
[2] Quoted in *Sir Arthur Sullivan*, by Arthur Lawrence (Bowden). The Duchess of Edinburgh was the only daughter of Tsar Alexander II of Russia.

In the same year (1873), visiting Oxford, he stayed with Dean Liddell, of Christ Church, whose daughter Alice was the original heroine in the recently-published *Alice in Wonderland*. Miss Liddell sang Sullivan's 'Orpheus with his Lute' for him, and in the evening he went to hear John Ruskin lecture. The next year we find him touring Germany with a party of noble friends, staying at the Duke of Coburg's castle, where he accompanies the great Swedish soprano Christine Nilsson, and receives from the Grand Duke the Order of Coburg (Knight 3rd class)—'so that I swagger about with a ribbon and star'.

Sullivan's main connection with the stage in these four years was when John Hollings-head asked him to write incidental music for *The Merry Wives of Windsor* at the Gaiety. Even the production in Vienna in 1874 of Johann Strauss's *Die Fledermaus*, packed with lively tunes, does not appear to have aroused in Sullivan any envious wish to return to comic opera.

As the year 1874 died who would have thought that there would ever be another Gilbert and Sullivan opera? *Thespis*, the one and only, was by now almost forgotten. Did no one want another? Not the public. Not the Queen ('*The Light of the World* is destined to uplift British music'). Not Mr Hollingshead at the Gaiety. Probably not Gilbert. Certainly not Sullivan.

Only one man wanted another. His name was Richard D'Oyly Carte.

TRIAL BY JURY.

AN OPERETTA.

SCENE.—*A Court of Law at Westminster.*

Opening Chorus of Counsel, Attorneys, and Populace.

HARK! The hour of ten is sounding,
 Hearts with anxious hopes are bounding,
 Halls of Justice crowds surrounding,
  Breathing hope and fear—
For to-day in this arena
Summoned by a stern subpœna
EDWIN, sued by ANGELINA,
  Shortly will appear!

LEFT:

Facsimile from Gilbert's ballad in the magazine 'Fun', the origin of the comic opera

BELOW:

The Defendant pleads with the chorus of bridesmaids

Chorus of Attorneys.

Attorneys are we
And we pocket our fee,
Singing so merrily, "Trial la law!"
With our merry ca. sa.,
And our jolly fi. fa.
Worshipping verily Trial la law!
  Trial la law!
  Trial la law!
Worshipping verily Trial la law!

1875

'TRIAL BY JURY'

RICHARD D'OYLY CARTE BACKS A WINNER

He combined knowledge of art and literature with organizing ability in a manner none too common among impresarios, and thanks to his qualities in this respect he was able not only to see the possibilities of Gilbert as an opera librettist, but to make a lifelong friendship with Sullivan, without which the Gilbert and Sullivan partnership would hardly have lasted as long as it did.

—Francis Toye in GROVE'S DICTIONARY
OF MUSIC AND MUSICIANS

RICHARD D'OYLY CARTE was indeed an out-of-the-rut young man. He was only thirty-one when he brought Sullivan and Gilbert together again. Sullivan was now thirty-three and Gilbert thirty-nine. W.S.G. once declared that no man creates anything worthy of himself until he is forty. These three, before any one of them had reached that age of maturity, soundly established Gilbert and Sullivan opera as a perfect art—for *Trial by Jury* is nothing less, a perfect little gem that flashes as sharply today as on the day when it was produced, 25 March, 1875. It is still hailed with glee wherever the D'Oyly Carte Opera Company goes on tour, and in America innumerable radio performances have made it a most popular sample of British humour. It is the only Gilbert and Sullivan work with no spoken dialogue; it is the shortest opera of the lot—for less than forty minutes it dances the gay fantastic, without a care in the world. There's not a solemn gesture in it, and yet its subject is one of the most solemn that Gilbert could have chosen, the British system of justice. Gilbert takes a look back at his own days at the Bar, but it isn't at all a level-headed look. *Trial by Jury* is quite crazy. Gilbert turns a cartwheel. Sullivan follows. And we all follow with them, gladly, into this cuckoo-court where the learned Judge enters to the strains of a mock Handel chorus, 'All hail great Judge!' . . . where the beautiful plaintiff in a breach of promise case attends in full bridal costume with bridesmaids . . .

Comes the broken flower—
Comes the cheated maid . . .

where the defendant accompanies himself on a guitar (Tink-a-tank) as he tells a hostile jury how

I used to mope, and sigh, and pant,
Just like a love-sick boy!
Tink-a-tank — Tink-a-tank.

But joy incessant palls the sense;
And love, unchanged, will cloy,
And she became a bore intense
Unto her love-sick boy!
With fitful glimmer burnt my flame,
And I grew cold and coy,
At last, one morning, I became
Another's love-sick boy!
Tink-a-tank! Tink-a-tank! Tink-a-tank!

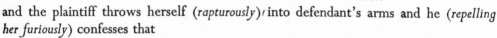

and the plaintiff throws herself (*rapturously*) into defendant's arms and he (*repelling her furiously*) confesses that

I smoke like a furnace—I'm always in liquor
A ruffian—a bully—a sot—

until the Judge intervenes—

The question, gentlemen—is one of liquor;
You ask for guidance—this is my reply:
He says, when tipsy, he would thrash and kick her,
Let's make him tipsy, gentlemen, and try!

Pandemonium in court as everyone objects to this experiment, except the defendant. And so to the final Gilbertian absurdity when the Judge (*tossing his books and papers about*) cries—

All the legal furies seize you!
No proposal seems to please you,
I can't stop up here all day,
I must shortly get away.
Barristers, and you, attorneys,
Set out on your homeward journeys;
Gentle, simple-minded Usher,
Get you, if you like, to Rus*sher;*
Put your briefs upon the shelf,
I will marry her myself.

How on earth had Sullivan and Gilbert been persuaded into this lark?—Sullivan, who for four years had apparently moved steadily away from the theatre, whose oratorios *The Prodigal Son* and *The Light of the World* were now in the repertoire of every Choral Society; and Gilbert, who in the period since his previous partnership with Sullivan had earned so much money with his plays that he was under no financial temptation to rekindle the spark of Gilbert and Sullivan opera.

The scene of the rekindling was the Royalty Theatre in Soho, the 'foreign' quarter of London.[1] The bills outside announced that the operetta *La Périchole*, starring Madame Selina Dolaro, was being performed. There was no great crush at the doors, and in his office Madame Dolaro's manager, Mr D'Oyly Carte, looked glumly at the box-office returns. *La Périchole* was gay enough and should be popular—it was very French, it was by Offenbach, but it was rather short as an evening's entertainment, and Mr Carte had the notion that what the Royalty needed was something even shorter to fill out the bill with *La Périchole* . . . something very English and just as gay as Offenbach (was this an impossible conjugation?). Mr Carte's thoughts dwelt on the problem. He remembered *Thespis*. And then, whether by design or accident we do not know, Mr Gilbert called at the Royalty Theatre. He was shown into the office and found himself facing a dark, alert little fellow whom he knew to be a shrewd and successful business man, for besides managing the Royalty for Madame Dolaro, Carte was running an operatic, lecture, and concert agency in Craig's Court, Charing Cross; on his books were celebrities such as Mario, the Italian tenor, Matthew Arnold, and (later) Oscar Wilde. Lecture and concert tours were arranged here for Europe and the U.S.A. But Carte was something more than a hard-headed executive; he was a man of artistic sensibility.

This is the key to the part he played in the Gilbert and Sullivan story, for without artistic insight Carte would not have remembered *Thespis* nor foreseen, in the then unlikely circumstances, a future for Gilbert and Sullivan comic opera.

As the D'Oyly Carte family, generation after generation, have continued to play a part in the fortunes and misfortunes of Gilbert and Sullivan and their operas, right down to the present day, and as indeed this dynastic combination of artistry and business acumen is to have at least as forceful an influence on our story as the varied qualities of Messrs Sullivan and Gilbert, let us pause for a moment to consider the Carte family origins.[2]

There were three successive Richard Cartes, father, son, and grandson. The first was quartermaster of the Blues in the Napoleonic Wars. He had many children and after the wars lived at Wain House, Welshpool—the house was said to be called

[1] The Royalty, built 1840, was demolished in 1955. Besides *Trial by Jury*, it was notable as the birth-place of *Charley's Aunt* (1892).

[2] Information from Miss Bridget D'Oyly Carte and Professor Daniel Jones, nephew of Richard D'Oyly Carte.

'Wain' (wagon) because it was full of Carts, as the name was then spelt. The old soldier's son, the second Richard, went to London and made a stir as an infant prodigy on the violin; then he took to studying the flute, which was extremely popular in the 1820's as a solo instrument. His ambition was to study in Germany but the family was poor—and now we first glimpse the Cartian combination of business initiative and art, for at twenty years of age Richard Cart the Second organized a series of concerts in the north of England and made enough money to pay his way to Germany. On his return he was in demand as a flautist: 'his tone was beautiful and varied'.[1] He added the *e* to his name to avoid confusion with another well-known flautist named Card. In 1840 he eloped with Eliza, the vivacious dark-eyed daughter of the Reverend Thomas Jones, for more than fifty years reader (chaplain) at the Chapel Royal, Whitehall, which no longer exists but was on the site now occupied by the United Services Museum.

The Joneses were a Welsh branch of the old Norman family of D'Oyly. The Reverend Thomas had cosmopolitan tastes and despite the hazards of shipwreck in those sailing-ship days, he regularly took his family to France for holidays and for education. They had many acquaintances among the Parisian professional class. The French language, and an interest in ideas outside England, thus became second nature to them. Eliza passed on this European outlook to her son, Richard the Third, when he came along (born in Soho, 1844). This was the future impresario of the Savoy Theatre. He grew up in a home where there was a constant stream of visitors, musicians, painters, explorers and travellers from Europe and America. His father, the flautist, wrote flute solos such as 'The Keel Row' which had a popular sale, and became a director of the flute-making business of Rudall, Rose & Carte: this firm, as agents for Adolphe Sax, introduced the saxophone into England. Music as an art and as a business was the background to the young life of Richard Carte the Third. A love of pictorial art, French as well as English, was also given to him, who in later years was to be the friend of Whistler and the patron of 'forward' movements in art and especially in theatrical décor. His mother took him for holidays to the Jones family home in Suffolk where the latent gastronomic interests of little Richard were stimulated by visits to glasshouses for the cultivation of pineapples and oranges: these were duly described in the diary of the boy who grew up to build the Savoy Hotel and to introduce from Paris such social and culinary revolutions as the after-theatre supper.

He was educated at London University and joined his father in the musical instrument business before setting up on his own as a theatrical manager and agent. He had a macabre humour (in later years he kept an untamed crocodile at his island home near Weybridge on the Thames)—a sense of humour which was to be a bond with Mr Gilbert. He was mad about the theatre and before he met either Gilbert or Sullivan had himself composed the music for operettas produced at St George's Hall (1868) and the Opéra Comique (1871). His cultured musical mind was to be a bond with Mr Sullivan.

[1] *Musical Opinion*, obituary, 1 January, 1892.

MANAGER MR R. D'OYLY CARTE. CHEF-D'ORCHESTRE MR SIMMONDS

ROYALTY THEATRE.

Dean Street Soho.

Licensed by the Lord Chamberlain to Miss Henrietta Hodson.

Directress

MRS Selina Dolaro.

Gilbert and Sullivan fly as cherubs on Richard D'Oyly Carte's programme

About 1869 he began evolving his great idea: 'The starting of English comic opera in a theatre devoted to that alone was the scheme of my life', he wrote in later years. In 1870 he suggested it to Sullivan, in 1874 to both Gilbert and Sullivan—'but it fell through because I was short of money'.[1]

And now, in 1875, Mr Gilbert stood in Mr Carte's office at the Royalty Theatre. Barely had Carte expressed his need for an operetta to go with Offenbach's *La Périchole* when Gilbert said that the libretto was already written. Gilbert explained that seven years previously *Fun* had published a ballad of his called *Trial by Jury*. More recently Gilbert had expanded it into a sort of musical mock trial with the idea of Mr Carl Rosa[2]

[1] Letter from Carte to Gilbert and Sullivan, dated 8 April, 1880, in Savoy archives.
[2] Carl Rosa had been a fellow student with Sullivan at Leipzig. He had now (1875) just founded the Carl Rosa Opera Company.

doing the music and his wife, Madame Parepa-Rosa, appearing in the leading part at Drury Lane Theatre. Madame Rosa's death had put the MS back in a pigeon hole in Gilbert's desk. Would Mr Carte like to see it?—and Gilbert fished it out of his pocket.

Mr Carte liked it very well, but suggested that Sullivan should set it, not Carl Rosa. Sullivan was certainly the only English composer who could stand beside Offenbach.

Gilbert went straight round to Sullivan's house, and over a blazing fire he read *Trial by Jury* aloud, apparently full of a chilling apprehension that Sullivan would not be interested, for Sullivan himself says:

'Gilbert came to my rooms and read it through to me in a perturbed sort of a way with a gradual crescendo of indignation, in the manner of a man considerably disappointed with what he had written. As soon as he had come to the last word he closed up the manuscript violently, apparently unconscious of the fact that he had achieved his purpose, inasmuch as I was screaming with laughter the whole time. The words and music were written, and all the rehearsals completed within the space of three weeks time.'[1]

Why the sudden conversion of Sullivan? His mercurial temperament, his love of the theatrical, may be accounted partly responsible, but the likeliest explanation of why both Sullivan and Gilbert came back so readily into partnership is that they respected D'Oyly Carte as a man who combined business acumen with artistic integrity. He was a good cut above the average theatre manager of the time.

Carte knew that in bagging Sullivan he had bagged a big-wig, a bigger wig in fact than Gilbert at this time, and this is reflected in the wording of an advance announcement in the programme at the Royalty Theatre, heralding

> A New Comic Opera composed expressly for this Theatre
> by Mr Arthur Sullivan, in which Madame Dolaro and
> Miss Nelly Bromley will appear.

A gentle protest from Gilbert was enough to remedy the omission of his name, but he must have been a bit annoyed when it was inserted at the next printing as 'W. C. Gilbert'.

From *The Times*, London, 29 March, 1875:

ROYALTY

Trial by Jury, the joint production of Messrs W. S. Gilbert and Arthur Sullivan, is a pleasant addition to the bill of fare at Madame Selina Dolaro's pretty theatre in Soho. Its success on Thursday night, when Mr Sullivan himself directed the orchestra, and both he and his colleague were summoned at the descent of the curtain, was thoroughly genuine . . . Many, doubtless, were curious to know what kind of impression a brief extravaganza, the united effort of two Englishmen, would create immediately after one of the productions, so much in vogue, of M. Offenbach and his literary coadjutors. To judge by the unceasing and almost boisterous hilarity

[1] *Sir Arthur Sullivan*, by Arthur Lawrence (Bowden), 1899.

At 7.30, the successful romantic Extravaganza by R. H. EDGAR
and CHARLES COLLETTE, entitled

Cryptoconchoidsyphonostomata

OR

WHILE IT'S TO BE HAD.

Plantagenet Smith (Champ-pack, Showman, Minstrel,
Scientific Lecturer, Photographic Artist, &c., &c.
With Patter-songs, Imitations and Burlesque Lectures. (By kind permission of
Mrs Bancoft.)

Toddlepit ... ... Mr GEORGE CHILDS
Sue ... ... (A hireling of romance) Mr C. CAMPBELL
Polly ... ... Miss LINDA VERNER
Scene—**The back parlour of Toddleposh's Shop,
at Sloeumbe-cum-Tiddlywink.**

To be followed by Offenbach's Opera, in Two Acts, translated from the French,
entitled

LA PERICHOLE.

CHARACTERS BY

Mme NELINA BOLARO

La Perichole ... ... Miss LINDA VERNER
Guadalena ... }
Berginella ... } (Three cousins) { Miss VERDONI
Mastrilla ... } { Miss LASSALLE

Manuelita ... ... Miss LINDA VERNER
Ninetta ... } (Ladies of the Court) { Miss BEVERLEY
Brambilla ... } { Miss LASSALLE
Frasquinella ... { Miss VERTON}
Don Andrès ... ... Mr FRED SULLIVAN
Don Pedro ... ... Mr C. KELLEHER

Panatelas ... ... Mr C. W. NORTON
Marquis of Tampo ... ... Mr C. CAMPBELL
Usher ... ... AND ... Mr J. BELLEVILLE
Piquillo ... ... Mr WALTER FISHER

ACT I.

THE MARKET PLACE OF LIMA.

ACT II.

PALACE OF THE VICEROY.

To conclude with a novel and entirely original Dramatic Cantata,
entitled

TRIAL BY JURY

Music by A. SULLIVAN, the Book by W. S. GILBERT.

The Learned Judge ... ... Mr F. SULLIVAN
Counsel for the Plaintiff ... Mr HOLLINGSWORTH
The Defendant ... ... Mr WALTER FISHER
Foreman of jury ... AND ... Mr KELLEHER
Usher ... ... Mr PEPPER

The Plaintiff ... ... Miss NELLIE BROMLEY
(Her first appearance this Season)

Bridesmaids, Mesdames VERNER, SASSALLE, GRAHAME,
DURRANT, PALMER, BEVERLEY, CLIFFORD, VILLIERS,
&c.

Gentlemen of the jury, Messrs CAMPBELL, HUSK, &c.

Chef-d'Orchestre ... ... Mr SIMMONDS

Scenic Artists ... ... Mr SPONG
Machinist ... ... Mr LITTLEBURNS
Costumes designed by "FAUSTIN," executed by Messrs. MAY

Prices of admission, Private Boxes, £2 2s. and £3 3s. Stalls, 7s. 6d. Dress
Circle, 6s. Upper Boxes, 3s. Pit, 2s. Gallery, 1s.

Seats may be secured at all the Libraries and at the Box Office, open daily from
Eleven till Five.

Box Office and Saloons under the direction of Mr J. W. CURRAN.

The first-night programme of 'Trial by Jury,' Royalty Theatre, London, 25 March, 1875

[127]

which formed a sort of running commentary on the part of the audience, *Trial by Jury* suffered nothing whatever from so dangerous a juxtaposition. On the contrary, it may fairly be said to have borne away the palm. Two more expert practitioners than Messrs Gilbert and Sullivan could hardly, it is true, have been invited to combine in the manufacture of so odd a piece of work—the designation of which, by the way, as 'a novel and original dramatic cantata' is as strange as anything else belonging to it.

The astute Mr Carte was quick to capitalize the success of Gilbert and Sullivan over 'Offenbach and his literary coadjutors'. He printed a programme (reproduced on p. 125) whereon cherubic figures of Sullivan and Gilbert fly around the 'directress'. This is *not* the first-night programme: it appeared a little later when Carte judged that the erstwhile champion, Offenbach, could be relegated to a niche at the top of the page. The first-night programme,[1] illustrated on p.127, shows that the bill at the Royalty was, first, a curtain-raiser called (believe it or not) *Cryptoconchoidsyphonostomata*, then *La Périchole*, and finally: '*Trial by Jury*, music by A. Sullivan, the book by W. S. Gilbert.'

Superior people were shocked by A. Sullivan's appearance at the Royalty Theatre. 'It is to be gathered from the public prints,' declared *The Musical Standard* pompously, 'that the versatile composer of *The Light of the World* has turned his attention lately to musical burlesque.' But real red-blooded musicians were delighted. Sims Reeves, the famous tenor, wrote to Sullivan:

I shall look forward with the greatest interest for a large Comic Opera. I trust Rosa will give you the opportunity of giving the world something that will astonish the nations, and make the teeth of the furreneers gnash, and tear their beards. Go on and win, old fellow . . . Yours ever, IL VECCHIO TENORE ROBUSTO SENZA IL TREMOLO.

Many years later Sir W. S. Gilbert looked back and said: 'When my collaboration with Sir Arthur Sullivan began, English comic opera had practically ceased to exist and such musical entertainments as held the stage were adaptations of operas of Offenbach, Audran, and Lecocq. Their treatment was crude, unintelligent, and sometimes frankly improper.'

There was nothing unintelligent about *Trial by Jury* and the only accusation of impropriety came from the Lord Chief Justice, Sir Alexander Cockburn. 'Although he was very fond of me personally,' said Sullivan, 'and very fond of music, he did not like the notion of our *Trial by Jury* at all, as he thought the piece was calculated to bring the bench into contempt! He went to see the piece once, remarking afterwards that it was very pretty and clever, and "all that sort of thing", but he would not go again for fear he should seem to encourage it.'[2]

John Hollingshead, of the Gaiety, where legs and lingerie were the vogue in burlesques, called Gilbert and Sullivan opera 'burlesque in long clothes' but *Trial by Jury*

---

[1] Now in Mr Reginald Allen's collection at the Pierpont Morgan Library, New York.
[2] *Sir Arthur Sullivan*, by Arthur Lawrence (Bowden), 1899.

marked a revolution much deeper than a return to decorum. Fifty years later Dr Dunhill, composer and critic, gave the verdict of posterity: '*Trial by Jury*, with its continuous musical activity and unflagging humour, is almost the only English comic classic which can, without irreverence, be fairly matched with Mozart's *Cosi Fan Tutti* in the playground of music'.[1]

In 1875 musicians delighted in Sullivan's fresh adroitness, and chortled at such clever parodies as the Handelian chorus and the Sextet 'A nice dilemma we have here', with its deliciously florid style, *à la* Italian grand opera. The man-in-the-gallery found he could enjoy it, too. That Italian opera take-off was a rare bit of a laugh, with its trills and rolling eyes, a proper tear-up. That Judge was a cough-drop, too, holding up the Court procedure to sing reminiscences of his love-life with a rich attorney's elderly, ugly daughter:

'You'll soon get used to her looks,' said he,
'And a very nice girl you'll find her!
She may very well pass for forty-three
In the dusk, with the light behind her!'

And the whole show stuffed with tunes you could whistle. And well dressed. The girls good to look at. Best of all, *Trial by Jury* turned on that love of ridiculing our betters and our national institutions which is a healthy English safety-valve (the Lord Chief Justice need not have worried on that account). This new kind of opera was ridiculous, and yet it was not rubbish. As entertainment it was far more intelligent than any of its rivals.

The unique secret of Gilbert and Sullivan opera is that it can be both ridiculous and intelligent at the same time.

From 1728, when *The Beggar's Opera* was produced, to 1875 and *Trial by Jury* is close on 150 years. The great significance of *Trial by Jury* was that it marked the re-awakening of English comic opera, almost dormant during all that time. Like *The Beggar's Opera*, all Gilbert and Sullivan opera is thoroughly native—it takes ordinary English character-types and institutions and guys them in a hearty, disrespectful good-natured English way, and its tunes are the distillation through Sullivan's genius of the same English folk-song tradition from which *The Beggar's Opera* plucked its music. Instead of highwaymen and the rough justice of Newgate, *Trial by Jury* gives us barristers and that curious practice of the Court of the Exchequer, a breach of promise action; instead of sweet Polly among the rogues and vagabonds we have a sweet Plaintiff ogled by jury and judge alike; instead of Macheath—

How happy could I be with either,
Were t'other dear charmer away!

we have the Defendant—

I'll marry this lady today,
And I'll marry the other tomorrow!

[1] *Sullivan's Comic Operas* by Thomas F. Dunhill (Arnold), 1928.

The Seasons Tapestry, by William Morris, typical of the new art of the 1870's. Compare with opposite . . .

A man who remembers the birth of *Trial by Jury* in London, Mr Charles E. Grigsby, states: 'In my boyhood my only recreation—besides Chapel twice a day on Sunday, and Sunday school morning and afternoon—was a ghastly form of entertainment known as the Penny Reading. How much torture I have endured at this enforced gaiety it would be difficult to say. How many times must I have heard "The Curfew shall not toll tonight" or "The Village Blacksmith" or "Excelsior"? . . . Theatres in those days were beyond our reach. Bus and tram services were bad and there was no catering for the suburbs as we have today. Still another obstacle to theatre-going was the stern, religious middle-class conscience that had no love for the theatre or regarded it, together with the dancing hall, as an ante-room to Hell. It was on such a world that Gilbert and Sullivan burst like a bolt from the blue.'[1]

That *Trial by Jury* succeeded where *Thespis* had failed is a mark of improved skill by its authors, but it also shows that the revolution into which Gilbert, in particular, had put years of work was at last having effect. Better standards of taste and performance were spreading on the stage. In a wider sense, the general public was becoming better educated—the 1870 Education Act was having gradual but great effects. Women were emerging from the strict confines of the Victorian home: in the year of *Trial by Jury* Newnham College for women was founded at Cambridge, and in the previous year Girton began; as more women—educated women—began to go to the theatre they influenced its standards. Again, parallel with Gilbert's efforts towards better standards

[1] 'When Gilbert and Sullivan Began', article by Charles E. Grigsby, the *Gilbert and Sullivan Journal*, London, July, 1927.

in scenery and costume design (in which he found a keen supporter in Richard D'Oyly Carte), there was a wider æsthetic crusade led by William Morris, the great artist and craftsman who in 1871 (the year of *Thespis*) had bought Kelmscott, the lovely manor house near Lechlade, and started the Kelmscott Press which became a symbol of good design. Morris set new standards in book production, in furniture, in dress design, in the colour and texture of materials, all of which were to have repercussions on the English stage. The dresses in *Trial by Jury* were the æsthetic modern clothes of the period, 1875, and they have retained that style ever since. (Percy Anderson redesigned them in 1920, but adhered to the period.) The leggy vulgarities of burlesque were gone; the stage was filled with the graceful and colourful costumes which were so charming a feature of mid-Victorian life.

William Morris was actively interested in experiments with new dyes and in weaving. The results were new fabrics, new and more subtle colours. When this 'new æsthetic movement' ran to seed later on, Gilbert satirized it in *Patience* ('Young ladies dressed in æsthetic draperies are grouped about the stage'), but just now we are dealing with

. . . *the new art burlesqued in 'Patience'. (Martyn Green as Bunthorne, with Marjorie Eyre and Kathleen Naylor, 1938)*

1875, and in that year this widespread tendency towards better standards was a move-ment of taste which helped Gilbert and Sullivan, and which they helped.

'In so far as they made the stage morally wholesome and intellectually fresher, and in that way more widely acceptable, they helped materially in the creation of the present great play-going public. It was not the least of their achievements.' So says a modern writer, Mr Godwin,[1] and it is a sensible judgment.

At the time when *Trial by Jury* brought a new sparkle and brilliance to the English stage, Benjamin Disraeli, who had succeeded Gladstone as Prime Minister, was giving government a new flamboyance, and Empire-building a new magnificence: he sent the Prince of Wales on a tour to India and he bought for Britain the Suez Canal shares, as preliminaries to making Queen Victoria 'Empress of India'. English history was rising to a peak. The Symphony of Victorian Life, after the dull, dreary, Dead-march Move-ment of the period when Albert the Good died, was changing now to a Movement more romantic, lively, ambitious. And in tune with this change went the theatre.

One of the improvements of *Trial by Jury*, compared with *Thespis*, was in the acting: Gilbert was beginning to make his players understand what he wanted. In particular, Fred Sullivan as the Judge was a brilliant comedy success in the grave new Gilbertian style. 'One of the secrets, if not the all-important one, of the phenomenal success of these operas', says a famous Savoyard, Rutland Barrington, 'lies in the serious manner in which the delineation of each and every part should be sustained, a truism which has not invariably been recognized by the artists concerned. What a monument of fun and whimsicality is *Trial by Jury* when so attacked! And yet on many occasions I have seen it distorted almost out of recognition by artists who insisted on being funny; indeed, at one performance, in which Gilbert himself was to appear as the Judge's Associate (an ornamental non-speaking part) this tendency was so marked at rehearsal as to result in a telegram on the day of performance, from the author, to the effect that he had "a severe cold and could not come to town". I wrote him a sympathetic letter to which he replied by return that he was "perfectly well, but dared not risk the effect on his health of such a performance!" '[2]

The first American performance of *Trial by Jury* was at the Eagle Theatre, New York, on 15 November, 1875, with G. H. McDermott as the Judge. This production was unauthorized by Gilbert, Sullivan, and Carte. A printed libretto which appeared on the American market was also a pirated edition. In 1948 a copy of this 1875 libretto was advertised for sale by a New York second-hand bookseller for sixty-five dollars. Its original price, in a paperback, can hardly have been more than twenty-five cents.

The Eagle Theatre performance marks the beginning of Gilbert and Sullivan in the U.S.A. (not, as is frequently stated, a production of *H.M.S. Pinafore* in 1878).

[1] *Gilbert and Sullivan*, by A. H. Godwin (J. M. Dent), 1926.
[2] Article on W. S. Gilbert by Rutland Barrington, in the *Bookman*, July, 1911.

In the same year as *Trial by Jury* Gilbert was rehearsing Mrs Kendal and John Hare in a revival of *Broken Hearts* at the Court Theatre, London, when he had a quarrel with Hare. The rehearsal was cancelled, and they both left the theatre in a temper—only to meet on a nearby railway station: 'Up and down the platform Gilbert and Hare tramped, each with a settled frown upon his brow and each ignoring the other as they passed, almost brushing shoulders,' says Mrs Kendal. 'The only notice they took of one another was a sniff as they passed by. At length the little train puffed in. Both of them made for the same door, which a passenger had opened in order to alight. Naturally, as the door was too narrow to admit them both at the same time, neither could get in. Suddenly, Gilbert's strong sense of humour came to the rescue of the absurd situation. He burst out laughing. Hare looked at him, and in his turn, burst out laughing . . . They returned to the theatre. "We've come back to rehearsal," they both exclaimed at the same time. "Oh, have you?" I said, quite complacently. "I think everybody's gone. You've been some time making up your minds and at the present moment I'm going home." I left them both gazing in astonishment at me . . . Hare and W. S. Gilbert were both in the habit of losing their tempers every minute and recovering them in a half a minute. Gilbert was aware of his peculiar proclivity, for, on one occasion, invited to a stag party, he exclaimed in astonishment on entering the room "A dozen men, and I'm on terms with them all!" '[1]

Having thrown off *Trial by Jury*, Sullivan went on holiday. He wrote from Lake Como to his mother:

The heat is so great as to make it almost impossible to do anything but sit about without movement in a chair until the evening, when we manage to saunter out a little or be paddled about in a flat-bottomed boat. Then it is delicious, absolutely lovely. The stillness of the water, the brilliant moon, throwing its glittering light on the lake, and making a long trail of little diamonds, the mountains all round looking grave and calm, little boats filled with men and women, some of them with mandolines and singing popular melodies, and the light from the villages and towns dotted round the lake contribute to form a scene which is enchanting, and unlike anything one has dreamed of.

After resting on his laurels in Italy, with Sir Coutts and Lady Lindsay, Arthur Sullivan returned to new conquests, conducting, composing, travelling.

I am dead tired today. Next week I shall be knocked up, I fear . . . There are so many things I want to do for music if God will give me two days for every one in which to do them.

From 1875 to 1877 he was conductor of the Glasgow Orchestral and Choral Union. Despite all his triumphs, he was not conceited or unapproachable: this is well illustrated by Sir Landon Ronald's experience. When still a young student Ronald had written an operette which was to be presented at a London theatre, but he knew little of the art of scoring for a small theatre orchestra so he got an introduction to that

[1] Article by Dame Madge Kendal in the *Cornhill Magazine*, September, 1933.

master of the art, Arthur Sullivan. 'I kept my appointment with the great man in fear and trembling,' says Sir Landon Ronald. 'He received me delightfully, placed me at my ease at once, and almost made me feel I was a brother colleague of his. I explained my mission, but he told me in his kindest manner that he never taught, and advised me to go to a friend of his, an admirable musician named Ernest Ford, which eventually I did. As I was taking leave of Sullivan, he asked me if I was going to the next Richter concert. I replied in the affirmative. "Well," he said, "the wonderful Mozart symphony in G minor is being performed. Go and buy a pianoforte copy of it. Take it with you to the concert, listen well to the orchestration, and the next morning score it yourself from the pianoforte copy. Then go and buy Mozart's full score, compare it with yours, and you'll learn much".'[1]

One day the Prince of Wales, the Duke of Edinburgh, and Sullivan met together to discuss a proposal which the Duke had at heart: the result was the founding in May, 1876, of the National Training School of Music with Sullivan as Principal (he held the post until 1881). This is now the Royal College of Music.

Sullivan had entered the circle of the Prince of Wales, of whom Disraeli said: 'He has seen everything and known everybody.' The rotund geniality of the heir to the throne, his interest in horse-racing, good food, good talk—these were common enthusiasms H.R.H. shared with the bouncing little musician from Lambeth. Meanwhile, Mr Gilbert was conducting an acrimonious feud, in public print, against an actress with whom he had fallen out; 'Mr Gilbert has yet to learn', declared the *Theatre* severely, 'that he is a servant of the public and amenable to public opinion, and Miss Hodson must be congratulated on the courage she has shown in appealing to her profession against him.'[2]

A doodle from Gilbert's notebook

After *Trial by Jury* had been running some time Mr D'Oyly Carte tried to bring Gilbert and Sullivan together again, by suggesting that they write a *full-length* comic opera, but it was not so easy to get this prancing pair to respond. Gilbert, dispensing with music, was now producing his farcical comedy *Engaged* at the Haymarket. This ran 105 performances. Gilbert advises his actors in a foreword to the play: 'It is absolutely essential to the success of this piece that it should be played with the most perfect earnestness and gravity throughout. There should be no exaggeration in costume, make-up, or

[1] *Variations on a Personal Theme*, by Sir Landon Ronald (Hodder and Stoughton), 1922.
[2] The *Theatre*, 5 June, 1877.

JUDGE.

When I. good friends, was call'd to the bar, I'd an

Fred Sullivan

appe - tite fresh and — hear - .ty, But I was, as many young bar - risters are An —

demeanour; and the characters, one and all, should appear to believe, throughout, in the perfect sincerity of their words and actions. Directly the actors show that they are conscious of the absurdity of their utterances the piece begins to drag.'

Sullivan was high-stepping in another direction, as a letter from Cambridge shows:

Dearest Mum. The deed is done and I am Mus.Doc. Now I am dressed in a black silk gown (evening dress) and a trencher hat and am going to dine in hall at my own college (Trinity) and then go for an evening party at the Master's.

The new Doctor of Music did discuss with D'Oyly Carte the idea of a new opera, but then came a tragedy. The composer's brother, Fred Sullivan, was not a fit man. His illness brought *Trial by Jury* to an untimely end when it had run 128 performances. Gilbert had already allocated to Fred Sullivan the principal comedy part in the proposed new opera when, on 18 January, 1877, Fred died. He was only thirty-nine, and had been full of fun and vitality. His mother and brother were inconsolable; Mrs Sullivan had been so proud of the two boys, the one England's leading musician, the other newly renowned as a leading comedian.

Extract from an interview with Sir Arthur Sullivan in the *Strand Musical Magazine*, 1895:

'I was nursing my brother through a severe illness,' said Sir Arthur, meditatively, 'and had hardly left his bedside for several days and nights. Finding one evening that

[135]

he had fallen into a doze, I crept away into a room adjoining his, and tried to snatch a few minutes rest. I found this impossible, however, so I roused myself to work, and made one more of many attempts during four years to set music to Adelaide Proctor's interesting words. This time I felt that the right inspiration had come to me at last, and there and then I composed "The Lost Chord". That song was evolved under the most trying circumstances, and was the outcome of a very unhappy and troubled state of mind.'

After that Arthur Sullivan laid down his pen, and for several months did not write a single note of music. The new comic opera was forgotten.

Antoinette Sterling, a favourite contralto of the period, introduced 'The Lost Chord' to the public at a London concert. When she rehearsed it, Sullivan handed her the manuscript with the remark 'It won't be a success, I'm afraid', and at the first perform-ance, the singer recalls: 'I shall never forget the anxiety felt by all of us as to how it would be received—least of all, perhaps, by myself. The composer himself was at the piano, and Sydney Naylor at the organ. What excitement when it was all over! What applause burst out on all sides! It was the greatest success that had ever been made by a new song.'[1]

'The Lost Chord' became the most popular ballad of the century. It was rated so highly that it was sung at—for instance—the Leeds Festival of 1877 ('with organ obbligato'). The penalty of success was that it also became the most hackneyed song of the century. It was played on B flat cornets at every street corner. But it was heart-felt in its origin, and when someone parodied it Sullivan protested: 'I wrote "The Lost Chord" in sorrow at my brother's death, don't burlesque it.'

Today, 'The Lost Chord' is still selling. The publisher's latest count, up to the end of 1947, showed that 800,000 copies had been sold.

It was during the period of mourning that Dr Arthur Sullivan received a letter from Christ Church, Oxford:

> I am the writer of a little book for children, *Alice's Adventures in Wonderland*, which has proved so unexpectedly popular that the idea of dramatising it has been several times started. If that is ever done, I shall want it done in the best possible way, sparing no expense—and *one* feature I should want would be good music. So I thought (knowing your charming compositions) it would be well to get two or three of the songs in it set by you—to be kept for the occasion (if that should arrive) of its being dramatised. If that idea were finally abandoned, we might then arrange for publishing them with music.
> In haste—
> Faithfully yours
> C. L. DODGSON
> ['Lewis Carroll']

[1] Quoted in *A Century of Ballads, 1810 to 1910*, by Harold Simpson (Mills and Boon).

Sullivan replied: 'I am very glad to get good words for music. But I do not accept commissions to set words, preferring to buy the right to use them.'[1]

So nothing came of this proposed collaboration of Arthur Sullivan and Lewis Carroll.

An intimate glimpse of Sullivan as his friends knew him is given in the memoirs of Mr de Lacy Lacy:[2]

From 1870 to 1876 I saw a great deal of Cecil and Freddy Clay and Arthur Sullivan. The two brothers Clay lived in a flat in Seymour Street, and there I used frequently to dine, together with Arthur Sullivan. And oh, the delightful evenings we used to have. Sometimes they would be in serious mood, and would sit down together at the piano, and play through an opera; more often they would be frivolous, and would sing each other songs, exaggerating such weak points as were to be found in them. For instance, Arthur would say, 'Now here is what Freddy calls a song', and he would sing an exquisite caricature of, say, 'She wandered down the mountain side' or some song of Freddy Clay's. Then Freddy would shove him away from the piano, and return the compliment by burlesquing some song of Arthur's.

Arthur Sullivan loved humming tunes, he was always humming. He would get hold of the latest music-hall song, and declare it was the finest tune ever written. 'Can't you see, you idiot,' he would say. 'It has the grandeur of simplicity, it has only got three notes', and he would crash out 'The Two Obadiahs', we will say, and make it sound magnificent. The next time you saw him, he would have got another tune which was the finest ever written. But he never varied from *the* grandest tune which was ever composed by mortal man, and that was 'The Old Hundredth'; and he would sit down and crash it out on an ordinary piano, until you felt you were listening to the massed bands at the Crystal Palace.

Arthur Sullivan used to be a great deal at Hanford,[3] almost as much as I was, and he wrote some of his well-known music there. Violet Ker Seymer, the second daughter, relates how Arthur wrote the music of the hymn 'Onward, Christian Soldiers' one Saturday afternoon, and how they had the maids in after dinner to practise it, in order to sing it in the Chapel on Sunday, and Arthur said that the children—there were the four Ker Seymer children and two Webber cousins staying there at the time—should choose a verse and sing it by themselves without the others. 'We chose the third verse', said Violet, and so this hymn, which has now been sung by countless millions, wherever the English language is spoken, had on the occasion of its first performance six small children's shrill voices singing:

'Like a mighty army
Moves the Church of God'.

[1] Letter in library of Harvard University.

[2] This hitherto unpublished extract is quoted through the kindness of Mr de Lacy Lacy's daughter, Mrs H. Hippisley-Coxe, of London.

[3] Hanford was a country house belonging to Ernest Clay (elder brother of the composer) who married Miss Ker Seymer and took her name.

'The Times', *November 19th, 1877*

Messrs W. S. Gilbert and Arthur Sullivan have once again combined their efforts with the happiest result. *The Sorcerer*, produced at the Opéra Comique on Saturday night, before an audience that crowded the theatre in every part, achieved a genuine success. The idea of the love potion exists from time immemorial, from Tristan and Iseult, the fate-struck lovers whom Wagner has resuscitated, to the Philtre of Auber and the *Elisir d'Amore* of Donizetti. Mr Gilbert's treatment of the subject, nevertheless is quite original.

The orchestra, according to Mr Sullivan's usual method of treating such subjects takes a conspicuous part in the humorous delineation of personages and incidents, and as he is thoroughly acquainted with every resource of that important element in operatic music, it need scarcely be added that it is invariably used with pointed and well-considered effect . . . A more careful first performance of a new work of its kind has rarely been witnessed. The orchestra and chorus were excellent and quite strong enough for the size of the theatre—the former numbering nearly 30, the latter upwards of 40.

Scene from *'The Sorcerer'* at the Opéra Comique—an engraving from the *'Illustrated London News'*, 23 February, 1878

The 1938 revival. The dress styles of 1878 have been retained. The dresses for the original production were designed by Wilhelm, famous costumier of the Empire Theatre ballets

1877

'THE SORCERER'

IT WAS CHRISTMAS, 1876. Dignified readers of the *Graphic* Christmas Number were chuckling over their nuts and port as they read an account of the quaint results of an entire English village having taken doses of a love potion. The short story, 'An Elixir of Love', a sketch from which is seen, above left, depicting the Bishop piping his heart out in the love-stricken village of Ploverleigh, was written and illustrated by the spell-binder, above right. W. S. Gilbert had a weakness in his writings for fairy spells, philtres, and magic lozenges. Nearly a year later, when a new Gilbert and Sullivan comic opera, *The Sorcerer*, was produced, the Bishop had become Dr Daly, Vicar of Ploverleigh, who 'enters pensively, playing on a flageolet', and as soon as he claps his eyes on the lovely Aline falls head over heels in love, chortling—

> Oh, joyous boon! oh, mad delight;
> Oh, sun and moon! oh, day and night!

In the *Graphic* short story the love-potion had been supplied at 1s. o½d. a bottle by Baylis & Culpepper, of St Martin's Lane, a firm of old-established magicians, astrologers, and professors of the Black Art: 'Their Curses at a penny per dozen were the cheapest things in the trade, and they sold thousands of them in the course of the year. Their Blessings—also very cheap indeed, and quite effective—were not much asked for.'

In *The Sorcerer*, Mr John Wellington Wells, of J. W. Wells & Co, Family Sorcerers, introduces himself to the village with similar sales talk, in fact some of it is the same, word for word, as that in the *Graphic*: 'Our sale of penny Curses, especially on Saturday nights, is tremendous. We can't turn 'em out fast enough . . .' And then follows the famous patter-song:

Oh! my name is John Wellington Wells,
I'm a dealer in magic and spells,
    In blessings and curses
    And ever-filled purses,
In prophecies, witches, and knells.

Sketches from the 'Illustrated Sporting and Dramatic News'

The Sorcerer was produced on 17 November, 1877, at the Opéra Comique, a theatre in a turning just off the Strand (demolished in 1904 to make way for the new Aldwych and Kingsway). Mr D'Oyly Carte, encouraged by the success of *Trial by Jury*, now hatched a scheme to make this theatre the Alma Mater of English comic opera. Gathering a number of financiers around him as directors, he founded in 1876 the Comedy Opera Company. Sullivan and Gilbert were *not* directors. In a letter canvassing for £5,000 to £6,000 capital, Carte wrote of the long and well-worn vogue of French *opéra bouffe*: 'But when one considers who are the most popular composers in England one finds that they are not M. Lecocq or M. Offenbach. On any pianoforte in any drawing-room in England one will find half a dozen songs of Mr Arthur Sullivan's to one of the French composers. I believe that there is in England no lack of appreciation of native talent and no lack of efficient artists . . . My plan is to secure the services of the most distinguished composers of the day to write the music for a series of light and amusing but interesting comedy operas.'

Burnand, Alfred Cellier, Albery, and Clay were among the English composers and authors Carte approached, but in the end the field was narrowed down to the following sheet of notepaper:

9, ALBERT MANSIONS,
S.W.

5 June 1877.

My dear Carte

Gilbert and myself are quite willing to write a two act piece for you on the following terms.

1. Payment to us of two hundred guineas (£210) on delivery of the MS. words and music - that is to say, before the piece is produced.

2. Six guineas a night performance (£6.6) to be paid to us for the run of the piece in London - from this will be deducted the two hundred guineas paid in advance so that the payment of the six guineas a performance will not really commence until about the 33rd or 34th performance.

3. We reserve the country right your right to play it in London on these terms to extend only to the end of the your season.

This is signed overleaf 'Yours truly, Arthur Sullivan'. Carte agreed the terms.

Sullivan and Gilbert had decided to make a completely fresh start. First, they would write a two-act opera. Second, they proposed to recruit a company from scratch, disregarding West End favourite actors, and seeking not grand operatic voices but singers who could do clear justice to the words as well as the music (this Gilbert insisted upon).

In casting *The Sorcerer* Gilbert and Sullivan (without knowing it, for how were they to foresee the future?) were casting *types* for nearly all their operas—the Major-General types, the Lady Jane types, the beautiful Mabels, the fleshly Don Alhambras. Future characters were fitted to the actors and actresses who now signed-on in Mr Carte's office. Some of them stayed with the company for years, others were replaced later by similar types. The longest-stayer proved to be portly Rutland Barrington. He says in his autobiography: 'I made the initial success of my career in one of the most important parts in a comic opera for the stupendous stipend of six pounds per week . . .' Barrington had previously been in melodrama, and could not quite understand why Gilbert booked him for the part of the moonstruck Dr Daly. 'As the time of production drew near I began to feel rather anxious about it, and confessed as much one day to

Gilbert, saying that I felt what a daring experiment it was to introduce a Dean into comic opera, and that I fancied the public would take either very kindly to me or absolutely hoot me off the stage for ever. He was very sympathetic, but his reply, "I quite agree with you", left me in a state of uncertainty.'[1]

This is what *Punch* thought about it after the first night:

The idea of placing a real live burlesque Vicar on the stage is a bold one. But I saw two Clergymen in the stalls who thoroughly enjoyed the joke, especially when his Reverence said, that, as a penance, he would spend the remainder of his days in the congenial gloom of a Colonial Bishopric.

Barrington

Though Sullivan was consulted about the musical capabilities of the new actors and actresses, Gilbert was really the Casting Director, and as St John Ervine says: 'Gilbert's sense of the stage was as sharp as Mr Noel Coward's. He could see an actor where other people could only see a wooden-faced fellow, as when he put Rutland Barrington into his cast.'[2]

Not only Barrington, but Richard Temple and George Grossmith were future stars who were now spotted and given parts in *The Sorcerer*.

Lady Sangazure in *The Sorcerer* is the first of the macabre procession of elderly and ugly ladies in Gilbert and Sullivan opera. Gilbert pins her down with a pun in the cast-list as 'a Lady of Ancient Lineage'. He booked for the part Mrs Howard Paul, who had had her own little touring show in which a young entertainer at the piano had appeared, one George Grossmith. As a youth Grossmith was a Penny Reader. He had been Press Reporter at Bow Street Police Court. He was now doing songs and recitations 'at provincial Literary and Mechanics' Institutes, often appearing in conjunction with his father'.[3] He had taken the part of a juror in a benefit performance of *Trial by Jury*, at the Haymarket Theatre, and there he met Arthur Sullivan. Later, in a hall in Bayswater, he played the Judge—and caught the eye of Mr Gilbert.

Sullivan to Grossmith:

Are you inclined to go on the stage for a time? There is a part in the new piece I am doing with Gilbert which I think you would play admirably. I can't find a good man for it. Let me have a line or come to 9, Albert Mansions tomorrow after 4, or Thursday before 2.30.

Mrs Paul to Grossmith:

Under any circumstances, and at some sacrifice, do not fail to accept the part . . .

[1] *Rutland Barrington*, by Himself (Grant Richards).
[2] Article in the *Observer*, on the centenary of Gilbert's birth, 1936.
[3] The *Theatre*, 1 November, 1879.

it will be a new and magnificent introduction for you, and be of very great service afterwards.

'Then came a week of awful anxiety,' writes Grossmith in his autobiography.[1] 'Should I cancel the provincial engagements which I had already made, and which were, of course, a certainty, in favour of a new venture which was not? My father said "Not". He did not think I had voice enough. Arthur Sullivan, however, thought I had. I went to consult him and he struck the D (fourth line in treble clef if you please), and said, "Sing it out as loud as you can." I did. Sullivan looked up with a humorous expression on his face—even his eye-glass seemed to smile—and he simply said— "Beautiful!"

'Sullivan then sang "My name is John Wellington Wells", and said, "You can do that?"

'I replied, "Yes, I think I can do that."

' "Very well," said Sir Arthur, "if you can do that you can do the rest."

'Then off I went to W. S. Gilbert, at Bolton Gardens, to see what the part itself was like. Mr Gilbert was very kind and seemed pleased that I meditated accepting the engagement . . . He read me the opening speech of John Wellington Wells, with reference to the sale, "Penny curses", etc, with which, of course, I was much amused, and said he had not completed the second Act yet; but the part of Wells had developed into greater

George Grossmith, 1877

prominence than was at first anticipated. I saw that the part would suit me excellently, but I said to Mr Gilbert, "For the part of a Magician I should have thought you required a fine man with a fine voice."

' "That," replied Gilbert, "is exactly what we don't want."

'I afterwards learned that the directors of the Comedy Opera Company, to a man, were adverse to my engagement. One of them sent the following telegram to Carte: *Whatever you do don't engage Grossmith.*'

Grossmith became their greatest star. He was an instant public success as J. W. Wells, whisking blithely around the stage with his absurd tea-pot full of the love-potion. This character is all the funnier a figure because after dosing the villagers with

---

[1] *A Society Clown*, by George Grossmith (Arrowsmith), 1888.

Love and observing its complicated and unsettling effects upon them he is overcome with remorse:

> Oh, I have wrought much evil with my spells!
> And ill I can't undo!
> This is too bad of you, J. W. Wells—
> What wrong have they done you?

at which point Lady Sangazure enters, and as this lady of ancient lineage has herself partaken of the aphrodisiac out of the teapot, Fate now has a Gilbertian revenge on the sorcerer:

Recitative

LADY SANGAZURE: What is this fairy form I see before me?
MR WELLS: Oh horrible!—she's going to adore me!
This last catastrophe is overpowering!
LADY SANGAZURE: Why do you glare at me with visage lowering?
For pity's sake recoil not thus from me!
MR WELLS: My lady, leave me—this may never be!
DUET—LADY SANGAZURE AND MR WELLS
MR WELLS: Hate me! I drop my H's—have through life!
LADY SANGAZURE: Love me! I'll drop them too!
MR WELLS: Hate me! I always eat peas with a knife!
LADY SANGAZURE: Love me! I'll eat like you!

and so on. Much has been written about Gilbert's elderly ugly ladies, from that day to this. Already in *The Sorcerer* we find that the tenderness and the humour of Sullivan's music takes away any bitter taste that might otherwise have been left. Grossmith says in his reminiscences how immensely he was impressed at his very first meeting with Sullivan by 'the intense humour in the man's face', and he describes how this quality (which has been rather underrated in books on Gilbert and Sullivan) came into action at rehearsal. At the end of Act One of *The Sorcerer* Sullivan asked the cast to parody the methods of Italian grand opera, singing with arms outstretched towards the gallery.

'We were unsatisfactory,' says Grossmith. 'Sullivan tapped his desk, and the orchestra stopped. The composer screwed his eyeglass into his eye and, addressing us individually, said:

"Don't you understand? I want you to think you are at Covent Garden Opera not at the Opéra Comique. I want you, Miss ——, to imagine you are Adelina Patti; and you, my dear Grossmith, are dreadful; there is not enough Mario about you."

'I saw what he meant and exaggerated the Italian mode, and nearly fell over the footlights into the orchestra. Sullivan, with a smile, said: "Ah! That's better. Capital! Do even more. You needn't consider your safety." '[1]

[1] *Souvenir of Sir Arthur Sullivan*, by W. J. Wells.

But both Sullivan and Gilbert had to be severe as they moulded their 'raw' cast into the Gilbertian style. 'My goodness, how we all stood in awe of them!' exclaims Rutland Barrington, and Grossmith gives a picture of Gilbert as 'a perfect autocrat' standing on the stage beside an actor or actress, 'and repeating the words with appropriate action over and over again, until they are delivered as he desires them to be.'

The Sorcerer ran 175 performances. It is not the best of the Gilbert and Sullivan operas, though it contains in John Wellington Wells one of their best comic characters; The Sorcerer's importance in this history is that as a full-sized comic opera (as distinct from the miniature Trial by Jury) it was the solid base on which Gilbert and Sullivan were to build their absurd castles of fantasy for the next dozen years; and now for the first time they were complete masters of casting, rehearsal, and production. Mr D'Oyly Carte gave them an absolutely free hand. As Sir W. S. Gilbert said many years later: 'To few authors indeed has such absolute control been accorded, and it is to that absolute control that I attribute a large measure of the success that those pieces achieved.'[1] The Sorcerer founded a new school of acting whose traditions and methods have lasted to the present time. Perhaps the outstandingly fresh quality which struck people about this opera in 1877 was its Englishness, in its characters, its scene, its dress, its humour—

FINALE
Now for the tea of our host—
Now for the rollicking bun—
Now for the muffin and toast—
Now for the gay Sally Lunn!

and, above all, in its music. In some of its numbers Sullivan sounds the note of haunting tenderness which floats down through our English music from the ballads and madrigals of Elizabethan times (as in a quintet to the unlikely words 'She will tend him, nurse him, mend him; Air his linen, dry his tears'); in other numbers he is as gay and cocky as a light-hearted Cockney could be.

The period of depression caused by Fred Sullivan's death was over. Arthur Sullivan's mother was now living with Fred's widow at Fulham. One day in the year of The Sorcerer Arthur Sullivan sent her a high-spirited note about a party he was planning:

Dearest Mum,—In for a penny, in for a pound. My Princess Louise is coming tomorrow, so I had better do all I can to make her happy! Bring a lot of roses— never mind what it costs—I don't get her here every day. I want nothing but roses about the rooms, masses of them and one in every single thing I have got. Hooray! Blow the expense. I hope neither you nor Charlotte will be late as there is a good deal to do. God bless you. Yr. Affec. A.

Princess Louise, the twenty-nine years' old daughter of Queen Victoria, had married

[1] Speech at a banquet in 1908 in honour of his knighthood.

the Marquess of Lorne,[1] and the list of guests that Sullivan wrote on the letter to his mother shows the sort of company he was now keeping.

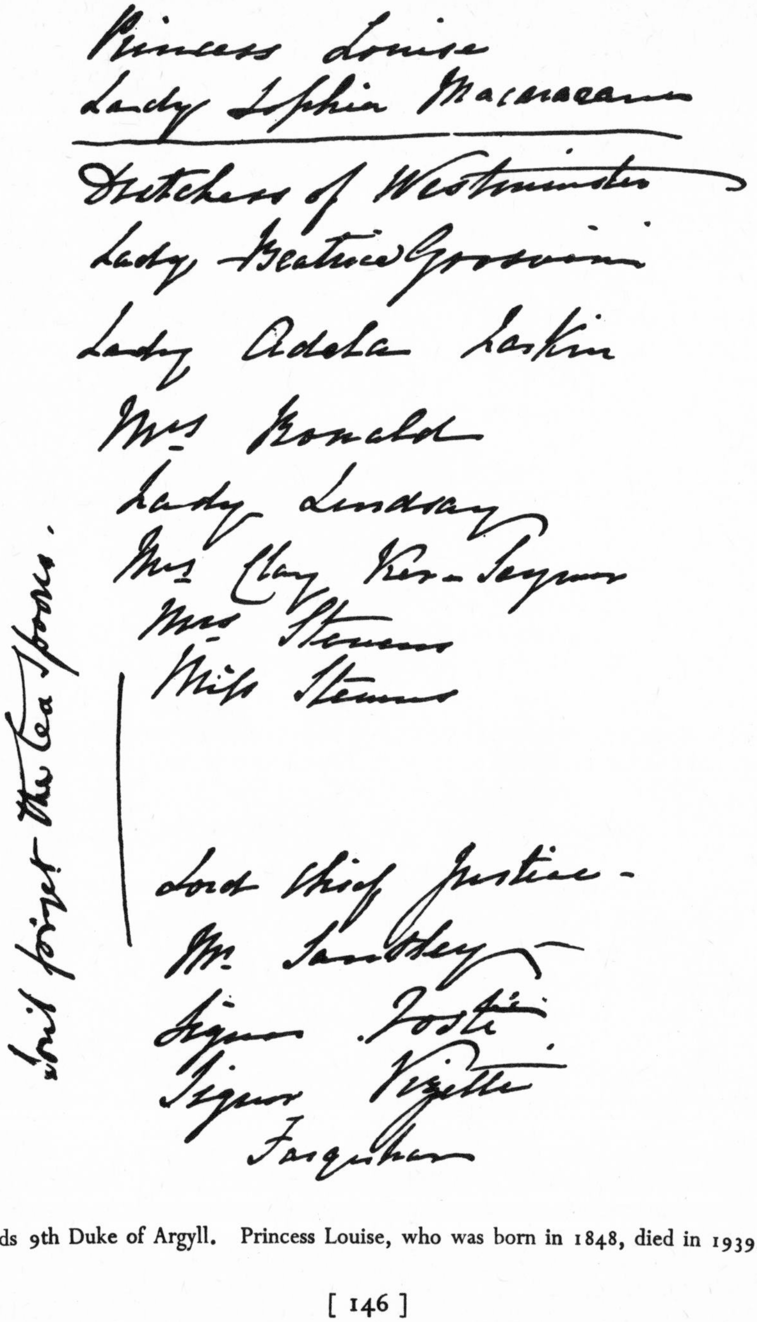

Princess Louise
Lady Sophia Macnamara
_____
Duchess of Westminster
Lady Beatrice Grosvenor
Lady Adela Larkin
Mrs Ronald
Lady Lindsay
Mrs Clay Ker-Seymer
Mrs Stevens
Miss Stevens

Don't forget the tea spoons.

Lord Chief Justice.
Mr Sambsey
Signor Tosti
Signor Vizetti
Farquhar

[1] Afterwards 9th Duke of Argyll. Princess Louise, who was born in 1848, died in 1939.

From now on the name of Mrs Ronalds occurs almost daily in Sullivan's diary.

From the *New York World*, 25 November, 1900:

> Mrs Ronalds was Miss Mary Fran-
> ces Carter, of Boston, many years
> ago, noted for her beauty, her tact
> and her exquisite voice. She was a
> member of an excellent family re-
> lated to New Yorkers of prominence.
> She was married on 6 November,
> 1859, to Pierre Lorillard Ronalds, a
> member of a well-known New York
> family. He is a direct cousin of Pierre
> Lorillard.
>
> The Ronalds's lived together eight
> years, during which four children
> were born to them. They were
> travelling abroad in 1867, when they
> finally decided that they were un-
> congenial. Mr Ronalds returned to
> America, while his wife made an ex-

'*I would travel the length of my kingdom to hear Mrs Ronalds sing "The Lost Chord"*'
—*The Prince of Wales*

> tensive trip through Algiers. Upon her return she made her home in London, where
> she soon became prominent in court circles, at a time, too, when Americans were
> little known except as curiosities. From the first Mrs Ronalds's graceful tact and
> perfect knowledge of the world made her a reigning favourite. She was not only a
> leader in the Prince of Wales's set, but she was the warm friend of the Princess of
> Wales. It is well remembered that Mrs Ronalds is one of the few persons not
> members of the royal family who are privileged to call informally upon the Princess
> of Wales.
>
> Mrs Ronalds took a pretty little house at No. 7 Cadogan Place in London, where
> she modestly returned the many entertainments given in her honour by a series of
> Sunday evening musicales at which one met the smartest people in England and
> listened to the greatest artists.
>
> For more than a decade Sir Arthur Sullivan was a visitor at Mrs Ronalds's house.

Such was the powerful personality and influence of this lady that they called her 'the
permanent ambassadress of the United States at the Court of St James's',[1] a singular
position in those decorous days for a woman living apart from her husband, and one
which says much for her qualities of charm and discretion. Presumably any idea of
divorce or re-marriage was impossible because of the damage such a course would have
done in those days to Sullivan's career, especially in the sphere of serious music where

[1] According to *The Story of Gilbert and Sullivan*, by Isaac Goldberg (John Murray), 1929.

he had won the Queen's personal admiration. Mary Ronalds, beautiful, ambitious, rich, musical, was for the next twenty years the strongest human influence in Sullivan's life, yet there was no public scandal; the charm and discretion of both of them prevented that. When Mrs Ronalds died in 1916, aged seventy-seven, the manuscript copy of 'The Lost Chord' was buried in her grave at Brompton Cemetery.

Sullivan to his mother, 11 April, 1878:

The party at Marlborough House was very small and very swell. The Prince and Princess were both very kind to me and Mrs Ronalds sang the 'Lost Chord' splendidly. I suppose if it is fine you will go to the Boat Race. I can't afford the time.

Arthur Sullivan was the nearest thing in Victorian times to a Court Musician; but W. S. Gilbert was never Court Jester. No newspaper conjectured upon a knighthood for him. To the circle of literary and theatrical folk who dined at the Gilberts' in The Boltons, W.S.G. was an enigma. He could be gruff. He could be genial. After a visit to friends for supper, he was asked if it had gone well. 'Admirably,' he replied, 'not a mouthful over.' Or he could bring down his victim with a wicked double-meaning. Sitting next to a lady who had striven over much to hide her years with artificial aids, Gilbert talked about the Crimean War.

'But I don't remember the Crimean War,' protested his companion.

'Don't you?' said Gilbert. 'I am sure you could if you tried.'

His word-juggling was apt to make slower-witted people feel that they were being scored over. Once, at a rehearsal a messenger carrying a parcel crossed the crowded stage, dodging in and out among the actors. 'Look at that agile creature, Mr Gilbert,' said an actress. 'One would think he was dancing a *pas seul*.'

'Yes,' returned Gilbert, 'a brown-paper *pas seul* obviously.'

There was occasionally a macabre touch to add to the Gilbertian enigma. Upon reading in the newspaper about a murderer who had disposed of several wives by burying their bodies in cement, Gilbert remarked: 'Dear me, a strange man: he seems to have made a hobby of marrying in haste and cementing at leisure.'

But there was one circle in which Gilbert mixed always genially, never gruffly, and to whom he was no enigma. Children loved him. After playing with a little girl whose name was Olive he returned her to her mamma with the remark: 'I thought olives were an acquired taste.' The Gilberts had been married ten years now, and there was no family, but the children's parties at their house were uproarious occasions when W.S.G. played like a big boy, recited the *Bab Ballads*, and gave everyone a royal time. His niece, Mrs Carter, of Salisbury, says: 'When I was a child I used to go up to London to the lovely children's parties held by Uncle Schwenck and Aunt Lucy. It was a tragedy they had no family of their own, for they both adored children. There were at least 200 children at his parties, and he gave presents to us all. And he was always up to practical jokes. This continued all through his life. We had a big brass door-knocker at our house in The Close, and I remember a neighbour once remarked "Oh, I wish I had a knocker on *my* door''—and next day when he returned to his house there *was* a knocker on the door. It had been painted there by W. S. Gilbert.'

At the end of 1877 Sullivan was resting on his oars in Paris. *The Sorcerer* was doing quite well in London, but the Opéra Comique was not always full. The education of the English public to the new school of comic opera was only slowly taking effect. What Gilbert and Sullivan needed now was a great world-wide success to establish their name for ever.

Gilbert, in London, wrote in his diary:

Carte called. Read plot of new opera to him. Much pleased. He is to send draft agreement. Business at Opéra Comique TX to EX. Only one week i.e. Xmas Week, below expenses.

(Gilbert used a code to conceal figures in his diary.)

Although *The Sorcerer* was covering expenses it was apparent that a new opera would soon be needed, and it was the never-flagging Gilbert who set the pace as always.

Gilbert to Sullivan:

I send you herewith a sketch plot of the proposed opera. I hope and think you will like it. I called on you two days ago (not knowing that you had gone abroad) to consult you about it before drawing it up in full. I have very little doubt, however, but that you will be pleased with it. I should like to have talked it over with you as there is a good deal of fun in it which I haven't set down on paper. Among other things a song (kind of 'judge's song') for the First Lord—tracing his career as office boy in cotton broker's office, clerk, traveller, junior partner, and First Lord of Britain's Navy. I think a splendid song can be made of this.

As Mr W. H. Smith, founder of the book-selling and newsagent firm, held the post of First Lord of the Admiralty in Mr Disraeli's government, Gilbert adds:

Of course there will be no personality in this—the fact that the First Lord in the opera is a radical of the most pronounced type will do away with any suspicion that W. H. Smith is intended . . .

—a rather Gilbertian way of asserting his innocent design, seeing that W.S.G. was notorious for seeing things upside down, or by their mirrored opposites!

The letter touches on casting: 'Barrington will be a capital Captain, and Grossmith a first-rate First Lord'—and concludes:

The manuscript, when it arrived, was the best libretto Gilbert had yet written. Sullivan could not resist it. Gilbert's witty words acted on him like champagne. The music of *H.M.S. Pinafore* bubbled out of him.

A contemporary artist's impression of 'H.M.S. Pinafore', 1878

1878

'H.M.S. PINAFORE'

THE SHIP THAT SAILED TO VICTORY

NELSON'S FLAGSHIP, H.M.S. *Victory*, made a gallant sight as she lay anchored in honourable retirement at Portsmouth. The tall man who had been roaming round her decks drew from his pocket a sketch-book and rapidly pencilled a few memoranda: an old salt or two, the outline of a deck-house, the curve of the poop. He cast a discerning eye over the rigging and sketched in its detail. He sniffed the sea air, and with relish scanned the shipping in the harbour, the uniforms of navy men (still little changed from Nelson's time), the formal ceremony on an adjoining ship as a gold-braided officer was solemnly piped aboard. This was Gilbert's element. The salty blood of his father (if not that of his alleged ancestor, Sir Humphrey) raced in his veins. In his mind's eye he could see a version of this scene on the stage at the Opéra Comique . . . H.M.S. *Pinafore* . . . he could hear the Gilbertian burlesque of naval occasions:

BOATSWAIN: My lads, our gallant captain has come on deck; let us greet him as so brave an officer and so gallant a seaman deserves.

Enter Captain Corcoran

CAPTAIN: My gallant crew, good morning.
ALL (*saluting*): Sir, good morning!
CAPTAIN: I hope you are quite well.
ALL (*as before*): Quite well; and you, sir?
CAPTAIN: I am in reasonable health, and happy
To meet you all once more.
ALL (*as before*): You do us proud, sir!

Into the notebook went the exact stage-movements by which the First Lord of the Admiralty would be piped aboard, together with 'the admiring crowd of sisters, cousins and aunts that attend him wherever he goes'. There would be a chorus of jack tars to greet them:

Sir Joseph's barge is seen
    And its crowd of blushing beauties,
We hope he'll find us clean,
    And attentive to our duties.

And a chorus of Sir Joseph's female relatives to respond:

        Gaily tripping,
        Lightly skipping,
Flock the maidens to the shipping . . .

Gilbert's diary shows that during that day at Portsmouth—13 April, 1878—he 'lunched on board *Thunderer* with Lord Charles Beresford. Went round ship. Went on board *Victory* and *St. Vincent*, making sketches, then pulled ashore to station'—and back in London in the evening he went to the Beefsteak Club for dinner, called at the Olympic Theatre, where his play, *The Ne'er-do-well*, was proving a flop, and then went home to his own little theatre: 'From the sketches he made on board the *Victory* he was able to prepare a complete model of the *Pinafore's* deck', writes François Cellier. 'With the aid of this model, with varied coloured blocks to represent principals and chorus, Gilbert, like an experienced general, worked out his plan of campaign in the retirement of his studio, and so came to the theatre ready prepared to marshal his company. The perfect state of preparedness in which *H.M.S. Pinafore* was launched showed Gilbert to be the master-absolute of stagecraft.'[1]

[1] *Gilbert, Sullivan and D'Oyly Carte*, by Cellier and Bridgeman (Pitman), 1927.

Gilbert's model stage, with an experimental setting for an opera.

BELOW: *The 'Characters'*

A photograph of Gilbert's model stage was published with this description: 'He has an exact model of the stage made to half-inch scale, showing every entrance and exit, exactly as the scene will appear at the theatre. Little blocks of wood are made representing men and women—the men are three inches high, and the women two and a half inches. These blocks are painted in various colours to show the different voices. The green and white striped blocks may be tenors; the black and yellow sopranos; the red and green contraltos; and so on. With this before him, and a sheet of paper, Mr Gilbert works out every single position of his characters, giving them their proper places on the model stage, and he is thus enabled to go down to rehearsal prepared to indicate to every principal and chorister his proper place in the scene under consideration.'[1]

Dr Arthur Sullivan accompanied Mr W. S. Gilbert on that visit to Portsmouth in April, 1878, when—with the production of *H.M.S. Pinafore* scheduled for May—they made a final check-up on accuracy and atmosphere aboard ship, and inspected the uniforms which were being made by a Portsmouth naval tailor (a typical touch of Gilbertian fastidiousness for detail). Sullivan had not been keen to come back to the grindstone when Carte and Gilbert called him over from France early in the year.

Sullivan to D'Oyly Carte, from Nice, 5 February, 1878:

Is *The Sorcerer* seriously on the wane—I mean is business bad? I hope not for I am not in very good cue yet for writing anything fresh and bright. I think the new piece ought to be very funny . . .

Good-bye, my dear D'Oyly. Keep good and virtuous. I shall be home at the end of the month. I have lost all my money gambling—a regular facer. Ever yours, A.S.

[1] 'Illustrated Interviews', by Harry How, *Strand Magazine*, 1893.

While at Nice, Sullivan received an invitation from the Leeds Musical Festival to compose an oratorio for first performance at Leeds, at the next Festival in 1880, but he felt 'so ill and worn' that he declined it. Later he changed his mind.

Sullivan to Fred R. Spark, secretary, Leeds Musical Festival:

I am much better now, and feel more disposed to entertain the proposal which the committee have done me the honour to make me. I could not, however, undertake the composition of an oratorio which should occupy the whole of a concert. For that I should have no time. But I should not be unwilling to write a work of the same length and character as *The Prodigal Son*—a work of about an hour or an hour and a half . . .[1]

The committee agreed, fee 100 guineas. Sullivan's mind was full of this oratorio—he was trying to find a subject which had not already been tackled by Handel or Mendelssohn—when he wrote at the end of February to Mrs Dockett, his London housekeeper, signalling his return home:[2]

(handwritten letter)

> Hotel Isotta. Genoa.
> Monday 25 Feb: 1878
> —
>
> Dear Mrs Dockett
>
> I am on my way home and hope to be in London the end of this week. I don't know the day precisely, but it will be Saturday Sunday or Monday. At all events when I get to Paris, I will write again and let you know the exact day & hour. I hope you have had the house well cleaned, and the mouse caught. You will be glad to know that I feel very much better now — fresher & stronger. But
>
> I was in bed, ill for a week at Nice. I caught a violent cold. I thought I was going to have a rheumatic fever. But it passed off.
>
> The weather here is not so warm as at Nice, but it is very fine nevertheless. I drove in a carriage a great part of the way from Nice here, sleeping one night on the road — The scenery is magnificent
>
> I enclose a cheque for five guineas.
>
> Yrs very truly
> Arthur Sullivan

Back in London Sullivan was faced with such a flurry of preparations for *H.M.S. Pinafore* that the Leeds oratorio was pushed aside.

[1] Quoted in *History of the Leeds Musical Festivals*, by Fred R. Spark and Joseph Bennett (Leeds), 1892.
[2] This letter now belongs to Mrs Dockett's granddaughter, Mrs Coquard, of Wembley.

Nobody would think that a sick man wrote the vigorous sea-salty tunes of *Pinafore*, which match so wonderfully the words of Gilbert's satire on the British Navy and British self-conceit:

> For he himself has said it,
> And it's greatly to his credit,
> That he is an Englishman!
> For he might have been a Roosian,[1]
> A French, or Turk, or Proosian,
> Or perhaps Itali-an!
> But in spite of all temptations
> To belong to other nations,
> He remains an Englishman!

The words are set to a gloriously pompous tune. The catchy waltz of 'He loves little Buttercup' is not sick-bed music. Nor is the perkiness of the First Lord's song:

> Now, landsmen all, whoever you may be,
> If you want to rise to the top of the tree,
> If your soul isn't fettered to an office stool,
> Be careful to be guided by this golden rule—
>> Stick close to your desk and never go to sea,
>> And you may all be Rulers of the Queen's Navee!

Sullivan to 'Dearest Mum':

Everyone is out of town for Easter except myself . . . I haven't been out this week except to dine, as I am in the full swing of my new work. It will be bright and probably more popular than *The Sorcerer*, but it is not so clever . . .

He did not tell her, as he disclosed later that 'I would compose a few bars and then be almost insensible from pain. When the paroxysm was passed I would write a little more, until the pain overwhelmed me again. Never was music written under such distressing conditions.'

Meanwhile, at the Opéra Comique Mr D'Oyly Carte was busy re-engaging (or dismissing) artists who had had their trial in *The Sorcerer*. In the archives at the Savoy is preserved a new contract engaging George Grossmith 'to sing and act' at a weekly salary of eighteen guineas. And they were still on the look-out for new talent:

Telegram, Carte to Jessie Bond, at Liverpool: WOULD YOU LIKE COMIC OPERA CALL ELEVEN O'CLOCK MY OFFICE.

---

[1] 'Some people . . . may be Rooshans, and others may be Prooshans; they are born so and will please themselves'—Mrs Gamp in *Martin Chuzzlewit* (Dickens), 1843.

In the original 'Pinafore' : Jessie Bond (Hebe)
and George Grossmith (Sir Joseph Porter)

'It was like a trumpet call,' writes this great star. 'To go on the stage, to play in a company which was doing something entirely new and original in light opera! The name of Gilbert and Sullivan was already ringing through the country, I knew well what chances of advancement association with it would give to me. But —it was the Victorian era, the stage was frowned upon by the respectable, and I had been trained in the strict conditions of concert and oratorio singing. Would not such a change in my life mean social downfall, and would not my parents think I had gone to perdition? I dared not tell them of Carte's offer, I knew too well beforehand how strong their objections would be. But in my eyes the prospect was too dazzling, I could not turn away from it. I made some excuse about a pressing engagement in London, packed in hot haste, and caught the first possible train. At eleven o'clock on the appointed morning I was in Mr D'Oyly Carte's office. He offered me an engagement in his company, and without hesitation I signed a contract for three years, at the princely salary— for me—of three pounds a week.'[1] She played Hebe, the First Lord's first cousin.

Rehearsals began at the theatre:

GILBERT: Miss ——, why are you taking the centre of the stage? Did I not tell you to stand over there?

ACTRESS: (*Indignantly*) Indeed, Mr Gilbert—I *always* took centre-stage in Italian opera.

GILBERT: Madam, this is not Italian opera. It is only a low burlesque of the worst possible kind.

'Gilbert says this sort of thing in such a quiet and serious way that one scarcely knows whether he is joking or not,' said Grossmith.

Rutland Barrington recalled that when rehearsing *Pinafore* Gilbert told him to sit on one of the ship's skylights, pensively. 'I did so, but the stage carpenter had only sewn the thing together with packthread, and when I sat on it it collapsed entirely, whereupon he said like lightning: "That's expensively."'[2]

---

[1] *The Life of Jessie Bond* (John Lane).

[2] *Rutland Barrington*, by Himself (Grant Richards).

Gilbert was nervous about *H.M.S. Pinafore*. He frequently sat up rewriting until two and three in the morning. Gout had begun to trouble him. 'Tried to work—couldn't' he notes several times in his diary. Three weeks before the first performance of *Pinafore* he was still revising it. He rehearsed so intensively that on the day before the production he was at the theatre all day and nearly all night as well—'Drove to Opéra Comique for night rehearsal. Everything smooth—dresses all right. Remained there till 3.35 a.m. then to Club for supper, then home at 4.30.'

Gilbert was up again in a few hours and off to the theatre to 'superintend the scene'. He dined and dressed at his club, and then departed for the first performance:

'To theatre at eight. Put finishing touches. Rowdy gallery, singing songs, etc. Piece went extremely well. I went in and out three or four times during evening. Enthusiastic calls for self and Sullivan. Then to Beefsteak Club.'

The opening night was 25 May, 1878. Sir George Douglas, who was present in the audience, writes:[1] 'There was no room for fault-finding whether in music, play, or acting. One heard that night for the first time words and airs that have remained with one ever since, and that straightway became a part of the national inheritance.' Next day, a Sunday, Gilbert went round in a hansom to call on Sullivan, they read the Sunday paper notices together, and decided to cut out a hornpipe in Act One and 'Barrington's Serenade, Act Two'. On the Monday the newspapers were very kind, except

the *Daily Telegraph*: 'A frothy production destined soon to subside into nothingness.'

Within a few days it looked as though the *Telegraph* was right. Receipts dropped below £100 a night. The most apparent cause was an unexpected May heatwave; then, during a blazing June, *Pinafore* was almost stifled to death; in July, London still sweltered, receipts were down to £40 and less. Jessie Bond blames 'the small, poor and inconvenient' building in which audiences 'perspired and gasped', and the fact that a theatre was still 'not quite the place for decent and respectable people to be seen in'.

And some respectable people who saw *H.M.S. Pinafore* were shocked for quite a new reason, not for the old one of the stage's sexy vulgarity. They could not stomach Gilbert's satire upon Things

'Pinafore' still going strong in the Nineteen Fifties: Ann Drummond-Grant as Little Buttercup

[1] In the *Gilbert and Sullivan Journal*, September, 1928.

[157]

British. Mr Disraeli—now Lord Beaconsfield—wrote that except at Wycombe Fair in his youth he had 'never seen anything so bad as *Pinafore*'.

It was not only Gilbert's satire on naval discipline, and his mockery of the British system of appointing non-technical civilians to the head of highly technical Services (e.g. W. H. Smith at the Admiralty, a Disraeli appointment), but *Pinafore* actually dared to poke fun at Class Distinction in the Senior Service.

SIR JOSEPH PORTER: I hope you treat your crew kindly, Captain Corcoran.

CAPTAIN: Indeed I hope so, Sir Joseph.

SIR JOSEPH: Never forget that they are the bulwarks of England's greatness, Captain Corcoran.

CAPTAIN: So I have always considered them, Sir Joseph.

SIR JOSEPH: No bullying, I trust—no strong language of any kind, eh?

CAPTAIN: Oh, never, Sir Joseph.

SIR JOSEPH: What, *never?*

CAPTAIN: Hardly ever, Sir Joseph. They are an excellent crew, and do their work thoroughly without it.

SIR JOSEPH: Don't patronize them, sir—pray, don't patronize them.

CAPTAIN: Certainly not, Sir Joseph.

SIR JOSEPH: That you are their captain is an accident of birth. I cannot permit these noble fellows to be patronized because an accident of birth has placed you above them and them below you.

CAPTAIN: I am the last person to insult a British sailor, Sir Joseph.

SIR JOSEPH: You are the last person who did, Captain Corcoran.

Many years later Sir W. S. Gilbert wrote a summary of the opera for children, in which he commented upon the First Lord: 'You would naturally think that a person who commanded the entire British Navy would be the most accomplished sailor who could be found, but that is not the way in which such things are managed in England. Sir Joseph Porter . . . knew nothing whatever about ships. Now as England is a great maritime country it is very important that all Englishmen should understand something about men-of-war. So as soon as it was discovered that his ignorance of a ship was so complete that he did not know one end of it from the other, some important person said: "Let us set this poor ignorant gentleman to command the British Fleet, and by that means give him an opportunity of ascertaining what a ship really is." This was considered to be a most wise and sensible suggestion, and so Sir Joseph Porter was at once appointed First Lord of the Admiralty of Great Britain and Ireland. I daresay you think I am joking, but indeed I am quite serious. That is the way in which things are managed in this great and happy country.'[1]

On top of this, some of the satire in *Pinafore* was so subtle that those who could not

[1] *The Pinafore Picture Book* (G. Bell & Sons).

understand it were annoyed—by, for instance, a character like Ralph Rackstraw, who though a common A.B. spoke in such uncommonly high-flown language as had never been heard from a jack-tar on the English stage:

RALPH: I am poor in the essence of happiness, lady—rich only in never-ending unrest. In me there meet a combination of antithetical elements which are at eternal war with one another. Driven hither by objective influences—thither by subjective emotions—wafted one moment into blazing day, by mocking hope—plunged the next into Cimmerian darkness of tangible despair, I am but a living ganglion of irreconcilable antagonisms. I hope I make myself clear, lady?

JOSEPHINE: Perfectly. (*Aside*) His simple eloquence goes to my heart.

The original Ralph Rackstraw was Mr (later Sir George) Power, who had been principal tenor at the opera house at Valetta. But in 1878 no amount of good singing could save *H.M.S. Pinafore*, apparently. For one cause and another, by midsummer it looked as though this opera must be written off. D'Oyly Carte, Sullivan, and Gilbert had faith in its quality: they only wished to weather the heat-wave. So did the cast, who voluntarily cut a third of their salaries; but the directors of the Comedy Opera Company wished to cut their losses. Several times they put up notices dismissing the cast. 'Carte would rush off to soothe the directors, and get them taken down again,' Jessie Bond tells us, 'but the Company was in a ferment of suspense and anxiety, and Carte's nerves became thoroughly rasped and irritated.'

If *H.M.S. Pinafore* had been shipwrecked, the indications are that there would never have been a *Mikado* or a *Gondoliers*. Sullivan and Gilbert would have been sufficiently discouraged to give up further collaboration in comic opera. Gilbert's diary shows that his mind was running again towards serious drama. Sullivan's thoughts were turning again north, to Leeds, to the more austere climate of oratorio. Although the partners now seemed to be in danger of splitting apart in one direction, they came together most unexpectedly in another, for in June the *Leeds Express* announced that Sullivan had found a subject for the new oratorio:

Taking counsel with his friend and co-worker, Mr W. S. Gilbert, he has selected the poem by the late Dean Milman, *The Martyr of Antioch*, which will be arranged and in fact rewritten by Mr Gilbert.

A Gilbert and Sullivan oratorio!—this was a far cry from the popular career they had appeared to be set upon. Had they given up *H.M.S. Pinafore* and that sort of thing? In July, Sullivan went off to France, as Commissioner for Music at the Paris Exhibition.

For his work in Paris, Sullivan was awarded the Légion d'Honneur. When he returned to London he appeared nightly as conductor of the Promenade Concerts at Covent Garden Opera House. It was an action of his in this more serious sphere of music (though not a very serious action) which, strange to say, blew new breath into the declining body of *H.M.S. Pinafore* and thus saved Gilbert and Sullivan comic opera for posterity. Sullivan included in the Promenade Concert programme a Selection from *H.M.S. Pinafore*. It was a tremendous success. He played it again and again. The charming tunes started people talking about the opera. Business freshened at the box office. By the end of August the theatre was full at every performance. D'Oyly Carte was organizing touring companies. The catch phrase 'What never?'—'Well, hardly ever', became a craze. Music shops sold 10,000 copies of the piano score in one day.

PINAFORE MANIA!

shouted the headlines. Messrs Gilbert, Sullivan, and Carte had struck a gold-mine. Carte rewarded the actors and actresses at the Opéra Comique by organizing a river picnic up the River Thames. Gilbert's diary records that they went in steam launches from Windsor to Cliveden Woods, where they landed and lunched, returning to London in the evening: 'One of the chorus sick—looked after her and put her in cab.'

Now it was prosperity all round. Gilbert bought himself a sea-going yacht, the *Druidess*, and had a sea-going adventure when he and 'Mrs' (as he refers to Mrs Gilbert in his diary) made their first voyage in her from the Isle of Wight to London:

Got under weigh at 12.30. At 2 heavy squall struck us. Topsail with difficulty taken in. After squall, fine. Determined not to put back. Pleasant run till 5 when wind and sea rose. Rough night. One sidelight went out. No binnacle light. One hand sick. Eventually made Dungeness by daybreak and ran for Dover. Should have had to anchor in bay if we had not found a tug to take us in. Got into Granville Basin —smashed our cutwater.

After this the diary records that he took a course of lessons in navigation!

D'Oyly Carte meanwhile had sailed for America to see what could be done to prevent unauthorized performances of *Pinafore* there. In a note to Carte, Sullivan refers to 'offers I've had from America to go over and conduct *Pinafore* whilst the rage is on. Ford offered me one thousand pounds to conduct in Philadelphia for a fortnight.'

But the surgeon's knife detained Sullivan in England.

The Duke of Edinburgh to Sullivan:

I cannot tell you how glad I was to read your letter that you were relieved from your sufferings by a successful operation. The Prince of Wales has asked me to join his congratulations to mine.

Sullivan to John Hollingshead:

I have been suffering martyrdom here for a fortnight, but on Monday last I underwent the operation of having the stone crushed, and I am now well enough to leave Paris tomorrow en route for rest and quiet in the Engadine.[1]

[1] This letter, in the collection of Mr Reginald Allen, of New York, is also interesting because in it Sullivan asks Hollingshead for the loan of band parts of *Thespis*—proving that at this date the music of that opera, since lost, was still at the Gaiety Theatre in Mr Hollingshead's charge.

But the kidney trouble was to dog his steps to his dying day.

While Sullivan was convalescing and Carte was away in America the headlines had a new sensation to scream about in England.

THE FRACAS AT THE OPÉRA COMIQUE

By an Eye-Witness

> Many people who have read the police-court proceedings of the recent riot at the Opéra Comique have laughed at the matter as being a good joke . . . but very few persons are really aware of the facts, and to what fearful danger the many hundreds of people who formed the audience at the above theatre on the eve of July 31st were most certainly put.

So begins a report[1] of this disgraceful affair, which sprang from a dispute between D'Oyly Carte and his fellow directors of the Comedy Opera Company. Ever since the directors had matched the heat-wave of 1878 with their own cold feet concerning *Pinafore*, their relations with Carte had been strained. Now that the opera was proving a gold-mine these financiers no longer wished to suspend it (they had invested £500 each, and were now drawing £500 a week). They made the extraordinary decision to split from Carte and open their own separate production of the opera at the Aquarium Theatre, and they arrived with horse-vans and an army of men at the Opéra Comique with the intention of taking away the scenery. They did not wait until the end of the performance. Says our eye witness:

> The actors on the stage were startled in the middle of their performance by cries of 'Come on! Now's the time!' They heard a rush of many persons down the stone steps which led direct to the stage, and immediately afterwards saw a number of roughs at the prompt entrance . . . The ladies on the stage became panic-stricken, and too much praise cannot be given to Miss Everard (playing Little Buttercup, the stout Portsmouth bumboat woman) for her presence of mind and the struggles she made to proceed with her part in the ordinary way. The ladies and gentlemen began to rise hurriedly and leave the stalls . . . The uproar behind the scenes increased, and scuffling and loud cries were heard.

Alfred Cellier, who was conducting, stopped the performance, there were cries of 'Fire!' and George Grossmith in his uniform as First Lord stepped forward and reassured the 'terrified audience'. What was happening behind the scenes is described by Sir George Power: 'There was a free fight of considerable fierceness. The intruders rushed down the narrow staircase leading to the stage, and quick as lightning our stage hands were summoned to keep them back. The two parties met on the stairs . . . The struggle lasted more than an hour before the invaders were thrown out.'

[1] The *Theatre*, 1 September, 1879.

Gilbert, writing to Sullivan a few days later, said that Mr Barker, Carte's manager, was knocked downstairs and seriously hurt, 'and has applied for summonses'.

The mutineers proceeded with their rival production of *Pinafore*, but Gilbert notes: 'I hear the performance at the Aquarium was wretched and that very few audience were present. J. G. Taylor plays Sir Joseph as a low comedy part and the soprano is a contralto who has to take her high notes an octave lower.'

Gilbert added that he arranged for sandwich-board men to patrol the streets notifying the public that *H.M.S. Pinafore* at the Opéra Comique was the only authorized production.

Presently the rival show had the effrontery to move to the Olympic Theatre, almost next door to the Opéra Comique, where it died for lack of public support. Its sponsors were mortified to find that the law-suits which ensued only served to advertise the 'official' version. Litigation dragged on into 1881, when we find the *Illustrated Sporting and Dramatic News* decorated by a drawing of '*H.M.S. Pinafore* in Court' with Henry Irving giving evidence, and a portly, eye-glassed, and worried-looking Sullivan sitting with Gilbert, immediately below the examining Counsel:

'*H.M.S. Pinafore* in Court'

The Comedy Opera Company thus broke up. In its place a memorandum of agreement was drawn up in Gilbert's handwriting:

Mem. It is proposed that Sullivan and Gilbert shall enter into partnership with Carte, in the Opéra Comique, from the date of the withdrawal of *H.M.S. Pinafore*. Each partner shall contribute £1,000 as trading capital. The profits of the speculation to be equally divided after all expenses have been paid. Carte's salary to be £15 per week—Sullivan's and Gilbert's fees to be four guineas per representation, each. These salaries and pay to be included in weekly expenses. The partnership to exist for the term for which Carte holds the theatre.

W.S.G.
R.D'O.C.
Arthur Sullivan.

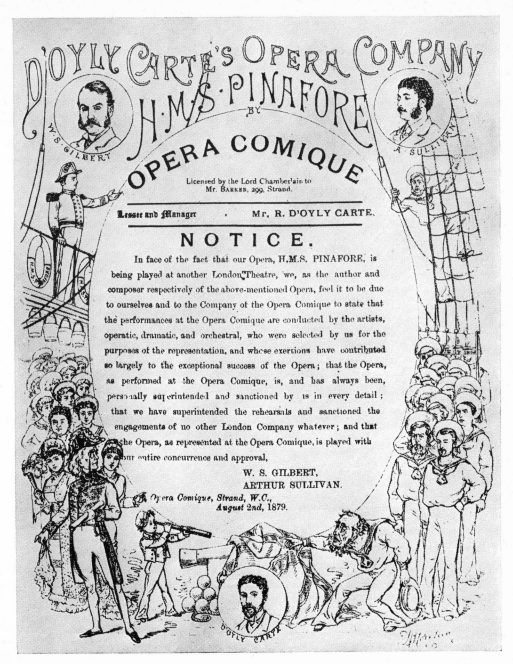

Public announcement issued after the fight at the Opéra Comique

This was the simple basis for a long partnership. Though amended by subsequent agreements it established the equal sharing of profits 'after all expenses have been paid' —a phrase which was to cause trouble at the time of the Carpet Quarrel twelve years later.

The Pinafore Mania continued for two years, right up to *The Children's Pinafore*, which opened at the Opéra Comique on 16 December, 1879, the entire cast being boys and girls. They acted (said the *Theatre*) 'without a tinge of juvenile precocity'. Mrs Jean Stevens, who is the wife of the curator of Salisbury Museum, recalls that when she was a small girl her father painted W. S. Gilbert's portrait and one day 'Mr Gilbert took me to the Children's performance of *Pinafore*. After the show he walked down to the Strand and went to a sweet shop, and every boy and girl in the play was presented with a huge box of chocolates.' But *The Children's Pinafore* roused the wrath of Lewis Carroll. He was 'sad beyond words' when he heard the juvenile Captain use

that 'big, big D——'. The author of *Alice* remarked that he could not understand how Gilbert could have stooped to write, or Sullivan 'could have prostituted his noble art to set to music such vile trash' as:

CAPTAIN: Though 'Bother it' I may
         Occasionally say,
      I never use a big, big D——.
ALL: What, *never?*
CAPTAIN: No, never!
ALL: What, never?
CAPTAIN: Hardly ever!
ALL: Hardly ever swears a big, big D——
       Then give three cheers, and one cheer more,
       For the well-bred Captain of the *Pinafore!*

Gilbert himself appeared as an amateur actor once in 1878. Quotation from *Punch*: 'The great event of last week in the theatrical world was

From the 'Illustrated Sporting and Dramatic News', 1879

unquestionably the Amateur Pantomime at the Gaiety Theatre, on Wednesday afternoon, 13 February, 1878. I give the date in full, for the sake of generations yet unborn. The subject of the pantomime was *The Forty Thieves* . . . written by Messrs R. Reece, W. S. Gilbert, F. C. Burnand, and H. J. Byron . . . Mr Gilbert was the Spanglest Mister Spangles that ever we did see—a very Titan among Harlequins—at least his dress was a very *tight 'un*—and he did his spiriting with a gentle firmness, a courteous determination of purpose, and an inflexible gallantry.'

W. S. Gilbert's geniality—and his inflexible confidence in W. S. Gilbert—come back merrily over the years to us in his own account of the amateur pantomime. He contributed it in verse to a magazine called *Mirth*. First he leaves home for the Gaiety:

> Go and call me a hansom, and see that the horse
> Seems to look at his fate as a matter of course;
> Is prepared to fly over the ground at a rate,
> Dealing danger to children, for hang it, I'm late . . .

then 'in metre suggestive of Bonnie Dundee' he describes his own entrance:

> There was laughing and cheering, and shouts of surprise
> As Gilbert in glittering garb met our eyes;
> And when the 'positions' he showed well he knew,
> A thrill of excitement ran the house through . . .

The performances of the other singers and dancers in the cast are genially described:

> And Gilbert through all danced and postured with grace,
> With a very determined expression of face . . .[1]

For recreation Gilbert was very fond of tennis. His diary records that he was often on the courts before breakfast. The volume for 1878 with its terse entries shows what a crowded life he led. Evenings at theatre, opera, or music hall; days crowded with writing, business interviews, rehearsals, coaching his stars. He had taken under his wing Marion Terry, the twenty-six years' old sister of Ellen Terry. 'Mr Gilbert had the courage to entrust the young and comparatively inexperienced actress with the principal part in a play he was then writing . . . From that time it could not be doubted that an important addition had been made to the list of English actresses.'[2] In 1878 'M.T.' figures very often in the diary: Marion Terry stayed with the Gilberts for long periods, and went on holiday with them at Margate.

Occasionally old William Gilbert came to stay, and on one diary page we have a pen-picture of W.S.G. reading *David Copperfield* aloud to the family circle (including 'M.T.'). On another we find W.S.G. and 'Mrs' taking a jaunt to France, and at Dieppe he has a dip every morning at one part of the beach, 'Mrs apart'—in accordance with the sea-bathing etiquette of the period.

At Rouen: 'Row with hotel porter. Offered him 3s. He asked 5s. Refused to give it him—he made me a present of it.' Rows with cabbies, actors, 'a man trying to steal a dog', were scrupulously admitted in the diary. On its final pages Gilbert made an

---

[1] *Mirth*, No. 5, edited by H. J. Byron, 1878.
[2] The *Theatre*, 1 November, 1878. The play was *Dan'l Druce*.

The Amateur Pantomime—W .S. Gilbert (CENTRE), '*the Spanglest Mister Spangles that
ever we did see' said 'Punch'*

elaborate list of code words to be used when cabling back to London, during his forthcoming visit to America:

> Approbation — I have arrived safely.
> Avalanche — We produce *Pinafore* in a week.
> Bayonet — Piece very successful.
> Billiards — Piece an absolute failure.
> Felicitation — Share of profits last week £300.
> Jacobite — Bookings good.
> Jessamine — Bookings fair.
> Journalist — Bookings bad.

After covering several pages with hundreds of these ciphers, W.S.G. evidently tired of
being serious, and ended the year's diary with some rather more personal phrases for
cabling back to 'Mrs':

> I am ill.
> I am very ill indeed.
> I am at the point of death.

[166]

I have broken my leg.
I have broken my arm.
I have fractured my skull.
I have been stabbed in the back.
I have been stabbed in the arm.
I have been stabbed in the leg.
I have been stabbed in the body.
I have been shot and stabbed.
I have been run over.
I have fallen downstairs.
I have been crushed.

New York Advertisement of (LEFT) *a pirate*
version, and of the English company, 1879

The D'Oyly Carte Company in New York again, 1934-5, at the Martin Beck Theatre:
Marjorie Eyre, Radley Flynn, Muriel Dickson, Derek Oldham, Dorothy Gill, Richard Walker

1879

WORLD-WIDE SUCCESS

DEPARTURE OF BRITISH EXPEDITION
AGAINST PIRATES IN U.S.A.

Wrote in morning. Then dressed for levee.
Called for Sullivan—went to levee with
him. Then to H.M. Theatre to see Maple-
son about Pinafore for America—offered it
to his friend for £70 per night, 50 nights
guaranteed. Then home.

—GILBERT'S DIARY, 3 May, 1879

THE PINAFORE MANIA had spread rapidly across the world. In America innumerable pirate-companies were playing the opera, or their perversions of it, within a few months of its London success—and not a dollar did they send to Gilbert, Sullivan, and D'Oyly Carte. 'I will not have another libretto of mine produced if the Americans are going to steal it,' said Gilbert. 'It's not that I need the money so much, but it upsets my digestion.'

From *The Times* Philadelphia Correspondent, 19 March, 1879:

H.M.S. *Pinafore* has fairly taken our leading cities by storm. In Philadelphia it has been successfully running at half-a-dozen theatres at one time. In New York and Boston it has been similarly successful, and it is running in the South and West. Its melodies are sung by everyone and its jokes have got firmly fixed in our news-paper literature. Such a furore as this opera has created I have never known before in the history of the American stage.

Catch phrases from the opera winged their way from Atlantic to Pacific. One Ameri-can newspaper editor called his reporters into his office and told them that 'What never? Well, hardly ever' had occurred twenty times in the previous day's issue. 'Never let me see it used again,' he thundered.

'What never?' was the inevitable question.

'Well, hardly ever,' boomed the editor.

[169]

First Lord in Australia: J. C. Williamson, from a photograph now in the Mitchell Library, Sydney

To Gilbert, Sullivan, and Carte it was now obvious that they had a property of international value, and they took steps to protect it. Cables round the world speedily fixed an agreement for the operas to be handled by J. C. Williamson, Ltd, a famous Australian theatrical firm, under a licence from Richard D'Oyly Carte (the arrangement still operates today). Mr J. C. Williamson himself played Sir Joseph Porter at the Theatre Royal, Sydney, in 1879, with Maggie Moore as Josephine. He sent several companies out to tour Australia and New Zealand.[1]

In New York eight theatres were playing *Pinafore* simultaneously—every one without authority of the authors. When a pirated piano score was published in the U.S.A. it bore the legend: '*H.M.S. Pinafore*, the reigning sensation throughout all theatrical circles all over the world!' Philadelphia had a negro version, and in Boston the chorus consisted of 'fifty voices from various Catholic churches'. The deviation from Gilbertian writ that such performances achieved may be imagined. One version interpolated a song about a new style in trousers. Another burlesque, Tony Pastor's *Canal Boat Pinafore*, invited to a matinée 'all the actors in *Pinafore* now riding at anchor in New York'— and the casts of all the other pirate versions filled the house!

Carte, reconnoitring the lair of the pirates, reported from 27 Waverley Place, New York, to his colleagues in London:

I saw *Pinafore* on Wednesday. The people had all excellent voices—surprisingly good some, but not the remotest idea how to play the piece. The acting, costumes, time of music, etc. were too atrociously bad for words to express. It is fair to say that this was not one of the best companies. It is clear to me that the 'business' of the piece has never been done. Everyone here thinks that the advantage of your rehearsing the piece will be enormous. Steinway says if you came with the original orchestration and business and a company from England the *Pinafore* would run another season.[2]

When Mr D'Oyly Carte hurried back to England for consultations, Dr Sullivan and

[1] A more detailed history is given in *Gilbert and Sullivan Opera in Australia, 1879 – 1931*, by Vinia de Loitte (Mrs Howard Vernon).

[2] This letter, in Mrs Bashford's collection, is dated 27 June, 1879.

Little Buttercup's dress styles: LEFT, *Rosina Brandram in the 1899 revival;* RIGHT, *George Sheringham's new costume design, 1929*

Mr Gilbert agreed that as soon as possible they must get across the Atlantic and carry the fight into the pirates' camp, by showing America just how much superior the genuine presentation could be. Carte found the Pinafore Mania still raging in Britain. The tunes were heard everywhere. 'A hundred thousand barrel organs were constructed to play nothing else,' exclaimed Sullivan (the composer of oratorio!).

Despite Mr Gilbert's protestations that he didn't really mean it, Mr W. H. Smith was now universally known as 'Pinafore Smith'. One day he, as First Lord of the Admiralty, visited Plymouth and launched a ship at Devonport Dockyard. On the dockside stood the Royal Marines Band. Just before Mr Smith was due the Bandmaster received a verbal message from the Port Admiral not to play any music from *Pinafore* on any account. The message was wrongly delivered and Mr Smith arrived on the scene to the strains of

> Stick close to your desks and never go to sea,
> And you all may be Rulers of the Queen's Navee![1]

---

[1] I am indebted to the son of the Bandmaster for this story. 'I was only a small child at the time,' he writes, 'but I heard my father tell the story several times.'—L.B.

At the Opéra Comique *H.M.S. Pinafore* went on to score 700 performances.[1] Mr Sullivan's coffers, so lately depleted at casinos in the South of France, were full again. Mr Gilbert bought another yacht, *Pleione*, and went sailing along the South of England. His only complaint was that his cook 'has an idea that the more you water gravy, the more gravy you get'.[2] He landed at Gravesend and, proceeding to London, produced his play *Gretchen* at the Olympic Theatre. Suffering from 'an acute attack of nervous debility' on the first night, he roamed the streets around Covent Garden during the performance, and on returning to the theatre he found that the audience had gone home. 'Is the play over?' he asked a bystander. 'Over!' was the reply. 'I should say it *is* over—over and done for. Never see'd such a frost in all my born days.'

[1] Including the children's performances.
[2] Letter to his friend Miss Beatrice de Michele, quoted in *W. S. Gilbert*, by Sidney Dark and Rowland Grey (Methuen).

Mr and Mrs Gilbert on board 'Chloris' with some young friends; INSET, *a bathing scene from his sketchbook! Gilbert bought 'Chloris', a 110-ton yawl, built by John Harvey (father of actor Sir John Martin-Harvey) for £5,000*

More and more it was being brought home to Gilbert that what the public now wanted was not plays by Gilbert, but comic operas by Gilbert and Sullivan.

The long run of *H.M.S. Pinafore* did not blind the partners to the need to have a successor ready for the moment when the Pinafore Mania should wane. When preparing a new comic opera their usual procedure was that Gilbert would first draft a synopsis, which he read to Sullivan. After discussion, Gilbert set about writing the libretto, not necessarily starting at the beginning of the first act. He sent bits of it—a song here, a chorus there—to Sullivan by post. If Sullivan encountered difficulty in setting the words, back they would go to Gilbert for revision. By midsummer 1879 they had worked out the general plan of their next comic opera, and Carte was at the same time urging them to go to America; in these circumstances their promise to have the Sullivan-Gilbert oratorio *The Martyr of Antioch* ready for Leeds in the following year was an embarrassment to them.

It happened that, mainly owing to a temporary slump in trade which led to unemployment and a shortness of money, the Leeds Festival Committee was considering whether to shift the Festival on to 1881, and when Sullivan heard of a postponement he wrote to the Festival Secretary:[1] 'It will be a great relief to me and a weight off my mind because in consequence of my approaching visit to America I should have very little time to write in the next six months, and I have been very seriously perplexed how to manage it.' This letter well illustrates Sullivan's lifelong dilemma in trying to follow two careers, the highest culturally (or what appeared so to be) and the most profitable financially. When, in America months later, he heard from Leeds that they were adhering to the 1880 Festival, *The Martyr of Antioch* became indeed a weight on his mind.

It was in 1879 that the long association began between the Gilbert and Sullivan operas and the amateur societies: a connection which has no equal in theatre history and has done a great deal to strengthen the hold of these operas on the British public. The first amateur performance in Britain was *H.M.S. Pinafore* at the Drill Hall, Kingston-on-Thames, on 30 April, 1879, by the Harmonists' Choral Society.[2]

But even in the amateur field the American pirates scored a scoop. On 28 and 29 April students of Columbia College presented *Pinafore* at the Union League Theatre, New York.[3]

Meanwhile, the new opera was on the way. Gilbert wrote to Sullivan, 7 August, 1879:

I have broken the neck of Act II, and see my way clearly to the end. I think it comes out very well. By the way, I've made great use of the 'Tarantara' business in Act II. The police always sing 'Tarantara' when they desire to work their courage to sticking-point. They are naturally timid, but through the agency of this talisman they are enabled to acquit themselves well when concealed. In Act II, when the robbers approach, their courage begins to fail them, but recourse to 'Tarantara' (pianissimo) has the desired effect. I mention this that you may bear it in mind in setting the

---

[1] 30 June, 1879. See *History of the Leeds Musical Festivals*, by Fred R. Spark and Joseph Bennett, 1892.
[2] According to Miss Rose Cellier, writing in the *Gilbert and Sullivan Journal*. Her father produced the opera.
[3] 'For all I know,' writes Mr Reginald Allen, of New York, 'there may have been earlier amateur performances in America, but this one I can prove. I have a copy of the programme.'

General's 'Tarantara' song. I mean that it may be treated as an important feature and not as a mere incidental effect. I need not say that this is mere suggestion. If you don't like it, it won't be done.

So began *The Pirates of Penzance*. They tried to keep the idea quiet, but somehow it leaked out, to the joy of the American pirates. In the words of a U.S. lawyer: 'With the taste of blood in their mouths, they pricked up their ears at the news of further prey; they even quarrelled among themselves, in advance, as to the distribution of the booty.'[1]

On 5 November, 1879, Gilbert and Sullivan sighted America from the liner *Bothnia*. Carte came over a week later. Their plan was to produce an authorized *H.M.S. Pinafore*. More—in their bags were the unfinished words and music of *The Pirates of Penzance*; they would themselves present it in New York. The première of a British opera in America!—it would be historic, unprecedented. And if they kept it strictly to themselves it would foil the pirates; for in Sullivan's own words: 'At that time there was no copyright between the two countries, and so we were compelled to retain possession of the whole work in manuscript. The moment any portion of the opera appeared in print it was open to any one in the States either to publish, produce, or do what he liked with it. Apart, however, from the absence of international copyright, the law concerning artistic questions was very involved and uncertain, and in a very unsatisfactory state altogether. Keeping the libretto and music in manuscript did not settle the difficulty, as it was held by some judges that theatrical representation was tantamount to publication, so that any member of the audience who managed to take down the libretto in shorthand, for instance, and succeeded in memorizing the music was quite at liberty to produce his own version of it.'[2]

This actually happened while they were in America, and Sullivan mentions that one of his orchestra was offered 100 dollars if he would supply the first violin part to a pirate publisher.

When the British expedition arrived in America they were given an unexpected welcome by the pirates in steamers off Sandy Hook. 'Every vessel in the motley squadron,' says the *Musical Times*, 'was dressed with American and English flags, and having on board a *Pinafore* band and chorus. The Standard *Pinafore* sent two tugs, and the Church Choir *Pinafore* one; another hailing from the Aquarium, another from Chickering Hall, another from Lexington Avenue, and another from some place where a German version of the operetta is played.' But the effect was spoiled by a 'pestilent little tug' sent out by a bitterly rival entertainment—the Nigger Minstrels—carrying a flag with the terrible legend NO PINAFORE! . . . 'The mission of this little tug, like that of the rift within the lute, was to spoil the music, and it did its work with all

[1] Article on 'Sir Arthur Sullivan and Piracy', by Alexander P. Brown, *North American Review*, June, 1889.
[2] Quoted in *Sir Arthur Sullivan*, by Arthur Lawrence (Bowden), 1899.

[174]

the perseverance and success of a first-class steam whistle. Whenever a band played or a chorus sang, the steam whistle of the Minstrels shrieked its loudest, and so were Messrs Gilbert and Sullivan escorted into New York Bay.'

The *New York Herald*, 6 November, 1879:

The appearance and manner of the two famous Englishmen greatly belie the published accounts which have found their way across the ocean, and which represented more especially Mr Gilbert as a man of austere and haughty temperament. On the contrary, two more amiable, modest, simple, good humoured and vivacious men could not easily be imagined. They fairly brim over with animation, high spirits and the jolliest kind of bonhomie, and it would appear to the most indifferent observer that they must shed gladness upon any company in which they happened to be. Mr Gilbert is a fine, well-made, robust man, apparently forty-five, above the medium stature, with the brightest and rosiest of faces, an auburn moustache, and short 'mutton chop' whiskers, tipped only slightly with grey, large and clear blue eyes, and a forehead of high, massive and intellectual cast. His voice has a hearty, deep ring, and his utterance is quick and jerky—as though he were almost tired of keeping up this business of saying funny things, which everybody more or less expects of him. Mr Sullivan is quite different. In his appearance gentle feeling and tender emotion are as strongly expressed as cold, glittering, keen-edged intellect is in that of Mr Gilbert. He is short, round and plump, with a very fleshy neck, and as dark as his 'collaborateur' is fair, with a face of wonderful mobility and sensitiveness, in which the slightest emotion plays with unmistakable meaning, with eyes which only the Germanic adjective of 'soulful' would fitly describe and the full, sensuous lips of a man of impassionate nature. With all this Mr Sullivan, who keeps a monocle dangling over one eye while the other twinkles merrily at you and whose dark whiskers and hair have an ambrosial curl, is also something of a polished man of fashion.

The conversation of course turned first upon *Pinafore* and Gilbert and Sullivan agreed in expressing their surprise at its enormous success in this country.

'It is rather hard,' said Gilbert, with great good humour, 'when one has done for years a serious work—or work, at least, aiming to be so—to find after all that a frothy trifle like this should here so far exceed in its success the work which one has held in far more serious estimation. For we really had no idea that it would be such an extraordinary success, you know.'

Mr Sullivan cordially chimed in with this sentiment and alluded to his oratorios and other compositions of a more classical and ambitious style, which, he was constrained to acknowledge, had not met with anything like the popular success that *Pinafore* had enjoyed.

The reporter asked how it was that the words and music of the Gilbert and Sullivan operas were so closely wedded. Gilbert replied: 'We have now been working together harmoniously for the last seven years, and have learned to understand each other so thoroughly that even the faintest suggestion of the one meets with a ready and sympathetic response from the other. In all this period of active co-operation it has never even once occurred that we have disagreed as to the way in which an idea should be carried out, be it either poetically or musically.'

'Did you expect these familiar quotations from *Pinafore* to become the popular catchwords which they now are?'

'Never', was Mr Gilbert's serious emphatic reply.

'What! Never?'

'Well, very seldom.'

During this interview Gilbert made a startling claim that until his partnership with Sullivan no operatic work by a British author and composer had ever had a longer run than three weeks. Presumably he did not count *The Beggar's Opera* because its music was not original, but rather a collection of traditional tunes. Nor did he count *The Bohemian Girl*: Balfe's opera had 100 performances at Drury Lane in 1843–4 but not in a consecutive run. *The Beggar's Opera* in 1728 had sixty-two performances; after that a good many plays without music had long runs, but no original British musical work achieved any notable run until *Trial by Jury* (128 performances), *The Sorcerer* (175), and *Pinafore* (700). All the now-famous titles, from *The Geisha* to *The Merry Widow* and *The Arcadians*, and from *The Maid of the Mountains* to *Me and My Girl* and *The Dancing Years*, have come on the playbills since Gilbert and Sullivan set the phenomenal example; and the same applies to American musical plays, from *The Belle of New York* to *Oklahoma!*

The party of British invaders that landed in New York in 1879 included Rosina Brandram, Blanche Roosevelt from Covent Garden, and Jessie Bond, who was astonished to find that in one of the pirated versions of *H.M.S. Pinafore* her own part of Hebe was played by a girl in ballet skirts 'as a sort of music hall dancer'.[1] They started at once on rehearsals at the Fifth Avenue Theatre.

Sullivan to his mother:

We have engaged a first-rate chorus, and the Principals are the best who have ever been got together for the immortal *Pinafore*. We open on Monday week and the rest depends upon the public . . . I must do the Americans the justice to say that they are most wonderfully kind and hospitable. The moment a man sees you, he wants to know what he can do for you, and means it too. Of course it is an exciting state of existence—too exciting for me. I live in a semi-public state all the time, everything I do watched, every word I say noted and publically commented on, so that I get bewildered and dazed, and long for a little rest and quietness, but I fear it is out of the question here.

[1] *The Life of Jessie Bond* (John Lane).

Gilbert, of course, produced the opera. The authentic Gilbertian polish was an eye-opener to the American critics: 'We've seen *Pinafore* as a comedy, we've seen it as a tragedy,' wrote one, 'but the play these Englishmen have brought over is quite a new play to us, and very good it is.'

Another was impressed by the animated first scene: 'Practicable shrouds were set, with sailors clambering up and down, and the chorus was skilfully divided, some on the gun deck, and some on the quarter deck, so as to destroy the usual unpleasant stiffness in the grouping. But the really noticeable difference in the interpretation was the orchestration. There was breadth, colour and tone, together with a harmonious blending with the vocalism which was utterly wanting in what may be called the home-made *Pinafores*.'

The authors were called before the curtain, and Mr Gilbert made a speech. 'It has been our purpose,' he said, 'to produce something that should be innocent but not imbecile.'

Sullivan to his mother:

A success unparalleled in New York. At last I really think I shall get a little money out of America. I ought to, for they have made a good deal out of me . . . In order to strike while the iron is hot, and get all the profit we can while everyone is talking about it, we are sending out three companies to other towns in America, and all these have to be selected, organized, and rehearsed.

An American manager named Stetson offered them £5,000 down for the rights in Boston, but the offer was declined. They preferred to send out their own companies— 'and,' said Sullivan, 'taking it all round, we did excellently well, more especially when one remembers that our attempt to retain possession of our own property involved us in a guerrilla warfare.'[1]

International copyright law was in such a state of chaotic uncertainty that the Gilbertian partners tried many expedients to protect their rights on both sides of

---

"PINAFORE."

Wherein It Is Pre-eminently the Attraction of the Day.

Tragedy and Comedy Paling Before Its Brightness.

Arthur Sullivan is greatly pleased with his success of "Pinafore" in this country; but he thinks that no American performance has yet given it the true orchestration, which, he adds, is to be found only in the English editions of his nautical, or naughtical, opera.

New York press comment, 1879

---

[1] Quoted in *Sir Arthur Sullivan*, by Arthur Lawrence (Bowden), 1899.

the Atlantic. One idea was simultaneous production in England and the U.S.A.

Plans were therefore set afoot for the next opera, *The Pirates of Penzance*, to make a quiet début at Paignton, in Devonshire, simultaneously with the New York première, which was now fixed for 31 December, 1879. A month before this date the music of *The Pirates* was not nearly finished. Sullivan and Gilbert had landed in America with about half the work done, and all through the *Pinafore* rehearsals Sullivan had been trying to finish *The Pirates*. Then he made an appalling discovery.

Sullivan to his mother:

I fear I left all my sketches of the last Act at home, as I have searched everywhere for them. I would have telegraphed for them, but they could not have arrived in time. It is a great nuisance as I have to rewrite it all now, and can't recollect every number I did. We hope to get it out in a fortnight from next Saturday.

A fortnight to go. In his hotel Arthur Sullivan set about this stupendous task, and now he was stricken again by his old illness. He was in tortures of pain as he dragged himself from his couch, writing, writing, writing, all day and long into the nights. Gilbert and Carte frequently came in for conferences, and Cellier helped Sullivan with copying out the orchestral scores, as did Sullivan's old friend Frederic Clay.

Sullivan's diary, 9 December, 1879:

Gilbert came in after dinner and returned home with me to arrange changes in 2nd Act. Cellier here also filling in accompaniment of 2nd Act to send to England. Went to bed at three.

Fred Clay was staying in New York with the Barlows, a well-known family, who had decided to impose a fine on anyone who used a catch-phrase from *Pinafore*. Clay went to church one Sunday with his hosts and the preacher concluded his sermon with the words: 'For he himself has said it.' Clay whispered to Sam Barlow, 'And it's greatly to his credit,' and promptly taking half a dollar from his pocket passed it to him.

In the interval between the production of the authentic *Pinafore* and that of the new opera, D'Oyly Carte had arranged for Gilbert's opera *Princess Toto* (music by Frederick Clay) to be presented at the Standard Theatre, New York, with Leonora Braham as leading lady. It was not a success, but everyone was agog with curiosity about the forthcoming Gilbert and Sullivan piece. A story had got around that its plot was about six burglars who made love to six daughters of a house they had burgled, and that it would be called *The Robbers*. Mr Gilbert told the *New York Herald* that he and Sullivan had originally thought of the amorous burglars as an idea for a one-act operetta like *Trial by Jury*—'and very likely we shall use it in the present work. But I cannot tell you anything more about the plot, because, to tell the truth, the piece is not yet thoroughly elaborated . . . The treatment of the new opera will be similar to that of *Pinafore*, namely, to treat a thoroughly farcical subject in a thoroughly serious manner.'

The Gilbert and Sullivan formula could not be more neatly stated!

Actually the opera was in a more finished state (or Mr Gilbert's share of it was) than he admitted. He had already created and cast and costumed those absurd creatures, the true-blue English pirates and the true-blue English policemen, all with a highly-developed sense of duty, who were to provide the 'farcical subject' for the new opera . . . and the Pirate King who was really a soft-hearted orphan boy:

PIRATE KING
Although our dark career
   Sometimes involves the crime of stealing,
We rather think that we're
   Not altogether void of feeling.
Although we live by strife,
   We're always sorry to begin it,
For what, we ask, is life
   Without a touch of Poetry in it?

ALL (*kneeling*)
Hail, Poetry, thou heaven-born maid!
Thou gildest e'en the pirate's trade:
Hail, flowing fount of sentiment!
All hail, Divine Emollient!

When the last four lines are sung, unaccompanied, to harmonies as serious as a chorus in any of Sullivan's oratorios, and with the entire cast solemnly kneeling, the audience is always hushed by the solemnity of the moment, and there is always great applause afterwards; but is this not a prime example of the Gilbertian formula—'to treat a thoroughly farcical subject in a thoroughly serious manner'?

The original costumes designed by Faustin for 'The Pirates of Penzance', seen in a contemporary sketch at the top, were retained with minor modifications until 1919 when Percy Anderson redesigned the women's dresses in the style of 1851. New costumes were again devised in 1929 by George Sheringham; these are shown above—Darrell Fancourt as the Pirate King, John Dean as Frederic, Dorothy Gill as Ruth

1880

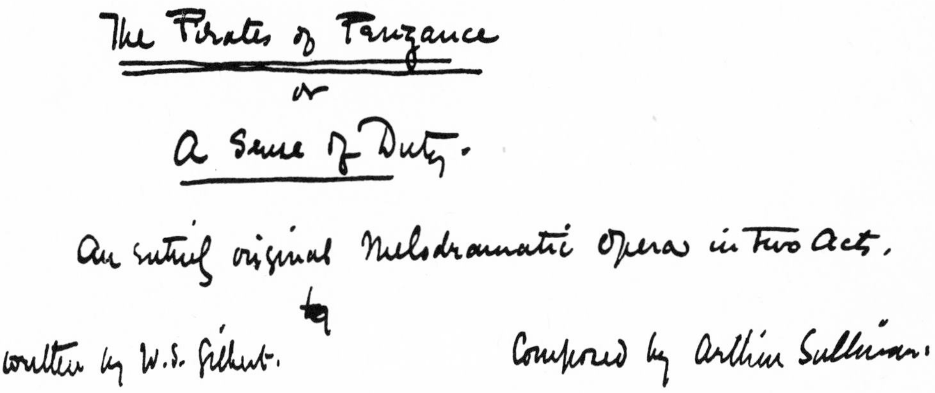

The Pirates of Penzance

or

A Sense of Duty.

An entirely original Melodramatic Opera in Two Acts,

written by W.S. Gilbert.   *Composed by Arthur Sullivan.*

Titles on W.S.G.'s original MS.

SOMEONE HAS SAID that *The Pirates of Penzance* is *H.M.S. Pinafore* transferred to dry land. Instead of satire on naval discipline and tradition there's satire on the army, the police, and the Englishman's sense of duty, a solemn enough subject for Mr Gilbert to treat in a 'thoroughly serious manner'. Instead of a dapper little landlubbing First Lord of the Admiralty there's a dapper little out-of-date Major-General of the Army . . .

> For my military knowledge, though I'm plucky and adventury,
> Has only been brought down to the beginning of the century;
> But still in matters vegetable, animal, and mineral,
> I am the very model of a modern Major-GINeral!

The basic formula is much the same. The treatment is very different. *The Pirates* is more elaborate in plot and presentation, in words and in music, and this is the more remarkable when we recall the conditions under which it was written in New York during the closing days of 1879, with a very 'seedy' (his own word) Sullivan writing against the clock, not only to meet the advertised date of production at the Fifth Avenue Theatre (31 December), but the simultaneous performance at Paignton.

Sullivan's diary records that on 17 December most of the music of Act 1 was shipped to England, then—'Went to rehearsal at theatre, 11 to 4. Came home tired, couldn't work, dined at the Betts'—very pleasant. Conducted at the theatre . . .'

He was conducting performances of *Pinafore* in the evening, rehearsals of *Pirates* in the daytime, and there was still quite a lot of music to compose.

'Returned to the Betts' until 12. Then home. Wrote Trio (2nd Act) and Ruth's song 1st Act, and went to bed at 5.'

This was Ruth's:

> When Frederic was a little lad he proved so brave and daring,
> His father thought he'd 'prentice him to some career seafaring.
> I was, alas! his nurserymaid, and so it fell to *my* lot
> To take and bind this promising boy apprentice to a *pilot* . . .

instead of which, being hard of hearing, she apprenticed him to a pirate (which was precisely the same mistake as was made with Captain Bang, a pirate in Gilbert's play *Our Island Home* in the old German Reed days). Such a jogtrot lyric as this was easy stuff for Sullivan to set; in this opera, as in the others, he was deliberately simple in some of his settings and those who deride these songs for their um-cha-um-cha accompaniments should bear in mind that Sullivan was deliberately 'keeping the music down', as he called it, so that Gilbert's all-important words should come over clearly. But elsewhere in the new opera Sullivan saw his chance to build up the music more ambitiously. *The Pirates of Penzance* was coming from his pen as the most *operatic* opera of the lot, so far, including some burlesquing of what he called 'the farm-yard effects' of Italian grand opera, notably in the waltz song, 'Poor wandering one'. This did not make his race against time any easier, of course. And it caused trouble with the orchestra, as Sullivan afterwards explained:

> We had been rehearsing *The Pirates* and it was but two or three days before the performance that the whole band went on strike. They explained that the music was not ordinary operetta music, but more like grand opera. Perhaps it is necessary to explain that their method is to charge according to a scale, so much per week for entr'acte music, with an ascending scale for operetta, and so on. Had they made their complaint earlier no doubt matters could have been arranged satisfactorily, but their going on strike for higher salaries at the very last moment in this way appealed to me as being a very mean thing to do. Under these circumstances I felt there was nothing for it but to grapple as best I could with the emergency. I called the band together and told them that I was much flattered by the compliment they had paid my music, but declined to submit to their demands. I went on to say that the concerts at Covent Garden which I conducted had just been concluded, and the orchestra there, which was the finest in England, had very little to do before the opera season began, and that I was certain that, on receiving a cable to that effect, they would come over to America to oblige me for little more than their expenses. In the meantime I told them I should go on with the opera, playing the pianoforte myself, with my friend Mr Alfred Cellier at the harmonium, and that when the Covent Garden orchestra did come, we should have a very much finer band than we could get in New York.

Then I went to my friend, the manager of the *New York Herald*, and asked him to write an article in the shape of an interview with me on the subject, which he did, and I launched out freely with my opinions. The upshot of it all was that the band gave in, and everything went along smoothly. Of course, the idea of getting the Covent Garden band over was hardly less absurd than the ludicrous idea of using the pianoforte and harmonium in a big theatre, but, fortunately, public opinion was with me, and my one game of bluff was successful.[1]

One thing which did save time during those last hectic weeks of 1879 was that the chorus 'Climbing over rocky mountain' which Sullivan and Gilbert had written for *Thespis* nine years previously was now salvaged for the gaily-tripping entrance of the Major-General's bevy of daughters, those 'pure and peerless maidens' who blunder into the pirates' cove and bowl over the impressionable pirate apprentice, Frederic.

Day after day the entries in his diary show Sullivan crawling to bed at 3, 4 and 5 in the morning. On 19 December: 'Wrote till 6. Cellier at work on overture, left at 5.30. Wrote letters to L.W., Mother, and the Duke of Edinburgh.'

'L.W.' (Little Woman) was his code for Mrs Ronalds.

On Sunday the 21st, with ten days to go, he went to church, made a full note in his diary of the service of music, then scored *Pirates* all afternoon. For the next three days he was hard at this truly superhuman effort to get the opera finished in time, with

only an occasional thought for the world outside his gaslit hotel room on East 20th Street, New York City: 'Sent 12 brace of ducks to Prince of Wales, ditto to Duke of Edinburgh, and 6 brace to Prince Christian.'

Christmas Day was spent writing music. At 7 a.m. on 28 December he finished the full score. Next day came full dress rehearsals: 'In despair because it went so badly.'

It went well at the final rehearsal on the 30th and Sullivan returned in better spirits to his hotel at 1 a.m. on the 31st with Cellier, Clay, and Gilbert. There was still work to do: the Overture was not yet written. The four of them set to, Sullivan and Cellier composing the Overture, the others copying the parts. 'Gilbert and Clay knocked off at 3 a.m. Cellier and I wrote till 5 and finished it.'

From 'Punch', 30 October, 1880

[1] *Sir Arthur Sullivan*, by Arthur Lawrence (Bowden), 1899.

A heavy strain on the physique of a sick man. We can sense the desperate screwing-up of courage for the ordeal of the first night when we read Sullivan's entry in his diary on that last day of the year, when after a morning spent at the Fifth Avenue Theatre rehearsing the orchestra in the Overture, on which the ink was hardly dry, he returned to his hotel for *breakfast* at 1.45 p.m. but felt too ill to eat; then . . .

Went to bed to try and get sleep - but
could not. Stayed in bed till 5.30.
Filbert came. Got up feeling miserably
ill - head on fire. Dressed slowly &
got to New York Club at 7.30. Had
12 oysters & two glasses of champagne.
Went to the Theatre. House crammed
with the élite of New York. Went into
the orchestra more dead than alive, but
got better when I took the stick in my
hand. Fine reception. Piece went
marvellously well. Grand success.
Went to Frank's afterwards, driving
élite home. Met Mrs Worley there,
to see old year out. Went afterwards
to Mrs Murray's (72 Fifth Av:) to
a reception. Then home - could not
sleep to 3 and not go to bed till
3.30. Felt utterly worn out.

A few hours *before* this New York première the copyrighting performance of *The Pirates of Penzance* had been given in England. At 2 o'clock in the afternoon of 30 December the curtain rose upon one of the queerest shows ever put on any stage, at the tiny Royal Bijou Theatre at Paignton, a quiet resort on the South Devon coast. In the depths of winter Paignton's few visitors, seeking the balmier climate of England's most southerly latitude, saw on the hoardings the posters announcing the first production in any country of a new Gilbert and Sullivan opera; but what they were offered was a very scrappy performance. It is certain that all the music of *The Pirates* had not arrived from New York, for Sullivan was working on it until the eleventh hour, as we have seen. Paignton was chosen for the English première simply because D'Oyly Carte's touring company happened to be touring in Devon with *H.M.S. Pinafore*—and most of them appeared in their *Pinafore* costumes because there had not been time to prepare the new wardrobe. The pirates were denoted by having handkerchiefs tied round their heads. The chorus of policemen marched on dressed as sailors. Instead of bull's-eye lanterns they carried copies of the music, which they hadn't had time to learn. In this thoroughly Gilbertian way, England first heard from that thoroughly Gilbertian character, the Sergeant of Police . . .

SERGEANT: When a felon's not engaged in his employment—
ALL: His employment,
SERGEANT: Or maturing his felonious little plans—
ALL: Little plans,
SERGEANT: His capacity for innocent enjoyment—
ALL: 'Cent enjoyment
SERGEANT: Is just as great as any honest man's—
ALL: Honest man's.
SERGEANT: Our feelings we with difficulty smother—
ALL: 'Culty smother,
SERGEANT: When constabulary duty's to be done—
ALL   To be done.
SERGEANT: Ah, take one consideration with another—
ALL: With another,
SERGEANT: A policeman's lot is not a happy one.
ALL: When constabulary duty's to be done—
                    To be done,
     The policeman's lot is not a happy one—
                  Happy one.

The actor who first played the part of the unctuous Sergeant was Fred Billington, a portly and much-loved member of the touring Gilbert and Sullivan companies from that date up to 1917.

In the absence of Richard D'Oyly Carte in America the organization of the Paignton première devolved upon Miss Helen Lenoir, a very remarkable Scots lady who at this date held the post of London secretary to Mr Carte, and who eight years later became his second wife. By his first wife he had had two sons—Lucas, who became a barrister and died in 1907, and Rupert, who eventually took over the opera business and died in 1948. Miss Lenoir was a sweet little thing with a quite formidable brain for business, at a time when most women took little part in such affairs. Helen Lenoir was a scholar, she spoke several languages, and she had been on the stage; Lenoir was in fact her stage name (she was the daughter of George Cowper Black, Procurator Fiscal for Wigtown-shire). With one day's rehearsal of *The Pirates* at Paignton, and with scraps of music coming across to her from New York, Helen Lenoir had to make the best she could of this extraordinary performance. It is quite likely that she had not even a final script, for W. S. Gilbert's manuscript of *The Pirates of Penzance* contains revisions and cuts made evidently at the last minute in New York. This original manuscript, still in existence, is neatly written in Gilbert's hand on sheets of quarto paper. The sub-title on the front page is *A Sense of Duty* (see head of this chapter). This was changed for the Paignton performance to *Love and Duty*, and later was again changed to *The Slave of Duty*.

Helen Lenoir (later Mrs D'Oyly Carte)

Duty is the theme of the libretto from the moment the curtain rises on the rocky sea-shore of the coast of Cornwall and the pirates 'pour the pirate sherry' to bid fare-well to Frederic. He is just twenty-one . . .

FREDERIC: Today I am out of my indentures, and today I leave you for ever.
PIRATE KING: But this is quite unaccountable; a keener hand at scuttling a Cunarder or cutting out a P. and O. never shipped a handspike.
FREDERIC: Yes, I have done my best for you. And why? It was my duty under my indentures, and I am a slave of duty . . .

Individually, he loves the pirate band with 'affection unspeakable', but collectively Frederic looks upon them with disgust and henceforth his sense of duty will require him to devote himself heart and soul to their extermination. Even when the chorus of General Stanley's daughters trips on to the sea-shore Frederic sings to them—of duty:

> Oh, is there not one maiden breast
>   Which does not feel the moral beauty
> Of making worldly interest
>   Subordinate to sense of duty?
> Who would not give up willingly
>   All matrimonial ambition,
> To rescue such a one as I
>   From his unfortunate position?

So it runs as the opera is performed today, but Gilbert's original manuscript has instead the following lyric, cut out during rehearsals:

FREDERIC: Oh do not spurn the pirate's tear,
            Nor deem his grief unreal and frothy,
       He longs to doff his pirate gear
            And turn tall-hatty and broad-clothy.
       He hates his life upon the wave,
            And longs 'on change' to try his luck, oh—
       He loathes this rude and draughty cave,
            And sighs for brick relieved with stucco.

ALL: We do not spurn the pirate's tear,
            Nor deem his grief unreal and frothy.
       He's right to drop his pirate gear
            And turn tall-hatty and broad-clothy.

Another change made by Gilbert was to cut out his original Finale to Act 1:

> King   For we all are Orphan boys
>
> all   We are!
>
>   Hurrah for the Orphan boys
>
> King   And it would be a kindly thing
>
>   To spare all orphan boys
>
> all   It is!
>
>   Hurrah for the orphan boys
>
> _Girls & General go up rocks & group while Pirates indulge in a wild dance of ecstacy on stage R & R.C. The General produces a British flag & the Pirate King (on arched rock RC) produces a black flag with skull & crossbones. Picture._
>
> End of act 1

It would be interesting to know whether these revisions arrived at Paignton in time for the first performance. However scrappy a show it was, the critic of the most authoritative drama journal of the day, Mr Clement Scott's *Theatre*, evidently felt

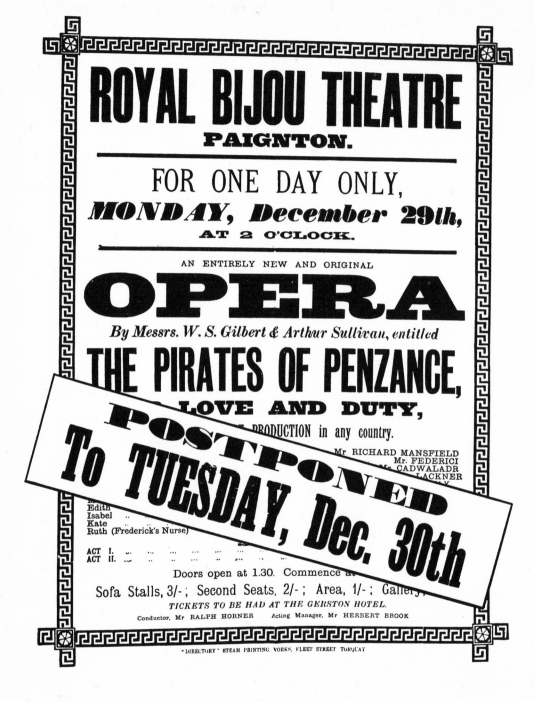

well rewarded for his journey from London to Paignton. He wrote three pages about the opera. He was pleased by its quaint humour, especially when at the end of Act I the Major-General tells a 'terrible story' to save his daughters from abduction by the pirates, informing these fierce fellows (all of whom are orphans) that he is himself an orphan boy, it being of course a strict rule that pirates never molest orphans.

When Frederic discovers that he was born on 29 February in a leap year and is therefore (reckoning by birthdays) not twenty-one but 'a little boy of five, ha! ha!' he has to return to his pirate apprenticeship, bidding Mabel farewell in what the *Theatre* critic considered 'the most charming song in the opera' . . .

Andante
MABEL

Ah, leave me not to pine A-lone and des - o-late; No fate seem'd fair as mine, No hap -

From
the 'Theatre', 1880

- pi-ness so great! And na-ture, day by day, Has sung___ in ac-cents clear,

This is indeed a lovely duet, weaving into the opera those soft, sweet cadences which so wisely give us a breathing space now and again from the topsy-turvy gaieties of Gilbert.

[189]

Sullivan to 'Dearest Mum', from 54 East 20th St. N.Y., 2 January, 1880:

At last I am out of my penal servitude and find a little breathing time to look around me, and write home . . . The whole opera was finished at last—even the Overture, and brought out the night before last with a success unparalleled in New York, as our telegram will have told you. We had long and wearisome rehearsals, but fortunately our Company and all the Chorus are charming people and devoted to us, and spared themselves no pains or trouble to do their work thoroughly well—all except the Tenor who is an idiot—vain and empty headed. He very nearly upset the piece on the first night, as he didn't know his words, and forgot his music. We shall, I think, have to get rid of him.

. . . The laughter and applause continued through the whole piece until the very end, and then there were thunder calls for Gilbert and myself after every Act. Its success was undoubted and instantaneous, and the next day (yesterday) both performances (being New Year's day there was a Matinée as well) were crowded, and the booking is already a fortnight ahead . . .

What do I think of the piece myself? The libretto is ingenious, clever, wonderfully funny in parts, and sometimes brilliant in dialogue—beautifully written for music, as is all Gilbert does, and all the action and business perfect.

The Music is infinitely superior in every way to the *Pinafore*—tunier, and more developed—of a higher class altogether. I think that in time, it will be more popular. Then the *mise en scène* and the dresses are something to be dreamed about! I never saw such a beautiful combination of colour and form on any stage. All the girls are dressed in the old-fashioned English style—every dress designed separately by Faustin, and some of the girls look as if they had stepped bodily out of the frame of a Gainsborough picture. The New York ladies are raving about them.

The Policemen's Chorus is an enormous hit, and they are cheered tremendously when they march on with their Bull's Eyes all alight, and are always encored. I am sanguine of its success in London, for there all the local allusions, etc. will have twice the force they have here.

We have to remember that this English invasion of America by a purely British style of stage show took place at a time when the American nation had not yet discovered its modern idiom of music and entertainment. The commercialization of jazz, ragtime, and swing has evolved a characteristically American style of stage and film show. In 1880 ragtime was still a little-known negro rhythm crooned in the cotton fields, it was the raw folk-music of New Orleans, the native idiom of the Deep South. Its commercialization had not begun. Irving Berlin was not born until 1888, George Gershwin not until ten years later. In 1880 Sullivan's diary contains not a reference to ragtime, and he almost surely heard not a bar of it, or he would have noted it down as he did the native music of (for instance) Egypt when he visited that country. But very soon the tunes of *The Pirates of Penzance* became so popular as to be absorbed into American minstrelsy. This one, for example, was turned by college students into 'Hail, hail, the gang's all here' . . .

Come, friends, who plough the sea, Truce to na-vi-ga-tion, Take an-o-ther sta-tion,

Sullivan's diary reflects the fact that New York Society in 1880 was very 'English' in many ways. He went by horse-carriage to polite parties, just like those in Kensington. New York City was quiet and comfortable, and everyone knew everyone else, rather like an English provincial city, and there was a great regard for anyone and anything from London, so it is not so surprising that New York should fall for so *English* an entertainment as this, with its bobbies, its major-general, its final quip in the last minute of the opera, when the pirates surrender immediately the police call upon them 'In Queen Victoria's name' . . .

PIRATE KING: We yield at once, with humbled mien,
Because, with all our faults, we love our Queen.

and Ruth reveals the truth about the pirate band:

RUTH: They are no members of the common throng;
They are all noblemen who have gone wrong!

MAJOR-GENERAL: No Englishman unmoved that statement hears,
Because, with all our faults, we love our House of Peers.
I pray you, pardon me, ex-Pirate King,
Peers will be peers, and youth will have its fling.
Resume your ranks and legislative duties,
And take my daughters, all of whom are beauties.

The U.S.A. in 1880 had less than fifty million inhabitants, only fifteen millions more than Great Britain. It was the Land of Promise. The pioneers were still opening up the Golden West. Hollywood was a place where they grew lemons. Mr F. W. Woolworth had just started his five- and ten-cent stores. Mr Alexander Graham Bell had invented the telephone four years ago, and Mr Edison had invented the talking machine three years ago, but hadn't yet started on his scheme to light and heat New York by electricity. Into this exciting new land Dr Sullivan and Mr Gilbert now plunged with all their zest, travelling up and down the States like conquerors.

Sullivan to his mother:

We anticipate immense business for the next few weeks—at the end of the eighth week from now we leave New York and go round to the big towns, Chicago, Cincinatti, St Louis, etc. where good business is to be done. We also send out another Company as soon as we can get it ready to the smaller towns—in New England first, then South—strike while the iron is hot. We may go across to San Francisco as there is money to be made there.

On 7 January, 1880, Sullivan was in Baltimore and went to a theatre with friends: 'Was taken to the proscenium box. As soon as I was comfortably settled I heard my name passed round through the theatre, and then the audience began to cheer me, so that I got up and bowed from the box. They were not satisfied with this, so I had to go on the stage and make my acknowledgments.'

He was pleased that his serious works were not ignored in America. At Baltimore they asked him to conduct a concert of his music, and at Boston *The Prodigal Son* was given under his baton by the highly esteemed Handel and Haydn Society.

Like an excited schoolboy Sullivan wrote up in his diary the sights he saw as he travelled with D'Oyly Carte to Washington: they paused to stay on a 450-acre farm where the negro servants were 'all dressed like Uncle Tom's Cabin' and Sullivan was surprised to find luxurious quarters in such an outpost—luxury, and music after dinner, and 'a grand piano and large harmonium, and a great deal of fun'. Part of the journey was in open horse carriages, and when they forded the Shenandoah River, with the carriage wheels jolting over the rocky bottom, Sullivan felt shaky in more senses than one, but they then wended up the Blue Ridge Mountains and the country was beautiful, and he declared he never enjoyed anything more in his life. America and the Americans he thoroughly enjoyed.

Mr Gilbert, in New York, was not a social lion. American hostesses who fawned upon him learned to beware of his prickles.

'Dear Mr Gilbert,' said one lady, 'your friend Sullivan's music is really *too* delightful. It reminds me so much of dear *Baytch*. Do tell me what is *Baytch* doing just now? Is he still composing?'

'Well, no madam,' replied Gilbert, 'just now as a matter of fact dear Bach is by way of decomposing.'

'Great reception when I entered the orchestra. Piece enormously successful,' wrote Sullivan in Philadelphia. Gilbert was rehearsing two companies in New York, in addition to one already performing there and one in Philadelphia. Sullivan travelled with the 'Western Company' to Buffalo, arriving in a snowstorm: 'Very bad performance—everyone nervous. I conducted and worked like a nigger—piece successful more at night performance when there was a packed house and very enthusiastic audience.'[1]

Next day Sullivan went to Niagara Falls. 'Walked across the river and back again on the ice—this is the first year it has been frozen over since 1865. At first the falls don't strike one as being so stupendous, but every moment their grandeur increases and now I think Niagara wonderful.'

Next day via Toronto to Ottawa: 'Drove into Ottawa with Lord Lorne. Very warm welcome. After lunch played lawn tennis in the court and tobogganed for the first time. Great parliamentary dinner at night.'

[1] From Sullivan's diary. All such quotations are by permission of Mrs Elena Bashford.

Three famous Major-Generals of successive generations: George Grossmith (a sketch from the 'Theatre', 1 May, 1880); LEFT, *Henry Lytton in the nightdress scene, production of 1924;* RIGHT, *Martyn Green, leading comedian of the D'Oyly Carte Opera Company until 1951*

[193]

Back in New York during February, 1880, Sullivan had a round of parties, business interviews with Gilbert, theatres, cards, splitting headaches in the morning and gay larks in the evening:

'Went to the theatre and demoralized everybody by larking. Gilbert came to tell me of a member of the orchestra having arranged a set of quadrilles from the *Pirates* and that they were printed by White, of Boston. Had a long talk with Carte. Oysters and bed.'

Next day: 'Breakfasted in Gilbert's room. Went down to William Street to consult Judge Shipman about piracy of music.'

Gilbert (aged forty-three) and Sullivan (thirty-seven) were now assured of lasting fame and fabulous fortune. A Mr Lothian offered them 25,000 dollars in February for the right to play *The Pirates of Penzance* in Boston and New England, but as usual they preferred to send out their own touring companies.

Sullivan had received from England an invitation which was to affect his life profoundly. The Leeds Musical Festival Committee offered him the conductorship of the next Festival. On 28 January, 1880, he accepted 'the honour they have done me'.

Sullivan's American tour came to a climax with his entertainment by the Governor-General of Canada. He then returned to New York, where Gilbert was quietly packing his bags for the journey home, and on 2 March, 1880, at the Hotel Brunswick, Sullivan threw a farewell dinner. Nineteen sat down, and the bill was 313 dollars (nearly £80). Next day Sullivan and Gilbert stood on the deck of S.S. *Gallia* homeward bound, watching the disappearing skyline of New York City (then not nearly so high and precipitous as now)—their conquest of American public opinion complete, the pirates of America not defeated, for a lax law protected them, but at least shown up as incompetent dealers in second-rate imitation.

To what were they looking forward?—Mr Gilbert to the London production of *The Pirates* (so far the only performance in England had been that at Paignton); Dr Sullivan to the Leeds Musical Festival. Previous Leeds Festivals had been conducted by Sir Michael Costa, the fashionable Italian-born composer who had once coached the choir-boy Sullivan, but Costa's imperious manner had alienated the Yorkshiremen. Difficulties had also arisen between the Leeds Committee and their alternative choice as conductor, Mr Charles Hallé, the German-born founder of the Hallé Orchestra. Now Leeds offered Sullivan 200 guineas to conduct the Festival in October, 1880, in addition to the 100 guineas already agreed for composing *The Martyr of Antioch*.

A Leeds newspaper gossip-writer remarked:

As a conductor, Mr Sullivan is regarded by those who have watched his career as possessing great ability—albeit, he is quiet and unobtrusive in the orchestra. No gymnastic exercises, no stamping of the feet, no loudly expressed directions, will he indulge in . . . There is one point about which I am particularly pleased. It is the

Chic fashions of the Eighties: stars of the original London production of 'Pirates'—Alice Barnett (LEFT) as the Pirate Maid, and Marion Hood as Mabel

fact that for an *English* Festival we are to have an *English* conductor. Too long have we in this country bowed down to foreign talent, even when it has been far inferior to English talent. On the selection of an Englishman over Costa and Hallé as conductor, an admirer of *Pinafore* sends me the following from that work, slightly altered:

> We might have had a Russian—a French, or Turk, or Prussian,
>   Or else I-ta-li-an,
> But in spite of all temptations to go to other nations
>   We select an Englishman!

Sullivan always regarded this post as the blue ribbon of his profession. When he first visited Leeds to meet the Committee in June, 1880, he told them they had conferred upon him 'almost the greatest honour that could be held by any man'. He was proud of his connection with the famous Yorkshire choir, and within a few days he asked the Committee to augment the orchestra to 120 players. The Duke of Edinburgh agreed to be President of the Festival.

Meanwhile, *The Pirates of Penzance* had been launched in London, at the Opéra Comique in April. Mr Gilbert had produced it. At one of the rehearsals when Mabel sang

Frederic, save us!

the tenor who replies 'I would if I could' was missing from the stage, so Gilbert piped up from the stalls:

I'd sing if I could, but I am not able . . .

and the pirates responded:

He would if he could, but he is not able.

After the first performance Mr Clement Scott wrote this penetrating analysis in the *Theatre* (1 May, 1880):

> The style of humour of which these Bab Ballad operas is composed has hitherto defied analysis and description . . . It has been called topsy-turvy, deformed, exaggerated, caricature, grotesque; it has been compared to the effect of a man looking at his face in a spoon, in a magnifying glass, or at the world through the wrong end of an opera-glass; but none of these things hits the mark. It is a kind of comic daring and recklessness that makes fun of things which most people would not dream of mentioning, and reveals to broad daylight the secrets of suggestiveness. In a dim, dreamy, and incoherent way we have all *thought* many of Mr Gilbert's ideas; but he *says* them. They are true, or they would not be so familiar to us. Most people suppress some of their funniest thoughts for fear of offending somebody. Mr Gilbert makes of his conscience, or inner guide, or daily companion, a friendly jester, who urges him to say the first thing that comes uppermost, careless of consequences. Now, how exquisite is the satire here of Duty. Ten out of a dozen men would hesitate to ridicule such a sentiment, believing that it is a good, a pure, and generous impulse. But Mr Gilbert can only see the humbug in it, and searches for its ludicrous aspect. In a comical way he shows us all that is mean, and cruel, and crafty, and equivocal even in the world's heroes; and he makes us laugh at them because we are convinced such faults are lingering in the breast of the best of us.

Clement Scott gave glowing praise to the cast, especially 'the true comedy, twinkling fun, and delightful gravity of Mr R. Barrington as the Policeman, who in the smallest part of the opera makes the greatest hit'.

'I only appeared in the second act,' writes Barrington, 'and my song, "The Enterprising Burglar", was such an immense success that I had always to repeat the last verse at least twice. It occurred to me that an encore verse would be very nice, and in a

Front cover of the programme of the first London production of 'The Pirates of Penzance',
1880

rash moment I one day presumed to ask Gilbert to give me one. He informed me that "encore" meant "sing it again".[1]

At the Leeds Festival in October, 1880, *The Martyr of Antioch* had its first performance, the composer conducting. Mr Gilbert, who had arranged the words, was not present at its début and the critics were at sixes and sevens about it. The *Athenaeum* wished that 'Mr Sullivan had taken a loftier view of his theme'. The *Guardian* considered it 'quite thrilling'. Sir Alexander Mackenzie said later that the solo parts were not uniformly strong: 'Probably excited by the promise of the effect which would be

[1] *Rutland Barrington*, by Himself (Grant Richards).

Net receipts (earned by my profession)
from 1st January 1880 to 31st December 1880

	£. s. d.
Metzler & Co. Royalties.	
Christmas '79. £900. Autumn '80 – 824.15	
	1724.15 –
Booaey & Co. ditto.	
373 – 11 – 3. and 304 – 12 – 11 =	678 – 4 – 2.
America – Pirates of Penzance. (net)	2637 – 9.
Opera Comique. Pinafore.	655 – 4.
Ditto. Pirate of Penzance.	2517 – 11.
ditto – Bal: of Pinafore + Children.	100 – 16.
Country right of pieces – half paid Xmas.	725 – 0
Australian ditto	150 .
India ditto . & Co. + Box.	41 –
School of Music – 2 terms.	266 – 13 – 4.
Tennyson Song. (Kegan Paul & Co)	42 – 0 – 0
Leeds Festival	315 –
Australian right – Pinafore. 2nd year.	135 .
£.	9988 – 12 – 6

A page from Sullivan's diary

produced by the famous Yorkshire choristers, Sullivan seems to have put all his strength into the choruses, of which there are many and of great variety.'[1] But if opinions were divided about *The Martyr of Antioch*, they were unanimous concerning Sullivan's directorship of the Festival. His conducting and his personality were praised to the skies. He was popular with artists, orchestra, chorus, audience. This, his first Leeds Festival, beat all records of attendance (14,854) and profit (£2,371).

After the Festival Sullivan gave Gilbert a silver cup inscribed 'Martyr of Antioch; W. S. Gilbert from his friend Arthur Sullivan' (now in possession of Gilbert's great-niece, Mrs Parker).

Gilbert to Sullivan, 3 December, 1880:

It always seemed to me that my particularly humble services in connection with the Leeds Festival received far more than their meed of acknowledgment in your preamble to the libretto—and it most certainly never occurred to me to look for any other reward than the honour of being associated, however remotely and un-worthily, in a success which, I suppose, will endure until music itself shall die. Pray believe that of the many substantial advantages that have resulted to me from our association, this last is, and always will be, the most highly prized.

Thus the year ended happily and prosperously. But some writers in the Press were beginning to stress, with irony, the fact that Arthur Sullivan, the one-time musical prodigy, was now winning most of his fame and fortune through his connection with W. S. Gilbert. In 1880 this parody of the Judge's song in *Trial by Jury* appeared in *Punch*:

> As a boy I had such a musical bump,
> And its size so struck Mr Helmore,
> That he said, 'Though you sing those songs like a trump,
> You shall write some yourself that will sell more'.
> So I packed off to Leipsic, without looking back,
> And returned in such classical fury,
> That I sat down with Handel and Haydn and Bach—
> And turned out *Trial by Jury*.
>
> But W.S.G. he jumped for joy
> As he said, 'Though the job dismay you,
> Send Exeter Hall to the deuce, my boy;
> It's the *haul* with me that'll pay you.'
> And we hauled so well, mid jeers and taunts
> That we've settled, spite all temptations,
> To stick to our Sisters and our Cousins and our Aunts—
> And continue our pleasant relations.

[1] *The Life Work of Arthur Sullivan*, by Sir Alexander C. Mackenzie (1900).

At the TOP *is a sketch from Richard D'Oyly Carte's publicity handbill for the original production of 'Patience';* BELOW, *Rupert D'Oyly Carte's company in 1939*

1881

'PATIENCE'
A CARICATURE OF THE FOLLIES
OF THE AGE

WHEN W. S. GILBERT looked around him in 1880–1 he looked at the languid ladies and affected men at fashionable salons, he looked at *Punch*, in which the 'aesthetic craze' was caricatured by George du Maurier's drawings of Postlethwaite and Maudle, and he noted that the movement towards Beauty in daily life which had been led so healthily by William Morris ten years earlier had swung to ridiculous extremes of 'greenery-yallery' fashions and mediaeval-English posturing, all ridiculously mixed up with a vogue for Japanese fans and jars which had come from Paris to London and had turned upper-middle-class England into something like an Oriental bazaar.

Back in the period of *Trial by Jury*, Gilbert and Sullivan Opera had helped in William Morris's reaction against tawdry design. Victorian homes and theatres, cluttered up with ugly what-nots, had felt the liberating swing of this movement; but now the sharp eye of Mr Gilbert observed that the pendulum had swung too far. To be an apostle

GALLANT COLONEL: *'And who's this young Hero they're all swarming over now?'*
HIS PARTNER: *'Jellaby Postlethwaite, the great Poet, you know, who sat for Maudle's "Dead Narcissus"! Is not he Beautiful?'*

Grosvenor adposing by the lake   *Lady Sane's High Art Dado.*

The 'Illustrated Sporting and Dramatic News' cartoons on the first night of 'Patience'

in the high aesthetic band you only had to 'Walk down Piccadilly with a poppy or a lily in your mediaeval hand'. How near this quip of Gilbert's was to the truth we may gather from Mr Francillon, the Victorian memoir-writer, who went to a party in Gower Street and saw 'a youth carrying throughout a whole evening, in melancholy silence, a tall white lily, with whose droop he was evidently doing his best to bring his own figure into imitation. At this same house a young woman, dressed as it seemed to me in nothing but an old-fashioned bathing-gown and an amber necklace, whom I was asked to take to the supper room, returned to my inquiry of what I could get for her the lugubriously-toned answer, "I seldom eat!" '

So the target Gilbert chose for the satire of his new opera was Affectation, as Duty had been that of the *Pirates*, and Discipline that of *Pinafore*. Right in the centre of the target was the fleshly figure of Oscar Wilde, twenty-five years old, who was just publishing his first slim volume of poems.

Oscar Wilde was once discussing the popular actor Henry Irving. 'Irving's legs,' said Wilde, 'are distinctly *precious*, but his left leg is a *poem*.'

Walter Pater declared: 'It does not matter what is said provided it is said beautifully.'

Such men were the models for Gilbert's Reginald Bunthorne who in *Patience* recites his poetry to admiring females who consider it 'Nonsense perhaps, but oh! what *precious* nonsense!'—

Oh, to be wafted away
    From this black Aceldama of sorrow,
Where the dust of an earthy today
    Is the earth of a dusty tomorrow!

But when left alone Bunthorne soliloquizes:
    Am I alone,
        And unobserved? I am!
    Then let me own
        I'm an aesthetic sham!
    This air severe
        Is but a mere
            Veneer!

    This cynic smile
        Is but a wile
            Of guile!
    This costume chaste
        Is but good taste
            Misplaced!

Henry Lytton as Bunthorne

    Let me confess!
A languid love for lilies does *not* blight me!
Lank limbs and haggard cheeks do *not* delight me!
    I do *not* care for dirty greens
        By any means!
    I do *not* long for all one sees
        That's Japanese.
    I am *not* fond of uttering platitudes
        In stained-glass attitudes.
    In short, my mediaevalism's affectation,
    Born of a morbid love of admiration!

When the curtain rises on *Patience* twenty love-sick maidens 'dressed in aesthetic draperies' are grouped about the courtyard of Castle Bunthorne. They are love-sick for the poet Bunthorne. Their attitudes, dresses, pastel colours, are all a Gilbertian gibe at cults. W.S.G. himself designed the costumes, he bought the fabrics at Liberty's, a shop in Regent Street which specialized in aesthetic robes and beads and potteries, and his décor and grouping of figures in various scenes of the opera was a skit on the contemporary art of the Pre-Raphaelites and the melancholy attitudes of a Burne-Jones painting—for Gilbert's target in *Patience* was not limited to the literary aesthetes, Oscar

*From a souvenir programme of the 250th performance
in London and 100th in New York*

Wilde & Co. The painters and art critics had recently been shaken by a bitter controversy, culminating in a law-suit, and this gave the subject a topicality which Gilbert was quick to seize upon. Whistler had sued Ruskin, supreme art critic of the day, for libel. The Pre-Raphaelites preached that true artists are those who draw and paint with exact fidelity to Nature, and some adopted quite a mediaeval manner ('How Botticellian! How Fra Angelican!' comments *Patience*). Quite a different view of Art was preached by the Impressionists in France, and in England notably by Whistler, who had exhibited some paintings called 'Nocturnes' at the Grosvenor Gallery . . .

> A greenery-yallery, Grosvenor Gallery,
> Foot-in-the-grave young man.

Ruskin went to see the exhibition and wrote: 'I have seen and heard much of Cockney impudence before now but never expected to hear a coxcomb ask two hundred guineas for flinging a pot of paint in the public's face.' That's why Whistler sued Ruskin for libel. Gilbert's diary reveals that W.S.G. took the keenest interest in the proceedings. On the morning of the first day of the trial he took breakfast with Whistler.

All this was the background to *Patience*. The three officers of Dragoons who, in an effort to win the affection of the love-sick maidens, abandon their uniforms and dress up in imitation of aesthetes, put the situation succinctly:

> It's clear that mediaeval art alone retains its zest,
> To charm and please its devotees we've done our little best.
> We're not quite sure if all we do has the Early English ring;
> But, as far as we can judge, it's something like this sort of thing:
> > You hold yourself like this (*attitude*)
> > You hold yourself like that (*attitude*)
> By hook and crook you try to look both angular and flat (*attitude*) . . .

'You hold yourself like this'— a snapshot (RIGHT) *from the wings in 1926—and the same pose in the original production, 1881*

CIRCULAR ISSUED BY RICHARD D'OYLY CARTE IN 1881:

I have the pleasure to announce that my opera company is about to visit your neighbourhood . . . The 'movement' in the direction of a more artistic feeling, which had its commencement some time since in the works of Mr Ruskin and his supporters, doubtless did much to render our everyday existence more pleasant and more beautiful. Latterly, however, their pure and healthy teaching has given place to the outpourings of a clique of professors of ultra-refinement, who preach the gospel of morbid languor and sickly sensuousness, which is half real and half affected by its high priests for the purpose of gaining social notoriety. Generally speaking, the new school is distinguished by an eccentricity of taste tending to an unhealthy admiration for exhaustion, corruption and decay. In satirizing the excesses of these (so-called) aesthetes the authors of *Patience* have not desired to cast ridicule on the true aesthetic spirit, but only to attack the unmanly oddities which masquerade in its likeness. In doing so, they have succeeded in producing one of the prettiest and most diverting musical pleasantries of the day.

They certainly did that, and more. *Patience* is a phenomenon in English history. Consider: it is only ten years since Gilbert and Sullivan began their partnership with *Thespis*, now they dare to go before the public with a comic opera on such a recondite subject as aesthetics. This almost-highbrow comedy of manners is a mark of the revolution in public taste. Here is Gilbert dipping his pen in acid and drawing upon the stage a caricature of the follies of his age. He has become the Hogarth, the Rowlandson, the David Low of theatrical art and of his own time.

But how long would the cartoon hold its point? This worried Gilbert. He knew that 'aestheticism' was a phase, and feared that *Patience* would pass out with it. He need not have worried. In our later years this opera still appeals to the public, not only for its incidental wit and music, but because its basic subject—Affectation—is always with us. The particular manifestations may have changed but we still have our *poseurs* of art and fashion, our 'miminy, piminy, *je-ne-sais-quoi* young men'. Today Reginald Bunthorne is recognized for what he is by audiences who do not know that as originally played by George Grossmith in 1881, and as still made-up today, he is a composite caricature made of Whistler's eyeglass and hairstyle (a white streak on one side), Walter Crane's velvet coat, and Oscar Wilde's knee-breeches and mannerisms—

> An ultra-poetical super-aesthetical,
> Out-of-the-way young man!

A modern audience can similarly recognize in the dairy-maid Patience the voice of naïve, sweet common-sense—

BUNTHORNE: It is a wild, weird, fleshly thing; yet very tender, very yearning, very precious. It is called 'Oh Hollow! Hollow! Hollow!'
PATIENCE: Is it a hunting song?
BUNTHORNE: A hunting song? No, it is *not* a hunting song. It is the wail of the poet's heart on discovering that everything is commonplace. To understand it, cling passionately to one another and think of faint lilies.

Patience also marks a command over theatrical effect which Sullivan and Gilbert had not hitherto achieved. After opening the opera in pastel shades, matched by music of a similarly mellow quality, it is a *coup de théâtre* to bring on the scarlet Dragoon Guards to that strapping, virile, brassy chorus—'The Soldiers of our Queen'. The entire atmosphere is transformed in a moment. The 35th Heavy Dragoons, in contrast to the aesthetes, are tough, unimaginative military men, conquerors of the world—and of feminine hearts. Here again Gilbert holds up his mirror to the world around him. The eighteen-eighties was a period when the British were bent on colonial conquest. They had just fought the Zulus (Gilbert had been invited by *The Times* to go as War Correspondent, his diary reveals). Queen Victoria had become Empress of India; from Egypt to Fiji the red-coats were making their presence felt. These plumed helmets and scarlet uniforms were designed to scare the fuzzy-wuzzies abroad, and flutter the hearts of the women at home: 'A uniform,' brags Colonel Calverley, 'that has been as successful in the courts of Venus as on the field of Mars!'

When I first put this uniform on,
  I said, as I looked in the glass,
'It's one to a million
That any civilian
  My figure and form will surpass.
    Gold lace has a charm for the fair,
    And I've plenty of that, and to spare,
      While a lover's professions,
      When uttered in Hessians,
    Are eloquent everywhere!'
    A fact that I counted upon,
    When I first put this uniform on!

Both in music and words this song echoes—and mocks—the
barrack-square bravado of these sabre-rattling he-men. It is a
sorry state of affairs for them when the ladies prefer Mr Bunthorne—

  Now is this not ridiculous—and is not this preposterous?
    A thorough-paced absurdity—explain it if you can.
  Instead of rushing eagerly to cherish us and foster us,
    They all prefer this melancholy literary man.

Darrell Fancourt
as Colonel
Calverley

In one respect *Patience* is not surpassed in the entire Gilbert and Sullivan series. This
is their peak so far as social satire is concerned. The commentary on aestheticism and
the counter-commentary on braggart militarism has a place in English history. And yet
Gilbert very nearly left the aesthetes out of *Patience*. Until he had the libretto two-
thirds finished the intended victim of his satire was the Church.

Taking an idea from a *Bab Ballad* called 'The Rival Curates', the original draft of
the comic opera concerns clergymen of adjoining parishes, competing in lamb-like
meekness for the admiration of the young ladies of the district; but then Gilbert had
misgivings. He says:

I became uneasy at the thought of the danger I was incurring by dealing so freely
with members of the clerical order, and I felt myself crippled at every turn by the
necessity of protecting myself from a charge of irreverence. So I cast about for a
group of personages who should fit, more or less nearly, into the plot as already
devised, and who should allow me a freer hand in making them amusing to my
audiences . . . As I lay awake one night, worrying over the difficulties that I had prepared
for myself, the idea suddenly flashed upon me that if I made Bunthorne and Grosvenor
a couple of yearning 'aesthetics' and the young ladies their ardent admirers, all
anxieties as to the consequences of making them extremely ridiculous would be at
once overcome. Elated at the idea, I ran down at once to my library, and in an hour

or so I had entirely rearranged the piece upon a secure and satisfactory basis.[1]

By early in 1881 (*Patience* was to be produced in April) Gilbert had it all rewritten, but getting the music composed was another question.

Sullivan's diary:

> The year 1881 opens when I am still at Nice. Having brought with me some numbers for the new Opera G. and I intend doing, I occasionally try to find a few ideas . . . but the sunshine and my natural indolence prevent my doing any really serious work. I enjoy myself doing nothing, with many visits to Monte Carlo.

When at last Sullivan returned to London, in March, his first engagement was to conduct *The Martyr of Antioch* at the Albert Hall. The Prince of Wales was present. Sullivan found it hard to concentrate his mind on comic opera. Gilbert had already started rehearsals. Every night the light in Sullivan's room in Victoria Street burned until quenched by the light of day.

Three days before the first performance he wrote in his diary:

> Rehearsal at twelve, then home to write Tenor song, afterwards cut out. Duke of Edinburgh called to see me, stayed while I wrote and dined. Went to theatre at 7.30 to dress rehearsal. Came home late. Scored Tenor song and sketched out Overture. To bed 5.30 a.m. Finished all scoring of the opera.

The military music came as second nature to one who had been born and bred in the world of military bands, and some of the delicate sequences of *Patience* give us Sullivan at his charming best, notably the duet 'Prithee, pretty maiden', but opinions about this opera provide an example of the changes that occur over the years in what is regarded as good music and good taste. In 1881 the *Theatre's* reviewer declared with approval that the unaccompanied sextet 'I hear the soft note of an echoing voice' was in the class and style of a seventeenth-century madrigal, and most Victorian critics agreed. In 1953 Miss Audrey Williamson calls it a bad lapse into churchiness, and most modern critics would agree. Miss Williamson writes that the music of *Patience* 'in spite of excellent moments, is overlaid with church harmonies and conventional sentimental melodies, and there is far less instrumental interest than in most of Sullivan's scores'.[2]

Musical analysis is not our concern in this book except where it illuminates our biographical analysis, and here it does. Sullivan, indulging in his 'natural indolence' in the South of France, got behindhand (even by his standards) with writing *Patience*, with consequent lapses in his orchestral inventiveness and flounderings into the churchiness and sentimentality which came so easily to him, and to many other Victorian composers. These lapses are shown up by the test of time.

So the music of *Patience* was conceived in an atmosphere of impatience: the impatience of Gilbert and the cast waiting at rehearsals for the arrival of newly-written sheets of music at the theatre; and the impatience of the publisher, Mr Tom Chappell,

---

[1] Preface to the American edition of *Patience* (Doubleday, Page & Co, Inc. New York), 1902.
[2] *Gilbert and Sullivan Opera: A New Assessment*, by Audrey Williamson (Rockliff), 1953.

Leonora Braham, creator of the
part in 1881

Rhoda Maitland in the provinces in
the Eighties

Three girls who played Patience
Centre in the modern costume is Margery Abbott

to have the piano score of the opera printed ready for sale in the music shops of Britain
on the morning after the première. Every day he would send a youth to Sullivan's rooms
with the proofs, and that messenger, young Goodman, grew up to be a Director of
Chappell's and has now given these reminiscences to this book:[1]

'I used to take the proofs with me, and catch a horse-bus to Victoria Street. Mr
Sullivan worked in the semi-basement. The butler would let me in. It was a plainly
furnished room. There was a piano, but I don't recollect ever seeing Sullivan playing it.
He wrote most of his music at his desk, smoking cigarettes and sipping weak gin-and-
water. Very often he would say to me: "Now, you call back tomorrow morning, my

[1] Since writing them Mr E. Goodman has died at the age of eighty-one.

[209]

boy, and I'll leave the MS. and the proofs with the butler for you.'' I knew this meant he was going to work through the night.

'There was always great excitement when a new Gilbert and Sullivan opera was published. Public interest grew with every opera. This was heightened by the secrecy. The titles of the operas were kept secret until the curtain went up, because Sullivan and Gilbert were afraid of the title getting to America and being pirated. At our printing works the vocal score would be set up, all ready to print, and the machines would be standing-by to turn out the thousands and thousands of copies the public clamoured for, when the title was finally inserted into the blank spaces. Then the machines would run, day and night. The music was always ready to be sold at the theatre on the first night of a new opera and in the shops the next day. I remember in Bond Street outside our offices there would be rows and rows of horse-vans and cabs lined up, waiting to be loaded, and railway vans too, ready to take the country deliveries. Our men had been working night after night packing the orders, and there was great excitement to get them out. Then, what a thunder of iron-shod wheels, what a cracking of whips and clatter of hooves, as these chariots bearing Gilbert and Sullivan's newest opera whirled away through the streets of London!'

In addition to the operas, Sullivan's ballads earned large sums for the composer, his heirs, and his publishers. Mr Goodman remembers a form of 'ballad-plugging' in Victorian times which will surprise those who imagine song-plugging to be a product of modern dance-band commercialism. In the days before gramophone records and radio and cinema, a new song depended to 'get known' upon being sung at ballad concerts throughout the country. The publishers paid singers anything from half-a-guinea to three guineas each time a given song was performed. 'When I was a young man,' says Mr Goodman, 'I was looking through the books one day when I found that we were paying certain sums of money to the famous baritone, Sir Charles Santley. By then Santley was past his prime, and I couldn't understand why we had been paying this money for so many years. Then I found that when one of Sullivan's ballads was first published we had promised Santley very exceptional terms if he would sing it . . . not merely a fee every time he sang it, but a royalty on the sales. Now that he had ceased singing the song for a long time, I thought we might stop the royalty; in my youthful enthusiasm I went to my chief and said so. But Mr Tom Chappell, who was the soul of honour and integrity, said we had made a promise to pay a royalty on the sales and this must go on to the end of Santley's life, even if he were not now singing the ballad. The song in question was the famous ''Thou'rt Passing Hence'' which was sung in St Paul's Cathedral at Sir Arthur Sullivan's funeral service.'

On 23 April, 1881, its first night in London, *Patience* had eight encores. The critic of the *Referee* noticed that some of Gilbert's shots went over the heads of the audience, perhaps because the fusillade was too rapid: this opera is packed with subtleties of humour—the very title *Patience, or Bunthorne's Bride* is a joke, for Bunthorne is the only one who is not married off at the end. Despite the jokes that were missed, the *Referee* predicted 'lasting popularity'.

The *Daily News* paid tribute to 'literary culture, with the absence of anything approaching to coarseness or vulgarity'.

But Richard D'Oyly Carte was nervous about the reception the new opera might get in America. According to Sir Johnston Forbes-Robertson's memoirs:[1] 'D'Oyly Carte, knowing that the American public was not familiar with the craze on which the play was built, sent Oscar Wilde on a lecture tour in order to prepare the ground for Bunthorne and his chorus of admiring ladies, and very successful this ingenious advertisement proved.'

[1] *A Player Under Three Reigns*, by Sir Johnston Forbes-Robertson (T. Fisher Unwin), 1925.

*Oscar Wilde as 'a sandwich-board man for Patience' in America:
a cartoon by Max Beerbohm*

The amusing truth of this matter is revealed in a private letter from Carte to Helen Lenoir in December 1881 when she was in New York managing his interests there:

> There have been stupid paragraphs in the *Sporting Times*, one saying that I was sending Wilde out as a sandwich man for *Patience*, and another one afterwards stating that he was not going as 'D'Oyly Carte found that he could get sandwich men in America with longer hair for half the money'.
>
> Wilde is slightly sensitive although I don't think appallingly so; I, however, suggested to him that it would be a good boom for him if he were to go one evening to see *Patience* and we were to let it be known beforehand, and he would probably be recognized. This idea he quite took to . . . I told him he must not mind my using a little bunkum to push him in America. You must deal with it when he arrives.

A few weeks later Carte followed Oscar Wilde to New York, and wrote to Sullivan:

> You will be glad to hear that *Patience* is still running here, doing now a fair jogtrot business. The receipts had gone down, but inscrutable are the ways of the American public and absurd as it may appear it seems that Oscar Wilde's advent here which has caused a regular 'craze' has given the business a fillip up.

Seven months after the London première, *Patience* was produced at the Theatre Royal, Sydney, the Australian Bunthorne being Howard Vernon, with Signor Verdi as Grosvenor. In London the opera ran for over a year (408 performances). As an example of a reviewer who was utterly wrong in his predictions, 'Our Captious Critic' (*Illustrated Sporting and Dramatic News*, 7 May, 1881) would be hard to beat:

> Messrs Gilbert and Sullivan have brought forth their aesthetic opera. This mountain of combined genius and intellect produced a—well, a tolerably large sized rat. England, let us hope, has always expected every man to do his duty and in these days of supposed success, England is very well satisfied with meagre results, madly enthusiastic over successes, pleased with moderate performances, and tolerant of absolute failures. Can it be wondered at, then, that the grand combination of musical and literary talent brought to bear upon the aesthetic opera known as *Patience* should have been rapturously received by the members of the general public? Nay, more, that the general public should stand out in the bleak street and meet the merriments of Messrs Gilbert and Sullivan half way with a hearty welcome? Such is the state of affairs, and in consequence the manager of the Opéra Comique finds himself in possession of an entertainment that is too big for his theatre, in other words, that overflows his coffers and leaves a disappointed crowd, coin in hand, grumbling at the door each evening because admission is an impossibility . . . Doubtless the thing is but a fashion of the moment and a short but sweet season may be the lot of *Patience*. The days of *Pinafore*, I think, are numbered by years, those of *The Pirates* by scores of weeks, but *Patience* will know none of these and long before Postlethwaite and his crew have cut their hair and their lilies *Patience* will be withdrawn in order to make room for a more congenial conceit.

It was true that the Gilbert and Sullivan entertainment was now too big for the Opéra Comique. This led to an important development.

The new Savoy Theatre—engraving from the 'Illustrated Sporting and Dramatic News', 1881. Note the electric lamps round the circle

Richard D'Oyly Carte was not the man to go on turning the public from his theatre door. Seeing that the Opéra Comique was too small and too old-fashioned, he now brought in the architects to plan for an even greater future. A prospectus he issued to the public is as interesting for what it reveals of the man as for what it describes of the plan:

The Savoy Theatre is placed between the Strand and the Victoria Embankment, on a plot of land of which I have purchased the freehold, and is built on a spot possessing many associations of historic interest, being close to the Savoy Chapel and in the 'precinct of the Savoy', where stood formerly the Savoy Palace, once inhabited by John of Gaunt and the Dukes of Lancaster, and made memorable in the Wars of the Roses. On the Savoy Manor there was formerly a theatre. I have used the ancient name as an appropriate title for the present one. The theatre is large and commodious, but little smaller than the Gaiety, and will seat 1,292 persons.

Proving that 'the new electricity' is safe by smashing an electric lamp without causing a fire: the incident of 1881 re-enacted in the 1953 film 'The Story of Gilbert and Sullivan' with Peter Finch as Richard D'Oyly Carte

I think I may claim to have carried out some improvements deserving special notice. The most important of these are in the lighting and decoration. From the time, now some years since, that the first electric lights in lamps were exhibited outside the Paris Opera-house, I have been convinced that electric light in some form is the light of the future for use in theatres, not to go further. There are several extremely good incandescent lamps, but I finally decided to adopt that of Mr J. W. Swan, the well-known inventor of Newcastle-on-Tyne. The enterprise of Messrs Siemens Bros. Co. has enabled me to try the experiment of exhibiting this light in my theatre. About 1,200 lights are used, and the power to generate a sufficient current for these is obtained from large steam-engines, giving about 120 horse-power, placed on some open land near the theatre. The new light is not only used in the audience part of the theatre, but on the stage, for footlights, side and top lights, etc. and (not of the least importance for the comfort of the performers) in the dressing-rooms—in fact, in every part of the house. This is the first time that it has been attempted to light any public building entirely by electricity.

Two years previously, 1878, the Thames Embankment had been electrified, and as long before that as 1869 John Hollingshead had fitted an electric lamp on the top of his Gaiety Theatre as an advertisement, but dismantled it for fear of frightening horses in the street.[1] Carte's enterprise at the Savoy was the first internal electrification of a theatre, but realizing that the public would be nervous of such an innovation he went on in his prospectus to assure them that gas light would be laid on as an alternative:

[1] *Gaiety Chronicles*, by John Hollingshead (Constable).

[214]

The greatest drawbacks to the enjoyment of the theatrical performances are, undoubtedly, the foul air and heat which pervade all theatres. As everyone knows, each gas-burner consumes as much oxygen as many people, and causes great heat besides. The incandescent lamps consume *no* oxygen, and cause no perceptible heat. Mr Carte further assured his public that the architects of the new theatre did *not* belong to the Gingerbread School of Decorative Art. Paintings of cherubim, muses, angels, and mythological deities had been discarded; the interior ornament consisted entirely of delicate plaster modelling, designed in the manner of the Italian Renaissance. And, determined to go the whole hog with his reforms, he announced the abolition of that fertile source of annoyance to the public—tipping. 'The attendants will be paid fair wages.' Programmes and cloakrooms would be free of charge.

Programme for the new Savoy Theatre. Note the electric lamps in the design

On top of all these innovations D'Oyly Carte introduced at the Savoy Theatre a new method for preventing scrums when the cheap doors were opened, until then a disgraceful feature of the English theatre. He had seen this innovation in America—the queue.

The new theatre was opened on 10 October, 1881, with a bigger and better *Patience*. The brighter light necessitated repainting the scenery, and with a larger stage Mr Gilbert mounted the production anew. Mrs Ronalds sat in the stalls, entranced, at the dress rehearsal. Sullivan conducted, and after the show went to Gilbert's house for supper and stayed until three a.m.[1] They discussed an exciting evening, but they realized that for once someone else had stolen their thunder. In the words of the *Electrical Times*:

When the curtain fell Mr D'Oyly Carte came on grasping an electric lamp in his hand and a hush fell upon the audience, who thought that electricity was always fatal. He then delighted with a sort of polytechnic lecture à la Professor Pepper, respecting the safety of the electric light to a theatre. Finally he placed a piece of muslin round the lamp and held it up to the audience as who should say: 'You see there is no deception.' He then took a hammer and smashed the lamp which, naturally, went out. But when he held up the muslin unburnt the effect on the audience was electric, in both senses of the word. D'Oyly Carte bowed himself off amidst enthusiastic cheers, which were so prolonged that he had to go on and take two calls.

From the *Continental Times*, Geneva, 29 October, 1881:

The striking novelties and undreamt of improvements at the Savoy Theatre were greeted by a crowded audience of London's elect with every visible and audible sign of enthusiastic approval. Mr Carte was summoned before the curtain to receive public recognition of his enterprising spirit and admirable taste . . . The chief sensation of course was the unquestionable triumph of the electric light, conclusively proved to be susceptible of discipline and not a whit less manageable than its forerunner, the malodorous, scorching, blinding, oxygen-consuming coal-gas, doomed, I hope and believe, to speedy extinction. Swan, by inventing the Incandescent Lamp, and D'Oyly Carte by adapting it to his splendid theatrical venture, have paved the way for the application of electricity to the lighting of private houses; and these meritorious achievements may without exaggeration be held to entitle them to the gratitude of civilized humanity.

Yet behind the dazzling façade of this theatrical innovation, trouble had set in between the three partners. From the moment when D'Oyly Carte built the Savoy, bickerings began on a note which was to recur harshly as the year passed. The new theatre was Carte's personal venture; he let it to the Sullivan–Gilbert–Carte partnership for the presentation of the operas, and when he put the rent at £4,000 a year Gilbert made a caustic comment on the price and Carte was hurt: 'Money is not everything to me,' he wrote to Sullivan, with whom he was on affectionate terms, 'and I feel more about this tone he has taken than I care to say.' The public knew

[1] Yet a few hours later he was travelling to Norwich where he had to conduct *The Martyr of Antioch* on the following evening at Norwich Musical Festival.

nothing of this insidious germ which had got into the bloodstream of a healthy partnership. To them all was gaiety and light.

From now on the Savoy Theatre, the most handsome theatre in Europe, was the Mecca of English light opera. To its spellbound audiences *Patience* seemed a perfect collaboration between Sullivan and Gilbert, and yet today we can see within this opera another cause of future discontents. Look at the character of Lady Jane, at whose autumnal charms Gilbert pokes a finger of fun ('my charms are ripe, Reginald, and already they are decaying') . . .

Fading is the taper waist,
  Shapeless grows the shapely limb,
And although severely laced,
  Spreading is the figure trim!

Sullivan, setting these words to music, deliberately softens the blow. Gilbert intended Lady Jane to have a ludicrous effect, sawing away at her 'cello, but Sullivan gave to Lady Jane, as though in compassion, one of his most fragrant melodies. This sense of disunity with

Lady Jane, played by Evelyn Gardiner

Gilbert was one of several embarrassments Sullivan was beginning to nurse concerning his work in comic opera.

Mr Chappell recognized that Lady Jane's song had possibilities if published as a drawing-room ballad, were it not for the words. The music was just right for the mellow, sentimental atmosphere of the after-dinner Victorian sing-song, but the words —*NO!*—too unkind to dowagers and grandmamas. So new words were set to Sullivan's tune, innocuous, sentimental, sad words by Hugh Conway, commencing—

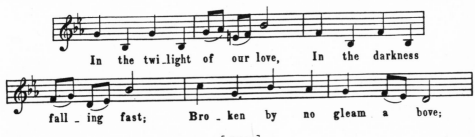

In the twilight of our love, In the darkness fall-ing fast; Bro-ken by no gleam a-bove;

and ending, so sadly, 'Would we two had never met!' This song, published separately, brought Sullivan a nice sum in royalties.

What Gilbert thought of this song is not recorded. He went on making fun of ageing ladies in his future operas and never uttered a word to explain himself, or defend himself against his critics, on this, the most hotly-debated of all aspects of the Gilbertian brand of humour.

Here are some modern comments on Gilbert's alleged sadism:

Sir Arthur Quiller-Couch: 'Gilbert was essentially cruel and delighted in cruelty.'[1]

Mr Guy Boas, writing in 1948: 'A fashion is current today, as absurd as any of Gilbert's deliberate absurdities, of saying this author is cruel . . . If one is repelled by Gilbert's "cruelty" one might as well be repelled by Falstaff's debauchery or the indelicacy of Sairey Gamp . . . Taste is a subjective matter, and if you are offended by a stout lady with a 'cello bewailing that there will be too much of her in the coming by-and-by, offended you are, but you are ascribing lack of chivalry to an author of fiction who in practice was a particularly chivalrous character, and, like those who make fun of Jane Austen, you ought to be in the book, not reading it.'[2]

Mr Leslie Woodgate, BBC conductor and chorus master, in a lecture to the Gilbert and Sullivan Society, 1938: 'It was Sullivan's great sense of humour that made him the ideal composer for the lyrics of Gilbert. There are many things in that great writer of polished lyrics that are frankly cruel, but Sullivan's music takes away the edge of satire and gives it a twist of humour that is nowhere excelled or even equalled. There has been no real successor to Sullivan, and I think there never will be.'

Mr Collin Brooks, writing in the *Norseman*: 'It is not (as Sir Alan Herbert has supposed) that Gilbert was a sadistical and cruel old man who could not refrain from exercising his wit on ageing women and plain-faced elderly virgins, as he did with Katisha and Lady Jane: it is that ageing women and plain-faced elderly virgins are apt as a rule to be too dignified, and Gilbert's task was the salutary one of showing that even an elderly English spinster—that impressive and intimidating social scourge—must bow before the ironic spirits of time and thwartation, just as his task was to show that elderly Ministers of State or great lawyers, or even monarchs themselves, cannot discard with their entry into high office the frailties of human nature.'

Dr Isaac Goldberg, an American, points out that Gilbert lived at a time when Britain was ruled by a Queen, and argues that his attitude was a form of resentment and resistance to feminine-led Victorian society! 'His cruel jibes at the elderly female of the species are not only the witticisms of a normal male untamed by social amenities; they are a retort to the rule of the petticoat and tight stays,' suggests Dr Goldberg in his *Story of Gilbert and Sullivan*.[3] This may be ingenious psycho-analysis but it is bad

[1] In *Studies in Literature* (Cambridge University Press), 1929.
[2] Article on 'The Gilbertian World and the World of Today', by Guy Boas, *English*, Spring, 1948.
[3] *The Story of Gilbert and Sullivan*, by Isaac Goldberg (John Murray), 1929.

history, both in regard to the generality of Victorian life and the particular circumstances of Gilbert's home life. 'The rule of the petticoat' indeed!

It may be that Gilbert himself would be more than surprised could he read these clever analyses. His only recorded remark about an over-stout lady, outside of the operas, is quite a kindly Gilbertianism: 'After all, she's quite nice, only I prefer a woman to be as long as she is broad.'

SPECIAL NOTICE.

THE arrangements for the production of the Electric Light are not yet perfected. The contractors hope to be able to light the *auditorium* by electricity this evening; but the *stage* will be lighted by gas as usual, as will also the Theatre generally, should everything not be ready. It has never before been attempted to light nearly so many as 1,200 incandescent burners as a single undertaking. A few days longer will probably perfect the arrangements, and the fact will be advertised.

R. D'OYLY CARTE,
Proprietor and Manager, Savoy Theatre.

A light and airy young thing

Early Effects of Electric Lighting

Cartoonists of 1881 had their fun with Mr Carte's innovation at the Savoy Theatre
CENTRE, *his first-night hand-out to the audience*

W. S. Gilbert in 1882, aged forty-six

Mrs Gilbert . . .
and the house that W.S.G. built:
Harrington Gardens, London

1882

'IOLANTHE'
WITH A CLOSE-UP OF GILBERT'S METHODS
AS A WRITER AND PRODUCER

Gilbert came this evening and sketched out an idea for a new piece—Lord Chancellor, Peers, Fairies, etc. Funny, but at present vague.

—SULLIVAN'S DIARY, nine days after première of *Patience*

GILBERT AND SULLIVAN were now rich. Each enjoyed an income of over £10,000 a year, or twice as much as the Prime Minister, Mr Gladstone. Sullivan spent freely on entertaining, race-horses, the casino, travel. Gilbert instructed an architect to design a large mansion to be built in Harrington Gardens, Kensington, equipped with such amenities (unusual in 1882) as central heating and four bathrooms. He was already trying out that remarkable innovation, the telephone, at 24, The Boltons.

Gilbert to Sullivan, 16 February, 1882:

My telephone is fixed and in working order—it costs £20 per ann. They are fixing one at the theatre, and it will be finished this week. Shall I order one for you? It takes some time, four or five weeks, to finish. I have ordered an instrument to be fixed at the prompt entrance so that I shall be able to hear the performance from my study—so will you, from your house, if you decide to have one . . . I am hard at work on Act 2 but have infinite difficulty with it.

These birth-pangs were in due course to provide the world with that delectable fairy-opera *Iolanthe*; but when the letter reached Sullivan he was in Egypt—the second foreign tour within a few months. Soon after the production of *Patience*, in 1881, Arthur Sullivan and Fred Clay had sailed in H.M.S. *Hercules*, as guests of the Duke of Edinburgh[1] on a voyage into the Baltic. At Copenhagen they were banqueted by the King of Denmark; in Russia the Tsar entertained them in opulent style, and Sullivan

[1] Admiral of the Fleet H.R.H. the Duke of Edinburgh was in command of the Reserve Squadron, British Navy.

was much impressed by the Imperial Chapel Choir: 'They have basses with the most wonderful voices going down to the low A, and the effect of their singing was thrilling.'[1]

Then they sailed to Kiel where Sullivan was greeted by the future Kaiser Wilhelm II: 'Prince Wilhelm bowed to me and sang "He polished up the handle of the big front door" from *Pinafore*. I burst out laughing and so did everyone. It was too funny.'[2]

Returning to London to move into a fine new residence at Queen's Mansions, Victoria Street, Sullivan was soon off again, to Egypt for three months. He was fascinated with native Arab music, and made some notes with a vague idea of composing an 'Egyptian' Symphony, but this never materialized. Sullivan was not in the mood for work. In Cairo he met two British princes, the future Duke of Clarence and the future King George V: 'We played riotous games and separated at midnight. The Princes enjoyed themselves very much, were in riotously high spirits, and knocked me about a good deal. I was in good spirits myself.'

He was just on forty.

[1] In a letter to his mother.
[2] Sullivan's Diary.

Peers and Shepherdess. 1936: Darrell Fancourt — Eileen Moody — Derek Oldham

Whilst all this junketing was going on, Gilbert was sitting at his desk at The Boltons struggling with the libretto that brought fairyland to Westminster and made fun of the sacred subject of British politics. The stillness of the room was disturbed by the tick of a grandfather clock, the fall of coals in the fire, the scratch of a quill-pen, as the characters were born into *Iolanthe*, the most subtle of all the Gilbert and Sullivan operas—for after the rather cutting social satire of *Patience* Gilbert was now writing a piece with a charming, pastoral quality and a more pawky political humour. In his quiet Kensington room he created Strephon, the Arcadian shepherd who is half fairy, half mortal ('from the waist downward'), and elected him to Parliament; and on this blotting pad of his the Lord Chancellor of England first gambolled in wig and robes, and was provided with one of the cleverest comic lyrics ever written in the English language:

> When you're lying awake with a dismal headache,
>   and repose is taboo'd by anxiety,
> I conceive you may use any language you choose to
>   indulge in, without impropriety;
> For your brain is on fire—the bedclothes conspire
>   of usual slumber to plunder you:
> First your counterpane goes, and uncovers your toes,
>   and your sheet slips demurely from under you;
> Then the blanketing tickles—you feel like mixed
>   pickles—so terribly sharp is the pricking,
> And you're hot, and you're cross, and you tumble and
>   toss till there's nothing 'twixt you and the ticking.
> Then the bedclothes all creep to the ground in a heap,
>   and you pick 'em up all in a tangle;
> Next your pillow resigns and politely declines to
>   remain at its usual angle!
> Well, you get some repose in the form of a doze,
>   with hot eye-balls and head ever aching,
> But your slumbering teems with such horrible dreams
>   that you'd very much better be waking;
> For you dream you are crossing the Channel, and
>   tossing about in a steamer from Harwich—
> Which is something between a large bathing machine
>   and a very small second-class carriage—
> And you're giving a treat (penny ice and cold meat) to
>   a party of friends and relations—
> They're a ravenous horde—and they all came on board
>   at Sloane Square and South Kensington Stations . . .

Note: The sketches here and later are from Gilbert's notebooks, by courtesy of the late Miss Nancy McIntosh.

[223]

And so on. So through the long hours Gilbert's pen scratched over the paper. Out of his inkwell arose the Fairy Queen, majestically corpulent and contralto-voiced, addressing that imperishable Guardsman, Private Willis, sentry on duty at Palace Yard, Westminster . . .

FAIRY QUEEN: To save my life, it is necessary that I marry at once. How should you like to be a fairy guardsman?

SENTRY: Well, ma'am, I don't think much of the British soldier who wouldn't ill-convenience himself to save a female in distress.

FAIRY QUEEN: You are a brave fellow. You're a fairy from this moment.

. . . and at this point Gilbert wrote a stage direction, 'Wings spring from Sentry's shoulders', and then he paused, thinking, and into the margin of the page his pen strayed and he sketched one of those doodles which ornament his manuscripts so amusingly.

Iolanthe is so delectable a combination of political satire and fairy magic, with the two sides—mortal and immortal—held in unique balance by Gilbert, that W.S.G. himself seems to have been caught in the spell of it, to judge by these doodles. But then Mr Gilbert was an immortal himself; at least half of him was Puck.

The other half of him was a hard mortal realist. At the end of a day's writing Mrs Gilbert would come softly into the study and lean over the dramatist's shoulder, and he would often read to her the pages he had written, and putting them in an envelope addressed to Sullivan, he would weigh it on his letter-balance and remark: 'I wonder what it will be worth to us? Fivepence postage, or five figures in the bank?'

The above picture of the final stages of writing a comic opera is a true one, but it would be an enormous error if the reader were to assume that Mr Gilbert sat down before a blank sheet of paper in the morning, and out of sheer inspiration instantly conjured the lyrics, speeches, and characters of his opera. The day he penned the final libretto was the last of many days, months, and years of gestation; and the pre-natal

Fairy Queen: 'You are a very fine fellow, sir'
Private Willis: 'I am generally admired'
Evelyn Gardiner and Sydney Granville, 1938 production

[225]

story of *Iolanthe* is a particularly good example of his methods. In his plot-books it is possible to trace the embryo of this opera through its stages of development. These plot-books are two-inch-thick leather-bound volumes of ruled paper into which Gilbert scribbled any ideas for operas or plays whenever they occurred to him; they are the reservoir of his fancies, to which he would turn when working out a libretto. But the first germ of *Iolanthe* is not to be found in the plot-book of 1881–2; it is in a *Bab Ballad* published in *Fun* some twelve years previously, 'The Fairy Curate':

> Once a fairy
> Light and airy
> Married with a mortal . . .

In the *Bab Ballad* this fairy came down to earth and chose an attorney of Ealing as her spouse, and then—

> Twelvemonths, maybe
> Saw a baby

—whom they named Georgie, and this half-man-half-fairy grew up to be a curate in the Church of England. In *Iolanthe* there is the same basic idea. The fairy Iolanthe marries the Lord Chancellor; their offspring is the Arcadian shepherd-boy Strephon whose upper half is immortal, but whose lower half grows older every day. We find him reaching the age of twenty-four when his fairy-mother is still a permanent sweet seventeen:

> I wouldn't say a word that could be reckoned as injurious,
> But to find a mother younger than her son is very curious,
> And that's a kind of mother that is usually spurious—
> Taradiddle, taradiddle, tol lol lay!

Between the *Bab Ballad* of 1870 and *Iolanthe* in 1882 comes the plot-book, in which the germ-idea is nurtured and expanded and given all sorts of new features. On page one of the book the scheme begins quite simply:

> A fairy has been guilty of the imprudence of marrying a solicitor. She has been sent to earth on a mission & has fallen in love with a prosaic lawyer of 45. Quite a matter of fact person.
>
> She is consequently banished summoned with her husband (who becomes a prosaic fairy from the fact of his marriage with her) into fairyland —

Then through hundreds of pages it is developed, amended, re-stated, elaborated. Many notions are introduced only to be abandoned. At first the Fairies (female chorus) fall in love *en bloc* with the barristers of the Northern Circuit (male chorus); the scene is a court of law. Then Ministers of the Crown begin to creep into the plot; during several pages the Fairy Queen is married to the Foreign Secretary; another fairy weds the Home Secretary; the scene shifts to Westminster, instead of the law court, which would have seemed repetitive of *Trial by Jury*.

[Handwritten manuscript note with a sketch:]

> Queen of Fairies marries ~~Prime Minister~~ Foreign Affairs
> Another principal marries Home Secretary
> Another principal marries Atty - Gen -
> Prime Minister is ~~already~~ married
> Scene House of Commons.
> Fairies &c.

All sorts of cross-currents of ideas gush into this plot-book. Some of them, though originally intended for *Iolanthe*, were omitted only to be used for other operas in the future; this one, for instance, came in useful eleven years later for *Utopia Limited*:

'The piece should show the miseries of a millennium:

All party strife	
All war	
All legal dissension	abolished
All religious differences	
All disease	

consequently—

All patriots	
All soldiers and sailors	
All barristers	are thrown out of work.'
All clergymen	
All doctors	

From such raw, even crude, material Gilbert crystallized his opera plots. After developing an idea through scores of pages of the plot-book, he would turn a clean page and start all over again, writing out the entire plot from beginning to end. One of these trial plots for *Iolanthe* begins with a scene on the rustic banks of the Thames 'with Naiads sitting about, whose duty it is to watch over and protect all counties through which the river flows'—a scheme which he abandoned, but the next idea was retained in the final opera—'They are very much distressed at the unsatisfactory character of British legislation and attribute much of this to the House of Peers which they consider should be abolished. They discuss the absurdities of hereditary legislature, and argue that a man should be legislator by reason of his own fitness rather than on account of the fitness of his ancestors.'

Gradually the plot takes its final form. The idea of the fairies marrying the Northern Circuit disappears when Gilbert scratches across the page:

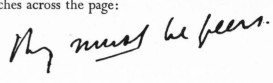

and from then on, peers they are. Gilbert, who always had the stock Savoy Company in mind when devizing characters, next scribbles down a cast-list:

Varine, Fairy Queen	Miss Barnett
Iolanthe, A Fairy Servant	Miss Bond
Lola ⎫	Miss Gwynne
Astarte ⎬ Fairies	Miss Fortescue
Lettie ⎭	Miss Braham
Sir H. Hartwright, Attorney-General .	Barrington
Ld. Chancellor	Grossmith
Commander-in-Chief	Lely
Admiral of Fleet	(baritone)
Trainbearer	Thornton

Later this is drastically modified—the roles of Attorney-General, Commander-in-Chief, and Admiral of the Fleet disappear altogether. The Fairy Queen loses her name, Varine. And a new character appears: 'Phyllis is a beautiful young shepherdess (Watteau), a ward-in-chancery and 19 years old. Corydon is a shepherd in the employ of Phyllis.' (Later he was renamed Strephon.)

Next Gilbert begins to write snatches of lyrics and dialogue into the plot-book, adorning them with neat little pen-sketches of the characters. Suddenly a new thought occurs to him, he decides to set Act 2 on the terrace of the Houses of Parliament, where the Peers are considering 'a Bill to Abolish All Existing Institutions, having for its object the reduction of civilization to its first principles—with the view of reconstructing Society anew on purely commonsense principles'.

But the hereditary Peerage did not appeal to Mr Gilbert as a very sensible element of the British constitution, so a few pages later in his plot-book he writes:

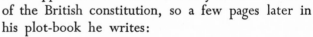

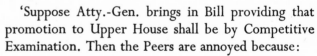

'Suppose Atty.-Gen. brings in Bill providing that promotion to Upper House shall be by Competitive Examination. Then the Peers are annoyed because:

(1) The prestige of House will be destroyed.

(2) A number of clever men will get into House who will entirely revolutionize its character.

(3) The existing members will be nowhere. They can't expect to contend with Wranglers and Double Firsts.

(4) The House will become a merely intellectual body.

(5) "Who ever heard of rewarding ability with a seat in the Upper House? It is unprecedented."'

Very little of which remains today in *Iolanthe*, where Gilbert narrows it into one gloriously ambiguous speech: 'It so happens that if there is an institution in Great Britain which is not susceptible of any improvement at all, it is the House of Peers!'

So, by this process of refining and rewriting, the plot is worked out, until at last it is crystal clear to Gilbert, then he turns a new page in his plot-book and sets about writing the final script. Only after all this does he come to that evening when he turns to Mrs Gilbert and says 'I wonder what it will be worth to us? Fivepence postage, or five figures in the bank?'

Sullivan and Gilbert wrote the operas by post. They were friendly but business-like letters.

Gilbert to Sullivan:

I enclose three numbers of Act 2. I have written more but these three can be set without the context, I fancy. I think you will like Iolanthe's ballad. I have tried to keep her tender and pathetic all through . . . I propose that Barrington shall be cast for Willis—a sentry (guardsman) on duty in Act 2.

SONG — PRIVATE WILLIS

When all night long a chap remains
    On sentry-go, to chase monotony
He exercises of his brains,
    That is, assuming that he's got any.
Though never nurtured in the lap
    Of luxury, yet I admonish you,
I am an intellectual chap,
    And think of things that would astonish you.
        I often think it's comical—Fal, lal, la!
        How Nature always does contrive—Fal, lal, la!
            That every boy and every gal
                That's born into the world alive
            Is either a little Liberal
                Or else a little Conservative!
                        Fal, lal, la!

This song 'stopped the show' on the opening night of *Iolanthe* (it was sung not by Barrington—who took the part of the Earl of Mountararat—but by a newcomer to the Savoy, Charles Manners, who later founded the Moody-Manners Opera Co.) and it has been a great favourite ever since, but when Sullivan first received the lyric he put it aside. *Patience* was doing very well at the Savoy and in America, and *The Pirates of Penzance* had been successfully launched by the Williamsons in Australia. There was no hurry, he thought. Then something happened to change his mood and wring music from him, as it had happened twice before; in 1866 it had been his father's death and *In Memoriam*, in 1877 his brother's death and 'The Lost Chord'. In 1882 soon after his return from Egypt:

'The blinds were all down. I rushed upstairs and was alone in the room—alone, that is, with dear Mother's lifeless body—her soul had gone to God.'

Mrs Sullivan was 71 when she died at the old Georgian house in Fulham where Arthur had set her up. She was buried in Brompton Cemetery, and it was the Rev. Thomas Helmore, Arthur's old teacher, who read the service.

Arthur Sullivan was heart-stricken by the blow. 'Home, feeling dreadfully lonely', says his diary on the day of the funeral. A few days later he plunged into the music of the new opera, and found forgetfulness.

The pastoral quality of *Iolanthe* appealed to Sullivan, it was a quality he could match to perfection . . . The fairy element was something he enjoyed, too; it took him back to the first great success of his youth, when he wrote fairy music for *The Tempest*. There is much of the sweet and gentle side of Sullivan's character in the music of *Iolanthe*. The persistent musical call of 'Iolanthe' haunts anyone who has seen this opera.

The summer of 1882 was hot and lazy. Sullivan went down to Cornwall to a country house party, but the guests saw very little of the celebrity whose tunes they all knew so well, and when he did join them he was absent-minded. 'I came across Arthur looking at the pigeons in the garden,' said one of his friends, 'and when I asked him where he'd been all the time he replied "It would be a good year for the cider".' Occasionally the piano in his private room was heard, and fragments of tunes that none of them knew drifted across the sun-bathed gardens, but usually no sound at all came from the room where Sullivan shut himself up for hours. Inside that room the bees were at the window, a beam of sunlight edged slowly across the floor, the light of day waned, and the bats dipped under the eaves, but all Sullivan saw was the stage of the Savoy and a proud procession of peers in their robes and coronets, and the notes on the paper before him as he wrote down the March of the Peers.

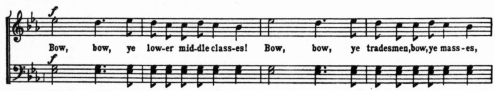

Meanwhile, D'Oyly Carte was in charge of *Patience* at the Savoy—but Gilbert kept a sharp eye on the business side, and suddenly he faced his partners with a demand for economy.

Gilbert to Sullivan:

The quarterly division has just been made, and I find that our nightly expenses are £130 per night! This is outrageous and I have written a letter to Carte of which I enclose a copy, and which will convey to you my ideas on the subject of retrenchment. A short code is appended, and I wish you would wire me according to the code that I may be sure that I am acting in accordance with your wishes. If you and Carte agree on any one point I shall of course consider it decided, and act accordingly.

This is a mild foretaste of the famous 'carpet quarrel' of years to come. In his letter to D'Oyly Carte, Gilbert demanded that expenses be reduced at once—'It is all very well while we are playing to £250 nightly but when business drops the consequences may be very serious'—and he compared the costliness of productions at the Savoy with those previously at the Opéra Comique: 'The gas bill at the Savoy costs £10 a week more than at the Comique—and this with electric light!'

Gilbert summed up: 'If we play for a year to an average of £120 nightly receipts, we make at the Opéra Comique £9,000 a year—and we lose at the Savoy £3,000 a year. You will see at once that this is simple ruination.'

Gilbert went yachting that summer off the Devon coast. One day he met Sullivan at the Half Moon, Exeter, and they spent the afternoon and evening in the coffee room discussing their affairs and reconstructing the first act of *Iolanthe*, about which Sullivan had been critical. They worked amicably, and Sullivan caught the night train to London with the final libretto in his bag. They intended to have the new opera ready by November. As usual the music was late. Sullivan had composed very little of Act 1 when Gilbert put Act 2 into rehearsal at the end of September, 1882, but thanks to Gilbert's strict preparedness with rehearsals, when *Patience* ended its long run on 22 November *Iolanthe* was ready to open only three nights later.

Durward Lely, a well-known Scottish tenor who had joined the Savoy Company for *The Pirates* and was now to play Lord Tolloller in *Iolanthe*, describes how at rehearsals the cast sat on the stage facing the author like a row of Christy Minstrels: 'Then Gilbert would read the "book" to

Cartoon by Linley Sambourne, of 'Punch'

us, saying as he went "This is your part, Grossmith," Barrington, or Lely as the case might be. He read exceedingly well, and gave full value to every word and every phrase, and it was quite an education in itself to hear him.'[1]

Next came Sullivan's music-rehearsals, the composer sitting at a cottage piano on the stage, while Gilbert listened and made notes—he never decided the stage 'business' exactly until he had heard how the lyrics had worked out to music. The smooth and rounded *Iolanthe* that the public knew was hammered out at subsequent rehearsals, Gilbert firing his instructions from a seat in the stalls. He had his prompt-book on his knee: an exercise book in which he had pasted the printed libretto on the right-hand pages, filling the left-hand sides with elaborate notes on the stage positions and move-ments of the characters (see pp. 240, 241). This prompt-book is now in the archives of the D'Oyly Carte Opera Co. On many pages the printed dialogue is crossed out and new lines pencilled into the margin. Lord Tolloller's solo 'Spurn not the nobly born', to which the Peers sing their haughty chorus of 'Blue blood', is thus written in as a revision.

The Savoy Company was now a superbly drilled team. Gilbert's whip needed to crack less frequently, but he watched the company with fatherly care—and sometimes was peculiarly strait-laced. Jessie Bond tells in her memoirs of one occasion when four young men in a stage box were sternly rebuked by Gilbert because they had dared to send a note round to ask the actress out to supper after the show. At other times Gilbert had just as quixotic a way of pouring oil on troubled waters. One day a chorus lady complained indignantly that she had been insulted: a dresser had told her she was 'no better than she should be'. Gilbert simply glowed with sympathy and said, 'Well, you are not, my dear, are you?'

'Why, of course not.'

'Ah, well, then that's all right,' said Gilbert. And the girl tripped happily away.

But when the whip did crack, it cracked without fear or favour. George Grossmith, who played the Lord Chancellor, was now one of the most famous figures of the English stage, thanks to Gilbert and Sullivan; but he was grumbling at rehearsal one day: 'We've been over this twenty times at least.'

'What's that I hear, Mr Grossmith?'

'Oh—er—I was just saying, Mr Gilbert, that I've rehearsed this confounded business until I feel a perfect fool.'

'Hmph . . . now we can talk on equal terms,' snorted Gilbert.

'I beg your pardon?'

'I accept your apology.'

It is Grossmith who tells the story of how Gilbert insisted that the peers in *Iolanthe* should all have the upper lip shaven. In an era of magnificent moustaches this was a devastating decree. So the chorus went on strike, but after being called before Gilbert

---

[1] Unpublished reminiscences of Durward Lely, communicated by his son, Cyril A. Lely. Durward Lely, whose real name was Lyall, was born at Arbroath, 1852.

'Iolanthe'—drawings in the 'Graphic' at the time of the original production, 1882

to give their reasons 'they all consented to obliterate the ornament, with the exception of one, who absolutely declined. In his case the moustache stayed on, but he did not.'

The entry of the peers caused Gilbert a lot of trouble in production, but as it turned out this scene caused a furore. Sullivan rose to the occasion with a magnificent processional chorus. A leading critic wrote:

Sketch by W.S.G.

> Now enters, preceded by the Grenadier Guards' band in full play, a procession of the most gorgeous beings that ever trod the boards of the Savoy or any other theatre. The British Peer, for the first time in operatic annals, is exhibited to the public in all his glory . . . Anybody suffering from curiosity with respect to honorific insignia can gratify his yearnings at the Savoy. There he will see Knights of the Garter, Bath, and Thistle, of St Patrick, SS. Michael and George, and the Star of India. Dark and light blue, crimson, pale green and rich purple mantles, embroidered with quaint devices and mottoes —ermine, velvet, pearls, strawberry leaves, enamel and glittering metal—all these and many other splendid emblematic gauds will meet the eye. The get-up of the Savoy Peers is correct to a ribbon end; and, taken as a body, they are much livelier than their Westminster prototypes. Singing a rollicking chorus, the refrain of which is 'Tarantara! Tzing! Boom!' they march round the stage to the braying of trumpets and the roll of drums.[1]

But it had not been easily achieved. At one stage of rehearsals Gilbert was heard crying out: 'For heaven's sake wear your coronets as if you were used to them!'

And there was anxiety about the Censor's attitude. This is shown in a letter from Carte to Miss Lenoir, who was in New York preparing the American *Iolanthe*; he warns her not to reveal anything to the Press, because 'if it gets over to the Lord Chamberlain's office that the sacred orders of the Garter, Thistle, Patrick and Bath are going on the stage the office may come down bang and forbid it being done'.

In a single night Sullivan wrote five songs, including the splendid 'When Britain Really Ruled the Waves'; his final rush to finish the music was aggravated by a plan of Carte's to send a fully-rehearsed company to open in New York on the same day as the London première which meant, of course, that the music had to sail with them, well in advance of the London first night. Alfred Cellier had to go on ahead to America, as conductor.

Sullivan left the music so late that he had to write to Cellier in America and ask him to compose an overture for the American production; Sullivan's overture for the London production was ready three days before the first performance.

[1] The *Theatre*, 1 January, 1883.

Piracy of their property in the U.S.A. was still depriving Gilbert, Sullivan, and Carte of many thousands of pounds a year, so they tried to put the pirates on the wrong path by rehearsing *Iolanthe* under a false name—'Perola'—which appeared in the printed libretti used at rehearsals. They also took legal action over incidents in the U.S.A. but the law was uncertain and variable from State to State, and several American judges ruled against them. Sullivan said, rather bitterly: 'It seems to be their opinion that a free and independent American citizen ought not to be robbed of his right of robbing somebody else.'

The old story that the name *Perola* was used at rehearsals has been challenged by sharp-eared listeners (to the BBC life of Gilbert and Sullivan, in which it was quoted) who point out that this name has three syllables and could not be sung, as frequently happens in the opera, to the four-note phrase of 'I—o—lan—the'. Further research in the archives of the Savoy shows that to overcome the difficulty of scansion the phrase used at rehearsal was actually 'Come Pe—ro—la' (Four notes).

Sullivan to Alfred Cellier:

> The name will definitely be I hope *Iolanthe*. This will remove all the 'Come Perolas'.

At the final rehearsal of *Iolanthe* at the Savoy, Sullivan addressed the assembled company: 'Ladies and gentlemen. You have been rehearsing *Perola* but when the curtain goes up the opera will be called *Iolanthe*. Will you please change the name Perola to Iolanthe throughout.'

Consternation and surprise. The name occurred many times. What if they made mistakes?

'Never mind,' said Sullivan, 'so long as you sing the music.'

One of the players feared she would forget the name of Iolanthe.

'Use any name that happens to occur to you! Nobody in the audience will be any the wiser, except Mr Gilbert—and he won't be there.'

Mr Gilbert was not there. He was nervously prowling up and down the Thames Embankment on the evening of 25 November, 1882. A Gilbert and Sullivan first night was now a Social Occasion. The new electric light had made it doubly exciting. The electric lamps—the sparkle of diamonds—the starchy sheen of dress shirts—the creamy shoulders of celebrated beauties—the turning and gazing and gossiping as the audience came in—the leaders of fashion, literature, politics, the law, science, art, and business in the stalls; and the galleryites singing choruses from the earlier Gilbert and Sullivan operas as they waited for the performance to begin—this became a ritual of Savoy first nights. The new theatre, cream and gold, was a lovely setting for such a thrilling occasion—and thrilling it certainly was as the audience lights went down, and every eye was turned towards the curtain, that rich creamy satin curtain heavily fringed with gold and embroidered in the Spanish style, of which one ecstatic journalist declared: 'Nothing so tenderly loving in colour and design has ever yet been seen in London.'[1]

And then the gallery burst into cheers as the man who had given them the tunes they loved mounted his rostrum and beamed through his eyeglass and bowed, and the *Iolanthe* overture began. The audience little realized that Sullivan was almost penniless. In the morning he had received the news that his brokers had gone bankrupt. Most of his savings were lost: £7,000. He gave no sign of the disaster throughout the evening; he and Gilbert were cheered at the end, but when he got home Sullivan confided to his diary that he felt 'very low'.

To the audience it had been a successful, even hilarious, evening. There was one unplanned incident which is thus described by Jessie Bond (who played Iolanthe): 'It was just a happy chance that set Captain Shaw, one of the best known and most popular men in London and Chief of the Metropolitan Fire Brigade, right in the centre of the stalls on that night of all others; and to this astonished man the Fairy Queen, advancing with outstretched arms, made her impassioned appeal . . .'

> Oh, Captain Shaw,
> Type of true love kept under!
>   Could thy Brigade
>   With cold cascade
> Quench my great love, I wonder!

Captain (afterwards Sir) Eyre Massey Shaw, an Irishman, ex-Chief Constable of Belfast, earned fame and the K.C.B. for turning the old-time independent fire-fighting teams, financed by insurance offices, into London's public fire brigade. He died in 1908. Today, when the public at large has forgotten his achievements his name obtains a curious immortality thus embedded, rather incongruously, in one of Sullivan's most romantic melodies.

Gilbert's idea of the 'cold cascade' was not quite original. In Planché's *King Charming* (produced in London 1850) these lines occur:

> My heart's on fire—not all the Fire Brigade could
> Subdue the flames, though led by Mister Braidwood . . .

Braidwood was a predecessor of Massey Shaw in London fire-fighting.

Another excitement on the opening night is remembered by Durward Lely: 'At the end of *Iolanthe* a novel and a very charming effect was made by the fairies at a given cue switching on the electric light on their foreheads, the battery being a small one carried on their backs, concealed by their flowing tresses.' This was the first time electric lamps had been so used. Great was the delight of the audience when Gilbert's resource as a showman capped this novelty with a 'trick' Finale: all the mortals were turned

---

[1] *Continental Times*, Geneva, 29 October, 1881.

into fairies, and wings sprouted from the shoulders of the Sentry, the Peers, and the Lord Chancellor himself. W.S.G.'s instructions for this were:

> "At off we go to fairy Land", Each principal pulls a string which is fastened to the pin which keeps his wings down — On being released, they fly up:
> The golden wings have appeared on his shoulders before this — that is to say when Fairy Queen says "you are a fairy from this moment".

Next day the world opened its newspaper. The thing the public was burning to know was what Mr Gilbert had decided to satirise this time. They found it was the Legislature.

> And while the House of Peers withholds
>   Its legislative hand,
> And noble statesmen do not itch
> To interfere with matters which
>   They do not understand,
> As bright will shine Great Britain's rays
> As in King George's glorious days.

In case the world should get the idea that Gilbert was thus taking sides with the Commons against the Lords, he had a gibe at the Lower House at the opening of Act 2:

> When in that House M.P.'s divide,
>   If they've a brain and cerebellum, too,
> They've got to leave that brain outside,
>   And vote just as their leaders tell 'em to.
> But then the prospect of a lot
>   Of dull M.P.'s in close proximity,
> All thinking for themselves, is what
>   No man can face with equanimity.

Most people took the critical humour of this well. The Prime Minister, a Liberal, himself went to see *Iolanthe* . . .

Mr Gladstone to Sullivan, from 10 Downing Street:

Nothing, I thought, could be happier than the manner in which the comic strain of this piece was blended with its harmonies of sight and sound, so good in taste and so admirable in execution from beginning to end.

Some people did not approve. *Punch* thought that the 'fairy-down-to-the-waist' whimsy was 'perhaps not quite pleasant' and concluded that '*Iolanthe* is not within a mile of *Pinafore*, not a patch on *Patience*'. But what really upset some of the critics was that at one point in the opera Gilbert went beyond his quipping at Lords and Commons and became class-conscious. We recall the incident now for the perhaps unexpected light it throws on Gilbert's character. He had a tender social-conscience, Dickens-like, unsuspected by those who knew him only as the rich autocrat of the Savoy. In the original production of *Iolanthe* he gave to Richard Temple, who played Strephon, a song in which the Arcadian shepherd-boy on entering Parliament rudely tells the Legislature to 'Fold its flapping wings', declares that he intends to bring in 'some rather urgent measures', and sings that 'crime begins at home':

> Take a wretched thief
>   Through the City sneaking,
> Pocket handkerchief
>   Ever, ever seeking:
> What is he but I
>   Robbed of all my chances—
> Picking pockets by
>   Force of circumstances?
>   I might be as bad—
>   As unlucky, rather—
>   If I'd only had
>   Fagin for a father!

This brought a protest from Mr Wm. Beatty-Kingston, critic of the *Theatre*:

When a first-night audience, prepared to laugh itself sore, and in great measure consisting of Mr Gilbert's avowed admirers, finds that gentleman exhibiting a tendency to impart pathos and politics into a book like that of *Iolanthe*, it may be excused for expressing disappointment as well as surprise—the more so because his pathos smacks of anger, a passion altogether out of place in a 'fairy opera', and his politics are bitterly aggressive . . . The libretto of *Iolanthe* has been utilized by its author as the vehicle for conveying to society at large a feeling protest on behalf of the indigent, and a scathing satire upon the heredity moiety of our Legislature. Advocacy and denunciation of this sort are all very well in melodrama, where telling points may always be made with the unmerited wrongs of the poor and the reprehensible uselessness of the aristocracy. But they jar upon the ear and taste alike when brought to bear upon us through the medium of a song sung by half-a-fairy in a professedly comic opera.

Mr Gilbert had of course scrupulously held the balance for the Peers in the song 'Spurn not the lowly born' in which Lord Tolloller argues that 'High rank involves no shame . . .'

> Hearts just as pure and fair
> May beat in Belgrave Square
> As in the lowly air
> Of Seven Dials!

but class-prejudice blinded the critics to this, Gilbert bowed to the storm, and took out the offending 'Fagin for a father' song. He had tried, not for the first time, to be serious, and was told his job was a jester's.

But in Gilbert's prompt-book may be found a song, scratched out at rehearsal, which would have horrified his critics even more than 'Fagin' had they heard it. Its theme is the snobbery of riches. It is about a Mr de Belville, who was highly talented as poet, and painter too, but nobody in civilized Britain could think of a way to reward this very gifted man. He tried being an inventor and proved himself to be a *very* great and *very* learned man, but remained penniless and unrecognized. And then:

> At last the point was given up in absolute despair,
> When a distant cousin died, and he became a millionaire!
> Then suddenly to all it seemed ridiculously clear
> Such a universal genius ought of course to be a Peer!
> And it's pleasant to reflect that his descendants by the score
> In the stately House of Lords will legislate for ever more;
> And who so fit to sit in it, deny it if you can,
> As the offspring of a very great and very gifted man?
> Though I'm more than half afraid
> That it sometimes may be said
> That we never should have revelled in that source of proper pride—
> However great his merits—if his cousin hadn't died!

This song was not heard in *Iolanthe*.[1] Even so, the satire in the opera gave Gilbert a bad name in certain circles. But the general public thought well of this political opera.

Sullivan's diary, 22 December, 1882:

Tom Chappell called to say that over 10,000 vocal and pianoforte scores of *Iolanthe* had been sent out from Bond Street the night before, all hands staying till nearly midnight.

Cables from America reported a wonderful reception over there. Mr Gilbert moved into his expensive new house in Harrington Gardens. Dr Sullivan quickly recovered his spirits and his bank balance.

[1] It was performed in early American productions of *Iolanthe*. Gilbert published it in full, in 1890, in his collection of *Songs of a Savoyard*.

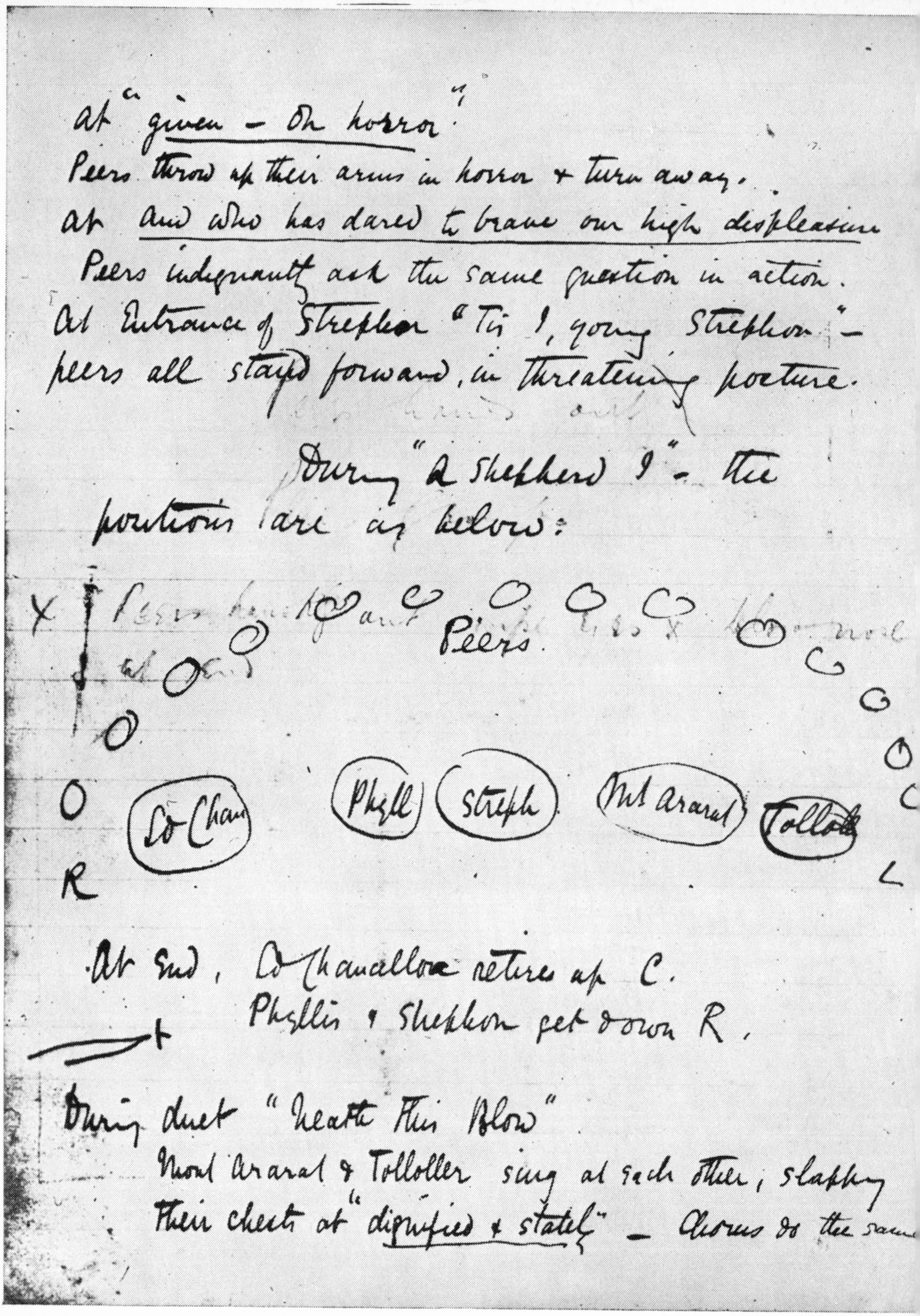

at "given — Oh horror"

Peers throw up their arms in horror & turn away.

at <u>and who has dared to brave our high displeasure</u>

Peers indignantly ask the same question in action.

At Entrance of Strephon "Tis I, young Strephon" —
peers all stand forward, in threatening posture.

During "A shepherd I" — the
positions are as below:

X

O

O

R

Peers &c &c and Peers

Ld Chan   Phyll   Streph   Ld Ararat   Tolloller

At end, Ld Chancellor retires up C.
Phyllis & Strephon get down R.

During duet "Neath this blow"
Lord Ararat & Tolloller sing at each other, slapping
their chests at "dignified & stately" — Chorus do the same

W. S. Gilbert's prompt-book for Iolanthe—

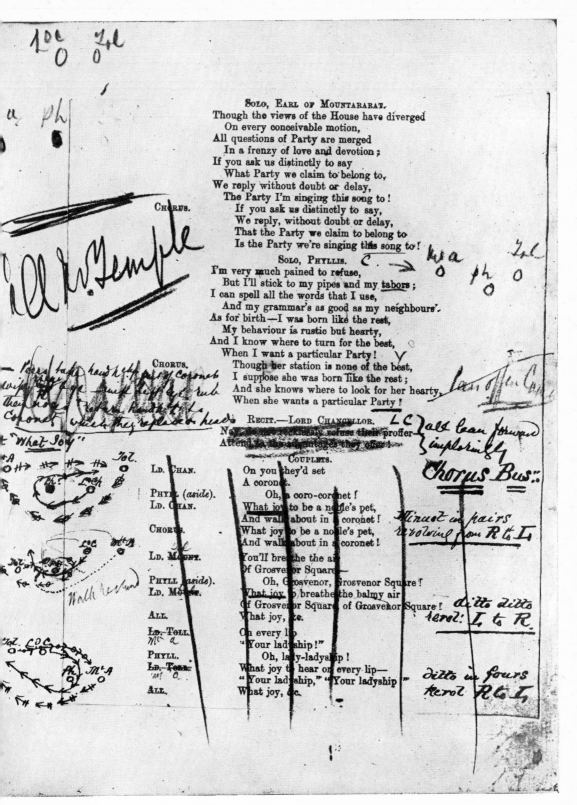

SOLO, EARL OF MOUNTARARAT.

Though the views of the House have diverged
  On every conceivable motion,
All questions of Party are merged
  In a frenzy of love and devotion;
If you ask us distinctly to say
  What Party we claim to belong to,
We reply without doubt or delay,
  The Party I'm singing this song to!
    If you ask us distinctly to say,
    We reply, without doubt or delay,
    That the Party we claim to belong to
    Is the Party we're singing this song to!

CHORUS.

SOLO, PHYLLIS.

I'm very much pained to refuse,
  But I'll stick to my pipes and my tabors;
I can spell all the words that I use,
  And my grammar's as good as my neighbours'.
As for birth—I was born like the rest,
  My behaviour is rustic but hearty,
And I know where to turn for the best,
  When I want a particular Party!
    Though her station is none of the best,
    I suppose she was born like the rest,
    And she knows where to look for her hearty,
    When she wants a particular Party!

CHORUS.

RECIT.—LORD CHANCELLOR.

~~Now that their~~ proffer
~~Attend to the advantages~~ they offer.

COUPLETS.

LD. CHAN.	On you they'd set
	A coronet.
PHYLL (aside).	Oh, a coro-coronet!
LD. CHAN.	What joy to be a noble's pet,
	And walk about in a coronet!
CHORUS.	What joy to be a noble's pet,
	And walk about in a coronet!
LD. MOUNT.	You'll breathe the air
	Of Grosvenor Square—
PHYLL (aside).	Oh, Grosvenor, Grosvenor Square!
LD. MOUNT.	What joy to breathe the balmy air
	Of Grosvenor Square, of Grosvenor Square!
ALL.	What joy, &c.
LD. TOLL.	On every lip
	"Your ladyship!"
PHYLL.	Oh, lady-ladyship!
LD. TOLL.	What joy to hear on every lip—
	"Your ladyship," "Your ladyship"
ALL.	What joy, &c.

—*Two pages from the author's own plan of stage-action*

10. Downing Street,
Whitehall.

May 3. 83

Dear Mr Sullivan

I have the pleasure to inform you that I am permitted by Her majesty to propose that you should receive the honour of Knighthood, in recognition of your distinguished talents as a Composer and of the services which you have rendered to the promotion of the art of music generally in this country.

I hope it may be agreeable to you to accept the proposal.

I remain

Faithfully yours

W E Gladstone

From the Prime Minister,
Mr Gladstone

1883

SIR ARTHUR SULLIVAN

A CLOSE-UP OF A DISCONTENTED COMPOSER

IT IS UNLIKELY that any but his most intimate friends—Frederic Clay, D'Oyly Carte, Mrs Ronalds—knew the real Sullivan. The public who cheered him at the Savoy saw the very picture of geniality. He hid his discontented state of mind from them as successfully as he concealed the physical illness which at times brought tears of agony to his eyes whilst conducting the orchestra through his gayest measures. Even on graver musical occasions Sullivan's good humour would come out. At the Leeds Musical Festival of 1883 he conducted the oratorio *King David* for the blind composer Sir George Macfarren, who sat at Sullivan's side during rehearsal. At one point the choir had to sing 'Fifty men, fifty men'. Macfarren touched Sullivan on the arm and whispered: 'Louder!—those "Fifty men" must be louder.' Sullivan turned to the chorus with a merry twinkle of the eyeglass and said: 'Those fifty men should be *forte*.'

At the Savoy Theatre many stories were told of Sullivan's good nature and quick wit. The seats for a Gilbert and Sullivan first night were always at a premium, and on one such occasion a member of the wealthy Sassoon family found that he had no ticket, nor could he buy one with all his riches, so he asked Arthur Sullivan to get him into the auditorium.

'It is impossible,' Sullivan told Sassoon, 'but if you will change the first letter of your name to B, I will find room for you in the orchestra!'

The difference between Sullivan and Gilbert, so far as it was seen by the audience at the Savoy, is well described in this reminiscence of their taking their bows on a first night: 'Sullivan came gracefully, all smiles, with a certain affable decorum and easy bearing which made his short, stout figure look less short and less stout than it really was. Gilbert had to be dragged on, and arrived in the presence of an applauding multitude with the air of a man who resents an indignity.'[1]

How surprised the audience would have been had they been told that of the two it was Sullivan who was dissatisfied with the success of their partnership, and who now

[1] Article 'English Men of Letters', by George W. Smalley, *McClure's Magazine*, New York, January, 1903.

[243]

began to hear in the applause of Savoy audiences a mockery of his life's deepest aspirations. Most carefully, Sullivan hid this sense of frustration from the actors and actresses at the Savoy Theatre.

The Savoy Company loved Sullivan as an amiable but fastidious master of their music —as meticulous as Gilbert, but more suave; although they found his last-minute habits of composition rather trying. George Grossmith tells us that it was Sullivan's way to compose the difficult choruses first, especially the finale to the first Act, then the quartettes and trios arrived at the theatre, and the duets and solos last: 'I have some-times received the tunes of my songs the week before production.' If a song had to be rewritten during rehearsal it might arrive only two nights before the performance: 'The difficulty then was not in rehearsing the new tune, but in *unlearning* the old one.'[1]

When the stars of the Savoy were invited to parties in Sullivan's rooms they came back to fill the dressing-rooms with stories of the celebrities they had met, and of the bonhomie of their host—and of his pet parrot which specialized in Little Buttercup's song from *H.M.S. Pinafore*.

'It may not be a perfect rendering,' said Sullivan, 'but it is certainly quite as good as Gilbert's attempts.'

Rutland Barrington reported of these parties: 'In addition to the honour of meeting Royalty, one had the great pleasure of hearing the *crème de la crème* of every branch of talent then before the public, for each and all were pleased with an opportunity to do ever so slight a service to the man whose geniality won all hearts. I have heard in his drawing-room Albani singing with Sullivan as accompanist, and the Duke of Edinburgh playing a violin obligato, to be followed by the latest and most chic of speciality artists, and then some trio or song from the piece then running at the Savoy.'[2]

On 13 May, 1883, there was a very special party. The Prince of Wales was at the head of a select gathering to celebrate Sullivan's forty-first birthday. W. S. Gilbert was present, having previously been let into the secret that Sullivan intended to astonish his guests with a demonstration of the Marvels of Science. By now the telephone had been installed at Sullivan's rooms and on this Sunday evening he switched it through at 11.15 to the stage of the Savoy Theatre, where the *Iolanthe* company had been assembled, at Sullivan's expense. Gathered round the theatre's telephone, they sang selections from the opera and at the other end of the wire, a mile away across London, His Royal Highness and friends passed the earpiece of Sullivan's telephone from man to man,

The Prince of Wales
(afterwards King Edward VII)

[1] *A Society Clown*, by George Grossmith (Arrowsmith).
[2] *Rutland Barrington*, by Himself (Grant Richards).

astonished by the wonder of what must have been one of the earliest feats of 'broad-casting'. (Within a few years the Electrophone was introduced in London, a system by which subscribers could be connected by telephone to a number of theatres.)

It was around the period of this birthday party that the following entries were made in Sullivan's diary.

29 April, 1883 (at a party at Rothschild's):

The Prince of Wales shook hands and said to me: 'I congratulate you on the great honour we have in store for you.' I suppose he means he is going to place me on the council of the Royal College of Music.

May 3: Received a letter from Mr Gladstone offering me knighthood.

May 7: Went to the opening of the Royal College of Music. Prince of Wales announced in his speech the intention of the Queen to knight me. Supped at the Lyceum Theatre with Prince of Wales and select party.

May 22: Went down by special train with some of the Ministers to Windsor to be knighted with Grove and Macfarren.[1] Met by Royal carriages and drove to the Castle . . . I bowed low, then knelt down, the Queen took the equerry's sword and laid it first on right then on left shoulder, said softly 'Sir Arthur' and gave me her hand to kiss, then I rose, bowed low again and backed out.

Knighted at forty-one . . . admired by high and low alike . . . conductor for the second time at the Leeds Musical Festival . . . his recent financial misfortune righted by the wonderful success of Iolanthe—why should this man be discontented?

At the beginning of the year, with Iolanthe safely launched, Sullivan had crossed to France for a holiday which he badly needed. 'Like an escaped schoolboy, he enjoyed the short holidays that hard work and ill-health allowed, in the south of France or Italy,' says a friend of his. 'I never knew him happier than when on a sunny morning he would start with a few friends, all on donkeys, and the "sumpter ass" following, to climb up to Gorbio or St Agnese for a long day in the open air. What days those were! Everything was a delight to him: the pungent smell of cut pine branches, the discovery of a mountain spring, the endless variety of wild flowers, but more than all, above and around us like a visible blessing, the glorious golden sunshine of a warm spring day. I remember his saying, one sunny morning on the Lung' Arno: "What sun worshippers we are! And no wonder, for the sun means light and warmth, and that is life and love, while its absence means darkness and hatred." His love of warmth and sunshine may have been inherited from his Italian grandmother.'[2]

Far away from London, Sullivan took stock of his position. The Leeds Musical Festival Committee had written asking if he would use his long-standing acquaintance

[1] All three knighthoods were conferred in connection with the opening of the Royal College of Music. George Grove became its first Director. George Macfarren was Principal of the Royal Academy of Music, 1875 to 1887.

[2] From article 'Sir Arthur Seymour Sullivan as an Old Friend knew Him', Argosy, February, 1901.

with Verdi to persuade the great Italian to compose a new work for the Festival in October; secondly, would Dr Sullivan himself write a symphony for Leeds? The invitation reminded Sullivan of what the musical world had long expected of him. Had he achieved the great expectations of his youth? What could he say, to Verdi for instance, of his own recent music? He had not composed a serious work since three years ago (*The Martyr of Antioch*); his last oratorio was ten years ago (*The Light of the World*). The grand opera which Rachel Scott Russell had urged him to write twenty years ago was still unwritten. Ah!—the soaring dreams and ideals of youth . . .

It had not escaped Sullivan's notice that the influential critic of the *Theatre* who had lashed out at Gilbert's share of *Iolanthe* took, in the same notice, a very flattering view of Sullivan's part:

Wagner parodied in 'Iolanthe':
the original Fairy Queen, 1882

I do not hesitate to say that the music of *Iolanthe* is Dr Sullivan's *chef-d'oeuvre*. The quality throughout is more even, and maintained at a higher standard, than in any of his earlier works. In fitting notes to words so exactly that the 'book' and its setting appears to be one and indivisible, our gifted countryman is without a rival in Europe, now that Offenbach is no more. His vein of melody seems inexhaustible, and in constructive skill he can hold his own with any contemporary composer. Increase of years has brought him augmented geniality of humour and grace of expression. His musical quips and cranks are every whit as effective as Mr Gilbert's literary jests; and to be instrumentally funny, without lapsing into vulgarity, is one of the most difficult feats in composition . . . All the fairy music is charming. Wagnerian extravagances are here and there lightly, not irreverently, caricatured. The parody of 'Die alte Weise' (*Tristan and Isolde*, Act 3), played whilst Iolanthe is rising from her watery prison, struck me as being uncommonly clever, and so did the Rhine daughter and Walkure reminders in the last scene . . . In every respect *Iolanthe* sustains Dr Sullivan's reputation as the most spontaneous, fertile, and scholarly composer of comic opera this country has ever produced.[1]

Very flattering; but at the same time rather disturbing to Sullivan, who envied Wagner. Another critic, in the *Globe*, had commented: 'Mr Sullivan's music is undoubtedly the work of a masterly musician, content for awhile to partially sacrifice himself rather than hinder the clear enunciation of the words . . .' This was meant

[1] Wm. Beatty-Kingston in the *Theatre*, 1 January, 1883. *Tristan and Isolde* had its first British production in the previous year at Drury Lane Theatre, Richter conducting. Offenbach had died in 1880. His *Tales of Hoffmann* was produced in Paris, 1881.

COLOUR PLATES

DUET– Nanki-Poo and Ko-Ko,
(with Yum-Yum, Pitti-Sing, and Pooh-Bah.)

SULLIVAN — CARTE — GILBERT
The greatest collaboration in the history of entertainment,
as seen by the Victorian cartoonists, Ape and Spy

'Princess Ida' re-dressed in 1954: James Wade's costume design for King Hildebrand

ST GEORGE'S OPERA HOUSE,
LANGHAM PLACE, OXFORD CIRCUS.

ENCORES NIGHTLY.

ROARS OF LAUGHTER.

(SCENE FROM THE)

CONTRABANDISTA
EVERY EVENING AT ½ PAST 7.
MORNING PERFORMANCE EVERY FRIDAY AT 2.

ADMISSION.
PIT 1/- BALCONY 2/-
STALLS 3/- ORCHESTRA STALLS 5/-

ADMISSION.
PIT 1/- BALCONY 2/-
STALLS 3/- ORCHESTRA STALLS &

1867: Sullivan's first comic opera, to words by F. C. Burnand. The names of neither composer nor author appear on this playbill. And BELOW—
Some twenty years later: Gilbert and Sullivan is a world-famed combination—the D'Oyly Carte Opera Company tours Germany

Mr. D'Oyly Carte's englische Opern-Gesellschaft.

Altes Theater.

Der Mikado
oder
Ein Tag in Titipu.
Burlesk-Oper in 2 Abtheilungen. Text von W. S. Gilbert.
Musik von Arthur Sullivan.

In the Eighties Mr D'Oyly Carte ran a children's company at the Savoy, and these quaint figures are from the programme of one of their productions. Master Stephen Adeson played the Pirate King; Master Edward Percy, Major General Stanley; and Miss Elsie Joel was Mabel. Prices were: circle, 4s.; balcony stalls, 7s. 6d.; stalls, 10s. 6d.; boxes, one guinea and *two* guineas

Designs for 'Patience' by
George Sheringham, 1929

The Buck and Blades in
'Ruddigore': (LEFT): Wil-
helm's original design, 1887;
(RIGHT): Peter Goffin's new
costumes, 1948

The cover and one of the pages of the elaborate programme for 'The Mikado' in 1885.
Inside were the cast-list, scenes from other operas such as 'Iolanthe', and advertisements.
Theatre supper at a famous restaurant cost 3s. 6d. Seats at the Savoy Theatre ranged
from a shilling in the gallery to boxes at three guineas

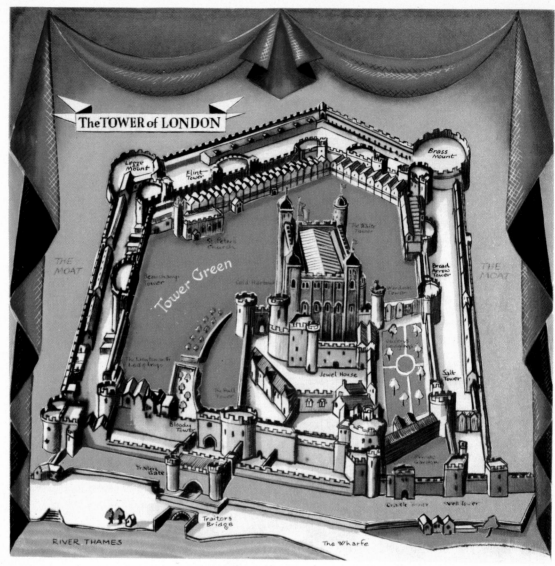

The TOWER of LONDON

Legge Mount — Flint Tower — Brass Mount — The White Tower — Broad Arrow Tower — THE MOAT — THE MOAT — St. Peter's Church — Beauchamp Tower — Cold Harbour — Wardrobe Tower — Tower Green — The Lieutenant's Lodgings — Jewel House — Queen's Lodgings — Salt Tower — The Hall Tower — Bloody Tower — Traitors Gate — Cradle Tower — Well Tower — Traitors Bridge — RIVER THAMES — The Wharfe

Chorus in Yeomen of the Guard

Drop Curtain for 'The Yeomen of the Guard' designed by Peter Goffin in 1939
(BELOW): *One of Percy Anderson's sketches for the re-dressing of this opera in 1919*

The Royal English Opera

Proprietor and Manager

R. D'Oyly Carte.

IVANHOE.
A Romantic Opera.

Words By
Julian Sturgis.

Music By
Arthur Sullivan

Cover of the souvenir programme for Sir Arthur Sullivan's grand opera at Mr Carte's new opera house

Special programme for the Royal Command performance of 'The Gondoliers', before Queen Victoria

(TOP): *George Sheringham's designs for 'The Pirates of Penzance', 1929*
(BELOW): *A Gilbert and Sullivan opera which few people have ever seen: these sketches were made by Percy Anderson when Rupert D'Oyly Carte was considering a revival of Utopia in the Nineteen Twenties. The project was abandoned*

Charles Ricketts' original designs for the new presentation of 'The Mikado' in 1926

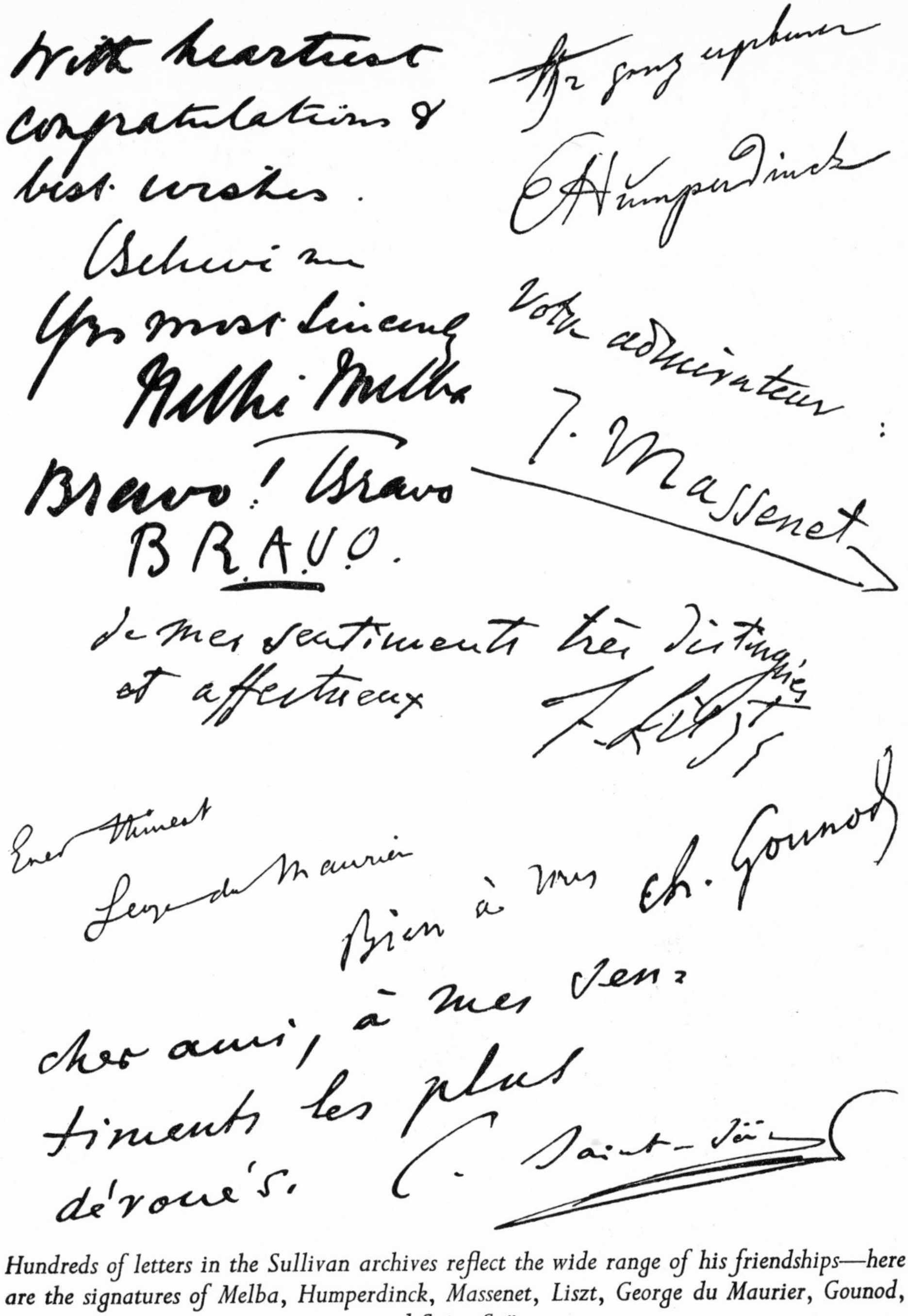

Hundreds of letters in the Sullivan archives reflect the wide range of his friendships—here are the signatures of Melba, Humperdinck, Massenet, Liszt, George du Maurier, Gounod, and Saint-Saëns

to be a tribute, but to Sullivan it was rubbing salt publicly into a private wound. He was getting tired of sacrificing himself to Gilbert's words. Wagner, whose death had just occurred and whose Rhinemaidens Sullivan had parodied in *Iolanthe*, had stirred the western world with a new kind of grand opera; Sullivan always said that *The Master-singers of Nuremburg* was the greatest comic opera ever written—and what he would have given to have written it!

In 1883 Sullivan returned to England, wondering what Gilbert would have to suggest for their next comic opera. When Gilbert outlined what became known as the Lozenge Plot, Sullivan protested that it was too artificial, too far-fetched, too much after the usual Gilbertian pattern. By swallowing a lozenge a character could be changed into another character.

The Lozenge haunted Sullivan and Gilbert from now on, like one of John Wellington Wells's evil spells, to sour their relationship. Gilbert craved to see it on the stage, and at last he had his way, but not with music by Sullivan. Alfred Cellier tackled Gilbert's lozenge in *The Mountebanks* in 1892 (*see* page 365). In 1883 Sullivan would not touch it. So Gilbert then suggested turning another of his earlier plays, *The Princess*, into a comic opera. Sullivan didn't like this at first either. He was feeling artistically frustrated. He wanted to take wings and soar higher. Perhaps his illnesses also affected his outlook. He was a disgruntled man just now, and had even confided to his great friend Frederic Clay that Gilbert's personal chaff, especially at social functions, was getting him down.

Typical Gilbert chaff: 'My cook gets £80 a year and gives me a kipper. Sullivan's cook gets £500 a year for giving him the same thing in French.'

Sullivan tried to get Bret Harte, the famous American short-story writer, to join him in partnership. Sullivan thought that with a Wild West story out of the same stable as *The Luck of Roaring Camp* he could break fresh ground. Then he thought better of it, and signed a new contract with Gilbert and Carte to continue writing comic operas for them for another five years.

Why did he not follow the course the Highbrows expected of him? Why not break away from comic opera altogether? Because (*a*) the genial streak in Sullivan simply could not resist comedy for long; (*b*) he was a close friend of D'Oyly Carte's; (*c*) the fact is that Highbrow Music could not pay for the High Life that Sullivan liked to live. The fee he received for conducting the 1883 Leeds Festival, three hundred guineas, was as much as he lost—or won—in a night at Monte Carlo. He knew that by composing another comic opera he could always refill his coffers, and this knowledge, comforting as it was financially, must often have pricked his artistic conscience.

He had what his diary calls some 'slight breezes' with Gilbert over the libretto for the next comic opera, but by midsummer Sullivan wrote: 'I like the piece as now shaped out, very much.' It was called *Princess Ida*, and Gilbert described it as a 'respectful perversion' of *The Princess* by Lord Tennyson, Poet Laureate.

This is the only Gilbert and Sullivan opera in three acts, and the only one in blank verse. There is a story of a Yorkshireman who saw it and said: 'Ah like t'music well enough; it's full o'toones as Ah can whistle. But t'words sounds too much like Shakespeare for t'likes of me to understand.' Perhaps that is one reason why *Princess Ida* did not win the success of most of the operas; yet George Grossmith and C. H. Workman both considered it the finest of them all, musically, and Durward Lely, who created all the leading tenor roles at the Savoy from 1881 to 1887, says: '*Princess Ida* is in my opinion one of the most charming of the series. I had a splendid Kissing Song which never failed to bring down the house, and for

'*Punch's*' view of Mr Carte, 1882

which on many occasions I had to give a double encore. The music all through was beautiful and the book, I always thought, was Gilbert at his very best; not quite so topsy-turvy as the others, but extraordinarily clever. What, for example, could be finer than Princess Ida's address to her girl graduates? As an example of mock heroics it seems to me unsurpassable.'[1]

Gilbert's satire was aimed this time at Women's Emancipation. At first sight the subject seemed perhaps a bit austere, not exactly a source of innocent merriment . . . Girton College for women had been founded in 1872, Newnham in 1875:

> With prudes for proctors, dowagers for deans,
> And sweet girl graduates in their golden hair.
> —Tennyson (*The Princess*), 1847.

Gilbert's journalistic eye had again seized on topical controversy: Girton and Newnham had been followed by the foundation of the London School of Medicine for Women, women were now admitted to degrees in London University, and feminists were beginning to agitate for the vote. When *Princess Ida* was revived in 1926 at the Prince's Theatre, London, *The Times* said: 'It was after the fairies of *Iolanthe* had wrought havoc in the British Constitution that Gilbert turned to the companion task of showing how fatal it would be if women ever presumed to be anything but fairies, and, cocking a cynical eye at Tennyson's *Princess*, wrote *Princess Ida, or Castle Adamant*. The theme spurred him to some of his best lines, and, quite apart from either the humour of the situation or Sullivan's delicious handling of it in music, the rhythm of his sonorous

[1] Unpublished reminiscences of Durward Lely, communicated by his son Cyril Lely.

Strikingly graceful attitude of the Girl-Graduates. 'Punch', 1884

blank verse in such things as King Hildebrand's first speech and the Princess's address to her neophytes is a thing to listen to.'

With the further passage of years, women's emancipation as a subject for satire has lost its topicality. Fully to appreciate *Princess Ida* we must measure it against its Victorian background, and against Gilbert's relationship with Sullivan in 1883. Gilbert was at heart a literary man and a serious-minded one ('I can do something more than wear the cap and bells')—and in *Princess Ida* he was, rather nervously, trying a recipe some-what different from the mixture as before. For all its frolics, this was a highbrow comic opera. Sullivan intended to make the music different, too. He was Sir Arthur Sullivan now. Just after his knighthood he had read—

The *Musical Review*, 1883:

Some things that Mr Arthur Sullivan may do, Sir Arthur ought not to do. In other words, it will look rather more than odd to see announced in the papers that a new comic opera is in preparation, the book by Mr W. S. Gilbert and the music by Sir Arthur Sullivan. A musical knight can hardly write shop ballads either; he must not dare to soil his hands with anything less than an anthem or a madrigal; oratorio, in which he has so conspicuously shone, and symphony, must now be his line. Here is not only an opportunity, but a positive obligation for him to return to the sphere from which he has too long descended.

And this was the comment of Sullivan's dear old friend Grove, now Sir George: 'Surely the time has come when so able and experienced a master of voice, orchestra, and stage effect—master, too, of so much genuine sentiment—may apply his gifts to a serious opera on some subject of abiding human or natural interest.'[1]

Another Savoy Opera was hardly what Grove meant by a 'subject of abiding human or national interest', yet this is precisely what the Savoy Operas have proved to be, for posterity. Sullivan's musical contemporaries were blind to his importance as a pioneer in the sphere of English light opera, but at this very moment four young men who were

[1] Article by Sir George Grove, in *Grove's Dictionary of Music and Musicians*.

to follow successfully in Sullivan's footsteps were closely watching his methods— Leslie Stuart (future composer of *Florodora*, etc.) was nineteen, and there were three young musicians who had reached the age of twenty-one, Edward German (later to write *Merrie England*), Sidney Jones (*The Geisha*), and Lionel Monckton (*The Arcadians*). Sullivan was the founder of this school. His own discontent with the comic opera work he was doing was now heightened by the emergence of a rival in the field of serious music, a younger man—another Irishman, too!—who was rapidly overhauling him in the estimation of musicians. 'By the eighties Stanford was established as executant, conductor, and composer . . . He was drawing crowds . . . He was composing music that was ahead of his time.'[1]

Princess Ida was scheduled for production at the year's end, 1883. In October Sullivan put it aside whilst conducting the Leeds Festival. Sir Arthur always thoroughly enjoyed himself at Leeds. His enthusiasm and musicianship had moved mountains since those early days when as a young man he first set out to travel the land with his baton: he had certainly raised the standard of good music among the working-class and business-class people of the provinces. In his choirs the mill-hands and mill-owners, the coal-miners and coal-owners, the shop assistants and shop-owners, the clerks and business men rubbed shoulders, and they sang with the greatest soloists in the land. At Leeds in 1883 (according to the *Daily Telegraph*) Sullivan elected to stand or fall by his interpretation of Beethoven's *Mass in D*, and he stood: 'It establishes his position among the "chefs d'orchestre" who are capable of producing the highest artistic results.' The Festival included a good deal of Handel, some Bach, Wagner and Mozart, Mendelssohn's *Hymn of Praise* and *Elijah*—but the only substantial work by Sullivan himself was his seventeen-years'-old overture *In Memoriam*. The second symphony he had been invited to write for the Festival was pushed on one side by *Princess Ida*.

The agreement signed by Gilbert, Sullivan and Carte on 8 February, 1883, for five years (subsequently extended) was to become the contract in dispute in the famous Carpet Quarrel of 1890. It gave Carte a licence for the performance at the Savoy Theatre of all operas composed by Gilbert and Sullivan, Carte agreeing to pay to each of them one-third of the net profit earned, after deducting £4,000 a year rent for the theatre, and necessary expenses, including 'repairs incidental to the performance', a phrase which contained the seeds of death for the great partnership.

[1] *Charles Villiers Stanford*, by Harry Plunket Greene (Edward Arnold), 1935.

This charming engraving from the 'Illustrated London News' of 19 January, 1884, shows the original décor. 'The three sets,' said the 'Theatre', 'are amongst the most beautiful pictures ever exhibited upon any stage. The graduate robes and Amazonian armour must be seen to be properly appreciated; the former are gravely gorgeous, the latter indescribably brilliant and splendid'

1884

'PRINCESS IDA'
THE FIRST QUARREL

Oh, don't the days seem lank and long
When all goes right and nothing goes wrong,
And isn't your life extremely flat
With nothing whatever to grumble at!

—*Princess Ida*

AFTER THE LEEDS FESTIVAL of 1883 Sir Arthur Sullivan rushed back to London, to a fight against time and his health. He flogged himself to complete *Princess Ida*. The year's end saw him in acute physical pain, and depressed by the sudden death of Frederic Clay who had a stroke whilst walking in the Strand. On New Year's Day, with the first performance only four days distant, Sullivan was at the Savoy Theatre for dress rehearsals. Two songs had yet to be written. He walked back to his rooms in a snowstorm, composed the songs overnight, and next day at a full rehearsal he collapsed. You may search the music of *Princess Ida* in vain to find any mark of all this. It contains much that is as gay, as delicate, as clever as his previous operas. The only significant difference is that here and there Sullivan seems to be feeling his way towards that grand opera which in his heart of hearts he longed to compose. There is a sober aria wherein Princess Ida implores Minerva (the rather militant goddess of the arts) to 'let fervent words and fervent thoughts be mine'; it has all the fervour and roundness of line of a grand operatic aria, and nothing of the slightness of accompaniment by which Sullivan often subordinates his music to Gilbert's words. Not

George Grossmith as
King Gama

[253]

that Sullivan lost his sense of humour in *Princess Ida*: his parody of Handel is a joy when the three young men throw off their armour before battle:

This helmet, I suppose,
Was meant to ward off blows,
It's very hot,
And weighs a lot,
As many a guardsman knows,
So off that helmet goes . . .

—with the chorus thundering a Handelian repetition:

Yes, yes, yes,
So off that helmet goes!

Sullivan's diary, 5 January, 1884:

Resolved to conduct the first performance of the new opera *Princess Ida* at night, but from the state I was in it seemed hopeless. At 7 p.m. had another strong hypodermic injection to ease the pain, and a strong cup of black coffee to keep me awake. Managed to get up and dress, and drove to the theatre more dead than alive—went into the Orchestra at 8.10. Tremendous house—usual reception. Very fine performance—not a hitch. Brilliant success. After the performance I turned very faint and could not stand.

From the *Globe* newspaper, two days later: 'Sir Arthur Sullivan fainted after presenting himself with Mr Gilbert on the stage to receive the congratulations of the audience. The following bulletin was issued yesterday afternoon: "1 Queen's Mansions, Victoria Street, S.W.—Sir Arthur Sullivan has passed a good night, and although suffering much pain from a muscular affection of the neck, is on the whole better. Absolute rest and quietude are strictly enjoined by his medical attendant, Dr Lynch." '

The 'affection of the neck' was his old kidney trouble.

Three weeks later D'Oyly Carte received a letter from Sullivan saying that he would write no more comic operas. Mr Carte and Miss Lenoir, full of surprise and concern, went to see Sullivan. They found him recovering from his illness—but not from his (to them) inexplicable decision. Sullivan went off, adamant, to France and Belgium for convalescence. Within three months the audiences of *Princess Ida* were dwindling. This opera ran for nine months at the Savoy, which in Gilbertian terms is a failure. After the first night the critic of the *Theatre* remarked: 'To me, music and words alike reveal symptoms of fatigue in their respective composer and author.' But most of the critics gave it a good send-off.

King Gama and King Hildebrand are rival kings in this opera. King Gama, a gnome-like creature, provided George Grossmith (and in later years Henry Lytton) with a splendid opportunity for macabre character acting.

Grossmith declared that King Gama's solo 'Yet everybody says I'm such a disagreeable man' was one of the best Gilbert ever wrote:

Princess Ida revived in the nineteen-twenties: Winifred Lawson and Bertha Lewis

I'm sure I'm no ascetic; I'm as pleasant as can be;
You'll always find me ready with a crushing repartee,
I've an irritating chuckle, I've a celebrated sneer,
I've an entertaining snigger, I've a fascinating leer . . .

King Gama is really a jocular self-portrait of Gilbert. At a rehearsal Gilbert told Grossmith: 'I meant it for myself: I thought it my duty to live up to my reputation!'[1]

To compliments inflated I've a withering reply,
And vanity I always do my best to mortify . . .

But although I try to make myself as pleasant as I can,
Yet everybody says I am a disagreeable man!
And I can't think why!

Princess Ida, King Gama's lovely daughter, runs a college for women. No men are ever permitted within the cloistered walls of Castle Adamant. Here Woman 'devotes herself to stern philosophies'—and W.S.G. gets in some jokes at the recently-opened women's colleges in England; and at the new blue-stockings, to whom Man is redundant:

They mock at him and flout him,
For they do not care about him,
And they're 'going to do without him'
If they can—if they can!

Castle Adamant is so feminist an establishment that although the ladies rise at 'cock-crow' every morning the crowing is done 'by an accomplished hen'.

1 'Recollections of Sir W. S. Gilbert', by George Grossmith, the *Bookman*, July, 1911.

But Gilbert is impartial. The New Woman is not his only target. In the solo 'The Ape and the Lady', built neatly on the Darwinian theory, Gilbert puts Man once and for all in his place among the monkeys (Charles Darwin, the English naturalist, had died two years earlier, 1882; his book *The Origin of Species* had caused a great controversy):

A Lady fair, of lineage high,
Was loved by an Ape, in the days gone by.
The Maid was radiant as the sun,
The Ape was a most unsightly one—
    So it would not do—
    His scheme fell through,
For the Maid, when his love took formal shape,
    Expressed such terror
    At his monstrous error,
That he stammered an apology and made his 'scape
The picture of a disconcerted Ape.

With a view to rise in the social scale,
He shaved his bristles, and he docked his tail,
He grew mustachios, and he took his tub,
And he paid a guinea to a toilet club—
    But it would not do,
    The scheme fell through—
For the Maid was Beauty's fairest Queen,
    With golden tresses,
    Like a real princess's,
While the Ape, despite his razor keen,
Was the apiest Ape that ever was seen!

He bought white ties, and he bought dress suits,
He crammed his feet into bright tight boots—
And to start in life on a brand-new plan,
He christened himself Darwinian Man!
    But it would not do,
    The scheme fell through—
For the Maiden fair, whom the monkey craved,
    Was a radiant Being,
    With a brain far-seeing—
While Darwinian Man, though well-behaved,
At best is only a monkey shaved.

[256]

Peter Pratt as King Gama in 'Princess Ida', revived again in the Nineteen Fifties; and (RIGHT)
as Bunthorne in 'Patience'

On the first night of *Princess Ida* Gilbert, for once, did not roam the streets. He sat in the green room reading a paper and trying to look unconcerned. During the third act a Frenchman, who had been employed to fit the cast with suits of armour, was so overjoyed by the reception accorded to the opera by the audience that he rushed in to Gilbert crying: 'Mais, monsieur, savez vous que vous avez là un succès solide?'

'It seems to be going very well,' replied the (apparently) phlegmatic Englishman. Gilbert said afterwards: 'I suppose he expected to see me kissing all the carpenters.'

During the run of the opera the box office clerk at the Savoy Theatre was instructed to telephone the day's takings to Gilbert's house every evening, but W.S.G. was worried by the possibility of eaves-dropping on the new telephone; he therefore wrote to D'Oyly Carte suggesting this cipher:

FAVOURITES

1 2 3 4 5 6 7 8 9 0

'In telephoning (say) £265, the clerk will say A R U pounds; so £128 would be F A T (but not very fat), and so on.' And the takings were not very fat. D'Oyly Carte wrote in March, 1884, to both Sullivan and Gilbert the letter reproduced overleaf.

[257]

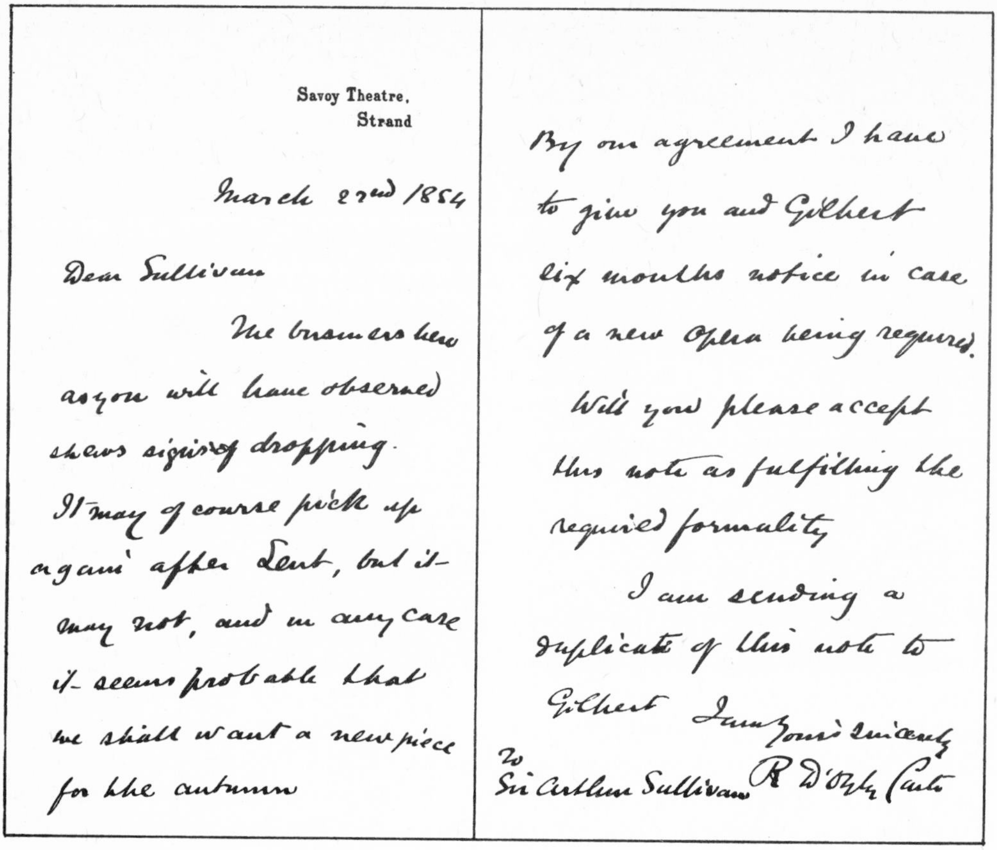

> Savoy Theatre,
> Strand
>
> March 22nd 1854
>
> Dear Sullivan
>
> The business here as you will have observed shews signs of dropping. It may of course pick up again after Lent, but it may not, and in any case it seems probable that we shall want a new piece for the autumn
>
> By our agreement I have to give you and Gilbert six months notice in case of a new Opera being required. Will you please accept this note as fulfilling the required formality
>
> I am sending a duplicate of this note to Gilbert
>
> I am yours sincerely
>
> R. D'Oyly Carte
>
> To Sir Arthur Sullivan

This was in accordance with their five-year contract signed only twelve months previously, but Sullivan replied from Brussels: 'I ought to tell you at once that it is impossible for me to do another piece of the character of those already written by Gilbert and myself.'

Already Gilbert had sketched out the libretto for a new opera when Carte told him about Sullivan's ultimatum. Gilbert's lawyer-mind at once seized on the fact that, by the terms of their contract, he and Sullivan would be liable to Carte for any losses that might result from default in supplying a new piece. He wrote to Sullivan to point this out, and his letter expressed his surprise and bewilderment that trouble should arise between them; they had worked together for years with good feeling, and—'I have invariably subordinated my views to your own.'

Sullivan, now in Paris, thought the opposite was the case.

Sullivan to Gilbert:

I will be quite frank. With *Princess Ida* I have come to the end of my tether—the end of my capability in that class of piece. My tunes are in danger of becoming mere repetitions of my former pieces, my concerted movements are getting to possess a strong family likeness . . .

I have looked upon the words as being of such importance that I have been continually keeping down the music in order that not one should be lost. And this my suppression is most difficult, most fatiguing, and I may say most disheartening, for the music is never allowed to arise and speak for itself.

I want a chance for the music to act in its own proper sphere—to intensify the emotional element not only of the actual words but of the situation. I should like to set a story of human interest and probability, where the humorous words would come in a humorous (not serious) situation, and where, if the situation were a tender or dramatic one the words would be of a similar character. There would then be a feeling of reality about it which would give fresh interest in writing, and fresh vitality to our joint work . . . I hope with all my heart that there may be no break in our chain of joint workmanship.

Gilbert to Sullivan:

Your reflections on the character of the libretti with which I have supplied you have caused me considerable pain. However, I cannot suppose that you have intended to gall and wound me, when you wrote as you did. I must assume that your letter was written hurriedly.

Meanwhile audiences at *Princess Ida* were falling off, causing both Gilbert and Carte the gravest concern as to what was to happen when this opera closed down, as soon it must.

As soon as Sullivan was back in London Gilbert called at his rooms and produced the 'new' libretto. It was the Magic Lozenge Plot which Sullivan had refused two years before.

Sullivan's diary:

I was obliged to reject the subject, as it makes the whole piece unreal and artificial. Long argument—no concession on either side—complete deadlock, though quite friendly throughout.

He thought the Lozenge too much like *The Sorcerer*, and said: 'It is going back to the elements of topsy-turvydom which I had hoped we had now done with.'

Gilbert could not see this at all.

Gilbert to Sullivan:

You will understand how faintly I grasp your meaning when I tell you that your objections to my libretto really seem arbitrary and capricious. That they are nothing of the kind I am well persuaded—but, for all that, I can't fathom them.

Bret Harte had meanwhile submitted a comic opera scenario to Sullivan, but Sullivan now returned it with this declaration: 'I have resolved to devote myself now, if not entirely, at least in a great measure to more earnest work. I have rather come to the end of my tether in that line (*comic opera*) . . . There are younger men rising to whom I would gladly give the chance of gaining success in that field, and if I did yield to

This helmet, I suppose,
Was meant to ward off blows,
It's very hot
And weighs a lot
As many a guardsman knows . . .
—'Princess Ida'

The players are Richard Walker, Darrell Fancourt, and Radley Flynn, in the Nineteen Thirties.

persuasion and write another I should feel bound not to sever myself from my collaborateur, Gilbert.'[1]

Generously, Gilbert suggested that perhaps Sullivan would like to work with another author 'for one turn'; perhaps he was stale through the length of their partnership?

Sullivan to Gilbert:

I yield to no one in admiration of your matchless skill and genius . . . Such a proposal as you make I could not entertain for a moment. Nor do I see why, because an idea which you propose to me fails in my judgment to afford me sufficient musical suggestion, we should necessarily come to a standstill.

But they were at a standstill. Meetings between Sullivan, Gilbert, Carte, and Miss Lenoir failed to break it. Gilbert tried to conciliate Sullivan by altering the new libretto, but Sullivan confided to his diary: 'I don't like the Lozenge. I stick to my objection.'

Sullivan's craving for grand opera, or at least for a story of 'human interest and probability', drove him to make this a show-down. He informed Gilbert that he simply could not force himself to do something which he felt unable to do well. Why should they not try something *quite new?* Unhappily, this letter reached Gilbert just when he was putting in some hard revision work on the Lozenge libretto.

Gilbert to Sullivan:

Anxious as I am, and have always been, to give due weight to your suggestions, the time has come when I must state—and I do so with great reluctance—that I cannot consent to construct another plot for the next opera.

Sullivan to Gilbert:

The tone of your letter convinces me that your decision is final and therefore further discussion is useless. I regret it very much.

It seemed like the end of the great partnership. A day or so later Gilbert was striding up and down his library in the new house at Harrington Gardens, fuming at the impasse, when a huge Japanese sword decorating the wall fell with a clatter to the floor. Gilbert picked it up. His perambulations stopped. 'It suggested the broad idea,' as he said later. His journalistic mind, always quick to seize on topicalities, turned to a Japanese Exhibition which had recently been opened in the neighbourhood. Gilbert had seen the little Japanese men and women from the Exhibition shuffling in their exotic robes through the streets of Knightsbridge. Now he sat at his writing desk and picked up the quill pen. He began making notes in his plot-book.

For several hours he scribbled down the pictures that were forming in his imagination. He saw the big Japanese sword carried across the shoulder of a diminutive Japanese executioner. He dipped his pen in the inkwell, and drew out a fat blob of unction: 'Pooh-Bah may be described without any hesitation as one of the most remarkable characters in ancient or modern history.'[2]

[1] *The Letters of Bret Harte*, edited by Geoffrey Bret Harte (Hodder & Stoughton), 1926.
[2] W.S.G.'s own description of the character, in *The Story of the Mikado*, written for children.

Recalling the recent arty-drawing-room craze for Japanese ornaments, his imagination applied it to the chorus men at the Savoy:

> If you want to know who we are,
> We are gentlemen of Japan.
> On many a vase and jar,
> On many a screen and fan.

Then he wrote a letter to Sullivan. He suggested that a Japanese opera would afford opportunities for picturesque scenery and costumes, and for unusual music, and nothing of the kind had ever been attempted in England. Next day, 8 May, 1884, came Sullivan's reply:

> Your letter is an inexpressible relief to me, as it clearly shows me that you, equally with myself, are loth to discontinue the collaboration which has been such a pleasure and advantage to us. If I understand you to propose you will construct a plot without the supernatural and improbable elements, and on the lines which you describe, I gladly undertake to set it without further discussing the matter, or asking what the subject is to be.

All unpleasantness was ended. The new opera was destined to be the most popular of all. Many people consider it the brightest jewel of all in the Savoy casket. Certainly this is the biggest Gilbertian joke of all: that the plot which was *not* to deal with 'the improbable' should be—*The Mikado*, of all Gilbert's grotesqueries the most far-fetched. Is this the story of 'human probability' that Sullivan had demanded, this Never-Never Land thinly disguised as Japan and filled with the wildest caricatures of humanity? Perhaps the joke was on Sir Arthur Sullivan. On the other hand, Mr W. S. Gilbert *had* abandoned the Lozenge—and Sir Arthur might very well claim that by his stubbornness he had got Gilbert out of a rut. He had provoked Gilbert into conceiving a story entirely fresh and original.

Everyone was relieved. But while they were quarrelling the weeks had flown by, and there was now no time to have *The Mikado* ready to replace the rapidly-collapsing *Princess Ida*, so stop-gap revivals were prepared at the Savoy: *The Sorcerer* and *Trial by Jury*, which had not been seen in London since the original productions at the old Opéra Comique. With the slickly-drilled Savoy Theatre company, Grossmith, Temple, Lely, Jessie Bond, Rosina Brandram, etc., *The Sorcerer* which had been a lukewarm success in 1877 became a red-hot favourite in 1884.

Time was flying, and the popular status which had been achieved by these stars of the Savoy was a reminder to the far-sighted Mr D'Oyly Carte that they would not last for ever. He held that the best training ground for new principals was in his chorus and his touring companies, so there was keen competition for even the humblest place in a D'Oyly Carte Company. It was in *Princess Ida* that a seventeen-year-old chorister now made his first appearance in Gilbert and Sullivan opera, at Glasgow. He was a Mr H. A. Henri. He was later to become famous as Henry A. Lytton.

An original sketch by W. S. Gilbert of the costumes to be worn under the armour of the three Sons in 'Princess Ida'. Gilbert seems to have drawn a self-portrait as the head of the figure

1885

'THE MIKADO'

KO-KO: *Well, a nice mess you've got us into, with your nodding head and the deference due to a man of pedigree!*

POOH-BAH: *Merely corroborative detail, intended to give artistic verisimilitude to an otherwise bald and unconvincing narrative.*

—The Mikado

IT IS REMARKABLE how many things of value and significance to us today are the harvest of a great outburst of Victorian productivity in the period 1884 – 5. Daimler invented the petrol engine. Gold was discovered in the Transvaal. The Fabian Society was founded in England. One of its founders, George Bernard Shaw, was writing his first play. Charles Parsons invented the steam turbine. Kipling was about to emerge as the Bard of Empire. *Parsifal*, which had its first British performance at the Albert Hall (Sullivan thought it 'gloomy, dull and ugly'), marked the peak of the Wagnerian revolution. And Gilbert and Sullivan completed their revolution with *The Mikado*, the keystone in the soaring arch of their theatrical genius.

Japan was just emerging from mediaeval obscurity. Anything Japanese seemed strange, romantic, exciting. 'The news that the next Savoy opera would be Japanese whetted the public curiosity and many were the efforts made to tap members of the company for information,' says Rutland Barrington,[1] who was cast for the part of Pooh-Bah. The timing of the new opera in conjunction with the Japanese Exhibition in Knightsbridge was a neat piece of Gilbertian showmanship.

'We are all being more or less Japanned,' wrote the *Daily Telegraph* theatre critic after the first night of *The Mikado*. 'Advertisements tell us every morning that we have Japan in London, and the quaint art of a strange people, who are getting rid of their

[1] *Rutland Barrington*, by Himself (Grant Richards).

[265]

national characteristics as fast as they can, is receiving from us that form of homage which the proverb describes as "the sincerest flattery".'

The quaint arts of Nippon are faithfully reflected in the Gilbertian looking-glass of *The Mikado*—in costume and scene, in the carefully-drilled flick of fans, the shuffling walk of the 'train of little ladies'—but when Mr Gilbert has taken you, like Alice, through his looking-glass and you gaze around expecting to find yourself in a foreign cherry-blossom land, you recognize things which are grotesquely familiar. Pooh-Bah, for example, that epitome of graft and patronage. Though this character is attired as a tremendously swell Japanese, the jibe is at condescending bureaucrats of any nationality:

POOH-BAH: 'Of course, as First Lord of the Treasury, I could propose a special vote that would cover all expenses if it were not that, as Leader of the Opposition, it would be my duty to resist it, tooth and nail. Or, as Paymaster-General, I could so cook the accounts that, as Lord High Auditor I should never discover the fraud, but then as Archbishop of Titipu it would be my duty to denounce my dishonesty and give myself into my own custody as First Commissioner of Police.

KO-KO: That's extremely awkward.

POOH-BAH: I don't say that all these distinguished people couldn't be squared . . .

There is, incidentally, an interesting parallel to this speech by Pooh-Bah to be found in Planché's play *The Sleeping Beauty* (1840) where Lord Factotum says:

As Lord High Chamberlain, I slumber never;
As Lord High Steward, in a stew I'm ever;
As Lord High Constable, I watch all day;
As Lord High Treasurer, I've the deuce to pay;
As Great Grand Cup-bearer, I'm handled queerly,
As Great Grand Carver, I'm cut up severely.
In other States, the honours are divided,
But here, they're one and all to me confided.

But how much more neatly is the joke handled by Gilbert! And in *The Mikado* he extends his satire from bureaucracy and plurality to a whole range of things English, to 'apologetic statesmen of a compromising kind', to the scientific theory of evolution. ('I am,' says Pooh-Bah, 'a particularly haughty and exclusive person, of pre-Adamite ancestral descent. You will understand this when I tell you that I can trace my ancestry back to a protoplasmal primordial atomic globule. Consequently, my family pride is something inconceivable.') The opera reflects sharply in its mirror both English sentimentality and English acquiescence in brutality. Gilbert himself was a kind man who could not bear to crush a beetle under his foot, but he knew that many of his fellow-countrymen made a spectacle of cock-fights, rat-fights, and other blood-thirsty sports, and though public executions had now been abolished the plight of a prisoner was treated as an exciting spectacle: columns of sordid crime reports in contemporary newspapers are evidence of this. Hence *The Mikado's* obsession with punishment ('something lingering, with boiling oil in it') and public decapitation—

> Oh, never shall I
> Forget the cry,
> Or the shriek that shriekèd he,
> As I gnashed my teeth,
> When from its sheath
> I drew my snickersnee!

The wonderful thing is that all this macabre satire, matched by Sullivan to music as witty as any he ever wrote, adds up to the most popular opera of all, a veritable feast of humour.

'In this play,' wrote G. K. Chesterton of *The Mikado*, 'Gilbert pursued and persecuted the evils of modern England till they had literally not a leg to stand on, exactly as Swift did under the allegory of *Gulliver's Travels*. I doubt if there is a single joke in the whole play that fits the Japanese. But all the jokes in the play fit the English.'[1]

Thus when Ko-Ko, the Lord High Executioner, produces his little list of things that never would be missed, it is in fact a catalogue of some of the tiresome features of English life in 1885, such as

> . . . the nigger serenader, and the others of his race,
> And the piano-organist—I've got him on the list!

At this period the piano-organ was ever-present on the streets of London, chirping out 'The Bluebells of Scotland' or Sullivan's most hackneyed tunes, whilst the nigger minstrel craze, sweeping across from America, was now at its height, so that the twanging of banjos and the corny jokes of the burnt-cork humorists never *could* be missed in the concert halls and pier pavilions of Britain. And then there was in 1885, as ever—

> . . . the idiot who praises, with enthusiastic tone,
> All centuries but this, and every country but his own;
> And the lady from the provinces, who dresses like a guy,
> And who 'doesn't think she waltzes, but would rather like to try';
> And that singular anomaly, the lady novelist—
> I don't think she'd be miss'd—I'm *sure* she'd not be missed!

The Mikado himself has a singularly Britannic list of antipathies for which he prescribes the 'punishment to fit the crime', ranging from the billiard sharp to the lady who 'pinches her figger', the amateur tenor, the advertising quack, and—

[1] 'Gilbert and Sullivan', article by G. K. Chesterton in *The Eighteen Eighties*, edited by Walter de la Mare (Cambridge University Press).

> The idiot who, in railway carriages,
>   Scribbles on window-panes,
>   We only suffer
>   To ride on a buffer
>   In Parliamentary trains.

This is a reference to nothing Japanese: 'Parliamentary trains' was an English nick-name arising from the Railway Regulation Act of 1844, in which Parliament laid down conditions such as fares at a penny a mile.

The opera is packed with such topicalities, some of which have become obscured by the passage of years. England had just been visited by a number of Lutheran evangelists from Germany:

> All prosy dull society sinners,
>   Who chatter and bleat and bore,
>   Are sent to hear sermons
>   From mystical Germans
>   Who preach from ten to four.

And again, it had not escaped Mr Gilbert's attention that the ballad-singer in the Victorian music-hall was capable, like the crooner of today, of the uttermost banality, so the punishment to fit the crime is thus prescribed:

> The music-hall singer attends a series
>   Of masses and fugues and 'ops'
>   By Bach, interwoven
>   With Spohr and Beethoven,
>   At classical Monday Pops . . .

*The original Mikado—
Richard Temple*

—the Monday Pops being the popular Monday night concerts sponsored by Chappell's and held at the St James's Hall, Piccadilly.

Having decided upon the Japanese camouflage for his satire, Gilbert went to infinite pains to perfect it. Most of the dresses 'of pure Japanese fabric' he ordered from Liberty's store in Regent Street, but 'the dresses worn by the principals were genuine and original Japanese ones of ancient date; that in which Miss Rosina Brandram appeared as Katisha was about two hundred years old. The magnificent gold-embroidered robe and petticoat of the Mikado was a faithful replica of the ancient official costume of the Japanese monarch; the strange-looking curled bag at the top of his head was intended to enclose the pigtail. His face, too, was fashioned after the manner of

Three little maids from school are we,
Pert as a school girl well can be,
Filled to the brim with girlisch glee,
Three little maids from school! etc.
Koko will feine Braut umarmen — ein kurzer
Streit über die Schicklichkeit dieser Zumuthung: doch
Pitti und Puh-Bah finden es ganz in der Ordnung,

Sybil Grey, Leonora Braham, and Jessie Bond as Peep-Bo, Yum-Yum and Pitti-Sing, the Three Little Maids in the first London production—and a page from a German brochure published in connection with the tour of 'The Mikado'

the former Mikados, the natural eyebrows being shaved off and huge false ones painted on his forehead.'[1] Antique suits of armour were brought over from Japan, only to be found useless because they would not fit any man taller than five feet four inches.

At the Japanese Exhibition W.S.G. found a geisha girl. Her English was limited to 'Sixpence please' (the price of a cup of tea at Knightsbridge), but Gilbert took her along to the Savoy rehearsals to teach the cast Japanese deportment. The spreading and snapping of fans to denote wrath, delight, or homage, the walk, the giggling and strange hissing of the girls—all this, which is still faithfully portrayed in modern productions of *The Mikado*, dates back to Miss Sixpence Please.

When Gilbert gave an interview to the *New York Tribune* in 1885 he was asked how he went about writing *The Mikado* and his answer must have been unexpected. He did *not* start by thinking out a plot. The first thing was 'to fit the company with parts . . . The accident that Miss Braham, Miss Jessie Bond, and Miss Sybil Grey, are short in stature and all of a height, suggested the advisability of grouping them as three Japanese

[1] *Gilbert, Sullivan and D'Oyly Carte*, by Cellier & Bridgman (Pitman), 1927. Alfred Cellier, whose recollection is quoted, had been resident conductor for Gilbert and Sullivan until 1878 when, during the run of *H.M.S. Pinafore*, he was succeeded by his brother, François.

schoolgirls who should work together throughout the piece.' Thus began the Three
Little Maids from School. Gilbert continues: 'The next thing was to decide upon two
scenes, which should be characteristic and effective. The respective advantages of a
street in Nagasaki, a Japanese market-place, a wharf with shipping, a Japanese garden,
a seaside beach, and the courtyard of a Japanese palace, were duly weighed; and the
courtyard and the Japanese garden were finally decided upon.'

Next Gilbert opened one of those weighty plot-books of his and wrote down the
story of the opera—in no less than eleven different ways, 'each presumably an improvement upon its immediate predecessor', and after that he began writing the lyrics of
songs for Act 1. The first that Sullivan set to music was 'Three Little Maids from School
are We', four days before Christmas, 1884—and less than three months before the first
performance.

The music follows a thoroughly English idiom. There is Gilbertian logic in this. To
have filled *The Mikado* with pseudo-Japanese tunes would have been to take away an
essentially familiar element of our excursion through the looking-glass into that
strangely familiar-yet-unfamiliar town of Titipu, where the Lord High Executioner
arrives to a pompous tune no more oriental than 'A Fine Old English Gentleman'—to
which it bears a comic resemblance. There is one exception to this rule: the Entrance
of the Mikado: 'Miya sama, miya sama, On n'm-ma no mayé ni . . .' etc.

The legend has grown up that Sullivan did not know the meaning of these words
and that it was only in later years that a Japanese told him it was 'the foulest song ever
sung in the lowest tea-house in Japan'; it is a nice story, especially when one thinks
of the innocent amateur societies who have chanted these 'foul words' so many
thousands of times . . . but it isn't true. The truth was told in a London newspaper,
the *Globe*, at the time of the controversy over the banning of *The Mikado* in 1907:
'Mr Diósy, the well-known authority on things Japanese,[1] says that it was at the
suggestion of Mr Richard Temple, the original Mikado in the opera, that he himself
supplied Sir Arthur with some real Japanese music in this particular tune, a famous
Japanese war march. Mr Diósy points out that the story of the opera is entirely fantastic,
having nothing Japanese in it except the name of the Lord High Executioner, Ko-Ko,
which means pickles, and the words of this particular chorus which are translated:

Oh, my Prince, oh, my Prince
What is that fluttering in the wind
Before your imperial charger?
Know ye not it is the imperial banner
Of silken brocade,
The signal for the chastisement of rebels?'

An official of the Japan Society in London has confirmed this: 'Miya Sama was the

---

[1] Arthur Diósy, F.R.G.S., 1856 – 1923, traveller and lecturer, Knight of the Rising Sun of Japan,
author of *The New Far East* (1898).

war song of the Imperial Army of Japan to which the troops of the Emperor went to victory in 1868. Except for the last four bars the music is the same as that used by Sullivan.'[1]

From the fortunate day when a Japanese sword fell from the wall of Gilbert's house and gave him an inspiration, to the rising of the curtain on the cleverest comic opera in the English language, a period of only nine months elapsed: in this time the whole of this work was created, a good accord once more held the partners in harmony, and the closest secrecy was preserved concerning the next opera at the Savoy.

The comparative failure of *Princess Ida* had given rise to a great deal of conjecture and criticism in the Press. Were Gilbert and Sullivan played out? Was their vein of genius exhausted? What was happening at the Savoy? As the first night approached, Press conjecture became more excited. Gilbert grew unusually anxious and fussy. He was for once unsure of his judgment, and at rehearsal he astonished the cast by announcing that he proposed to cut the Mikado's song . . .

> My object all sublime
> I shall achieve in time—
> To let the punishment fit the crime—
> The punishment fit the crime;
> And make each prisoner pent
> Unwillingly represent
> A source of innocent merriment!
> Of innocent merriment!

'Cut it was, there and then,' Barrington tells us, 'but when the choristers heard the news they went in a body to Gilbert and implored him to reinstate it. This was done, with what success we know.'

Before a distinguished audience, which included the Duke and Duchess of Edinburgh, Sullivan conducted the first performance of *The Mikado* while Gilbert nervously prowled the streets of London, mentally chewing upon the gloomy prognostications of the Press ('his vein of topseyturveydom is exhausted').

'What I suffered during those hours no man can tell,' he said. 'Agony and apprehension possessed me.'

Sullivan's diary, 14 March, 1885:

New opera *The Mikado, or The Town of Titipu*, produced at the Savoy Theatre with every sign of real success. A most brilliant house. Tremendous reception. All went well except Grossmith whose nervousness nearly upset the piece. A treble encore for 'Three Little Maids' and 'The Flowers that Bloom in the Spring'. Seven encores taken—might have taken twelve.

[1] Quoted from the *Nineteenth Century* magazine. See also a letter in the *Gilbert and Sullivan Journal* from T. Baty, Japanese Foreign Office.

Barrington writes: 'Never during the whole of my experience have I assisted at such an enthusiastic first night as greeted this delightful work. From the moment the curtain rose on the Court swells in Japanese willow-plate attitudes to its final fall it was one long succession of uproarious laughter at the libretto and overwhelming applause for the music . . . "Three Little Maids" was received with such enthusiasm and insistent encores as no musical number in my experience, or I believe anyone else's, has ever equalled.'[1]

Yet, incredible as it may seem now, before the curtain went up there was an uneasy suspicion in the dressing-rooms at the Savoy that *The Mikado* might be a failure. Of the Three Little Maids it is recorded: 'They were all three very young and as they waited off-stage for the men's chorus to end it seemed an age, and they were almost sick with fright; to go on and sing their little song was an ordeal, but when they sang it judge their surprise when the audience rose and cheered and clapped, and they had to sing it again.'[2]

The Mikado was (and still is) the biggest fortune-maker of all. Mr Beatty-Kingston, the eminent critic of the *Theatre*, declared that the music consisted of a string of 'musical jewels of great price all aglow with the lustre of pure and luminous genius'.[3] High praise, but most people would still support it today, whether we think of Yum-Yum's exquisitely melodious ballad 'The sun whose rays are all ablaze', or the sheer joy of the delicate 'Three Little Maids from School', or the world-famed 'Flowers that bloom in the Spring', or the enchanting glees and choruses, or the wry humour of Katisha's love-duet with Ko-Ko, 'There is beauty in the bellow of the blast'. And as this evergreen opera

Durward Lely, the first Nanki-Poo—the caricature is from the 'Illustrated Sporting and Dramatic News'

goes on year after year one is constantly astonished by the cleverness of Gilbert's libretto—even though today some of it seems dated, more so than the music.

The Sullivan-Gilbert dispute of the previous year had the effect of putting both men on their toes. But Gilbert was uneasily aware of Sullivan's desire to 'let the music speak for itself'. The first Nanki-Poo, Durward Lely, tells of a rehearsal when Gilbert

[1] *Rutland Barrington*, by Himself (Grant Richards).

[2] According to Mrs V. B. Thompson, of Birmingham, whose aunt, Sybil Grey, was one of the original Three Little Maids (in a letter to the author).

[3] The *Theatre*, 1 April, 1885.

[272]

Oh, never shall I
Forget the cry,
Or the shriek that shriekèd he,
As I gnashed my teeth,
When from its sheath
I drew my snickersnee!

Henry Lytton George Grossmith Martyn Green

Ko-Ko through sixty years—three famous Lord High Executioners: Martyn Green in the modern costume by Ricketts, Grossmith in the original by Liberty's. The sword carried by Grossmith was actually the weapon that fell from the wall in Gilbert's study

[273]

said to him: 'Very good, Lely, very good indeed, but I have just come down from the back seat in the gallery and there were two or three words which failed to reach me quite distinctly. Sullivan's music is, of course, very beautiful, and I heard every note without difficulty, but I think my words are not altogether without merit and ought also to be heard without undue effort. Please pay particular attention to the consonants, the M's, the N's, and especially the S's.'

Gilbert was furious at the way Mr Beatty-Kingston commented on the plot, and certainly this critic took *The Mikado* over-solemnly at its face-value when he wrote that the characters:

. . . are carefully shown to be unsusceptible of a single kindly feeling or wholesome impulse; were they not manifestly maniacal they would be demoniacal. This view of them is rendered imperative by the circumstance that their dearest personal interests are, throughout the plot, made dependent upon the infliction of a violent death upon one or other of them. Decapitation, disembowelment, immersion in boiling oil or molten lead are the eventualities upon which their attention (and that of the audience) is kept fixed with gruesome persistence; what wonder that their brains should be unsettled by such appalling prospects, or that their hearts should be turned to stone by the petrifying instinct of self-preservation? . . . Having resolved to deal with the grimmest subject ever yet selected for treatment from the comic point of view by any dramatic author, and to exhibit his fellow-men to their con-temporaries in the most disadvantageous light imaginable, Mr Gilbert has done his self-appointed work with surpassing ability and inimitable *verve*.

Soon after the opening of *The Mikado* Gilbert had a serious dispute with Carte. It should be explained that the working arrangement between the three partners was as follows: Sullivan and Gilbert had a veto on engagement of artists, and they themselves engaged all principals, but Carte held the preliminary auditions, and he always engaged the chorus and understudies. Sullivan and Gilbert had entire control of rehearsals, but after the first night Carte was expected to keep a nightly eye on the standard of per-formance. Carte, as manager of the Savoy Theatre, controlled its day-to-day business, both back-stage and at the box-office: he paid the cast and stage staff, supervised advertising, purchased equipment, and kept the theatre in good order. It is important to bear all this in mind, in view of the deteriorating relationship of Gilbert and Carte from now to the time of the Carpet Quarrel. Gilbert now said that he thought Carte had too much control.

Carte replied: 'It seems to me that we are not all of the same opinion as to our respective positions under the contract framed some time ago,' and he denied that this contract implied equal management of the three men in the Savoy Theatre. A tripartite management, with daily meetings over every detail, would be impossible. 'I cannot see how you and Sullivan are part managers of the theatre,' said Carte, 'any more than I am part-author or part-composer of the music.' At which, Gilbert exploded.

Gilbert to Carte. 1 June, 1885:

I am at a loss to express the pain and surprise with which I read your letter. As you decline to permit me to have any voice in the control of the theatre that Sullivan and I have raised to its present position of prosperity and distinction, and point out to me that, by our agreement, I am merely a hack author employed by you to supply you with pieces on certain terms, I have no alternative but to accept the position you assign to me during the few months that our agreement has got to run. Henceforth I will be bound by its absolute and literal terms. If this course of action should result in inconvenience or loss to yourself you will do me the justice to remember that it is of your own creation.

Carte to Gilbert:

Your note grieves me more than I can say. Must a dramatic author be considered a 'hack' author if he does not arrange the number of stalls in the theatre where his opera is played? What is my position compared to yours? I envy you your position, but I could never attain it. If I could be an author like you I would certainly not be the manager. I am simply the tradesman who sells your creations of art.

Carte was conciliatory. But Gilbert also wrote to Sullivan, insisting that they should share in the management of the theatre, because if Carte were left alone and unfettered, he might do ill-advised and foolish things and perhaps ruin the business!

Carte to Gilbert:

Of course you run this risk. But my reply is that I stand the whole risk of pecuniary loss.[1] It is possible that you and Sullivan might write something for the Savoy that, instead of being the great draw your pieces are, would draw the people out of the theatre and ruin the business: I run the risk of your doing this. When we made the five-year contract I had such faith that your success would continue that I was well pleased to take this risk. You had sufficient belief in my capacity to trust the business organization to me. What is the *raison d'être* of our triumvirate? As I understand it, it is that you and Sullivan do not wish to undertake the laborious duties of managing a London theatre, from four to six provincial tours, the American and Australian business, etc. and the pecuniary risks thereto pertaining. What I do I am enabled to do by long experience in the practical business of the theatre. If I had to consult you and Sullivan on all points, to hear your opinions and argue them out, and have meetings for this purpose, I could not possibly get through the mass of work.[2]

With that the trouble blew over, for the time being. Sullivan had avoided being drawn into the dispute, but its effect was to draw him closer to Carte, for Sullivan could never have been bothered with day-to-day management and was content with the existing arrangement. This did not improve Gilbert's temper. Nor did the fact that some of the most influential London critics were kinder to Sullivan's share in *The Mikado* than to Gilbert's; the *Daily Telegraph*, for instance:

The most beautiful things in *The Mikado* come when the composer appeals rather

[1] The three partners shared the profits of the operas equally, but not the losses.

[2] From correspondence in the archives of the Savoy Theatre.

to tears than to laughter. Sometimes he does this in situations where seriousness is greatly mixed with comic elements, as in the music sung by an elderly and rejected female of the Lady Jane type. Katisha's song, 'Hearts do not break', strikes us as, in its way, a masterpiece of expression, and with it may be bracketed the tragical-mirthful madrigal . . .

> Brightly dawns our wedding day;
> Joyous hour, we give thee greeting!

*　　*　　*　　*　　*　　*

It is perhaps the oddest thing about this very odd opera that one of the most popular numbers in it is this beautiful madrigal which belongs to the English village-green rather than the Oriental garden, and in which Gilbert ceases to be the clown and writes quite seriously in a mood akin to Herrick, and finds an answering note in Sullivan's love and understanding of the idiom of seventeenth-century madrigal music. The result is as un-Japanese as could be imagined.

Similarly, the wistful 'Tit Willow' has its roots in England. Nicholas Rowe, poet (1674 – 1718), wrote:

> To the Brook and the Willow that heard him complain,
> Ah Willow, Willow,
> Poor Colin sat weeping and told them his pain,
> Ah, Willow, Willow; ah Willow, Willow.
> Sweet stream, he cry'd sadly, I'll teach thee to flow;
> And the waters shall rise to the brink with my woe,
> Ah Willow, Willow.

Compare Gilbert's

> On a tree by a river a little tom-tit
> Sang 'Willow, titwillow, titwillow!'
> And I said to him, 'Dicky-bird, why do you sit
> Singing "Willow, titwillow, titwillow"?'
> 'Is it weakness of intellect, birdie?' I cried,
> 'Or a rather tough worm in your little inside?'
> With a shake of his poor little head, he replied,
> 'Oh, willow, titwillow, titwillow!'

It was now that Sir Arthur Sullivan was asked by the Leeds Festival Committee to write a symphony for the next Festival, 1886. He replied: 'I should very much like to do a short choral work, not necessarily sacred, but of an earnest character.' The result was the oratorio *The Golden Legend*. Sullivan was again engaged to conduct the

Forty years after its original production—'The
Mikado', with Henry Lytton as Ko-Ko, Bertha
Lewis as Katisha

entire Leeds Festival. He had been short-listed for the conductorship of the Birmingham
Festival; the other candidates were both foreigners, Randegger and Richter. When
Richter was chosen some people said it was because Birmingham was jealous of Leeds
and would not share the same man, but Sullivan remarked that 'In England there is still
a curious preference for musical foreigners'. This was in an interview with the
Magazine of Music, February, 1885.

If England had a preference for musical foreigners in serious music, foreign countries
and the Dominions had a preference for English comic opera. Even before *The Mikado*
sensation burst upon the world, *Princess Ida* had a big success in New York, in Sydney,
and in Melbourne, and over the next two or three years Gilbert, Sullivan, and Carte
were, as *Punch* had it, 'monarchs of all they Savoy'. Their kingdom was world-wide.
Shillings, dollars, pesos, marks, francs, poured into their coffers.

[277]

In South America Leonora Braham made triumphant appearances as Phyllis, Mabel, and Yum-Yum, 'three of the eight parts in which I appeared in Buenos Aires, Montevideo, Valparaiso, Lima, and other places with never failing success.'[1] She was one of several London stars who were sent across the oceans by D'Oyly Carte. Australia saw Grossmith and Temple in *The Sorcerer*. Alfred Cellier went out there to conduct.

Cellier to Sullivan, from Melbourne:

I opened with *The Mikado*, really a magnificent performance in every way. It is beautifully mounted, a capital large chorus, and small but very efficient orchestra of twenty-two. The Yum-Yum and Ko-Ko[2] are the best performances of those two characters I have seen anywhere . . . We expect to run ten weeks, six being the average, then we go to Adelaide, then to New Zealand, Sydney, Brisbane, and back here.

Having thoroughly planted the operas in the colonies, Mr D'Oyly Carte now turned his attention to the continent of Europe. Mrs Swinhoe (stage name Jessie Vince), a member of the first company to tour Holland and Germany with *The Mikado*, *Patience*, and *Pinafore*, sends the following memoir:[3]

I was twenty-two when I had an audition at the Savoy Theatre in London, and was given a place in the chorus, and immediately sent out to join the company in Hamburg. We played there a week, we had six weeks in Berlin, and one week in Amsterdam. They loved the operas, especially *The Mikado*. In Germany they didn't quite understand the satire of *Patience*. Books of words in both English and German were sold in the theatre, so that they could follow even if they didn't know English. In Berlin children used to run after us in the streets shouting 'Mikker-doo! Mikker-doo!' In Hamburg one evening an artist came behind the scenes and made a sketch of some of us as we waited in the wings—I think it's rather lovely, don't you? But then, those were lovely days . . . it was so thrilling to help to make theatrical history and to find ourselves the cause of tremendous interest wherever we played . . .

In the correspondence of the famous German philosopher Nietzsche (who had just published his *Thus Spake Zarathustra*) there is a letter to his disciple, the composer Peter Gast, in which he thanks Gast for his account of a visit to *The Mikado* at Munich. 'Its simple charm and beauty enchanted and moved me in an extraordinary way,' wrote Gast, and Nietzsche responded: 'How your remarks about Sullivan and his Japanese music rejoiced me! What you like in music I like also, there can be no doubt about that.'[4]

The *North German Gazette* said:

'We are conscious of entertaining a very pronounced predilection for all our home

[1] Article by Leonora Braham in the *Gilbert and Sullivan Journal*, October, 1926.
[2] Howard Vernon, the Ko-Ko, continued to play this part in Australia for twenty years.
[3] Mrs Swinhoe, aged eighty-two, heard the BBC's *Gilbert and Sullivan* series in 1947 in her cottage near Brighton, and sent these notes to the author.
[4] Information supplied by Mr Stanley Godman and Mr A. M. Ludovici, translator of Nietzsche.

"Gossip"

Sketched behind the scenes at Hamburg—Jessie Vince with members of the chorus of
'The Mikado' in Germany

products, but we scruple not to confess that, as a performance, *The Mikado* surpasses all our operettas.' The world-famed conductor Arthur Nikisch directed a German presentation of *The Mikado*. Several of Gilbert's libretti were translated into German. The famous Policemen's Song from *The Pirates of Penzance* 'When a felon's not engaged in his employment . . .' became:

Lied des Sergeanten.

SERGEANT: Wenn der Schurke grad' beruflich unbe-
schäftigt –
ALLE: unbeschäftigt,–
SERGEANT: Oder sonst wie freie Zeit sich
nehmen kann
ALLE: nehmen kann,
SERGEANT: Dann durch Sport im Frei'n auch er
sich gern erkräftigt –
ALLE: gern erkräftigt,
SERGEANT: Ebenso wie jeder andre Ehrenmann –

THE SECRET JOURNEY TO NEW YORK

A document in the D'Oyly Carte archives at the Savoy tells an astonishing story of the lengths to which Mr Carte went in his desire to prevent the pirating of *The Mikado* in the U.S.A. News of the opera's success in London and dreams of fortunes to be made in America sharpened the covetousness of the Big Bosses of the American stage. With two of them Mr Carte discussed, separately, a contract for an authorized production in New York, using a company of artists to be sent out from London. Mr Stetson of the Fifth Avenue Theatre was chosen. The rejected showman, a Mr Duff, thereupon hurriedly set about preparing to mount a pirate version of *The Mikado* at the Standard Theatre, New York. Duff had his agents in England from whom he could obtain copies of the book of words, which were on sale as usual, but the music was a different matter. The full orchestral score was not (and never has been) published. Only a piano score was on the market; using this as a guide, the pirate producer had to get his own musicians to arrange an orchestral accompaniment. News of these activities reached D'Oyly Carte in London. The worst part of the news was that whereas Carte and Stetson had planned to present their 'official' version in October, Duff was hoping to forestall them by his pirated version in August.

Carte got busy. Drastically, he speeded up preparations for his New York company to sail from England. He in turn would forestall Duff! He found that cables sent to Stetson were being tapped by Duff's agents, so the expedition was organized with absolute secrecy. He wrote a letter marked 'Very Private' to the Cunard Line, booking fifty passages. An agent of Duff's arrived in London to buy Japanese costumes at Liberty's, but when Liberty's found that the agent was unauthorized by Carte, they refused to do business, so off went Duff's man to Paris. Carte sent an agent ahead of him—to buy up every Japanese costume in Paris! 'I don't mind how much money I spend to smash Duff', said Carte.

He wrote to Stetson, in New York: 'The moment you let me know when Duff proposes to open, I will swoop quickly across with my company and be before him.'

One day Stetson cabled that Duff had started rehearsals. Carte cabled back. 'Hear that detectives are watching you and theatre—put one on Duff.' Then, at the end of a rehearsal of one of his companies at the Savoy Theatre, he informed them that they were not bound for the English provinces, as they had assumed. They were going to New York.

He swore them to secrecy; they must not have relatives to see them off at the station. The company ('cheering loudly' says the Savoy Theatre document) fell in with the idea, and at midnight two days later slipped out of London by the boat train for Liverpool. Then:

> They breakfasted together at a small commercial hotel, where none of them was known, and were then conveyed by a special tug to the Cunard steamship *Aurania*. She was to start that afternoon, and, when the passenger tender was seen approaching, all the Company retired to their cabins and shut themselves in, so that they might not be seen and recognized by any persons who were coming out to bid farewell to their friends. The berths of the members of the Company were all booked under fictitious names, and Mr Carte himself was entered on the ship's books as Mr Henry Chapman . . .
>
> With so many chances of discovery to be escaped, it seems almost a miracle that nothing about the Company's having sailed for New York was cabled to that city; but when the *Aurania* anchored off Quarantine, at Staten Island, at midnight on 16 August, and Mr Carte's New York agent ascended a rope ladder from a small steamer that came out to meet the vessel, and the momentous question, 'Is anything known in New York?' was put to him, his answer was, 'Not one word.'

Mr Duff already had a poster out announcing the presentation of the pirate version at the Standard Theatre about a week later, and 'great was the consternation at the Standard when it became known that the enemy, supposed to be three thousand miles away, were actually in the citadel'. Although Mr Duff advanced his opening date a day or two, Mr Carte beat him to it: on 19 August the authentic *Mikado* was produced at the Fifth Avenue Theatre, and its success was immediate and triumphant.

The pirate versions continued, so D'Oyly Carte went to law against them in the American courts. A test case was heard by Justice Divver, of New York City. Divver was a strong Tammanyite and a native of Ulster. His decision included the following classic ruling: 'Copyright, or no copyright, commercial honesty or commercial buccaneering, no Englishman possesses any rights which a true-born American is bound to respect.'

In other courts and in other cities of the United States rulings were given in some

The transatlantic association of the D'Oyly Carte Company still continues: here embarking at Montreal in 1929, are (FROM LEFT) *Beatrice Elburn, Blossom Gelsthorpe, Leslie Rands, Marjorie Eyre, Henry A. Lytton and Bertha Lewis*

cases for Carte, in some for the pirates. When Duff extended his piratical operations to Chicago and Boston and elsewhere, D'Oyly Carte threatened to pursue him with law suits all over the United States, so Duff appealed to the Supreme Court. 'He charges,' reported the *New York Mirror* 'that the purpose of these threatened suits is to harass and annoy him, so as to induce him to desert his intended productions.' Precisely—and the Supreme Court found in Duff's favour.

The 'official' company performed *The Mikado* 430 times in New York, with George Thorne as Ko-Ko and Fred Billington as Pooh-Bah. Touring companies were sent out across the United States. Sir Arthur Sullivan, visiting relatives in California, found himself a hero wherever he went. He conducted a gala performance in New York on 24 September, 1885, and made a speech to the audience: 'We should have been grieved indeed if you received the first impression of our work from a spurious imitation—an imitation in which the authors' intentions are ignored for the very good reason that the performers don't know what our intentions are, and in which the music, through having been patched up from a pianoforte arrangement, must necessarily be mutilated,

And in 1955: the D'Oyly Carte Company arrive at San Francisco. The men are (FROM LEFT)
*Peter Pratt, Donald Adams, Isidore Godfrey, Fisher Morgan, Alan Styler, Jeffrey Skitch, Leonard
Osborn, Nevile Griffiths. The ladies are Cynthia Morey, Muriel Harding, Joyce Wright, Ann
Drummond-Grant*

and a misrepresentation of the meaning of the composer . . . Tonight you see our work
exactly as we intended it should be performed.'

During his tour Sir Arthur had visited Salt Lake City, bathed in the lake ('The water
is so salt you can hardly swim in it,' he wrote to his secretary, Mr Smythe), and
attended a service at the Mormon Tabernacle: 'The hymn tune was my arrangement of
St Ann's tune! They had a very fine organ and I played upon it for an hour.' At San
Francisco he would have enjoyed his stay 'but for the ceaseless and persistent manner
in which I was interviewed, called upon, followed, and written to'.

Gilbert had stayed behind in England. A very long run such as *The Mikado* was
enjoying is apt to lure the best of players into moods of slackness and of irresponsibility,
so every now and then W.S.G. would drop in at the Savoy to check up on discipline
and performance. He found that Rutland Barrington, who had one day borrowed four
shillings from Jessie Bond to pay a cab fare, was returning it in pennies, half-pennies,
and postage stamps which he handed to her one by one, night after night, *on the stage*
though unseen by the audience. It was not unseen by Gilbert. Barrington was repri-
manded for this piece of private frivolity. George Grossmith was also on the mat—

GILBERT: I am told, Mr Grossmith, that in last night's performance when you and Miss Bond were kneeling before the Mikado she gave you a push and you rolled completely over on the floor.

GROSSMITH: Yes. You see, I—in my interpretation of Ko-Ko—

GILBERT: Whatever your interpretation, please omit that in future.

GROSSMITH: Certainly if you wish it, but I got a big laugh by it.

GILBERT: So you would if you sat on a pork pie.

This conversation is highly significant. It reveals the mastery that Gilbert had now obtained over all he surveyed. As Mr Punch remarked, times had changed since Albert Smith said that 'there was only one person in the theatre lower than the call-boy, and that was the author'. At the Savoy, said *Punch*, 'Gilbert and Sullivan have only themselves to please . . . The result is that the ensemble is about the most effective thing in London—or in Paris for that matter.'

The lesson was not lost on other producers, managers, and authors. A most astute student of the Savoy school was D'Oyly Carte's manager, George Edwardes, who was soon to set up on his own as producer of the famous musical comedies at the Gaiety and Daly's. In the more serious theatre Bernard Shaw was soon to take a leaf out of Gilbert's book by producing his own plays and imposing his own discipline.

Gilbert and Sullivan had transformed the English musical theatre from a grubby hobbledehoy Cinderella into a dainty, charming Princess; they set a standard of taste and of musical technique infinitely higher than anything before their time. They were disciplinarians but that did not make them louts; they were men of culture, and their treatment of actors and actresses had something to do with the new position that theatrical folk were now assuming in the eyes of the public. A bishop could say how d'ye do to an actress without public scandal, and it was no longer expedient for musical plays to be disguised as 'illustrations' as in the German Reed days of Gilbert's apprenticeship.

These are among the things of value and significance to us today arising from that period of rich development which gave us *The Mikado*; and in all this Sullivan and Gilbert were aided and held together by Richard D'Oyly Carte, who was personally tasting the fruits of his labour: out of his profits from the operas he built the Savoy Hotel. As usual, he was ahead of his time—the plans for the hotel included so many bathrooms that the builder asked: 'Do you think your guests are going to be amphibious?'

The Mikado ran 672 performances at the Savoy Theatre.[1] Today it still beats all records all over the world as Gilbert and Sullivan's best seller. The music publisher, Chappell,

[1] This remained a record at the Savoy Theatre until *Paddy the Next Best Thing* broke it in 1922.

1936—and 'The Mikado' still goes on. Derek Oldham as Nanki-Poo sings 'Were you not to Ko-Ko plighted' to Sylvia Cecil as Yum-Yum

says: 'The vocal scores still sell very well. Of those published by Chappell's[1] I should place them in order of largest sales as follows: *The Mikado* first, always the most popular; then *The Gondoliers, Yeomen, Iolanthe, Pirates, Trial by Jury, Patience, Princess Ida, Ruddigore, The Grand Duke,* and *Utopia.*'

[1] *The Sorcerer* and *H.M.S. Pinafore* were published by Metzler, now Cramer & Co. In 1888 Mr A. E. Bosworth, who was with Chappell's, was asked by Sullivan if he would go to the Continent, to be his agent there. Mr Bosworth set up in business in Leipzig, his principal object being to spread Sullivan's music in Europe; this was the foundation of the modern publishing firm of Bosworth & Co.

Mad Margaret—(LEFT), Jessie Bond in 1887; (RIGHT), Marjorie Eyre in 1932

The original 'Ruddygore': from the 'Illustrated Sporting and Dramatic News', 1887

1886-7

'RUDDIGORE'
and
'THE GOLDEN LEGEND'

How am I to get through this year's work? Do they think me a barrel-organ? They turn a handle and I disgorge music of any mood to order!

—SULLIVAN'S DIARY

AFTER *The Mikado*, Sir Arthur Sullivan was temperamentally disposed to rest on his comic-opera laurels, and to devote himself to a setting of Longfellow's *The Golden Legend* which he had promised the Leeds Festival for October, 1886, but at the opening of the year Mr Gilbert again proposed that they should work on the Lozenge Plot. Again it was rejected, but within a few days the indefatigable Gilbert dropped in at Sullivan's place with an alternative idea, an operatic version of the old-fashioned blood-and-thunder kind of stage melodrama. Gilbert could remember when this sort of thing was prevalent on the English stage—

"*Carses! carses on ye both!*"   "'*Umbly I take my leave.*"   "*I may, perchance, yet be in time.*'   "*Agony! agony! agony!*"

In 1886 it was still by no means uncommon; so Gilbert proposed to burlesque it—as when Sir Despard Murgatroyd, the wicked baronet of Ruddigore Castle, strides across the stage and the chorus of Bridesmaids fly from him in horror:

SIR DESPARD: Poor children, how they loathe me—me whose hands are certainly steeped in infamy, but whose heart is as the heart of a little child! But what *is* a poor baronet to do, when a whole picture gallery of ancestors step down from their frames and threaten him with an excruciating death if he hesitate to commit his daily crime? But ha! ha! I am even with them! (*Mysteriously*) I get my crime over the first thing in the morning, and then, ha! ha! for the rest of the day I do good—I do good—I do good! (*Melodramatically*) Two days since, I stole a child and built an orphan asylum. Yesterday I robbed a bank and endowed a bishopric. Today I carry off Rose Maybud and atone with a cathedral! This is what it is to be the sport and toy of a Picture Gallery! But I will be bitterly revenged upon them! I will give them all to the Nation, and nobody shall ever look upon their faces again!

This picture gallery idea was a throw-back to Gilbert's play *Ages Ago*, at the Royal Gallery of Illustration in 1868.[1] Its nostalgia must have appealed to Sullivan's sentimental soul, for was it not at a rehearsal of *Ages Ago* eighteen years previously that the now-famous partners had first met?—and now, in 1886, as they sat over the fire and talked for hours Sullivan and Gilbert agreed upon *Ruddygore*, as it was originally spelt.

Sullivan now received a letter from Potsdam, from the German Prince William (the Kaiser of the 1914 war). Referring to *The Mikado* in Berlin, the Prince regrets that an attack of severe earache will keep him at home in the palace but—'Today the first performance will be viewed by my parents and all my sisters whom I envy immensely their good fortune to see this charming piece. I often think of our nice evenings at Kiel and the charming musick on the yacht, which gave me the lucky opportunity of making your acquaintance.'

Later in the year the Prince attended a gala performance of *The Mikado*, and declared he was 'exhausted from laughing'.

Richard D'Oyly Carte was of course delighted that the Gilbert and Sullivan business had won such universal and distinguished patronage. In ten years it had made him very rich, but money was by no means the only satisfaction to a man of his artistic sensibility; having helped

A letter from the future Kaiser

[1] See p. 96.

to carry out a revolution in the English theatre he regarded himself as the guardian of its standards of good taste.

Letters that now passed between Carte and Helen Lenoir throw a charming and amusing light on their relationship. He told her he could not have done the business at all, at any rate on the same scale, without her help; and he now (1886) suggested a new arrangement by which he should pay Miss Lenoir £1,000 a year plus ten per cent commission on business in all theatres. It was a princely income for a working woman in Victorian times, and Miss Lenoir replied that it was too much.

Carte to Miss Lenoir:

Knowing your peculiar disposition as I do, I can quite understand your hesitation in receiving this amount. Probably most outsiders would think your line of conduct absolutely quixotic but I fully appreciate your motives. You object to receive more than you think you have fairly earned. I am quite willing to fall in with your views in this respect, I do not desire that you should be under any obligation to me.

He then suggested that the proposal should be referred to arbitration by a business acquaintance of them both. Unfortunately there is no record of the outcome of this remarkable proposal.

The venerable Franz Liszt was paying London a visit in 1886, and Sullivan as England's musical figure-head had to entertain him at a round of functions. And everywhere in Society Sullivan in his turn was shown-off by the elegant Mrs Ronalds—at race meetings in the spring, yachting at Cowes in the summer, at garden parties, at concerts and theatres she loved to parade her lion. Then one day Gilbert and D'Oyly Carte called at Sullivan's rooms to remind him of *Ruddygore*.

Sullivan's diary:

Gilbert attacked me for delay in new piece—gave it him back—finally arranged to defer production of new opera until September or October.

The new oratorio for Leeds was also promised for October, so all that summer Sullivan was composing the music for two utterly different works side by side. Regularly the postman brought the familiar packets of lyrics from Gilbert—

I know a youth who loves a little maid—
(Hey, but his face is a sight for to see!)
Silent is he, for he's modest and afraid—
(Hey, but he's timid as a youth can be!) . . .

and side by side came the instalments of libretto from Joseph Bennett who was arranging *The Golden Legend*:

In snow-white robes uprising,
The ghostly choirs respond,
And sadly and unceasing
The mournful voice sings on . . .

and soon at Leeds Town Hall the not-so-ghostly Yorkshire choirs in their snow-white

[289]

robes were responding to the beat of Sullivan's baton on that exciting evening when all his work on *The Golden Legend* came to its zenith, work which seems to have swept him off his feet in an intensity of composition, and relegated *Ruddygore* into a forlorn second-place.

Gilbert to Sullivan:

I congratulate you heartily on the success of the Cantata which appears from all accounts to be the biggest thing you've done . . . I don't expect you will want to turn to our work at once without any immediate rest, but if you do I can come up any day and go through the MS with you.

It had been a brilliant Leeds Festival. Sullivan was conductor-in-chief (at three hundred guineas); Dvořák was present to conduct his *St. Ludmila*, and Stanford's *The Revenge* was another new work conducted by its composer.

Stanford's diary:

I heard Humperdinck say to Sullivan after a very smooth reading of a new work that he supposed that there were many foreigners in the band, and Sullivan was able to answer 'Not one' with an amused and not untriumphant smile.[1]

The Golden Legend came at the end of the week, and capped all. 'How can we describe the scene which followed the last note of the cantata!' exclaimed the *Leeds Mercury*. 'Let the reader imagine an audience rising to its multitudinous feet in thundering approval; a chorus either cheering with heart and soul, or raining down flowers upon the lucky composer; and an orchestra coming out of their habitual calm to wax fervid in demonstration. Never was a more heartfelt ovation.'

In 1947 a member of that chorus wrote: 'It is many years since I sang in two Leeds Festivals (I am now eighty-five) and I shall never forget the thrill I got when Sullivan overtook me coming from a rehearsal and told me he wished me to lead the second sopranos! I felt it was a great honour from a great man as I was the youngest member of that grand chorus and had had very little training. After the performance of *The Golden Legend* Sullivan was very visibly affected when he asked the chorus and band to meet him in an anteroom at the Leeds Town Hall to hear his thanks and certainly many of us were on the point of tears. Linked with his musical talents were great charm of manner and a strong personality which we, in the North, thoroughly appreciated and loved. I remember when rehearsing 'The Fire Descends from Heaven', the male voices put so much stress on 'fire', pronouncing it in the usual robust North Country way, 'fy-yer', that Sullivan was very amused and begged them not to put quite so much 'yer' into it, at the same time showing just how it should be sung which vastly amused us all, including himself.'[2]

Another recollection:[3] 'My mother was a member of the Festival chorus. As a small

[1] Quoted in *Charles Villiers Stanford*, by Harry Plunket Greene (Arnold), 1935.

[2] Letter from Mrs F. Chapman, of Newmarket, written in 1947 after hearing the *Gilbert and Sullivan* BBC series.

[3] From Mrs E. R. Nelson, of West Wickham, Kent.

Mᴹᴱ ALBANI.   Mᴹᴱ PATEY.   Mᴿ SANTLEY.   SIR ARTHUR SULLIVAN.   ALFRED BROUGHTON CHORUS MASTER.

LEEDS MUSICAL FESTIVAL.

"THE GOLDEN LEGEND."

[FROM AN OCCASIONAL CORRESPONDENT.]

The Victoria Hall never presented a more animated appearance, no more eager, expectant audience ever gathered within its walls, and perhaps on no former occasion has the world-renowned "Leeds" chorus met together with stronger determination to achieve honour for itself, its work, and its conductor, than on the last morning of the Festival-week, 1886. Great as had been the triumphs in connection with noble works performed earlier in the week, it was felt on all hands that so far as the popular taste was concerned "The Golden Legend" would command an attendance and interest

Sullivan's Triumph: the correspondent of the 'Yorkshire Post' and the artist of the 'Illustrated London News' were among the many Press observers who treated this as a great event in music

[291]

girl I was taken to one of the rehearsals and was much intrigued by the Sullivan eyeglass which was constantly falling from its appointed place. Mother said that after conducting Bach's *Mass in B minor* at this Festival, Sullivan remarked that he would have given all he had ever written to have composed the "Sanctus" in that work.'

The music critics from London were unanimous about *The Golden Legend*. The *Daily Telegraph* said: 'A greater, more legitimate, and more undoubted triumph has not been achieved within my experience.' The *Musical World* remarked stiffly that it had hitherto been difficult to find a place in the foremost ranks of English music for the author of *The Pirates of Penzance* but now Sullivan's fame rested on 'a very different basis'.

The *World* went so far as to label Sullivan 'the Mozart of England'.

The *Times* said: 'The Leeds Festival may boast of having given life to a work which, if not one of genius in the strict sense of the word, is at least likely to survive till our long expected English Beethoven appears on the scene.' This has proved to be a shrewd judgment, for Sullivan's serious music lasted only until Elgar's over-mounted it. Yet it is interesting to know from Elgar's daughter, Carice Elgar-Blake, that 'My father always spoke with great feeling and respect for Sullivan, and admired *The Golden Legend*. He was also very fond of the Overture *Di Ballo*.'[1]

Another great English music-maker, Dame Ethel Smyth (1858 – 1944), tells of a personal friendship with Sullivan which was 'a perfect blend of chaff and seriousness (the exact perfection of cadence there is in his work) . . . One day he presented me with a copy of the full score of *The Golden Legend*, adding: "I think this is the best thing I've done, don't you?" and when truth compelled me to say that in my opinion *The Mikado* is his masterpiece, he cried out: "O you wretch!" But though he laughed I could see he was disappointed.'[2]

The hard verdict of posterity on Sullivan as a serious composer has been more recently expressed by Dr Ernest Walker in his *History of Music in England*: 'The sacred cantata *The Martyr of Antioch*, apart from a certain amount of a sort of mildly pleasant picturesqueness, alternates between dullness and vulgarity, and sometimes attains both at once; while the more ambitious oratorio *The Light of the World* has hardly enough vitality even to be vulgar . . . In *The Golden Legend* Sullivan no doubt pulled himself together to some extent . . . but for the best-known English composer in the very prime of life, and putting forth his full powers, *The Golden Legend* is, as a whole, a melancholy production.'[3] Dr Walker goes on to analyse Sullivan's artistic character and concludes that he lacked steadiness of artistic purpose.[4]

[1] Letter from Mrs Elgar-Blake to the author.
[2] *Impressions that Remained*, by Dame Ethel Smyth (Longmans, Green), 1923.
[3] *A History of Music in England*, by Dr Ernest Walker (Milford), 1924.
[4] Dr Percy Scholes has pointed out in his invaluable reference book *The Mirror of Music* that whereas there were seventeen performances of *The Golden Legend* by British choral societies in the season 1886–7, this had fallen to six in 1926–7. I find that in 1949–50 there were two performances.—L.B.

What posterity should remember about Sullivan is that although his serious music has lost prestige until the passing years have brought it a dusty oblivion, in the nineteenth century it did help the musical awakening of masses of English people; that is why it was eulogized in terms that now seem extravagant. Present-day standards cannot be applied to the Victorian world. '*The Golden Legend* brought up purely English art to a level never before dreamed of,' said a lecturer at the Musical Association, Dr Charles Maclean, in 1902.

MR GEORGE GROSSMITH AS ROBIN OAKAPPLE.

As the year 1886 drew to its close *The Golden Legend* had musical England by the ears, and Sullivan was sought to conduct it whilst at the same time rehearsing *Ruddygore* at the Savoy Theatre. The first performance of the comic opera there was postponed until 22 January, 1887. A week before this date, Sullivan finished the score. On 19 January, *The Mikado* had its last performance, an extra-hilarious one ('pranks were played', says one newspaper report, 'that might have made the Mikado's hair stand on end had it not been too tightly braided to do so.') This left the theatre free for three days of final rehearsals for *Ruddygore*, ending usually around five a.m. The tricky business of bringing the portraits of the Ancestors to life in Act 2 ('A baronial hall'), and the multiplicity of costumes and uniforms of the period 1810, made this opera one of the most difficult productions Gilbert had ever attempted. The uniforms of twenty British regiments were represented and Gilbert had them all inspected for accuracy by Sir Arthur Herbert, Deputy Quartermaster of the British Army. One little problem was that of making Sullivan's baton visible when the stage was blacked-out for the Ancestors' reincarnation. Phosphorescent paint proving unsuccessful, a glass tube baton containing a platinum wire which glowed a dull red was devised.[1]

MR RICHARD TEMPLE - AS SIR RODERICK MURGATROYD

Durward Lely, who played the part of Richard Dauntless, a young jack-tar, tells us:[2] '*Ruddygore* was in many respects a new departure. There were many gems in the musical numbers, some of them, as, for instance, "The Ghosts' High Noon" (admirably sung by Dick Temple) being worthy of grand opera at its best. When the music was played to us at rehearsal Gilbert happened to be sitting

[1] The *Siemens Magazine* (Siemens Bros, Woolwich), 1927.

[2] Unpublished reminiscences of Durward Lely, communicated by his son Cyril A. Lely.

Note: The sketches on this page and overleaf are from the *Illustrated Sporting and Dramatic News*, February 5, 1887.

by me, and Sullivan played the "Parlez-voo" song, saying "This is yours, Lely" . . .'

I shipped, d'ye see, in a Revenue sloop,
    And, off Cape Finistere,
        A merchantman we see,
        A Frenchman, going free,
So we made for the bold Mounseer,
            D'ye see?
We made for the bold Mounseer.
But she proved to be a Frigate—and she up with her ports,
    And fires with a thirty-two!
        It come uncommon near,
        But we answered with a cheer,
    Which paralysed the Parley-voo,
            D'ye see?
    Which paralysed the Parley-voo!

Lely continues: 'I remarked quite unthinkingly to Gilbert: "It seems to me that Dick should follow that breezy song with a sailor's hornpipe", and thought no more about it. Next day Gilbert asked me without any preface, "Look here, Lely, can you dance a sailor's hornpipe?" and like the man when asked if he could play the fiddle, I replied, "I don't know, I never tried." I soon found out; Paul Valentine (the maître de ballet at Drury Lane) after putting me through several steps one morning in his studio, said, "Yes, tell Mr Gilbert that you can dance a hornpipe all right." No sooner said than done. Sullivan wrote a hornpipe—really the old stereotyped sailor's hornpipe musically inverted—and I set to work to learn the ten or twelve steps. It was the success of the opening night. The "Parlez-voo" went well but the dance that followed brought down the house. I understand that the tenors touring in the provinces cursed me, as they all had to go through the hornpipe whether they could dance or not. Courtice Pounds (my understudy) had no trouble as he was a beautiful dancer, but of some of the others perhaps it is better to be discreet and say nothing.'

The first night of *Ruddygore* was not a great success. The theatre was packed as usual with the cream of Society. In the centre of the stalls were Lord and Lady Randolph Churchill (parents of Winston, then a boy of twelve). The Lord Mayor of London was in the royal box. Whistler, Millais, and Leighton were among the eminent artists who came, dramatists like Burnand and Pinero, lawyers like Sir Charles Russell, and famous ladies such as Madame Albani. Some of the audience started whispering that the title of the new opera was not quite nice. Then as the plot unfolded they were plunged to-and-fro between the heat of enthusiasm for its frequently brilliant and charming scenes, and the cold bath of disappointment at its lapses into familiar Gilbertianisms. The *Illustrated Sporting and Dramatic News* rudely dubbed the piece a resurrection pie: 'The joint we have enjoyed hot from the spit may still be relished when presented cold with pickles. But when we find it persistently served up again, now spiced with curry, now hashed with sauce, our palled palate revolts at it.'

The end of the second act dragged. Rutland Barrington, who played the wicked baronet, Sir Despard Murgatroyd, says: 'There is no getting away from the fact that it was, for the Savoy, a very stormy first night, some of the malcontents in the gallery shouting "Take it away—give us back *The Mikado*"; in spite of which, however, it achieved a run of some twelve months, a thing that many modern managers would consider quite good enough.'[1]

When Sullivan and Gilbert met next day for an 'inquest' on the opera, and read through a pile of Press criticisms, they decided to remodel Act 2, and to change the title. The *Graphic* said: 'The sterner and less mealy-mouthed sex, safe in the club smoking-room, might pass such a name with a smile. But it is different in the case of ladies, to whom Savoy operas largely appeal, and on whose lips such a title would scarcely sound pretty.'

The sub-title of the opera is *The Witch's Curse*. The stage mechanism went wrong on the first night. Then the criticisms of the malcontents in the gallery and of the prudes in the parlour gave the opera a poor start. Yet fifty years later, in 1937, the *Manchester Guardian* declared: 'It is incomprehensible that *Ruddigore* should ever have been considered less attractive than the other comic operas in the Savoy series. The libretto gives us Gilbert at his wittiest, and in the music we hear Sullivan not only in his most tuneful vein but also a master of more subtle rhythms than he commands

[1] *Rutland Barrington*, by Himself (Grant Richards).

A mixed reception for the new opera

elsewhere'—an opinion not universally agreed, but one nevertheless which shows that there is more worth in this opera than appeared in 1887 when it seemed indeed to be under a curse—and that curse bedevilled anew the relationship of Sullivan and Gilbert. The *Weekly Dispatch* man at the first performance wrote: 'Somewhat more than half the success which *Ruddygore* is certain to attain will be due to the music.' It must have galled Mr Gilbert to find that such praise as there was went to Sir Arthur, not because Gilbert denied the merit of the music but because he thought it was the wrong sort of music for this comic opera.

'My own impression,' he wrote, 'is that the first act led everyone to believe that the piece was going to be bright and cheery throughout, and that the audience were not prepared for the solemnity of the ghost music. That music seems to my uninstructed ear to be very fine indeed, but—out of place in a comic opera. It is as though one inserted fifty lines of *Paradise Lost* into a farcical comedy. I had hoped that the scene would have been treated more humorously by Sullivan, but I fancy he thought his professional position demanded something grander and more impressive than the words suggested. I am not trying to shift the responsibility of failure onto his shoulders, for I think the dead weight of it should rest on mine.'[1]

More trouble for this unlucky opera came from Paris. *Figaro* announced that the 'Parlez-voo' song was an insult to the French Navy and nation. Gilbert replied with a friendly letter to the newspaper, pointing out that his mockery was without malice, it was meant genially, in the same way as the terms 'rosbif' and 'goddam' were used in French burlesques to ridicule 'les Anglais'.

Another mishap was a serious illness which struck down George Grossmith within a week of the opening night. The understudy who was called upon to step into the great Grossmith's shoes was Henry Lytton. The audience was 'disappointed and chilling' when it found an unknown stripling in the part of Robin Oakapple.[2] But the charm of Lytton won them over, and the evening ended with an ovation. Gilbert gave Lytton a gold-mounted walking stick as a memento. He also gave the young man a lecture. Lytton was hurrying one of his speeches when the great man pulled him up: 'That speech is now a short speech, but originally it consisted of three pages of closely-written manuscript. I condensed and condensed. Every word I could I removed until it was of the length you find it today. Each word that is left serves some purpose—there is not one word too many. So when you know that it took me three months to perfect that one speech, I am sure you will not hurry it. Try to remember that throughout your career in these operas.'

As to the criticisms of the title, Gilbert first suggested changing it to *Kensington Gore; or, Robin and Richard were Two Pretty Men*, but Sullivan and Carte disagreed. Then Gilbert

---

[1] Letter from Gilbert quoted in *A Sporting and Dramatic Career*, by Alfred E. T. Watson (Macmillan), 1918.

[2] See *The Secrets of a Savoyard*, by Henry A. Lytton (Jarrolds).

'*That is one of our blameless dances . . .*'

'*Ruddigore*' *as the cartoonists saw it: in* '*The Queen*', *1887, an artist sketches Jessie Bond and Rutland Barrington; in* '*The Tatler*', *1924, Nerman gives an impression of Eileen Sharp and Leo Sheffield in the same roles*

turned up at the Savoy and declared that it should be *Kensington Gore; or, Not so Good as The Mikado*. To Gilbert ruddy gore meant simply red blood, and he was irritated that his innocent attempt to mock the hyperbole of theatrical melodrama should be mistaken for the language of a Billingsgate fish-porter; one of his best witticisms was provoked when he met a friend soon after the first night:

FRIEND: How is *Bloodygore* going on?

GILBERT: It isn't *Bloodygore*, it's *Ruddygore*.

FRIEND: Oh, it's the same thing.

GILBERT: Is it? Then I suppose you'll take it that if I say 'I admire your ruddy countenance,' I mean 'I like your bloody cheek!'

Finally, it was decided merely to alter one letter, but this involved printing a new edition (the third) of the libretto, *Ruddigore*, in place of those that Chappell's had on sale with the offending word *Ruddygore* throughout. The first edition is now a rarity: a copy in the archives at the Savoy contains extensive alterations in Gilbert's handwriting towards the end of Act 2. These were put into effect, Sullivan scored a new Finale in twenty-four hours, and *Ruddigore* pulled itself together as an effective entertainment.

> 1 Queen's Mansions,
> Victoria Street, S.W.

Dear Jessie,

The Prince of Wales is coming here on Sunday night. Please come and help me entertain him. I think if you do the duet from Ruddigore with Barrington it would be very funny. I have seen Barrington this morning and he agrees with me. Come, like a dear child, and settle with him tonight about getting the dress from the wardrobe. Please don't say a word to anyone at the theatre.

> Yours affectionately,
> ARTHUR SULLIVAN

P.S.—You can dress and undress in my bedroom.[1]

So Jessie Bond as Mad Margaret and Rutland Barrington as Sir Despard, both dressed in sober and penitent black, performed for the Prince that deliciously prim song and dance:

> I once was a very abandoned person—
> Making the most of evil chances.
> Nobody could conceive a worse 'un—
> Even in all the old romances.
> I blush for my wild extravagances,
> But be so kind
> To bear in mind,
> We were the victims of circumstances!
> *(Dance)*
> That is one of our blameless dances.

Looking back on his life in later years, Gilbert regarded *Ruddigore* with special affection. He even thought it one of his best libretti, 'but I gave it an unfortunate name', he said.[2] Of course, he had a passion for the sea, and this burlesque, set in the Cornish fishing village of Rederring, is full of sea-going types and sea-faring metaphor, like Richard's 'I'm a poor man-o'-war's man, becalmed in the doldrums'. Then, he felt he had succeeded in his main object, to burlesque heavy melodrama—in other words, to burlesque a burlesque, which is always a risky thing to attempt. The opera certainly contains a few of Gilbert's most dramatic effects, and some delicious lyrics and happy tunes. But the troubles with writing and staging it had betrayed a lack of unity behind the scenes. *Ruddigore*, in fact, had shown that with ten operas to their

[1] Letter in the collection of Mr Reginald Allen, of New York.
[2] To Mr Willmott Houselander, of London (letter to the author).

The fishing village of Rederring in Cornwall—'Ruddigore' with scenery and dresses newly designed by Peter Goffin in 1948

credit the partners were now at the cross-roads. Gilbert had blunt opinions about 'what the public wants'. He put them on record:

> The dramatic author is in the position of a caterer, who has to supply one dish of which all members of every class of society are invited to partake. If he supplies nothing but *crème de volaille*, he may please the epicure in the stalls, but he will surely irritate the costermonger in the gallery. If he supplies nothing but baked sheep's heads, the costermonger will be delighted, but the epicure will be disgusted. Probably, the dish that will be acceptable to the largest number of every class is rump steak and oyster sauce, which is, after all, a capital thing in its way, and may be taken as a type of the class of piece which is most likely to succeed. It does not call for a very high order of merit on the part of the chef, but it requires a good deal of practical skill nevertheless.[1]

Sullivan was hankering to show how well he could cook *crème de volaille*, yet his own mode of life held him back. Joseph Bennett, librettist of the oratorio which had triumphed at Leeds, writes: 'With the production of *The Golden Legend* in 1886 my friendship with Sullivan reached its climax. From that time till his death there was a gradual declension . . . As far as I was responsible for this state of things, I attributed

[1] *New York Tribune* interview, August, 1885.

it in part to disappointment naturally felt at Sullivan's failure to go on to the "higher things" of which he spoke. I saw him immersed in West End life, which is never healthy for an artist; I saw him, as I thought, striving for such poor honours as the Turf can bestow; in these pursuits wasting time which was precious not only to himself but to the nation. Moreover, I felt that gifts so exalted as his were not turned to best account in the writing of comic operas, however popular and charming, and all this must have tinged my public remarks upon him with a feeling which a man so sensitive would quickly discern. Thus it came to pass that, without the slightest quarrel, we fell slowly apart.'[1]

So Sullivan's world got out of joint. He gave up his conductorship of the Philharmonic Orchestra, which he had held for two years, and wrote to Grove:

I loved my orchestra, and was proud of our performances, but I was obliged to let it go. In the first place, it tied me down too much—to be compelled to be in London for four or five consecutive months in the year doesn't at all suit my restless nature. Second, although I look tough enough I am not strong, and I used to worry and fret about things—either a passage wouldn't come out as I thought it ought to, or if it did after much pains the beastly Press would swear at or ignore all we had done. I found it was a hopeless, uphill fight with the Press. I thought I would let someone else have a try . . . I expect Mrs Ronalds back today. I will give her your love. Bless you.[2]

In the gloomy chill of an English February, Sullivan packed his bags and left his frustrations behind him—he fled to the South of France, to the sunshine and the casinos. He was thrilled by an earthquake at Monte Carlo, and by an invitation to conduct *The Golden Legend* at a gala performance in Berlin. What a triumph, that his work—his serious work—should be thus chosen to celebrate Kaiser William I's ninetieth birthday! But Sullivan could not escape from comic opera—even at Potsdam.

Sullivan's diary:

Berlin, 12 April, 1887. Being Princess Victoria's birthday, I took her a basket of roses at ten. Met the Kaiser and Royal Family standing on a landing listening to the Kaiser Frantz regimental band playing *The Mikado* in the courtyard. Prince of Saxe-Meiningen sent for the bandmaster (Otto John) and introduced him to me. After them came the band of the Cuirassiers and also played *The Mikado*, same selection!

When he returned to England, to the blazing summer of Queen Victoria's Jubilee, he was asked by his friend the Prince of Wales to compose an Ode for one of the many functions celebrating 'the fiftieth year of a reign prosperous and glorious beyond any recorded in the annals of England'.[3] This was very much to Sir Arthur Sullivan's taste. The success of *The Golden Legend* had restored his musical self-esteem. He sat down to

[1] *Forty Years of Music*, by Joseph Bennett. Bennett was the music critic of the *Daily Telegraph*.
[2] Letter in the possession of Mrs C. Garrett Smith.
[3] *The Times*.

write the Jubilee Ode; all 'trivial' music was put out of his thoughts. And then came a cold awakening.

Dear Carte,

I'm coming up to town on Thursday next. Can I see you then? Try to get Sullivan to meet us. He ought to attend to business a little.

Very truly yours,
W.S.G.

One day Carte and Gilbert came driving down to Sullivan's rooms in a cab. They wished to see him about a successor to *Ruddigore*—and Gilbert suggested the Lozenge! . . . with modifications, to be sure, so that Sullivan wearily agreed to 'a sort of provisional compromise' whereby Gilbert was to write part of the Lozenge Opera and if it still proved unacceptable 'no more should be said about it'.

During four months the collaborators saw nothing of one another. Gilbert was in his study sorting out his Lozenges. The Queen was in her parlour, telling the Prince to thank Sir Arthur for his 'delightful Ode'. It had been pompously performed while she laid the foundation stone of the Imperial Institute, South Kensington. Then, as the Jubilee summer waned, Gilbert took Sullivan into his study one evening after dinner and read the newly revised scenario.

Sullivan's diary:

It is a puppet show, and not human. It is impossible to feel any sympathy with a single person. I don't see my way to setting it in its present form.

This cutting, found among Sullivan's papers when he died, is typical of opinions which had fanned his self-discontent; it is from the 'Magazine of Music's comment on 'The Mikado'

All the music, indeed, is so pleasing that some may think it hyper-critical if we venture to question whether Sir Arthur Sullivan is quite doing justice to himself by continuing to write in this style. There is, of course, no doubt that it pays, while symphonies *don't*; but there is also no doubt that enduring fame and a place among the great composers cannot be gained by a long course of setting verses of refined burlesque to music pretty and graceful, but of a character that must of necessity be ephemeral.

The Savoy Company's annual picnic up the Thames, recreated in the film 'The Story of Gilbert and Sullivan' (1953). Gilbert, played by Robert Morley, is in festive mood conducting the singing on the foremost steamer

1888

'THE YEOMEN OF THE GUARD'

THE YEOMEN OF THE SAVOY.

Tower Warders,

Under orders,

Gallant pikemen, valiant sworders!

IT WAS A WARM September afternoon. The prows of three handsome river steamers cut the mirrored surface of the Thames in the neighbourhood of Maidenhead, in those lovely reaches of the river where the woods of Cliveden descend to touch the water's edge. Elaborately over-dressed men and women lolling in punts and skiffs along the banks looked up at the approaching steamers with surprise as the sound of singing voices drifted across the water; very beautiful voices they were, too, and surprise gave way to delight as the steamers drew level and the singers were recognized as the stars of the Savoy, and then the excitement of the spectators burst all bounds of decorum as they spotted, one in each of the three vessels, the legendary figures of Mr Gilbert, Mr Carte, and Sir Arthur Sullivan, all sporting cigars, and exceedingly genial. The vessels stopped; the Savoyards scrambled ashore and there in the woods, from Mr Grossmith to the call boy, they fell upon the salmon and the lobster salad and pigeon pies (catering by Carte).

These periodic river picnics were a happy means whereby the Savoy Company celebrated its success and indulged in a general sociability.

'Coming home by moonlight,' says Mr Barrington, 'we sang all the choruses and concerted music from the different operas, and the effect was perfectly delightful, drawing quite large houses at the different locks we passed through.'[1]

Boisterous witticisms were shouted from boat to boat. Mr Gilbert conducted a Limerick competition:

> There was a young lady from Malta
> Who strung up her aunt with a halter.
> She said: 'I won't bury her,
> She'll feed my fox terrier,
> And keep for a month if I salt her.'

Sir Arthur, taking a turn at the steering, dropped his eyeglass and nearly ran down a punt. 'Sorry!' he exclaimed. 'I always thought I was rather a good contrapuntalist'.

It was all very amiable. Nothing to show even the Savoy players that their chiefs had disagreed, that no new opera was being written to follow *Ruddigore*.

When it was at length announced that the next production would be a mere revival of *H.M.S. Pinafore* people looked at one another and shook their heads. So the partnership was ended . . .? Rehearsals began; it was noticed that the partners saw little of one another. Each looked after his own side of things. Gilbert took immense pains, redesigning sets and dresses, making models, and with characteristic economy warning Carte not to buy lanyards for the jack tars from the usual theatrical suppliers because he (Gilbert) had found an old salt 'who will knot them elaborately, thirty-eight of them, for two shillings each'. Such instructions he sent in dozens of letters to the Savoy. He chose a new scene-painter:

Gilbert to Carte:

   I think Emden will be the best person to employ to do the whole thing—he paints well enough. Bruce Smith says that if *he* don't paint the whole scene people will think he can't paint—well, people will be right—he can't.

It seemed almost unbelievable that Sullivan and Gilbert were unable to find a new opera. It seemed especially tragic in the late eighties because there was a strong feeling of well-being, of achievement, strength, progress, in all walks of British life at this time: it was the high summer of the Victorian era, preceding the decline and decadence of the nineties. A picture of national well-being had been focused before the public by the Jubilee celebrations, and not merely by the drums and bands, the prancing parades, the stirring sight of the old Queen emerging from her retirement and mourning; people looked around further and realized to what power and influence Britain had grown during this reign. In 1888 the British had recently occupied rich Burma

---

[1] *Rutland Barrington* by Himself (Grant Richards).

and Egypt; even from remote Tibet came news of the red-coats capturing native forts. India and Africa had been 'opened up'. Kipling and Kitchener were the new symbols of Imperialism. At home 'the development of railways, steam navigation, and electricity in its various practical uses is the work of our own time', said a *Times* leader, 'and the men who have done that work are among the ornaments of the Victorian age. The immense extension of industry and spread of trade could not have been possible without the aid of science.' Such a rampant industrialism had impelled Britain to look across the oceans for new sources of raw materials, and new markets for her products. 'Trade follows the flag,' they said. Not since the reign of Queen Elizabeth had there been such an expansionist feeling. The modern Drakes and Raleighs were now empire-builders like Cecil Rhodes in South Africa, and the engineers driving the Canadian Pacific Railway through the Rockies to the Pacific. As in Elizabethan England, the Victorians were proud of their poets and artists. Browning, Tennyson, R.L.S., still lived and wrote. As for music, Sullivan himself declared in an address at Birmingham Town Hall that England was now at the entry of the Promised Land. He recalled that for nearly two hundred years Britain had lost its leading world-position in music. 'My belief is that this was largely due to the enthusiasm with which commerce was pursued, and to the extraordinary way in which religious and political struggles, and, later still, practical science, have absorbed our energies . . . Now, however, the condition of things is changing—it *has* changed. And yet I cannot but feel that we are only at the entry of the Promised Land. Habits of mind and modes of action are still to be found which show that we have much to do before we become the musical people that we were in the remoter ages of our history.'

Arthur Sullivan had the satisfaction now of reading in a leading article in *The Times*: 'The middle classes and even the working classes, which had no opportunity of appreciating either art or music fifty years ago, cannot now complain that these whole-some enjoyments are monopolized by a fashionable aristocracy.' Gilbert and Sullivan had been notably connected with the spreading of 'wholesome enjoyments' . . . what a sad pity that they should fail in their collaboration at this glorious hour. Rider Haggard, cashing-in on the mysterious spell of Africa, had just had great success with his novels *King Solomon's Mines* and *She;* Conan Doyle had just invented Sherlock Holmes (*A Study in Scarlet*—1887); and the Gaiety Theatre in the Strand was thronged every night for *Dorothy* (music by Alfred Cellier, words by B. C. Stephenson). Some people said that this light opera marked the eclipse of Gilbert and Sullivan.

It is amusing to find that soon after Sullivan had so flatly rejected the revised Lozenge, Gilbert revived at the Savoy his old Lozenge play-without-music *The Wicked World*, the prototype of all his excursions into Lozengery! On 4 July, 1888, the Savoy Theatre presented 'A special morning performance of Mr W. S. Gilbert's original fairy comedy *The Wicked World*, the first time for fifteen years, in aid of the funds of the Victoria Hospital for Children.' George Alexander, Lionel Brough, and Julia Neilson were in

Sketch from Gilbert's Notebook

the cast. This single charity performance of Gilbert's pet Lozenge play no doubt gave him some meagre satisfaction, but the fact that Sullivan would now have nothing to do with setting any such theme to music gave him none.

Mr Gilbert was very sensitive of their failure. One day, waiting for a train on Uxbridge station, he found himself staring at a poster of the Tower Furnishing Company, depicting the Tower of London. What a wonderful title for an opera—*The Tower of London* . . . As he climbed into the London train Gilbert dwelt on its possibilities. 'I thought a beefeater would make a good picturesque central figure for another Savoy opera, and my intention was to give it a modern setting, with the characteristics and development of burlesque—to make it another *Sorcerer*. But then I decided to make it a romantic and dramatic piece, and to put it back into Elizabethan times.'[1]

The Tudor period was one for which Gilbert felt an affinity, and so did Sullivan. The decision against burlesque may have been influenced by a paragraph in the *Sporting Times*:

A *real* comic opera, dealing with neither topsy-turveydom nor fairies, but a genuine dramatic story, would be a greater novelty and a more splendid success than anything we are at all likely to see during the present dramatic season.

Perhaps the time *was* ripe for such a thing, thought Gilbert, and when he arrived in London that day he went to the Savoy for a rehearsal of *Pinafore*, and as he walked on the stage he bumped into Sullivan.

Sullivan's diary:

Gilbert told me that he had given up the subject over which there had been so much dispute (charm and clock-work) and had found another about the Tower of London, an entirely new departure. Much relieved.

Gilbert went home that day and started writing the opera he called *The Tower Warden*. Meanwhile, the revival of *Pinafore* brought a letter to Sullivan from Captain (later Admiral) Lord Charles Beresford:

From 'Illustrated London News', 1888

[1] Interview with Gilbert, the *Daily Mail*, 30 October, 1906.

Admiralty
14/12/87.

My dear Arthur,

I was perfectly delighted with *Pinafore* last night, quite excellent. You told me to tell you anything I saw which offended the eye of an expert. I do it, don't be X. They are minor details but make the difference in perfection and not absolute perfection.

1. All the men's trousers are VERY BAD, they don't fit, and appear to be made of drill or calico, and not plain honest scrubbed duck which always fits and sets well.

2. The ratlings want squaring and for good effect ought to be squared every night or morning after a performance.

3. One or two of the blue-jackets' stripes and badges ought to be put on higher up the arm and not in the joint of the elbow, most are in the right place.

4. Your marines are far too young in appearance, and tend to depreciate the most valuable and splendid corps. (The Stage has an enormous amount of Sentiment attached to it, which should be guided the right way.)

5. Manning yards VERY BAD. Men should stand up and look proud of themselves, heels together, and hands interlocked across each other on the life line.

6. Rigging should be set up tauter.

These are a few details, the rest is quite excellent.

Yours ever,
CHARLIE

After all his care on production, Gilbert might have been annoyed that such a letter was sent to Sullivan, but his own letters at this period show that now he was writing the new opera he was not in a fratchety mood. He was enjoying the work.

39 Harrington Gardens,
South Kensington.
12 Dec., 1887.

Dear S.,

I've got the plot of the new piece pretty well combed out—and I'm glad to hear you can dine with us on Wednesday, as we can go carefully into the matter after dinner. It is quite a consistent and effective story, without anachronisms or bathos of any kind, and I hope you will like it.

Yours very truly,
W. S. GILBERT

After hearing the plot Sullivan confided to his diary that he was immensely pleased: 'No topsy-turveydom, very human, and funny also.' Now preparations went ahead like a house afire. All through the first half of 1888 Gilbert was absorbed in his story of Jack Point, the tragi-comic jester in whom undoubtedly we may read more of W.S.G.

THE SOCIETY CLOWN

George Grossmith

himself than he put into any other of the creatures of his imagination:

> I've wisdom from the East and from the West,
>   That's subject to no academic rule;
> You may find it in the jeering of a jest,
>   Or distil it from the folly of a fool.
> I can teach you with a quip, if I've a mind;
>   I can trick you into learning with a laugh;
> Oh, winnow all my folly, and you'll find
>   A grain or two of truth among the chaff!

For the first time in his operas, Gilbert was not tilting at any British institution in *The Tower Warden*. It was a tale of how Jack Point and his sweetheart Elsie went as strolling players to the Tower, and there the jester lost his sweetheart to Colonel Fairfax. The single scene for both acts was Tower Green. A prominent artist, Percy Anderson, was employed to design the costumes (some of his designs may be seen at the Victoria and Albert Museum, London), but this did not prevent Gilbert sketching out the basic ideas.

Gilbert to Carte:

Elsie should change her dress to something like a wedding dress at the end of the piece. It should not be a wedding dress of a modern type (of course), but a dress of Henry VIII time that will suggest something of a matrimonial nature to the spectator. White silk or satin, and white bows, and a wreath of white flowers would do—but kept 'bourgeoise' in cut. I hope I make myself clear.

To keep the Savoy Theatre open while the new opera was in preparation, *Pinafore* was followed by reappearances of *The Pirates of Penzance* and *The Mikado*. 'Mr D'Oyly Carte's revival of *The Pirates of Penzance* was in every way a brilliant success,' reported a gossip-writer in the *Theatre*. 'Arthur Sullivan, alas! was not in his accustomed place, as usual upon such occasions, at the conductor's desk. His state of health has been unsatisfactory for some time past; when I last heard of him he was at Monte Carlo, just about to start for Algiers in search of still more warmth and a yet drier air.'

Sullivan took with him some of the new lyrics of the Tower of London opera. Gilbert, weaving his tapestry of sixteenth-century England with words more serious and poetic than he had ever used before, was to be seen walking about the Tower day after day, absorbing the atmosphere of the old fortress . . .

> The screw may twist and the rack may turn,
> And men may bleed and men may burn,
> O'er London town and its golden hoard
> I keep my silent watch and ward . . .

Such words hardly belong to comic opera. But Gilbert was bewitched by the period of the Tudors; he was writing in the spirit of the Tudor poets. He believed that the new libretto would satisfy Sullivan's musicianly yearning for 'better things'. And now, at this unlikely moment, came a letter from Monte Carlo which rocked the partnership. It provoked the following masterly reply:

Gilbert to Sullivan:

> I can't, for the life of me, understand the reasons that urge you to abandon a theatre and a company that have worked so well for us, and for whom we have worked so well . . . Why in the world we are to throw up the sponge and begin all over again because *Dorothy* has run 500 nights beats my comprehension. The piece that we are engaged upon has been constructed by me with direct reference to the Savoy Company. Every member of it has been fitted to the ground, and now that the piece is half finished you propose to scatter the Company, abandon the theatre, and start anew with a new company in (I suppose) a new theatre . . .
>
> We have the best theatre, the best company, the best composer, and (though I say it) the best librettist in England working together—we are world-known, and as much an institution as Westminster Abbey—and to scatter this splendid organization because *Dorothy* has run 500 nights is, to my way of thinking, to give up a gold mine. What is *Dorothy's* success to us? It is not even the same class of piece as ours. Is no piece but ours to run 500 or 600 nights? Did other companies dissolve because *Mikado* ran 650 nights?

It has been assumed from this, in previous books on Gilbert and Sullivan, that the composer had made a sudden unexpected decision to abandon light music. Letters now made available put a different complexion on the story. They show that the success of Alfred Cellier's comic opera *Dorothy* at the Gaiety Theatre had shaken not only Sullivan but D'Oyly Carte, and that these two had worked out a plan to lift Gilbert and Sullivan opera on to a new level, to which the *Yeomen* was a stepping stone. 'Grander' Gilbert and Sullivan—this was their answer to *Dorothy*.

Dorothy was a musical play which could beat the Savoyards at their old game, judging by the box office. It was now piling up hundreds of performances at the Gaiety, and even threatening to beat the record of *The Mikado*. It was an opera of undoubted charm, with a bewitching young leading lady—Marie Tempest, who was destined to become one of the great adornments of the English stage, but for once Mr Gilbert's eye for discovering new talent had failed him:

Carte to Sullivan:

> Gilbert has been to *Dorothy* to see Miss Tempest at my request. I was quite

satisfied to engage her, as I proposed to you in my letter to Naples, for a limited or at any rate for an undefined period. However, G having seen her has only confirmed his former objection to her and does not like her at all. He says that she 'screeches'.

In the provincial tour of *Dorothy* the leading lady was Lucy Carr Shaw, sister of George Bernard Shaw, the music critic of a new halfpenny newspaper, the *Star*. She also played in Gilbert and Sullivan opera in the provinces.

Eventually *Dorothy* achieved 931 performances at the Gaiety: more than any Savoy opera. Sullivan's reaction was that because other men were now exploiting a field which had been his own, the time had come for him to leave it altogether. But Carte had a different strategy; he persuaded Sullivan, just before he went to the Riviera, that rather than give up comic opera they should beat their own standards (and *Dorothy's*) by taking, or even building, a larger, more sumptuous theatre, recruiting an even better company, and 'making a fresh start', as he had put it to Sullivan on 13 February, 1888:

> If you wish the scheme to go through you will not delay writing to Gilbert at once and putting your views with that decisive clearness which is always at your command. If I do not speedily let the Savoy to a good tenant, or sell it, our scheme cannot I fear go through at all. Gilbert is not fully reconciled to the plan, but he is I think in that frame of mind in which your letter would probably decide him in favour of it.
>
> My speaking of not letting other people get ahead of us, and of a certain other theatre, and a certain other opera, and company, was evidently distasteful to Gilbert, as indeed it must be to us, yet I cannot but think that it does good. We have to take unpleasant medicine sometimes.

The unpleasant medicine was *Dorothy*. It is clear from this that Carte had already consulted Gilbert, but his judgment on Gilbert's receptive frame of mind proved wrong. The emphatic reply by Gilbert already quoted, in which he compared the Savoy Company as a world-wide institution to Westminster Abbey, settled the issue for the time being: Carte and Sullivan obviously could not go on with their new scheme without Gilbert. But it was only for the time being.

Why did Gilbert back down so stiffly? His was a sensible conclusion, that they need not put up the shutters at the Savoy merely because of the success of *Dorothy*, but it was expressed somewhat huffily in the letter to Sullivan ('I can't, for the life of me, understand the reasons', etc.). Could it be that, finding Sullivan and Carte with their heads together, Gilbert was annoyed?—it could very well be so, for we now know that Sullivan's letter from Monte Carlo setting out the new scheme arrived at a most unfortunate moment when Gilbert was indulging in a row with Carte over quite another matter. These are the facts. By a misunderstanding Gilbert came late to a rehearsal of *The Pirates of Penzance* revival at the Savoy; as a result the entire company and orchestra were kept hanging about for an hour, and when the author arrived he was in an ill-humour, and publicly scolded Carte in a way which (the Manager complained) 'you might adopt if I were either incompetent or had not the interest of the theatre at heart'. Gilbert retorted that Carte was 'dictatorial'. They set about each other angrily—by post. Carte telegraphed to Sullivan, now at Marseilles:

Serious row on with author don't really see how things are to go on. You must stick to me. Present revival artistic success but no money don't believe any other revival will be much better only chance of running present establishment seems to be rush on new piece. If this is impracticable must try to let theatre.

And two days later:

Row made up all is peace for the moment will write do stay at Monte Carlo till I come.

The storm had blown over—but it had shown strains in the old Triple Alliance, tending to isolate Gilbert. Three weeks later the close friendship of Sullivan and D'Oyly Carte was underlined when they returned to London for the event thus noted in Sullivan's diary:

April 12, 1888—Went to Savoy Chapel at 11.30 to be best man to D'Oyly, who married Helen Cowper-Black, otherwise Lenoir.

Richard D'Oyly Carte's first wife had died three years previously. With his ex-secretary Helen, partner now in his life as in his business, he set up a new London home at 4 Adelphi Terrace. Ever in the advance guard of every movement for the civilized and sophisticated amenities of life, Mr Carte installed a lift—a rarity in a private house—and he invited his artist friend Whistler to help decorate the new home. Whistler painted the entire billiard room the colour of the billiard cloth! There was one evening later when Whistler had just returned from Paris and he dined at 4 Adelphi Terrace; peremptorily, he waved away the sauce, then checked himself with: 'My dear D'Oyly, I forgot I was in your house. I always refuse sauces at other English houses!' With the chefs of his nearby Savoy Hotel at his beck and call, Mr D'Oyly Carte was setting up new gastronomic standards in the hotels of London, with the same flair for the good and the profitable as he had applied to new artistic standards in her theatres.

Arthur Sullivan, still unmarried, was caught up in the social round of London with Mrs Ronalds. Sir Henry Wood writes: 'I often saw him at Mrs Ronalds' Sunday afternoon musical At Homes where I shared duties of accompanist with Wilhelm Ganz and Henry Bird. At her house in Cadogan Square every artist of the day was to be seen; indeed, it was a *rendezvous* for musicians of every nationality.'[1]

Sullivan sat for his portrait to the fashionable Sir John Millais (it hangs now in the National Portrait Gallery, London). Fat royalties from *The Mikado*'s success all over the world paid for Sir Arthur's generous entertainment of his friends, and his flutters on the racecourse. A letter to him from a diplomat at the British Embassy in Berlin

[1] *My Life of Music*, by Henry J. Wood (Gollancz).

describes a State banquet given there to a visiting Japanese Prince at which the band struck up a selection from *The Mikado*: 'At the first sound Prince William held up his glass to me and we emptied a bumper to the air of "Taken to a county gaol"—not quite appropriate, but no matter. However, having done this by me I suppose the Prince suddenly recollected that he had toasted the wrong man first, for he smiled over to the Japanese Prince and down went another bumper to the tune of "Miya sama".'

Then the Duke of Edinburgh, sailing in the Mediterranean on a British battleship, sent to his friend Sullivan a decoration which the Sultan of Turkey had asked him to forward to Sir Arthur as a mark of His Imperial Majesty's pleasure in the Sullivan music played by the Sultan's band at Constantinople—'notably selections from your operettas'.

And then in May came the wonderful occasion of a performance of *The Golden Legend* at the Albert Hall, by command of the Queen. Wonderful . . . 10,000 people rising in the vast auditorium and turning to the royal box as Sullivan conducted the National Anthem . . . more wonderful as the oratorio rose to its climax, and Sullivan bowed and bowed again to the applause of his public and of his Queen. Still more wonderful, as he hurried to the royal presence and heard Her Majesty say: 'At last I have heard *The Golden Legend*, Sir Arthur! You ought to write a grand opera—you would do it so well.'

Sullivan's Diary

1888 31 Days   8 TUESDAY [129–237]   **74**
May

Grand Performance of the "Golden Legend" at the Albert Hall
by command of the Queen who was present. Very good
performance. Afterwards the Queen sent for me & expressed her
great pleasure at having heard the work. Her first words were
"at last I have heard the Gold: Legend, Sir Arthur!" Later she
said "you ought to write a grand opera — you would do it so
well". Her Majesty was very gracious & kind. Afterwards
I took a flying view of the "new gallery", opened today.
Dined at No 7. Received a telegram from Empress Victoria
& P'ss Victoria wishing they could be present at the Gold: Legend.
Dined back of the performance.

A wonderful day in Sullivan's life, and a significant one in the story of Gilbert and Sullivan, for to Sir Arthur that royal remark was as good as a command. Long ago Rachel Scott-Russell had urged him to write grand opera . . . then Grove . . . now the Queen. He determined to set himself to the task.

But meanwhile Mr Gilbert came with the completed libretto of the new Tower of London opera round to Sullivan's rooms, and they went through it together. Gilbert was unusually anxious to placate his partner. Extensive alterations were made to improve what Sullivan called 'the musical

The original Shadbolt and Phoebe
(Mr Denny and Miss Bond)

requirements'. Inspecting W.S.G.'s first manuscript, we find several lyrics which never got so far as to be set to music. There is a Rabelaisian ditty—or shall we say a song in the appropriate spirit of Bluff King Hal—originally intended for the King's jailor at the Tower, Wilfred Shadbolt, which might have raised an eyebrow in the Victorian theatre had Gilbert not on second thoughts deleted it . . . Shadbolt sings to Phoebe:

> The kerchief on your neck of snow
> I look on as a deadly foe—
> It goeth where I may not go,
>   And stops there all day long!
> The belt that holds you in its grasp
> Is, to my peace of mind, a rasp!
> It claspeth what I cannot clasp
>   (Correct me if I'm wrong).

> The bird that breakfasts at your lip—
> I would I had him in my grip,
> He sippeth where I may not sip,
>   I can't get over that!
> The cat you fondle, soft and sly,
> He lieth where I may not lie!
> We're not on terms, that cat and I!
>   I do not like that cat!

[313]

How painstaking Gilbert was, and how anxious to help Sullivan, is shown when he posts to Sullivan a lyric in alternative rhythms: the meaning of each verse is the same, but he leaves Sullivan to set the one he prefers—

Trio (alternative metres)

1st Verse (Leonard)

A headless bridegroom why refuse?
    If truth the poets tell
Most bridegrooms, ere they marry, lose
    Both head & heart as well.

or

What matter, though
    His head should fall
His trifling blow
    Need not appal
Most men who wed,
    So poets tell,
Have lost both head
    And heart as well.

Sullivan preferred the verse on the left. It appears in the final opera in the delightful trio 'Temptation, oh, temptation'.

The music of *The Yeomen of the Guard* was composed at Fleet in Hampshire. Concurrently, Sullivan was writing incidental music for *Macbeth*, to be produced at Christmas at the Lyceum by Henry Irving, and from the Leeds Festival Committee he now received a letter reiterating their suggestion that he should write a symphony. This was yet another prick to his musical conscience. He told his secretary to reply that his 'inclination' was to write a symphony, but his engagements were so heavy that at present he could not commit himself. He put all the art he knew into *The Tower Warden* which had several changes of name:

Gilbert to Sullivan:

The more I think of it the more convinced I am that *The Beefeater* is the name for the new piece. It is a good, sturdy, solid name, conjuring up picturesque associations.

During rehearsals the title was changed again to *The Yeomen of the Guard*, or *The Merryman and his Maid*, and as the opera was carefully prepared it became clear to all that the astounding Sullivan and Gilbert had found a remarkable way out of their former discontents.

Sullivan proved himself more than able to catch the Tudor spirit in his music. The exquisite madrigal 'Strange Adventure' might well belong to that age when Henry VIII could despatch a wife to the axe at one moment and write a madrigal at the next, that age of mingled beauty and brutality; this strange combination of opposite sensitivities is well expressed in *The Yeomen of the Guard*. Grim words these are that Gilbert wrote,

Colonel Fairfax (played by John Dean) and the Tower Warders

but the beauty of Sullivan's melody and harmony gives them a pathetic spell that haunts the ear . . .

> Strange adventure! Maiden wedded
> To a groom she's never seen—
> Never, never, never seen!
> Groom about to be beheaded,
> In an hour on Tower Green!
> Tower, Tower, Tower Green!
> Groom in dreary dungeon lying,
> Groom as good as dead, or dying,
> For a pretty maiden sighing—
> Pretty maid of seventeen!
> Seven-seven-seventeen!

Here at last was the 'human element' that Sullivan had been craving for, over so many years. But there were still frictions . . .

Sullivan's diary:

August 16: I attended rehearsal of chorus (new opera) for 1st time, Savoy. Haughty letter from Gilbert declining to reconstruct his piece, etc. Wrote him back a snorter and asked whether the rehearsals were to be continued as I wouldn't set the piece as it was.

August 21: Rehearsal at Savoy. Gilbert there, mild and conciliatory. All arranged satisfactorily.

The accompanist at the Savoy Theatre rehearsals was young Henry J. Wood, later to become the famous Sir Henry of the Proms. 'The Yeomen of the Guard', he tells us, 'was Sullivan's own favourite opera. He told me he thought it his best. I remember how worried he was over "I have a Song to Sing-o". I played several versions of it, none of which satisfied Gilbert, rhythmically, from the point of view of his lyric.'[1]

It was over this song that Sullivan went to Gilbert and admitted for the first time in their partnership that he was stumped.

'You've often told me,' he said, 'that when writing your lyrics you sometimes have an old tune in your head which gives you the rhythm. I've always asked you not to tell me the tune, or I shouldn't be able to get it out of my mind, but this time I'm stuck. Was there any tune that prompted you to write "I have a song to sing-o"?'

Yes, said Gilbert; he had heard the sailors on board his yacht singing shanties in the dog-watch, and had been struck by the curious style of one which he believed to be a corruption of an old Cornish carol:

> Come and I will sing to you—
> What will you sing to me?
> I will sing you one, O!
> What is your one, O!
> One of them is all alone,
> And ever will remain so . . .

Gilbert hummed the shanty to Sullivan, and thus gave him the 'feel' of it. Sullivan went away and wrote a new tune to Gilbert's words:

> I have a song to sing, O!
> Sing me your song, O!

with a lingering refrain which became the 'theme-tune' of this opera:

From 'Illustrated London News', 1888

> Heighdy! heighdy!
> Misery me, lackadaydee!
> He sipped no sup, and he craved no crumb,
> As he sighed for the love of a ladye.

[1] *My Life of Music*, by Henry J. Wood (Gollancz).

When the curtain came down on the first performance Sullivan went home and wrote in his diary:

> Crammed house—usual enthusiastic reception. I was awfully nervous and continued so until the duet 'Heighday' which settled the fate of the opera. Its success was tremendous, three times encored! After that everything went on wheels, and I think its success is even greater than *The Mikado*. Nine encores.

But more than once during the last rehearsals it had looked as though there would never be a *Yeomen*.

Sullivan's diary:

> 28 September. Full rehearsal, band and voices at the theatre. Had a regular flare-up with Gilbert between the parts. He worried everyone and irritated me beyond bearing—in one of his worst moods. I can't stand it any longer, and get as angry and irritable as he is. Eventually we made it up.

Gilbert's irritability was due, apart from gout, to his increasing anxiety as the first night approached about the seriousness of the opera; he feared they had over-stepped the mark with its tragic element.

On 3 October, 1888, the day of the first performance, Gilbert wrote a letter in the morning to Sullivan, placing on record his conviction that unless certain further alterations were made the success of the first act would be most seriously imperilled. He was desperately worried because the first five numbers in the opera, beginning with Phoebe's song at her spinning wheel, were in turn tearful, serious, grim, sentimental, and again sentimental in character—this in a 'professedly comic opera'. Shortly before the rise of the curtain Sullivan and Gilbert met at the theatre, and one of the sentimental songs (for Meryll) was cut out. Says Jessie Bond, who played Phoebe: 'We were all suffering from nerves and wondering how things would go. As I had the additional ordeal of having to open the opera alone I was probably as nervous as anyone. Before the curtain went up I sat down by my spinning wheel ready to sing "When Maiden Loves". Gilbert rushed on very agitated. "Is everything right, Jessie?" he asked. "Is everything right?"

'I told him it was and off he went. Within a few seconds he was back again.

' "Are you sure you're all right, Jessie?"

' "Yes, yes!" I stammered, anxious only to be left to myself. "I'm *quite* all right!"

'With that he kissed me, danced about the stage in a sort of panicky excitement, and vanished again. But once more he came on, and there were more kisses, more dances, and more inquiries. All this time we could hear the orchestra on the other side of the curtain and knew that the overture must soon be finished. The fussing interference became intolerable. At last I simply had to insist that he should leave me. "Please go, Mr Gilbert," I demanded, "Please go." In another minute he had left the theatre and my song had begun.'[1]

[1] Article by Jessie Bond, 'Behind the scenes at the Savoy', the *Gilbert and Sullivan Journal*.

And the opera opened on the note of innovation it was to hold to the end: Phoebe
alone on the stage, singing a plaintive song
as she spins—

When maiden loves, she sits and sighs,
  She wanders to and fro;
Unbidden tear-drops fill her eyes,
And to all questions she replies
  With a sad 'heigho!'
'Tis but a little word—'heigho!'
So soft, 'tis scarcely heard—'heigho!'
  An idle breath—
  Yet life and death
May hang upon a maid's 'heigho!'

From 'Illustrated London News', 1888

Gilbert spent that evening watching a rival show, a pageant-play of the Elizabethan period called *The Armada* at Drury Lane Theatre, but he walked down to the Savoy in time to take his curtain call with Sullivan. Next day he anxiously examined the Press notices.

Gilbert to Sullivan:
    The notices have been very gratifying. H—— sneers at me, of course. But then I never lose a chance of sneering at him.

Sullivan was delighted when the *Theatre* pronounced his latest music to be 'of a higher form' than hitherto. Gilbert was furious when *Punch* accused him of stealing the plot from *Maritana*.

One of the Old Guard at the Savoy, Rutland Barrington, was notably missing from *The Yeomen of the Guard*; he had decided to go in for stage-play production and had prevailed upon Gilbert to write him a 'straight' play, *Brantinghame Hall*. Gilbert did more—he brought to Barrington, at the St James's Theatre, the latest of his discoveries, Julia Neilson, a lovely upstanding girl with red-gold hair, twenty years of age. So convinced was Gilbert of her talent that he dedicated the play to her, but it was torn to pieces by the critics, whereupon Gilbert fell on them in wrath:

    You have crushed the hope out of the life of a poor girl who, paralysed with nervousness, was appealing practically for the first time in her life to the men who were to decide her destiny.
    I am determined not to expose myself again to your insolent jibes. I have written my last play.[1]

[1] Letter in the collection of Mr Reginald Allen, of New York.

In spite of these exclamations, Julia Neilson survived to adorn the English stage for sixty years.[1] And Gilbert wrote another play or two. But Barrington went back to the Savoy as soon as he could.

Rhoda Maitland was the heroine of an exciting incident at Manchester in 1888. Miss Maitland—now Mrs Bull, and over eighty—sends us these reminiscences:

'I took the leading soprano parts in the No. 1 touring D'Oyly Carte company, which visited all the big towns in Great Britain. Actually, there were two

The original Dame Carruthers, Housekeeper at the Tower —Rosina Brandram

companies, to cover the North and South. I went up to Manchester to watch the Northern company open *The Yeomen* in 1888, prior to our beginning the Southern tour at Bristol. My job at Manchester was simply to watch, but on the second night a printed slip was inserted in the programmes:

'Miss Cockburn, being unfortunately seriously ill today, is quite unable to appear tonight. Miss Rhoda Maitland has kindly undertaken to go through the part of Elsie Maynard to the best of her ability, at very short notice, and the kind indulgence of the audience is requested for her under these circumstances. This being only the second night of the production on tour of *The Yeomen of the Guard*, it will be seen that it is impossible that any substitute could have been sufficiently rehearsed.

R. D'OYLY CARTE

'At nine a.m. that day Mr Carte had come rushing round to my hotel and said: "Will you play Elsie tonight? The place is sold out. Will you save us?" I declared I didn't yet know the part. He advised me not to attempt to learn it; he said I could carry the book on the stage and quite openly read it. I told him to leave it to me. All that day I rehearsed. When the curtain went up I saw Mr and Mrs Carte in a box, as white as death. I don't know how I did it, but I didn't have to refer to the book at all. At the final curtain the stage was full of people shouting and shrieking, the audience was on its feet, and my dressing-room was filled with flowers and champagne. I called

[1] Julia Neilson, b. 1868, married Fred Terry; Dennis Neilson-Terry was their son, Phyllis their daughter. In 1948 Julia Neilson, then eighty years of age, wrote to the author her 'congratulations and appreciation' of the radio *Gilbert and Sullivan* series. *See also* p. 452.

THREE GENERATIONS OF ELSIES
Geraldine Ulmar, the creator of the character, 1888, in centre; Ruth Vincent, in the London production of 1897 (ON LEFT); and Helen Roberts, 1948, in the costume redesigned by Peter Goffin

the chorus down and told them to help themselves. As for me, I went straight back to the hotel, tired out.

'After this I played Elsie hundreds of times. It became my favourite part. My Jack Point, in the Southern company, was Henry Lytton—and Jack Point was *his* favourite part.'

One of those curious controversies which have grown up around the Savoy Operas—forming a sort of folk lore over which many books are written and many debates are held in the stalls and gallery—concerns the question whether Gilbert intended *The Yeomen of the Guard* to be a thorough-going tragedy. At the end of the opera there is a final stage direction: 'Fairfax embraces Elsie as Point falls insensible at their feet.' What did Gilbert mean by insensible? A swoon or a death? According to Rhoda Maitland, confirmed by Henry Lytton,[1] the original jester, George Grossmith deliberately toned-down this tragic ending. He was so much the accepted funny man of his day that the public might have laughed at a stark ending—or been mystified. But younger actors, in the provincial companies, could take a bolder line. Both George Thorne, in the above Manchester production, and Henry Lytton, in the Southern company, were young men with no established reputations to keep up like Grossmith. Lytton tried out a more tragic version of the part at Bath. Rhoda Maitland was Elsie that night.

[1] See *The Secrets of a Savoyard*, by Sir Henry A. Lytton (Jarrolds).

JACK POINT

as differently portrayed by George Grossmith (LEFT)—the comic; George Thorne (RIGHT)—the pathetic; and (CENTRE) Henry Lytton, here seen with Rhoda Maitland in 1888

Courtice Pounds as 'Fairfax'　　　*Richard Temple as 'Sergeant Meryll'*

'And how poignant it was,' she says. 'I always cried at the end of the *Yeomen* because Lytton, robbed of the love of his lady, stumbled and fell and kissed the hem of my dress . . . his hand in mine, he kissed every one of the ribbons round my dress, made the sign of his blessing, and then lay dead. It was a wonderful piece of acting. But the stage manager was horrified by this departure from the London version; he wired to D'Oyly Carte: LYTTON IMPOSSIBLE FOR POINT. WHAT SHALL I DO? Mr Carte came down to Bath, saw the performance, and approved, and later when Lytton asked the author's opinion on the death scene Gilbert replied: "It is just what I want. Jack Point should die and the end of the opera should be a tragedy." '

This approval of tragedy may appear oddly inconsistent of W. S. Gilbert, who had been so fearful of the seriousness of the opera on its London first night!—but it is confirmed by a statement sent to the author of this book by Mr Rupert D'Oyly Carte, pointing out that Gilbert was so impressed by Henry Lytton's 'new' interpretation of Jack Point that when *The Yeomen* was revived in 1897 he altered the finale of the opera from the song of a merrymaid 'who laughed aloud' to one 'who dropped a tear'. A small point, perhaps, but one which shows that Gilbert's apparent inconsistency was really an ability to revise his judgment in the light of experience; and experience showed that the public would accept a tragic ending.

Courtice Pounds, the original Colonel Fairfax, has revealed[1] that Sullivan had three shots at setting music to 'Is Life a Boon?' The first time Gilbert said: 'I know nothing about music, but it seems to me the wrong tune for an Elizabethan lyric.' The second time Gilbert still objected, 'puckering his brow and puffing out his cheeks', but Sullivan refused to write it again. Gilbert insisted, and Sullivan gave in, with the result that has charmed generations of theatre-goers.

'I know nothing about music' . . . Sullivan knew Gilbert well enough to take this with reserve. He told his biographer, Arthur Lawrence: 'When anyone assumes a tone of lofty superiority, and boasts that he knows nothing about music, and pretends not to be able to distinguish one tune from another, you may either accept his statement with a considerable amount of reserve, or conclude that there is something wrong in his physical or mental faculties, and recommend him to consult an aurist.'

In his old age Gilbert was tackled on the point by William Archer:[2]

GILBERT: I suppose I may claim a fairly accurate ear for rhythm, but I have little or no ear for a tune.

ARCHER: But you are not, like Dr Johnson or Charles Lamb, incapable of distinguishing one tune from another—or like Dean Stanley (was it not), who took off his hat when the band played 'Rule Britannia,' under the impression that it was 'God Save the Queen?'

GILBERT: Oh, no, I am not so bad as that. On the contrary, I am very fond of music up to a certain point. I care more for the song than for the singer—for the melody than for the execution. I would rather hear 'Annie Laurie' sung with feeling, than the greatest singer in the world declaiming a scene from *Tristan und Isolde*. I used to be exceedingly fond of the light French and Italian operas that were popular in my youth and that are never heard now—*Don Pasquale, Fra Diavolo, La Sonnambula, La Figlia del Reggimento,* and *L'Elisir d'Amore*. I believe they might be popular again if they were neatly translated and well done.

There was nothing wrong with Gilbert's mental faculties, and in fact his knowledge of music, at any rate in the light operatic field, was much greater than he let people believe. An example of this occurred soon after the launching of *The Yeomen*, when Carte ventured to re-open with Gilbert his scheme for moving to a new theatre. They were now back on friendly terms. Carte had written to a prospective tenant for the Savoy Theatre: 'I have commenced the building of my new theatre and am going ahead at full speed. If Gilbert and Sullivan agree with me to transfer our entertainment to my

[1] Interview in *Northern Daily Telegraph*, 1925.
[2] *Real Conversations*, by William Archer.

W. S. Gilbert's original manuscript of 'Is Life a Boon?'

new theatre I shall be in a position to let the Savoy. I think there is very little doubt that we shall arrange to move to the new theatre.'

But Gilbert again refused. He suggested instead that he should rearrange some of Offenbach's operas, to be presented at Carte's new theatre under his personal supervision. His correspondence displays a keen appreciation of the light French and Italian operas which had been popular in his youth.

Carte was not keen on this idea, and it fell through.

Sullivan and Gilbert, it was agreed, must stay at the Savoy. But what to do with Carte's new theatre, now that his original proposal for a more grandiose Gilbert and Sullivan presentation there was ruled out?

*Henry Lytton and Bertha Lewis as the Duke and Duchess of Plaza-Toro in the
nineteen-twenties*

1889

THE 'CIPHER' QUARREL
AND
'THE GONDOLIERS'

You ought to write a grand opera, Sir Arthur
—you would do it so well.
—QUEEN VICTORIA

SULLIVAN HAD NOT forgotten the Queen's advice. Nor had Richard D'Oyly Carte. It was Carte who now gave Sullivan the opportunity to achieve his heart's desire. He conceived an ambition to do for grand opera what the Savoy had done for comic opera: the opportunity presented itself behind a forest of builder's scaffolding in Shaftesbury Avenue, London. Carte decided to call his new theatre the Royal English Opera House. He invited Sullivan to compose a grand opera for its opening. But who was to write the words? Sullivan sent an invitation to his old collaborator, Gilbert. The ensuing correspondence shows that Gilbert took a very sensible, realistic view. He argued that grand opera would afford him no chance of doing his best work because his greatest successes had been those comic operas which were the most reckless and irresponsible:

> Personally I prefer a consistent subject—such a subject as the *Yeomen* is far more congenial to my taste than the burlesque of *Iolanthe* or the *Mikado*—but I think we should be risking everything in writing more seriously still. We have a name, jointly, for humorous work, tempered with occasional glimpses of earnest drama. I think we should do unwisely if we left, altogether, the path which we have trodden together so long and so successfully.

Gilbert warned Sullivan in this letter: 'I don't believe in Carte's new theatre. The site is not popular, and cannot become popular for some years to come.'

As things turned out, Gilbert was right.

Gilbert next suggested that Sullivan should get a serious librettist like Julian Sturgis to collaborate on the grand opera (which he did) and that simultaneously Sullivan should write a new comic opera with W.S.G.: he was quite capable of doing the two things at the same time. Sullivan's answer to this compliment was that he had now lost all taste for comic opera, at any rate with the stock Gilbertian company of characters: 'It is not too much to say it is distasteful to me.'

When Gilbert called at Sullivan's rooms on 9 January, 1889, Sullivan repeated that he wanted to tackle 'a dramatic work on a larger musical scale' and that 'the music must occupy a more important position than in our other pieces'. They continued the argument by post. Gilbert wrote to Sullivan:

> The success of *The Yeomen*—which is a step in the direction of serious opera—has not been so convincing as to warrant us in assuming that the public want something more earnest still.

Sullivan to Gilbert:

> I confess that the indifference of the public to *The Yeomen of the Guard* has disappointed me greatly, as I looked upon its success as opening out a large field for works of a more serious and romantic character. If the result means a return to our former style of piece I must say at once, and with deep regret, that I cannot do it. I have lost the liking for writing comic opera.

Sullivan went off to France with the Prince of Wales during this correspondence, and in the casinos, hotels, and sunshine of the Riviera he was having a 'right-down regular royal time' while Gilbert was trying to cope in London with trouble at the Savoy, where the principals were getting big ideas and the company was tending to break up. George Grossmith was planning to go back to his one-time job of piano-entertainer (and with his Savoy-won fame he did so to the tune of earning £10,000 in seven months).[1] Barrington had left the company. Temple and Ulmar wished to go, Bond was demanding more money. It is quite clear that Sullivan did not really wish to dissolve his partnership with Gilbert, for he now suggested that the tendency of the stock company to break up offered them a chance to restart their partnership on new lines. But in the course of correspondence Gilbert touched Sullivan on a sore spot: 'The librettist of a grand opera is always swamped in the composer,' complained Gilbert. This set a spark to the fire.

Sullivan to Gilbert:

> You say that in a serious opera you must more or less sacrifice yourself. I say that this is just what I have been doing in all our joint pieces, and, what is more, must continue to do in comic opera to make it successful . . . Hence the reason of my wishing to do a work where the music is to be the first consideration—where words are to suggest music, not govern it, and where music will intensify and emphasize the emotional effect of the words. Now is there any 'modus vivendi' by which my requirements can be met . . .?

[1] Grossmith's salary at the Savoy Theatre had been about £2,000 a year, big money in those days.

Gilbert to Sullivan:

If you are really under the astounding impression that you have been effacing yourself during the last twelve years—and if you are in earnest when you say that you wish to write an opera with me in which 'the music shall be the first considera-tion' (by which I understand an opera in which the libretto, and consequently the librettist, must occupy a subordinate place) there is most certainly no 'modus vivendi' to be found that shall be satisfactory to both of us. You are an adept in your profession, and I am an adept at mine. If we meet, it must be as master and master—not as master and servant.

THE GONDOLIERS: *Act* I

Sullivan was in Venice (unwittingly absorbing atmosphere for the next opera, *The Gondoliers*) when this outburst reached him and—very significantly—his immediate reaction was to write to his friend D'Oyly Carte at the Savoy Theatre. This letter is still in the archives at the Savoy. It reads:

There is one point in Gilbert's letter on which I cordially agree with him: 'If we meet it must be as master and master and not as master and servant'. If in the future this could be carried out it would probably smooth many a difficulty and remove a great deal of unnecessary friction, for excepting during the vocal rehearsals and the two orchestral rehearsals I am a cipher in the theatre.

A cipher. This was the fatal word. This put the fat right into the fire, for Carte immediately took a cab to Harrington Gardens and showed the letter to Gilbert. Previously Gilbert had alleged that Sullivan 'interfered' at rehearsals. Sullivan's letter from Venice now retorted that the trouble was that Gilbert's methods at rehearsal wasted everybody's time and 'ruined' Sullivan's music. This had got to stop, said Sullivan, and if he was to work any more in any way with Gilbert he must have more share in arranging the stage presentation, the attitudes and business, of the musical parts of the operas:

They are Gilbert's pieces with music added by me. You can hardly wonder that twelve years of this has a little tired me and that unless a change in the construction of the piece and in the manner of rehearsing and producing it is made I should wish to give it up altogether . . . You had better bring the substance of this letter to Gilbert's notice. If he thinks all I say unreasonable there is an end of the matter. If he is disposed to meet my views in all these matters we can see about a new piece at once. I write to you because I hate quarrelling with old friends and I should certainly say something unfortunate if I wrote to Gilbert.

When Carte showed this to Gilbert the first draft of *The Gondoliers* was already in the plot-book: W.S.G. had been working on it for the past ten days. Now he shut up his plot-book and informed Sullivan (by post) that the letter to Carte:

. . . teemed with unreasonable demands and utterly groundless accusations, the very least of which, if it had the smallest basis of truth, would suffice to disqualify me absolutely from collaboration with you . . . You say that our operas are Gilbert's pieces with music added by you, and that Carte can hardly wonder that twelve years of this has tired you. I say that when you deliberately assert that for twelve years you, incomparably the greatest English musician of the age—a man whose genius is a proverb wherever the English tongue is spoken—a man who can deal 'en prince' with operatic managers, singers, music publishers and musical societies—when you, who hold this unparalleled position deliberately state that you have submitted silently and uncomplainingly for twelve years to be extinguished, ignored, set aside, rebuffed, and generally effaced by your librettist, you grievously reflect, not upon him, but upon yourself and the noble Art of which you are so eminent a professor.

The trouble with Sullivan and Gilbert was that their personal characteristics tended to fly off the wheel of their merry-go-round at opposite tangents. But there was a greater magnetic force which held them on it. The cynic might define this force by saying that they knew where the money lay (in the box office at the Savoy, and a thousand similar box offices all over the world); but a closer examination shows that they had a genuine appreciation of each other's gifts, and it was this—sheer good horse-sense plus admiration—with which for many years they covered up their disharmony and built upon it that world of harmony, the Savoy Operas. The estrangement of 1889 lasted for many weeks, but in the letters which continued to fly to and fro there was a growing desire on both sides to find a friendly way out. Courtice Pounds, who overheard Gilbert talking about the trouble to Brandon Thomas, has left it on record[1] that his grievances seemed to be more against D'Oyly Carte than against

[1] In the *Strand Magazine*, December, 1925.

Clara Dow as Gianetta during revivals before the first World War
(RIGHT) *Jessie Bond, the original Tessa*

Sullivan. Gilbert and Carte were not happy partners, whereas Carte and Sullivan were bosom pals. And it seems likely that Gilbert resented Carte's grand opera house scheme as having thoroughly and finally unsettled Sullivan.

When the heat of anger subsided, Gilbert remembered Sullivan's argument that the break-up of the Savoy Theatre company gave the chance for a break-away from conventional stock parts. He was himself having a disagreement with Jessie Bond about her salary. She writes: 'Gilbert snapped out that he was tired to death of artists who thought that they were responsible for the success of the operas, and that he intended to put a stop to the whole thing. "We'll have an opera," he exclaimed, rather angrily, "in which there will be no principal parts. No character shall stand out more prominently than another." Surely enough, when *The Gondoliers* was written a little later, we discovered that it contained more than the usual number of big parts. In case we missed the significance of that, he gave the two gondoliers their duet which told that "all shall equal be".'[1]

The quarrel between Gilbert and Sullivan was healed at a meeting on 9 May, 1889, when Sullivan's diary records that they 'shook hands and buried the hatchet'. This meeting is said by Dr Goldberg[2] to have taken place at Mrs Ronalds' house in Cadogan Place, on what evidence is not clear. A letter written a fortnight previously from Carte

[1] 'Memories of an Old Savoyard', by Jessie Bond, *John O' London's Weekly*, 7 December, 1929.
[2] *The Story of Gilbert and Sullivan*, by Isaac Goldberg (Crown, New York), 1935.

[331]

to Gilbert, and not hitherto published, shows that it was D'Oyly Carte who played the peace-maker:

I went to Paris to see Sullivan and came back with him and after much conversation and negotiations the position is now this. Sullivan is prepared to write with you at once another comic opera for the Savoy on the old lines, if you are willing also . . . His aspirations in another direction (*the grand opera*) being satisfied, he will be, and is, the more ready to write a piece of the character we have hitherto found so successful. I think too that he really wishes to keep up the old collaboration, as I do. At one time as you know I was desirous of transferring the whole thing to the new theatre but as you objected I gave up the idea, and have today declined an offer of £5,000 a year for the Savoy. Sullivan says he is ready to start work energetically as soon as you give him the material.

Sullivan agreed to write comic opera and grand opera at the same time. But he still insisted that in comic opera his music must be more prominent; the opening of *The Gondoliers* is a continuous cascade of music for some eighteen minutes, unbroken by dialogue, music which brilliantly builds up the atmosphere and plot of that exuberant scene on the Piazzetta at Venice in 1750; and throughout the opera Sullivan's contribution is by no means subordinate, it is not 'music added by me'.

The Gondoliers is a joyous opera, happy, kindly, exuberant, the sweet fruit of reconciliation after the bitter quarrel. And in it there is almost a reflection of the Gilbert–Sullivan personal situation, for in *The Gondoliers* there appear two humble gondoliers

The original gondoliers—Rutland Barrington, a portly Giuseppe, and Courtice Pounds as Marco
[*Cartoon from 'Illustrated Sporting and Dramatic News'*]

of Venice, Marco and Giuseppe, one of whom is 'no less a personage than the only son of the late King of Barataria' but until the end of the opera we don't know which is which . . . so 'I have arranged that you will reign jointly,' says the Grand Inquisitor, Don Alhambra del Bolero, 'so that no question can arise hereafter as to the validity of your acts.'

'As one individual?' asks Marco.

'As one individual,' confirms Don Alhambra.

Marco and Giuseppe link arms and strike a pose: 'Like this?'

'Something like that.'

And it was something like that in real life. The relationship of Sullivan and Gilbert became in the next year a deliberate show of equality; they were more 'one individual' than they had been for years.

'Once upon a time there were two Kings'
—'*Punch*'

It was a very human twist of Sullivan's psychology that as soon as he was actually writing a grand opera for the Royal English Opera House —Sir Walter Scott's *Ivanhoe* was now chosen as the subject—back came his old dash and zest for comic opera at the Savoy. There is no attempt in *The Gondoliers* to follow up the more solemn pretensions of *The Yeomen of the Guard*. *The Gondoliers* is a happy return to the gay-hearted spirit of true comic opera, the spirit in which Sullivan and Gilbert had set the pace with *Trial by Jury* long ago.

Gilbert to Sullivan:

Don't you think we ought to mark Grossmith's departure by a present of some kind? He is a d——d bad actor, but he has worked very hard for us, and has endeavoured in every way to meet our wishes during the thirteen years of his engagement. If we presented him with (say) a piece of plate, value about £50, it would be a graceful recognition of his unvarying zeal and good will.

Some time later, when G.G. was giving his songs-at-the-piano show at Torquay, W.S.G. tried to entice him back to the Savoy, not without sarcasm: 'You shall have a thousand a week and then the entire receipts', he vowed! Grossmith never came back to the Savoy company, but Rutland Barrington did, in *The Gondoliers*.

Gilbert to Jessie Bond:

I am distressed to learn that you decline to renew under £30 a week—distressed because, though nobody alive has a higher appreciation of your value as a most accomplished artist than I, no consideration would induce me to consent to such a rise. While I do not forget how much of the success of our pieces has been due to you, you must not forget how much of your success has been due to the parts written for you by Sullivan and myself—you have been most carefully measured by both of us, and, I think you will admit, not unsuccessfully. Finally, it would distress me greatly to lose you after so many years' association, undisturbed, as far as I am concerned, by a single unpleasantness, but I cannot let personal regard and esteem blind me to the fact that my partners have to be considered.

'The fact remains,' says Jessie Bond, 'that Gilbert did have to reconsider the matter, and very annoyed he was, so much so that when I came for the next rehearsal he shouted for everyone to hear: "Make way for the high-salaried artist." '[1]

Sir Arthur Pinero once said: 'A peculiarity of Gilbert's, exquisite humorist as he was, was that he was apt to be exceedingly tetchy, even over trifles, in matters affecting his personal dignity . . . On one occasion he was accosted in the foyer of a theatre by a well-known amateur, a Mr H. Such Granville. "Excuse me, Mr Gilbert," said the gentleman, "excuse me for speaking to you without an introduction. You may have heard of me—my name is Such, but I act as Granville." "Oh, do you," retorted Gilbert, resenting the liberty, "then I wish your name was Granville and you acted as such." This encounter took place at the Garrick Theatre. Gilbert built the Garrick as a speculation, and leased it to his friend John Hare. To the dismay of everybody concerned, when the digging of the foundation had reached a certain depth a copious spring was discovered, and for a while it was feared that the building could not be proceeded with. "Well," said Gilbert, with more philosophy than he usually displayed, "at least we shall be able to let the fishing." '[2]

The Garrick was opened in 1889, the year of *The Gondoliers*.

One of several newcomers to the Savoy company for *The Gondoliers* was delicious Decima Moore, who had never been on the stage before and made her first entry as Casilda—

> *Flourish. A gondola arrives at the Piazzetta steps, from which enter the Duke of Plazo-Toro, the Duchess, their daughter Casilda, and their attendant Luiz, who carries a drum. All are dressed in pompous but old and faded clothes.*

DUKE: From the sunny Spanish shore,
            The Duke of Plaza-Tor'—
DUCHESS: And His Grace's Duchess true—
CASILDA: And His Grace's daughter, too—
LUIZ: And His Grace's private drum
            To Venetia's shores have come:
ALL: If ever, ever, ever
            They get back to Spain,
            They will never, never, never
            Cross the sea again—

[1] Article in *John O' London's Weekly*.
[2] Article by Sir Arthur W. Pinero in *T.P.'s Weekly*, 27 April, 1929.

Decima Moore, now Lady Moore-Guggisberg, C.B.E.,[1] sends the following notes for this book:

'My earliest recollection of Sullivan and Gilbert is of when I went to the Savoy for an audition. I was very young— under seventeen. I had a high coloratura voice, and wrote asking Sullivan to hear me. When I entered the theatre I saw some people sitting in the stalls. My first impression was of a very beautiful woman sitting next to Mr Gilbert. It was Julia Neilson. Mr Carte was there, and Mrs Ronalds was with Sir Arthur Sullivan. I went on the stage feeling very raw and young, but I sang them "Caro Nome", hit the top F at the end very well, and felt better. Sullivan said: "Can you sing anything English?"

'I replied: "Orpheus with his Lute."

' "Have you the music with you?"

' "I'm afraid I haven't, Sir Arthur."

' "All right, I'll play it"—and he sat down and played that old song of his for me. At the end he looked up and smiled and said "You know, Miss Moore, I was so frightened I should forget it. I haven't played it for years."

'Mr Gilbert next came up on the stage and spoke to me. He looked down from his great height and was really rather terrifying.

' "Have you ever acted, Miss Moore?"

' "No."

' "So much the better for you. You've nothing to unlearn."

'When we started rehearsals I discovered what Gilbert meant by that last remark. His method of training his actors was unique. Exact diction; every word to be heard at the back of the dress circle; the rhythm of the lines to be scrupulously followed. He would read a line of dialogue out, clapping his hands between the words to emphasize their rhythm, thus:

' "I've no patience (*clap*) with the presumption (*clap*) of persons (*clap*) in his plebian (*clap*) position (*clap*)."

Decima Moore as Casilda

[1] Decima Moore married Brigadier-General Sir Gordon Guggisberg in 1905, lived for many years in West Africa where her husband was a colonial governor, and in the two World Wars she founded and ran the British Navy, Army and Air Force Leave Club in Paris. She was originator of the Women's Emergency Corps, in 1914.

' "Now, Miss Moore," he would say, "again please!" . . . and his hands would go clap . . . clap . . . clap. "And keep your voice up at the ends of sentences!"

'I remember he asked me to his house in Harrington Gardens, and coached me privately there in diction by taking me through his play *Broken Hearts*. One day he suddenly rolled off to me this limerick:

> There was a young lady named Decima
> Whose conduct was quoted as "pessima",
> But her sins she forsook
> And the sacrament took
> On a Sunday they called Quinquagesima.'

'On the first night of *The Gondoliers* I was in a whirl. I walked on, took one look at the audience, and gulped. Then I saw Sullivan's face beaming up at me from the conductor's stand, and my confidence returned. I was always very fond of Arthur Sullivan. He was a dear little man, so kind, and so cheerful in spite of his burden of sickness.'

*   *   *   *

Sandringham, Norfolk.
2 May, '89.

Dear Sir Arthur Sullivan,

I am desired by the Prince and Princess of Wales to invite you to pay their Royal Highnesses a visit at Sandringham, from Friday, 10 May, to remain till Monday, 21st, to have the honour of meeting the Empress Frederick of Germany.

Will you please travel down by the 2.35 train from St Pancras and kindly send your luggage and servant by the three minutes past twelve train.

Conveyances will be sent from this to meet both trains.

Yours truly,
FRANCIS KNOLLYS

P.S. Slight mourning will be worn during the visit.

*   *   *   *

Marlborough House,
Pall Mall, S.W.

Dear Sir Arthur,

Francis Knollys has asked me to send you an answer to your question about champagne.

I have high authority for saying any champagne will suit H.R.H. as long as it is not too sweet.

Yours sincerely,
STANLEY CLARKE

[336]

During the summer of 1889 Sullivan was living at Weybridge. Unhurriedly he worked on *The Gondoliers*, at the same time composing *Ivanhoe* to a libretto by Julian Sturgis; and getting some occasional recreation rowing a skiff on the Thames. Gilbert's manuscript arrived by post in bits and pieces, and Sullivan noted in his diary that it was 'Bright, interesting, funny, and very pretty'. The two men were now working as 'master to master'; like their two reigning gondoliers, they seemed now to be 'combined with absolute equality':

> Dear S,—Here is the entry of the Duke and Duchess. I fancy you will like the spirit of it. Would you like a short episodic aria for Carlotta introduced into it? If so, it can be done. Or a duet for Carlotta and Luiz (aside)? Luiz is not on, as at present arranged, but I could bring him on if you wished him.
>
> Yours very truly,
>
> W.S.G.

(Carlotta was later renamed Casilda). Thus Mr Gilbert was at pains not to upset the apple-cart again, and referred everything scrupulously to his partner:

> Dear Sullivan—will this do? If it don't do, send it back and I'll try again. Yours very truly, W.S.G.

Enclosed, a lyric in longhand. Sullivan would put it aside for a week or a month, and then most likely he would set it to music in an hour or two one warm summer's morning on the lawn, as he did this one for the Grand Inquisitor:

This verse is in Gilbert's writing, the metrical suggestion '6/8 or 2/4' having been added in pencil by Sullivan.

[337]

Gilbert postponed writing the Finale until Sullivan had decided on a rhythm which would bring the opera to an exhilarating climax—this is the famous Cachucha, but at first Gilbert intended to preface it with a gallop, to these words, later deleted:

> With the cymbals clanging,
> And the trumpets tooting,
> And the tabors banging,
> And the fluters fluting,
> And the drummers drumming,
> And the harpers twiddling,
> And the hautboys humming,
> And the fiddlers fiddling—
> Let us sing, let us shout, let us ring, let us rout,
> Let us drink, let us dance, let us prink, let us prance . . .

Sullivan was able to make the cachucha gay and exciting enough without this, though it would have given him some amusing musical opportunities had it been retained:

> From the country of the thistle
> Bring the bagpipe's drone,
> And the little penny whistle
> And the loud trombone!

Another drastic alteration came after Gilbert had suggested that it would make a comic scene if the Grand Inquisitor were to teach the two clumsy gondoliers some court etiquette, and take them through the movements of an eighteenth-century minuet, for which he proposed these words:

GRAND INQUISITOR: Now I'm about to kiss your hand,
> Look haughty, proud, and rather freezy—
> Yet gracious, affable and bland—(*They attempt to do so*)
> It's not particularly easy.
> Humph, pretty well—it's not supreme.
> If anything, it's TOO unbending (*They unbend*)
> Now that's the opposite extreme—
> Don't be so deuced condescending!

MARCO AND GIUSEPPE: Oh, hard to please some people seem—
(*depressed*) > At first our pose was too unbending,
> Then came the opposite extreme,
> We were too deuced condescending!

GRAND INQUISITOR: Now try a cold Imperial air—
> Half-close your eyes and stick your nose out.
> Assume a blank and vacant stare,
> Shut up your mouth and turn your toes out (*They do so*)

That's very good—that's very fair—
　　That's dignified, yet very winning,
Upon my honour I declare
　　That's very good for a beginning!
MARCO AND GIUSEPPE: That comes of taking proper care—
　(*cheerfully*)　　　We're dignified yet blandly winning:
　　　　　　　Upon my honour I declare
　　　　　　　That's very good for a beginning!

But Sullivan preferred a gavotte to a minuet, the above lyric was scrapped, and the whole thing was altered into the now-celebrated—

Tempo di Gavotte. Allegretto.

I am a courtier grave and serious
　　Who is about to kiss your hand:
Try to combine a pose imperious
　　With a demeanour nobly bland . . .

The Gondoliers is an example of how careful Gilbert was to base even his wildest nonsense on fact. This time his original idea had come from a history book. In an early letter to Sullivan, sketching out the plot, he writes: 'The Venetians in the fifteenth century were red-hot republicans. One of their party is made king and invites his friends to form a Court. They object because they are Republicans. He replies that he has considered that and proposed to institute a Court in which all people shall be equal, and to this they agree. In Act 2 the absurdity of this state of things is shown.'
This is finally distilled as this sort of thing:

　　　Lord Chancellors were cheap as sprats,
　　　And Bishops in their shovel hats
　　　Were plentiful as tabby cats—
　　　　In point of fact, too many.
　　　Ambassadors cropped up like hay,
　　　Prime Ministers and such as they
　　　Grew like asparagus in May,
　　　　And Dukes were three a penny . . .

and he draws the Gilbertian moral:

　　　The end is easily foretold,
　　　When every blessed thing you hold
　　　Is made of silver, or of gold,
　　　　You long for simple pewter.

How Gilbert enjoyed writing such words! Politics had always been his favourite joke, and now the rising tide of agitation against class distinction gave it a new twist. The French Revolution ('Liberty, Equality, Fraternity') was still fresh in Gilbert's memory. Socialist-revolutionaries were active now in Germany and Russia. Anti-monarchist voices were heard in England where Queen Victoria was ruthlessly lampooned in some sections of the Press. In London Karl Marx had died in 1883 and here the second volume of *Das Kapital* (completed by Engels) had only recently been published. So W.S.G. dipped his quill-pen in the inkwell, and reduced equalitarianism to the final absurdity:

> When everyone is somebodee,
> Then no one's anybody!

The sub-title of the opera, *The King of Barataria*, he borrowed from *Don Quixote*, in which we read: 'After having travelled a certain distance, Governor Sancho, with his attendants, came to a certain town that had about one thousand inhabitants, and was one of the best in the duke's territories. They gave him to understand that the name of the place was the island of Barataria.' Gilbert, himself tilting at windmills, took a thrust in *The Gondoliers* at what are now called Rackets. The ludicrous Duke of Plaza-Toro (Ltd.) is a nobleman 'blazing in the lustre of unaccustomed pocket money' acquired from ambitious commoners whom he has helped—

> Small titles and orders
> For Mayors and Recorders
> I get—and they're highly delighted—
> M.P.'s baronetted,
> Sham Colonels gazetted,
> And second-rate Aldermen knighted . . .

but the real windmill of the opera is the Abolition of Class Distinction. In the original manuscript Gilbert had an opening chorus about—

> A people, dignified and polished
> Who class-distinctions have abolished,
> And one and all with zeal combine
> To make their monarch toe the line.

This disappeared from the opera, together with a Baratarian National Anthem in which the courtiers told the King to—

> . . . knuckle down with humble mien
> And keep your crown and sceptre clean,

but the idea of the working-class monarch remains to delight *Gondoliers* audiences to this day in the scene where Giuseppe is discovered in the Palace of Barataria, clad in his royal robes and carefully polishing the sceptre as he sings 'Rising early in the morning, we proceed to light the fire', and recites to Sullivan's aptly pert music the many little duties of a monarch's day, which include writing letters for his private secretary ('He is shaky in his spelling, so we help him if we can') and taking turns at sentry-go

DON
ALHAMBRA

DOWN
THE YEARS

A cartoon of the originator of the part, W. H. Denny; and (LEFT) *Leo Sheffield in the nineteen-twenties, with Sydney Granville in the nineteen-thirties after 'The Gondoliers' had been re-dressed by Charles Ricketts, R.A.*

('While the warrior on duty goes in search of beer and beauty'), for as Giuseppe says: 'We quite understand that a man who holds the magnificent position of King should do something to justify it. We are called "Your Majesty", we are allowed to buy ourselves magnificent clothes, our subjects frequently nod to us in the streets, the sentries always return our salutes, and we enjoy the inestimable privilege of heading the subscription lists to all the principal charities. In return for these advantages the least we can do is to make ourselves useful about the Palace.'

Oh, philosophers may sing
Of the troubles of a King;
Yet the duties are delightful and the privileges great;
But the privilege and pleasure
That we treasure beyond measure
Is to run on little errands for the Ministers of State.

The bubbling, champagne-quality of the libretto brought out the gayest Sullivan, and the Italian setting called up a warm, southern response from his own ancestry. The *Graphic* (14 December, 1889) pointed out that the music contains not only an English idiom but 'the composer has borrowed from France the stately gavotte, from Spain the Andalusian cachucha, from Italy the saltarello and the tarantella, and from Venice itself the Venetian barcarolle'. This genial quality in *The Gondoliers* amazingly conceals Sullivan's private agony. At Leeds in October he had conducted the Festival but he was so ill that a deputy, Joseph Barnby, had to take over the chorus rehearsals. *The Golden Legend* was revived on the final day,[1] and with the cheers ringing in his ears for 'The finest performance I have ever heard' Sullivan returned to London, but not to the rest and quiet his body craved. Much of *The Gondoliers* had yet to be composed. Gilbert wrote:

Dear Sullivan,

I didn't want to bother you while you were away, so I have worked at the piece myself, taking my chance of your finding it all right or otherwise. I have now finished it, subject, of course, to any alterations you may require, and it is set up in type that you may see and judge of it in a concrete form. I have found it necessary to make a few alterations and modifications, but none of them, I think and hope, will give you any trouble. I have written a nice little ballad for Pounds in Act 1 (he had no ballad), and a good rattling song for Barrington. I found that Denny had two songs in Act 2, so I have taken a song from Denny ('Now I'm about to kiss your hand') and transferred it to Wyatt. I could not consult you about this, as you were busy at Leeds, so have done it on the chance of your agreeing to it. If you don't it can be restored to Denny . . .

And so on, and so on. All through November Sullivan worked at *The Gondoliers*, night after night until the dawn, and his diary is now milestoned with pathetic little entries: 'Very seedy all day' . . . 'Too tired to go to rehearsal' . . . 'Home very tired.

---

[1] That Sullivan wrote no new oratorio was a disappointment to a section of the musical public, but at this period he was considering setting *The Dream of Gerontius*, later set by Elgar.

Scored Nos. 7 and 8. To bed at four. Only slept an hour.'

Yet in *one* such night he wrote 'Take a Pair of Sparkling Eyes' and the jaunty 'There lived a King, as I've been told, in the wonder-working days of old', and rewrote two other numbers.

This sort of thing scared Gilbert and D'Oyly Carte, both for Sullivan's sake and for the opera. Gilbert wanted the opera postponed. But as usual Sullivan came through in time—'I am out of prison at last!' he noted on 26 November, having finished the music (except the overture) and the next day he signed an agreement accepting £500 from Carte for 'all my rights of representation in the United States of America of the New Opera, for five years'.

Five days before the first London performance Sullivan had his first orchestral rehearsal, and after dining at home he composed and scored the Overture, finishing at three a.m. That same day he and Gilbert decided on the title. It was rushed round to Chappell's and set up on the printing presses which immediately started rolling off seventy thousand copies of the various arrangements which were required to meet the public's first orders for this new opera.

Corno di Bassetto, the critic of the *Star*, refused to attend the first night of *The Gondoliers* because, he said, 'We know the exact limits of Mr Gilbert's and Sir Arthur Sullivan's talents by this time as well as we know the width of the Thames at Waterloo Bridge' . . . but Mr Shaw admitted he had seen only two of the Gilbert and Sullivan operas.

OUR CAPTIOUS CRITIC.

"THE GONDOLIERS."

WHILE others rush wildly for a first glimpse of the latest Gilbert and Sullivan piece, I always put off my going as long as I can ; I want as much grace as possible between whiles in order to forget the previous production and the production before that. I ought no doubt to be burnt as a heretic or confined as a lunatic, but nevertheless I cannot bow down and worship blindly simply because I am told by the critics that it is the right thing to do. I am tired as an all round playgoer of the perpetual sameness of the Savoy methods they weary me to the point of absolute dulness. They were well enough when they were new, and may be well enough now to those who do do not go to theatres very often. But the hobby has been flogged until pretty nearly all the fun has been flogged out of it, and surprise is no longer surprise, because topsy-turvy is the only principle recognised. In short, the unexpected is developed with a matter of course regularity like serious incidents in a serious play, and with serious effect too, in *The Gondoliers*. I have seen no other piece of late which made me feel so little lively, except *The Dead Heart* at the Lyceum. I was more amused by the public than by the opera. The house was crowded, but it seemed to me less like an audience than a congregation. They had heard of Gilbert and Sullivan, and

SOME OF THE SAVOY CONGREGATION

had come to worship at their shrine as they would go on Sunday to sit under Stopford Brooke or Dr. Parker or Mr Spurgeon. They offered one another half their books of the words as good people do when you are put into a strange pew at church What is more, they looked at their books rather than at the stage, and followed the songs with awe, and the singularly wordy dialogue with reverence. Sometimes they smiled

A heretical notice from the 'Illustrated Sporting and Dramatic News', 1890

Mr Gilbert was nervous that some ingredients of *The Gondoliers* might be recognized as having been on the menu before, so after completing the libretto he told Sullivan that he intended to alter the *dénouement* of the opera because the situation was too much like that at the end of *H.M.S. Pinafore*, where Little Buttercup explains that she has changed the children at birth . . . but he never altered it. *The Gondoliers* still turns on the stealing and swopping of babies at birth! This *idée fixe* dates back to Gilbert's own experience at two years of age when, it will be remembered, he was stolen—in Italy; so it is hardly surprising that it had to be echoed in his Italian opera:

> I stole the Prince, and brought him here,
> > And left him gaily prattling
> With a highly respectable gondolier . . .

Most of the audience at the first night of *The Gondoliers*, on 7 December, didn't care a rap about familiar ingredients. Their idolatry annoyed Our Captious Critic, of the *Illustrated Sporting and Dramatic News* (see previous page), but as his colleague of the *Illustrated London News* declared:

> Mr W. S. Gilbert has returned to the Gilbert of the past, and everyone is delighted. He is himself again. The Gilbert of *The Bab Ballads*, the Gilbert of whimsical conceit, inoffensive cynicism, subtle satire, and playful paradox; the Gilbert who invented a school of his own, who in it was his own schoolmaster and pupil, who has never taught anybody but himself, and is never likely to have any imitator— this is the Gilbert the public want to see, and this is the Gilbert who on Saturday night was cheered till the audience was weary of cheering any more.

Now Gilbert wrote to Sullivan:

> I must thank you for the magnificent work you have put into the piece. It gives one the chance of shining right through the twentieth century with a reflected light.

And Sullivan replied:

> Don't talk of reflected light. In such a perfect book as *The Gondoliers* you shine with an individual brilliancy which no other writer can hope to attain.

The *Daily Telegraph* said so rightly: '*The Gondoliers* conveys an impression of having been written *con amore*.'

So the year 1889 went out in a blaze of amity. Sullivan's heart was warmed by a letter from his old colleague F. C. Burnand, now Editor of *Punch*, with whom he had written his first comic 'trifle', *Cox and Box*, twenty-two years previously:

> My dear Arturo Sullivano,
> Magnificento! Just seen *Gondoliers*. I delighted in the Italian recitatives. 'In a contemplative fashion' is a triumph. How did you arrive at it? Whence came the suggestion of the musical treatment? . . . I envy you and W.S.G. being able to place a piece like this on the stage in so complete a fashion.

In a contemplative fashion,
And a tranquil frame of mind,
Free from every kind of passion,
Some solution let us find. . .

'In a contemplative fashion' is a clever example of a favourite Sullivan trick—several vocal themes chattering away at the same time. He claimed to have invented this form of musical humour. He said: 'You get the germ of it in *The Sorcerer* and it is afterwards worked in a greater degree in *The Pirates* (the policemen's chorus with the counter theme for the sopranos). In *The Mikado* there is amongst others the Trio for the three men in the first act, with all three different themes going at the same time. The most ingenious bit of work (certainly the most difficult) is the quartet in *The Gondoliers*, "In a contemplative fashion".'[1]

The humorist in Sullivan was expressed in full measure and overflowing in *The Gondoliers*, its rippling, fast-flowing gaiety interspersed with those occasional pools of sentiment which reflect the other side of the composer—the poet in him. 'Take a Pair of Sparkling Eyes' is of course the most famous of these tender numbers, and one of the most popular songs Sullivan ever wrote. It has been vulgarized in every possible way, played all round the world on radios, bandstands, piers, fair-grounds, on every kind of instrument from cinema organs to mouth organs, and sung by tenors of every possible and impossible kind, and yet one has only to hear it sung by a singer of real quality and all its hackneyed reputation falls away, and one is left with a gem of the first water.

One evening during *The Gondoliers* Sir Arthur Sullivan dropped in on the Old Madrigal Society, which met monthly in Willis's Room, St James's Street. After dinner the members sang madrigals, supported by six boys from the Chapel Royal and six from Lincoln's Inn Chapel, in the treble parts. Sullivan listened to the singing, then spoke to a boy named Hanson of the Chapel Royal, patted him on the head

A modern Tessa (Nellie Briercliffe) and Giuseppe (Leslie Rands)

[1] Letter to B. W. Findon, quoted in the *Play Pictorial*, No. 309.

—and gave him half a sovereign.[1] It was an exact flash-back to his own receipt of benevolence as a Chapel Royal boy.[2] It was a sentimental touch typical of Sullivan. And a letter which the Editor of the *Globe* newspaper received at the end of the year had an impish touch typical of W. S. Gilbert:

> Sir, I am much indebted to your dramatic critic for the very flattering remarks upon the literary qualities of *The Gondoliers*. At the same time, I think I may be allowed to defend my word 'coyfully'. Your critic takes exception to it because one cannot be full of 'coy'. That is quite true; but is it a conclusive argument against the use of the word? We use the word 'manfully', though one cannot be full of 'man'. We use the word 'bashfully', though one cannot—at least I don't think one can—be full of 'bash'.

No doubt about it, Gilbert and Sullivan still had a world-wide 'pull'. When *The Yeomen of the Guard* was produced in Berlin at Christmas, 1889, Professor Ehrlich, a leading German critic, went so far as to say: 'It is far superior to all other operettas of the present day.' In Australia *The Yeomen* and *The Gondoliers* were greeted with joy.

But it was a different story when D'Oyly Carte sent a *Gondolier* company to America. They sailed on Boxing Day, 1889, in secret, once again to forestall the American pirates, but the English production in New York had a calamitous start. Seven actors in quick succession were tried in the role of the Duke of Plaza-Toro, so that the line about Dukes being three a penny earned a derisive laugh. Mr Reginald Allen, of New York, has recently carried out research into this débâcle, unique in D'Oyly Carte history. He sends us the following notes:

'The English company arrived in New York only two or three days before their opening night (7 January 1890) at the New Park Theatre. As usual, they were in a hurry to beat the pirate production, and they did so by about a week. But the *New York Times* gave them a downright panning, criticising not *The Gondoliers* as an opera but the company as inept. Esther Palliser was the only cast member who had a good notice. The *New York Times* said: "The other persons were sad specimens of the genus known in their native country as 'duffer'. It is an inelegant word, and its application to any person is rude; but nothing could be ruder than the attempted singing and misguided acting of these well-meaning but small-witted human beings from London."

'The company's manager cabled an S.O.S. to Mr D'Oyly Carte (continues Mr Allen). Mr Carte arrived by the next boat and gave a long interview to the Press, defending his company. From what we know of this company, they appear to have been hand-picked but they lacked the greatest single feature of a true Gilbert and Sullivan company—team work. So the unique disaster occurred. A widely-heralded

---

[1] For this information I am indebted to Dr P. W. Millard, of London, who was one of the choirboys present.—L.B.

[2] See p. 35.

Gilbert and Sullivan première was a flop. Judging by Mr Carte's defensive statement to the Press, what most incensed him was the adjective "cheap" which one paper had applied to his New York production of *The Gondoliers*. Carte, the business man, might have accepted philosophically such a term as "duffer", but he *did* know his company was not cheap, and he said so. In fact, he said that the company cost 500 dollars a week more than his first American *Mikado* company.

'Carte proceeded to summon a new company from London, and they arrived to open at Palmer's Theatre on 19 February, replete with such first-class talent as Fred Billington, Henry Lytton and Richard Temple; but the damage was done. *The Gondoliers* was dubbed "the gone-dollars".'

Meanwhile, the pirate production had opened in New Jersey. What it was like may be judged from the recollection of a member of the D'Oyly Carte company, Lindsay Harman[1]: 'We went to see a matinee. It was a wonderful copy, but Gilbert's humour was scarcely broad enough for them. Their Don Alhambra was of the low comedian order—very low. Besides his aspirates, he "dropped a Grand Inquisitor's tear"—and the splash was worked in the wings. In the opening of Act 2, Marco and Giuseppe were discovered ironing their shirts instead of polishing crown and sceptre. The whole opera ran along the same lines: never mind about author and composer—make it go!—get there!'

'What struck me particularly,' adds this D'Oyly Carte singer, 'was the class of lady and gentleman I was associated with in the chorus. Three of the fellows had graduated, one at Oxford and two at Cambridge. Most of the ladies and gentlemen were excellent musicians. It was an exception to find a person in the company unable to play the piano or violin well. Most of the ladies had studied at the Royal Academy, or similar institutions.' They were all, he remarks, what was in those days called 'refined'. This word had not acquired its modern implication of the pseudo-cultured, the genteel; it meant, simply, not-vulgar. And surely in the words and music of *The Gondoliers* the same refinement stands out—Gilbert and Sullivan got their effects of gaiety and of movement and colour without vulgarity, without the splash worked in the wings.

[1] *A Comic Opera Life*, by Lindsay Harman (Wm. Barlow, West Hartlepool), 1924.

W. S. Gilbert's last home: Grim's Dyke, on the heights of Harrow Weald, north of London. Here, surrounded by extensive grounds, with a boating lake, tennis courts, and croquet lawns, a lofty music-room [LEFT], and a lifetime's collection of bric-a-brac, the dramatist spent the autumn of his life

1890-1

THE CARPET QUARREL

But now they met with scowl and grin
In every public place,
And often snapped their fingers in
Each other's learned face.

It almost ended in a fight
When they on path and stair
Met face to face. They made it quite
A personal affair.

And when at length the case was called
(It came on rather late),
Spectators really were appalled
To see their deadly hate.

—*The Bab Ballads* ('Damon v. Pythias')

WITHIN NINE MONTHS of their brilliant return to comic opera the Savoyards were at loggerheads in the law courts. After *The Gondoliers* première Mr and Mrs Gilbert had taken a cruise to India. Sir Arthur Sullivan went wandering around southern Europe with a retinue comprising Clotilde (a Belgian, now his housekeeper), his man-servant Louis, and his parrot. Before coming to the Carpet Quarrel let us for a moment make a flash-forward fifty years, to the period of the Second World War: A very old lady dies in London, in a rather dingy flat where she has lived alone for many years. This recluse, in her black Victorian-style dress, was a mystery to the neighbours—she appeared to have no friends, she neglected her food and lived on mere odds and ends, she told the oddest tales of how she was once the best cook in London, improbable stories of life in high Society. She even claimed that she had been kissed by the Prince of Wales. They laughed at the old lady . . . but when Clotilde died £19,000 was found in her flat, most of it in notes laid like sandwiches, layer by layer, between clothing in the moth-balled drawers.

When Sullivan, Clotilde, Louis, and the parrot came back from Europe in April, 1890, Gilbert had been home from India a short time. Mr and Mrs D'Oyly Carte had not been away: they were in charge at the Savoy Theatre. There was an immediate crisis.

Gilbert to Sullivan:

I have had a difficulty with Carte. I was appalled to learn from him the preliminary expenses of the *Gondoliers* amounted to the stupendous sum of £4,500 ! ! ! This seemed so utterly unaccountable that I asked to see the details and last night I received a resumé of them. This includes such trifles as £75 for Miss Moore's second dress—£50 for her first dress—£100 for Miss Brandram's second dress (this costly garment has now, for some occult reason, been sent on tour); £450 for the wages of the carpenters during the time they were engaged on the scenery; £460 for the gondola, the sailing boat, the two columns and the two chairs and fountain for Act 2; £112 for timber, £120 for ironmongery, £95 for canvas—and so forth. But the most surprising item was £500 *for new carpets for the front of the house!*

The Savoy Trinity had always shared the profits of the operas equally, after deductions of expenses, which—in the words of their long-standing agreement—included 'repairs incidental to the performance'.[1] Gilbert now argued that new carpets could not possibly be 'repairs', nor could carpets in the lobbies and staircases at the front of the Savoy Theatre be considered as 'incidental to the performance'. He expected that Sullivan would back him up in demanding 'a distinct understanding' with Carte. During a stormy meeting at the Savoy Theatre offices Gilbert demanded the drawing-up of a new agreement. Carte replied that the only alteration he would accept would be to put the rent for the Savoy Theatre at £5,000 instead of £4,000 and that if W.S.G. was dissatisfied with the existing state of things he had only to say so:

Gilbert to Sullivan:

I replied that I *was* dissatisfied and he said 'Very well then—you write no more for the Savoy Theatre—that's understood.' I left him with the remark that it was a mistake to kick down the ladder by which he had risen, a sentiment which I hope will meet with your approval.

But Sullivan did not back him up. He disagreed with Gilbert's aggressive attitude. He arranged a peace conference at the Savoy offices. Mrs Carte was also there. Richard D'Oyly Carte's version of this meeting, in a statement he issued to the Press, was that Gilbert alleged that expenses were unwarrantable and excessive, and said to Carte: 'You're making too much money out of my brains'. Sullivan again upheld Carte, Gilbert lost his temper, called them both blackguards, and rushed from the room.

A fuller story of this historic and lunatic quarrel can now be told by reference to the letters of Mr and Mrs Carte. For lack of them, the affair has always been rather

[1] *See* p. 251, the agreement of 1883.

mystifying; Carte has been written down by more than one author as a Napoleonic personality whose power went to his head (but then why did Sullivan support him?), a big business man who indulged in unscrupulous practice by taking advantage of a loosely-worded phrase—'repairs incidental to the performance'—to the extent of £500. The first item of truth that we discover is that the carpet cost not £500 but £140. Carte writes to Gilbert a few days after the quarrel:

> I pass by the observation in your letter that the cost of restoring the carpets is £500, which sum I see you have reduced to £330 in your second letter, the actual amount being £140, merely remarking that this is a fair sample of the general inaccuracy of your letters, due no doubt to your not having properly examined the accounts.

Carte puts up two main defences to the Gilbertian attack. First, he agrees that the preliminary expenses of *The Gondoliers* were 'enormously and unnecessarily' high, but he blames Gilbert. He himself would never give orders without getting estimates, but when this opera was in preparation, he says, Gilbert gave orders 'blind'—he instructed the costume designer, and rejected and ordered costumes and materials 'without consulting me'. Carte tried to get estimates, but was told that Gilbert had not yet settled this or that. 'To save discussion', writes Carte, 'I quietly accepted the situation. The proof of my statement is in the fact that the provincial tour bills incurred under the sole control of myself and Mrs Carte show no such preposterous expenses, although the dresses are equally as good.'

His second defence is that the carpet was rightly charged as expenses: if a person rents a theatre he is expected to bear the cost of keeping it in good order. The opera-producing trio, Gilbert–Sullivan–Carte, rented the Savoy from its owner (Carte) for £4,000 a year, and the internal wear and tear on the premises therefore figures as expenses of Gilbert–Sullivan–Carte.

The long letter in which Carte sets out these defences is full of resentment at Gilbert's statements:

> You asked what I had done for the share I have got out of our very successful enterprise. I have devoted the greater part of my time and energies during the best years of my life to the management of the theatre in London, and the tours in the country and abroad. I and my wife have worked loyally in your interests, our first thought has always been to give a performance satisfactory to you and Sullivan, and that would be a credit to our management. We have thought more of this than of any money we might expect to make.
>
> If you do not know, or have forgotten, what I have done, the first passer-by in the street could probably tell you. You appear to forget this, and although the Savoy Theatre has always been charged against you one-fifth less than the market value, you have not charged less than the full market value of your pieces against me. I scarcely imagine that any solvent responsible manager would, taking good and bad times

The house that Carte built, 1890: the Royal English Opera House, birthplace of Sullivan's opera 'Ivanhoe'. Today, as the Palace Theatre, it is a popular home of musical comedies

A view of the theatre during the run of Emile Littler's 'Lilac Time'

together, agree to hand over more than two-thirds of the profits to any author and composer, even to yourselves.

'You have had much the best of it,' writes Carte, and he goes on to say that he has just lost thousands of pounds in America (on *The Yeomen*), and when there is a loss he bears the whole of it. While Gilbert has been holiday-making, Helen and D'Oyly Carte have been 'working like slaves' in America—

When you return all you do is to come to the Savoy Theatre and create disturbances. I should be very sorry to lose the pecuniary advantage of the productions of future operas of yours, but the earth does not contain the money that would pay me to put up with this sort of thing.

To conclude. If you are dissatisfied with the accounts, every facility can be given you to check them. The question, if it can be called a question, as to what should be charged against profits seems to be a very simple one and I cannot conceive how it could be argued that the restoring of carpets worn out, upholstery, and painting, etc. where necessary, should not come under the heading of repairs necessitated by 'wear and tear' just as much as the renewals of electric lamps as they wear out.

[352]

I believe it is the custom for all lessees of theatres to pay out such expenses. The Savoy is put out at *less* than a lease price and out of that reduced price I could and should certainly not undertake to pay such expenses, as I have never agreed to. The agreement speaks for itself.[1]

In later letters Carte reminded Gilbert that on many occasions in the past he had agreed to such expenses as electric lamps and interior painting. But Gilbert had not been consulted about the carpet, and he evidently thought the time had come to take Carte down a peg.

While *The Gondoliers* danced its gay cachucha to ever-delighted audiences during the spring of 1890, the partnership dragged itself thus into despair. 'It is hopeless for us to try and convince each other,' wrote Sullivan to Gilbert, in May. 'Will it not therefore be better to cease correspondence on the subject entirely?' He was living at Weybridge, trying to concentrate on *Ivanhoe*. He wrote to Ethel Smyth, then thirty-two:

Grove House, Weybridge.
14 June, 1890.

Dear Miss Smyth,
    Me voila. In the same house I occupied last year. Not very far from you, only two stations. When you want some tea come and have it with me; I generally strike work about five. Had I not been ill and in pain on that eventful Saturday[2] I should have been a gratified witness of your success. I had made all arrangements to go but I had a combined attack that day, my old physical trouble and . . . Gilbert! Nevertheless I was really pleased to read such nice things about the work of the gracieuse jeune fille, and I hope that you are beginning a brilliant and dignified musical career.

Ever yours sincerely,
ARTHUR SULLIVAN[3]

Gilbert said in later years: 'I had no quarrel with Sir Arthur Sullivan, though a coolness existed between us for a time in consequence of his declining to interfere in the difference between Mr Carte and myself.'[4] Nevertheless, a 'coolness' could be a dreadful business when anger, Gilbert's gout, Sullivan's kidney trouble, and Carte's accounts were all mixed up in the witches' cauldron along with traces of the old poison over Sullivan's 'grand' ambitions, now renewed in potency as Carte's bricklayers finished their work on the Royal English Opera House and Sullivan was head-over-heels in *Ivanhoe*. Acrimonious postal exchanges led to the break of 5 May, 1890:

Gilbert to Sullivan:
    The time for putting an end to our partnership has at last arrived . . . I am writing a letter to Carte giving him notice that he is not to produce or perform any

---

[1] This letter is dated 26 April, 1890, and together with much else in this chapter has not previously been published.
   [2] The performance of Ethel Smyth's *Serenade* at the Crystal Palace.
   [3] From *Impressions that Remained*, by Ethel Smyth (Longmans, Green), 1923.
   [4] Quoted in *My Table Cloths*, by Mrs Alec-Tweedie, New York, 1916.

of my libretti after Christmas 1890. In point of fact, after the withdrawal of *The Gondoliers*, our united work will be heard in public no more.

And now Helen Carte stepped into the ring as would-be peacemaker. A letter she wrote to Gilbert shows both the tact and the firmness of this remarkable woman:

When we opened the theatre nearly nine years ago it was freshly decorated and fitted up with entirely new carpets, furniture, etc.—the property of, and paid for by, Mr Carte alone. Of these carpets, etc. you have had the use ever since, they have been used and worn by the people who came to see your operas (out of which money you receive your one-third share)—in fact by 'wear and tear incidental to the performance'. At the end of your term here you would certainly have had to leave the theatre, as you would any other theatre—in as good a state as regards wear and tear as you found it, or reasonably near it.

Mr Carte *might* have done nothing meanwhile to keep the furniture, etc. in repair. He might have let the paint and paper get dirty, the carpets in holes, the place generally looking like some neglected provincial theatre. But I think had your friends told you the place was in this disgraceful state that you would have been the first to come to Mr Carte to say that he ought to have had these things seen to, and that you on your part had not the slightest objection to being charged with your share of the necessary expenses. To attend to these things seems to me to be entirely in the province of the manager of the theatre, and certainly a subject in which he should not necessarily require to consult or bother you or Sir Arthur.

I am sure that no theatre in London has been kept so bright and clean as this one for so small a cost. Most lessees in so long a time as eight or more years have had to redecorate their theatre thoroughly several times. You have never had to do more than clean and repair here and there . . .

By the agreement there is no question that Mr Carte is not called upon to do at his own expense more than substantial (that is, constructional) repairs. The substantial repairs have frequently come to large sums—in this year £500 to £1,000—and have been paid by Mr Carte and you never knew anything about them.

Both Gilbert and Carte had been rubbing salt into their wounds by postal repetitions of insulting phrases used at their first quarrel over the carpet. Helen Carte now tried a soothing balm:

I know, of course, that both of you believe absolutely in what you say you said. But you must remember that you were very excited indeed on that occasion—you burst out so suddenly and addressed Mr Carte in a way that you would not have used to an offending menial. All I was able to say myself was 'I'm sure you are not thinking about what you are saying, Mr Gilbert'. I really felt you did not think fully what you were saying. When you first burst out you said we were robbed right and left and that Mr Carte did not even check his carpenter's accounts, and that you had made him what he was. All this you said in a very violent and insulting way, although no one had said or done anything to provoke it. You then went on to the carpet matter and finally said there must be a new agreement. Mr Carte had by that time not unnaturally got annoyed and said 'Very well he would put the rent at £5,000 instead of £4,000'. Then *you* said 'If so, he must get another author for the Savoy'. The first words as to not writing any more for the Savoy came from you. Mr Carte did not then or at any time say 'Then you write no more for the Savoy' or anything to that effect. On this point I'm perfectly clear. I was quite calm myself and very grieved that the conversation should be taking such an unpleasant tone.

Further conversation followed and you asked Mr Carte very heatedly what *he* did for the share he got and he said he must decline to discuss that. He asked if you were dissatisfied with the existing state of things and wished to break it off. You said you were, and he then said you'd better go and see Sir Arthur Sullivan and talk to *him*. You then left the room with the remark about the ladder.

You seemed so different from your usual self and it all came so suddenly and was really so entirely unprovoked. You have always been so courteous to me personally that I do not like writing anything that may annoy you but it seemed to me to be quite as much due to you as to Mr Carte that I should say what occurred at the interview. The fact that you *believe* Mr Carte said the words you impute to him must have been, and has evidently been, an annoyance to you, as you believe yourself to have been deliberately insulted. It is right therefore *to you* as well as to Mr Carte that your mind should be disabused of this mistake so that you may be able to look at the business matters before you in a calm way. Anything in the conversation that might be considered insulting was certainly in some of the things you said to Mr Carte, not in anything he said to you, although as I have stated, he was of course more or less excited towards you because of the conversation.

Gilbert respected such straight speaking, but it was too late. By now he had put all dealings with Carte into the hands of his solicitors. Carte followed suit. The time had come round for the payment to Gilbert and Sullivan of their quarterly profits, from *The Gondoliers*, but Carte's solicitors advised him that the accounts should not be settled until all this trouble with Gilbert over expense items was cleared up. Gilbert thereupon decided to go to law. He issued a writ. Sullivan was shocked. Typically, he pleaded with his partners for conciliation.

Carte to Sullivan:

What concession and conciliation do you suggest I should offer? My feeling is this. I come back after a most imperfect holiday and ought to be able to devote my energies to the new theatre business (which wants all the time I can give it). I tumble into the middle of the Gilbert bother. This I should not grumble at, and would work everything straight, but if *you*, my friend of long standing with whom I have been working so long, who has advised me through this worry, for whose great work I have actually built my new theatre, if you are not going to back me up thoroughly in the trouble, then it is hard and I feel disheartened for the first time in a way that nothing else could make me. What you should have written to Gilbert was that if *he* did not behave in this outrageous manner then trouble would not arise.

Of course, the law-suit was a sensation. The popular Press howled a macabre chorus of merriment at the sight of be-wigged barristers gravely pleading the case of Gilbert v Carte and Sullivan. Gilbert asked the court to appoint a Receiver of the takings of *The Gondoliers*, and for payment of his share of the profits. Sullivan's counsel said Sir Arthur did not wish to be mixed up in the dispute at all but the appointment of a Receiver would be prejudicial to the property in which he was interested. It was stated that in the second quarter of 1890 the takings had been £20,000 and the expenses £11,000, leaving £9,000 to be divided as profits, so Gilbert's share was £3,000—for three month's performances. It was also mentioned that during the past eleven years Carte had paid Gilbert £90,000. Counsel for Carte now made an offer for settlement which was accepted. Only a day or so afterwards Gilbert wrote to Helen Carte, on 6 September, 1890:

Madam,

You will no doubt be surprised at receiving a letter from me and still more surprised when you find that it is an overture of reconciliation. But we have so thoroughly understood and appreciated each other in byegone days that I cannot believe that, notwithstanding what has passed, you and your husband can be anxious to maintain the unhappy relations that now exist between us . . . I propose that we should all withdraw the angry expressions which under the influence of strong irritation we may have used, and generally look upon byegones as having gone by.

I am faithfully yours,

W.S.G.

Helen Carte rejected a Gilbertian proposal that the outstanding differences should be referred to an arbitrator ('a legal person' said Gilbert), but offered herself to meet Gilbert privately at 4 Adelphi Terrace, the Cartes' home. On 15 September this man-to woman conference occurred, in strict secrecy. Sullivan and D'Oyly Carte were not

---

THE STAR,

"W. S." AT LAW.

The Gilbert-Sullivan-Carte Trio are Fighting it Out in the Courts.

When Mr. W. S. Gilbert expressed the opinion that "the law is the true embodiment of everything that is excellent," he was probably poking fun at the law. Doubtless he didn't dream then that he would before long have to seek its uncertain aid. But recently strange differences have arisen to divide the famous Savoy triumvirate, and Mr. Gilbert's heart has said to him, "W. S." (it calls him "W. S." because it has know him from a baby and they were at school together)—"W.S., you'll have to go to law." Accordingly, among the motions before Justice Lawrence sitting in the Chancery Division to-day was the one on behalf of Mr. Gilbert against Mr. D'Oyly Carte and Sir A. Sullivan, asking for the appointment of a receiver in respect of the librettist's alleged share in the takings arising from the performance of "The Gondoliers." Mr. Fischer, Q.C., appeared for Mr. Gilbert, and with him was Mr. Charles Mitchell (who ought to be

A GOOD FIGHTING JUNIOR,

well up in the upper-cutting and knocking-out styles of pleading if he wishes to be considered worthy of his name). These counsel were instructed by Messrs. Bolton and Mote. Mr. Martin, Q.C., led for Mr. D'Oyly Carte (instructed by Mr. Stanley); and Mr. Macnaghten (who was looked after by Messrs. Lewis and Lewis) appeared for Sir Arthur Sullivan. Considering who the parties were, it would have been a pretty little piece of courtesy if the judge had opened the proceedings in the proper comic opera style laid down by the librettist

"A nice dilemma we have here
That calls for all our wit."

Whereupon counsel would have responded :—

"And at this stage it don't appear
That we can settle it."

present. Helen told Gilbert that, though her husband was glad of this step towards a settlement, the application for a Receiver was deeply resented, and had been injurious to Carte's business, especially just when he was making mortgage arrangements for the Royal English Opera House.

Gilbert told Helen that his original statements about the carpet were made in anger: had he been aware of all the facts he would not have made them. But then, from conciliation, he turned to an astounding demand. He wondered whether there might have been other occasions in the past when Carte had charged expenses without Gilbert's knowledge; he suggested that all the accounts *back to the start of the partnership* be re-opened and examined! Helen said she must refer this to her husband.

Carte said that if there was a post-mortem it would be found that many sums not normally shared with an author—such as bar receipts and programme advertisements—had been put down for years as profits and shared between the three partners, though, by theatrical usage, Carte as the theatre proprietor was entitled to keep the lot. He had shared these profits because of his friendship: 'I thought it a fair and right thing to do.' But if Gilbert insisted on re-opening the eleven-years' accounts and deducting all repair expenses, he (Carte) would insist on deduction of all such incidental profits. Gilbert dropped the suggestion.

'I strongly object', wrote Carte in a memorandum to his wife, 'to Gilbert's taking the line that he and Sullivan have made my fortune. They have made their own as well, and it has been beneficial all round . . . I shall be very glad when the day comes, if it does come, when Gilbert and I can shake hands and forget that all this ever occurred.'

Mr and Mrs Gilbert were in the habit of renting a house in the country not too far from London during the summer months, as they both loved country life, and the next letter comes from:

Breakspears,
Uxbridge.
24 September, '90.

Dear Sullivan,

A letter that I wrote to you before I left for Carlsbad contains an expression that I desire to retract. In that letter, written angrily and under an acute sense of injustice, I applied an epithet to Carte which, on reflection, I consider to be unjustifiable. I am sorry that I used it and I unreservedly withdraw it.

Yours faithfully,
W. S. GILBERT

In a dignified and moving letter, Sullivan told Gilbert that although for old time's sake he would like to forget the quarrel he was only human and was still smarting from recent treatment. A reconciliation must be a thorough one, not merely a hurriedly patched-up truce:

I am physically and mentally ill over this wretched business. I have not yet got over the shock of seeing our names coupled not in brilliant collaboration over a work destined for world-wide celebration, but in hostile antagonism over a few miserable pounds.

Then back he went to *Ivanhoe*! 'The most important work I have yet written, not only from its magnitude but also from the strength of the musical work I have put into it.'[1] Its magnitude was represented by an orchestra of sixty-three, a splendid chorus, a duplicate cast of the finest English singers Carte could engage (duplicated so that they could comfortably give six performances a week), nine elaborate scenes, and a score about which a friend of his said: 'Sullivan wrote *Ivanhoe*, so to speak, with his lifeblood. He slaved at it steadily from May to December, and put into it only of his best. For weeks before he finished it he was inaccessible; the Christmas of 1890 was no holiday for him.'[2]

D'Oyly Carte, too, threw everything into the new venture. 'Nothing that is asked for is refused', said Sullivan. The new theatre was splendidly equipped. Rose Cellier, daughter of François (musical director of *Ivanhoe*, under Sullivan), says: 'I remember so well the first night. A new and gorgeous theatre, a new grand opera written by an English composer, royalty occupying two boxes, and a full house of London's best audiences, all expectant!'[3] On the previous day Sullivan had received a letter from Sandringham, from the Prince of Wales's private secretary, notifying that H.R.H. would be present, and that 'I am particularly desired to mention that the Princess of Wales had no intention of going to London tomorrow, but does so on purpose to attend the first performance of your opera, feeling that she ought to give every encouragement in and of the advancement of the English Opera'.

Every member of the audience was given a printed statement by D'Oyly Carte, setting out his policy: 'To establish English Grand Opera.' He pointed out that no other country had endeavoured to play grand opera all the year round, as was now intended, 'except with the convenient, if sometimes repressive, assistance of a subsidy from the State; which, it is unnecessary to say, this theatre does not enjoy'.

31 January, 1891, was a gala night for Sullivan. He was cheered when he climbed on to the conductor's dais at five minutes past eight; he spent one of the intervals in the Prince's private room smoking cigarettes with H.R.H. and the Duke of Edinburgh; he was cheered again when the final curtain fell at two minutes to twelve. He gave five shillings to each of the stage hands, and got home at four o'clock in the morning. And then—

[1] Letter to Mr Stephens, in D'Oyly Carte archives.
[2] *Thirty Years of Musical Life in London*, by Herman Klein (Heinemann).
[3] Article in the *Gilbert and Sullivan Journal*.

Osborne.

2 Feb., '91.

Dear Sir Arthur,

The Queen wishes me to write and tell you, with what pleasure she sees in the papers of today, that your Opera met with such a great success on Saturday.

It is a particular satisfaction to her, as she believes that it is partly owing to her own instigations that you undertook this great work.

What a gratification it must be to you, to feel that your work is so satisfactorily completed, pray let me congratulate you with all my heart on this, your greatest triumph. I cannot tell you *what* a disappointment it was to me, to have been prevented from going to one of your rehearsals which you had so kindly arranged for me to do, owing to my having such a bad cough. I am looking forward all the more anxiously to hearing *Ivanhoe* very soon.

Believe me,

Even Yours very sincerely Louise[1]

W. S. Gilbert was not present at the first night. He had declined an offer of stalls. The Gilberts were now living at Grim's Dyke, an elaborate mansion at Harrow Weald. During their stay in the country in the previous summer they had looked around for a permanent home; as they drove in a horse-carriage through the lovely grounds of Grim's Dyke and up to the house, which had been built in 1875 in the Tudor style to the designs of Norman Shaw, they immediately decided that here they must come to rest, to enjoy the fruits of W.S.G.'s labours. Within three days Grim's Dyke was theirs. Miss Nancy McIntosh, who lived there with them for many years, wrote[2] that Gilbert 'did many things to improve the grounds, adding tennis courts, a fine lawn for croquet, which became a great favourite after the tennis days were over; and the little lake for bathing which was perhaps his greatest pleasure. He took a great interest in growing fruit and added many houses for grapes, peaches and melons, but left all the gardens and flowers in his wife's hands as she had great knowledge and beautiful taste.'

Within a month of the opening of *Ivanhoe* Gilbert went to see the opera, and wrote a repentant note to Mrs Carte from Grim's Dyke: 'I am, as you know, quite unable to appreciate high-class music, and I expected to be bored—and I was not. This is the highest compliment I ever paid a grand opera.'

It had 155 performances, which is still a record for a continuous run for an English grand opera. And yet *Ivanhoe* has hardly ever been seen or heard since then, and only

[1] Princess Louise, Queen Victoria's sixth child, b. 1848, d. 1939. She was a keen patron of music, and a friend of Sullivan's.

[2] In a letter to the author.

one of its numbers is now well-known ('Ho, Jolly Jenkin', which might just as well have come from a comic opera). *Ivanhoe* did not establish Sullivan's star in the eternal heavens of grand opera; it was a rocket, bursting merely to disappear. Musicians differ about its quality. Sir Hubert Parry went to see it 'eager to be pleased . . . but was thoroughly disappointed . . . most of it is flat, characterless, and inadequate.'[1] On the other hand Sullivan had struck up a friendship with Debussy, and an article in the *Musical Times* says:

Debussy's opinion of Sullivan's music was that there were three Sullivans—Sir Arthur Sullivan the Society gentleman, Sullivan the imitator of Mendelssohn, Auber and Gounod, and Sullivan the pioneer of modern English comedy opera. *The Tempest* was pure Mendelssohn, but the *Henry VIII* music was influenced by Auber. *The Light of the World* was a combination of the styles of Mendelssohn and Gounod, and the weakness of this oratorio lay in its lack of cohesion, the result of the two styles not blending satisfactorily. *The Golden Legend* was Sullivan's best effort in cantata form, being pleasing and melodious, and the opening scene a hundred times more satisfactory than Liszt's noisy setting of the same words. *Ivanhoe*, he said, was equal in merit to the majority of Massenet's operas produced at the Paris Grand Opera, though more vigorous and manly. Debussy thought there was no phase in the history of music to compare with the enormous success of the comic operas. These were, he said, in reality comedy operas and not comic operas, and unlike the opéras-bouffes of Offenbach had outlasted all political changes.[2]

For the first time in his life D'Oyly Carte made a professional miscalculation. He expected *Ivanhoe* to have a very long run (much longer than its 155 performances), and was caught unprepared. He had invited Frederick Cowen to write a grand opera as the next production at the new theatre, but Cowen says in his autobiography that 'Fine as much of the music of *Ivanhoe* was, the opera's power of attraction after the first novelty had worn off was by no means as great as Carte had expected . . . My own opera was commissioned too late for me to complete it in time to follow Sullivan's, therefore, having no other English work ready, Carte was obliged to resort to a French light opera as a stop-gap,[3] with but a poor result. By this time his pockets had been considerably depleted, and not being disposed to incur further risk, he abandoned his scheme and gave up the theatre, which building, much to the regret of all music-lovers, was reopened later as the Palace Music Hall.'[4]

Gilbert had been proved right in his judgment: 'I don't believe in Carte's new theatre.'

It is ironical that though Queen Victoria was responsible for the writing of *Ivanhoe* she never saw it; and yet while it was still running she ordered a Command Performance

[1] *Hubert Parry*, by Charles L. Graves (Macmillan), 1926.
[2] From an article by Andrew de Ternant in the *Musical Times*, December, 1924.
[3] Messager's *La Basoche*.
[4] *My Art and My Friend*, by Sir Frederick H. Cowen (Edward Arnold).

of a comic opera by the D'Oyly Carte Company. They were the first theatrical company to receive a Command to Windsor since the death of the Prince Consort.

From the Queen's Diary, 6 March, 1891

At nine we went over to the Waterloo Gallery where all the seats were filled by the Ladies and Gentlemen of the Household. All the Princes and Princesses sat with me in the front row. *The Gondoliers*, the last of Sir A. Sullivan's comic operas, was performed by D'Oyly Carte's company of the Savoy Theatre, and lasted about two hours and a half. The music, which I know and am very fond of, is quite charming throughout and was well acted and sung. The opening scene with the contadini singing and binding flowers, with a lovely view of Venice and the deep blue sea and

DEMOCRATIC ROYALTY

Perfo⁻mance of "The Gondoliers' Before Good Queen Vic.

———

A SUCCESS IN EVERY RESPECT

———

The Queen and Her Family Set an Example of Royal Freedom So Well Celebrated by That Opera.

———

The Waterloo Gallery at Windsor Castle prepared for the Royal Command performance of 'The Gondoliers'. This event caused widespread interest, not only in Britain but in America, as may be gathered from the headlines in the 'Minneapolis Journal'

[361]

sky, was really extraordinarily pretty. The dancing which often comes in was very graceful and pretty. The dialogue is written by Gilbert and very amusing. The Grand Inquisitor (Mr Denny) was excellent and most absurd, also Mr Rutland Barrington, who is very fat and one of the gondolieri. Miss Jessie Bond is a clever little actress and sings nicely. The dresses are very gay and smart and the whole ensemble brilliant and well put on the stage. In the last scene there were eighty people on the stage, which for an extemporized one was wonderful. I really enjoyed the performance very much. Afterwards I spoke to Mr D'Oyly Carte and complimented him. We then went to .the Drawing-room, into which all the company came, but I only stayed a short while. Everybody was much pleased.[1]

Sullivan and Gilbert were not present. François Cellier conducted. Decima Moore, who was in the cast, tells us: 'The Queen was a little, squat figure in black.' She was seen to be beating time as they sang 'Then one of us will be a Queen and sit on a golden throne . . .'

> Oh, 'tis a glorious thing, I ween,
> To be a regular Royal Queen!

and she *was* amused when Barrington described the daily duties of the monarch of Barataria:

> First, we polish off some batches
> Of political despatches,
>   And foreign politicians circumvent:
> Then, if business isn't heavy,
> We may hold a Royal *levée*,
>   Or ratify some Acts of Parliament.
> Then we probably review the household troops—
> With the usual 'Shalloo humps!' and 'Shalloo hoops!'
> Or receive with ceremonial and state
> An interesting Eastern potentate.
>   After that we generally.
>   Go and dress our private valet—
> (It's a rather nervous duty—he's a touchy little man)—
>   Write some letters literary
>   For our private secretary—
> He is shaky in his spelling, so we help him if we can.
>   Then, in view of cravings inner,
>   We go down and order dinner;
> Then we polish the Regalia and the Coronation Plate—
>   Spend an hour in titivating
>   All our Gentlemen-in-Waiting;
> Or we run on little errands for the Ministers of State.

Bab

[1] From Queen Victoria's diary. Quoted by permission of His Majesty King George VI.

From the *Era*, 14 March, 1891:

Her Majesty, who followed her copy of Mr Gilbert's libretto closely, observed that certain additions were made to the text by the leading performers. Mr Carte was summoned to the elbow of Royalty and the Queen graciously inquired of him the meaning of these interpolations which she had noticed.

'These, your Majesty,' said Mr Carte, 'are what we call gags.'

'Gags?' replied the Queen, 'I thought gags were things that were put by authority into people's mouths.'

'These gags, your Majesty,' answered the manager, bowing profoundly, 'are things that people put into their own mouths without authority.'

The Queen smiled benignly and seemed perfectly satisfied with the ready reply.

So pleased was the Queen that when she was at Balmoral Castle six months later she asked for *The Mikado*. Mr Carte sent his touring company, then playing in Aberdeen, into the Highlands on what one of them describes as a very romantic, exciting and tiring journey. Rhoda Maitland, the soprano, says: 'On 4 September, 1891, we left Aberdeen after lunch and went by train to Ballater where we were met by a string of coaches and wagonettes and conveyed to Balmoral. The weather was perfect, we were a very happy company and very thrilled as we first saw the turrets of the castle in that exquisite setting amid the Scottish mountains. A large room had been set aside for *The Mikado* and in the afternoon we had a rehearsal. After the performance we were presented, and long after midnight we got into the brakes in the courtyard and before we left we stood up and in the light of flaming torches we sang the National Anthem, and the Queen came out on a balcony and waved us farewell.'[1]

It was now eighteen months since the break-up of the Savoy Trinity. Although during the carpet quarrel Gilbert had cancelled Carte's licence to perform 'any of my libretti' after Christmas 1890, he had in fact climbed down and *The Gondoliers* ran on until 20 June, 1891. That appeared to be the end of the Gilbert and Sullivan story. But now Tom Chappell came to Sullivan's rooms in the role of peacemaker. He told Sullivan that Gilbert wanted a complete reconciliation. In the meantime they had both been flirting with new partners. Sullivan had agreed to set *Haddon Hall*, by Sydney Grundy. Described as 'light opera', it was said to be a compromise in musical style between *Ivanhoe* and *The Gondoliers*. Sullivan had rejected a proposal by D'Oyly Carte that he should team-up with two rising young novelists, J. M. Barrie and Conan Doyle, who had concocted a script called *Jane Annie*. Eventually this was set to music by Ernest Ford; its production at the Savoy was notable only for the introduction to the public of Walter Passmore, soon to become a D'Oyly Carte star.

Gilbert had got Alfred Cellier, of *Dorothy* fame, to do the music for his *The Mounte-banks*, a piece of old-fashioned nonsense replete with the magic charms and potions

[1] Statement by the late Mrs Bull, *née* Rhoda Maitland, to the author.

He 'first put this uniform on' . . . in 1891: W. S. Gilbert as Deputy Lieutenant of the County of Middlesex

which Sullivan had spurned. This version of the ill-famed Magic Lozenge was produced by Gilbert at the Lyric Theatre, *not* at the Savoy, on 4 January, 1892. The Lozenge had now become a liquid which (writes W.S.G.) 'has the effect of making every one who drinks it exactly what he pretends to be. The hypocrite becomes a man of piety; the swindler, a man of honour; the quack, a man of learning; and the braggart, a man of war.'

[364]

The wildly complicating effect of this potion on Gilbert's characters and plot may be imagined!—but the fact that *The Mountebanks* enjoyed quite a good run (229 performances) showed that Gilbert's old faith in the Lozenge idea was not unjustified; and it also gave the lie to those who declared that Gilbert could not succeed without Sullivan. Nevertheless, nothing that either Gilbert or Sullivan wrote during the interruption of their partnership has lived in later years. Today *The Mountebanks* is forgotten; so is Sullivan-and-Grundy's *Haddon Hall* (204 performances at the Savoy in 1892); so is Gilbert's play *Rosencrantz and Guildenstern* (Vaudeville Theatre, 1891), a burlesque of *Hamlet* which Sir Arthur Quiller-Couch has since denounced as 'vulgar levity'.[1]

D'Oyly Carte, after *The Gondoliers* ended its wonderful run, had been forced for the first time to put on at the Savoy a comic opera *not* by Gilbert and Sullivan. This was *The Nautch Girl* by George Dance and Edward Solomon, and such was the faithfulness of Carte's public that they fell down and worshipped 'the new Indian idol at the Savoy', as a cartoonist called it. *The Nautch Girl* ran two hundred performances.

Despite the natural tendency of each partner to go on by his own momentum, and to enjoy some immediate public success, in truth and at heart the old Savoy partners were unhappy apart, and anxious to be reunited. When the stage properties left over from *The Yeomen of the Guard* were put up for auction in 1891, Gilbert bought the executioner's axe and block, and wrote to Helen Carte: 'I should like to have them as a relic of the best of our joint work at the Savoy.'

THE NEW INDIAN IDOL AT THE SAVOY

Tom Chappell's olive branch was typically Gilbertian. He told Sullivan that W.S.G.'s idea was that the causes of the rupture should be submitted to arbitration and the party who was thus found guilty should confess himself in the wrong, after which friendly relations would be resumed. Sullivan refused to talk over the old grievances: 'I am quite ready to let bygones be bygones, and to meet you at all times in the most friendly spirit, provided that the disagreeable events of the past eighteen months are never alluded to.'

Gilbert was inclined to wrangle over details. He ended a long letter: 'If you can suggest any reasonable means whereby this cloud can be removed, it will give me infinite pleasure to adopt it.'

It was Sullivan who now showed a sense of humour. He replied: 'Let us meet and

[1] *Studies in Literature*, by Sir Arthur Quiller-Couch, 1929.

shake hands. We can dispel the clouds hanging over us by setting up a counter-irritant in the form of a cloud of smoke.'

A week later, 12 October, 1891, Mr Gilbert called at Sir Arthur Sullivan's rooms in Victoria Street. He was there two hours.

What all their friends were eager to know was whether out of the cloud of smoke that drifted over Sullivan's hearth that day there would emerge, as had happened so often before, a new comic opera. If so, would it be the old Gilbert—'something with boiling oil in it'? Or the new Sullivan—a compromise between *Ivanhoe* and *The Gondoliers?*

It is said that one night Sullivan was watching *Ivanhoe* with Reginald de Koven, a young composer, who said: 'I like it.'

'That's more than I do,' replied Sir Arthur. 'A cobbler should stick to his last.'[1] Now the cobbler returned to his last.

[1] Article on de Koven, by Rennold Wolf, *Green Book Magazine*, December, 1913.

The composer in the last years of his life

FROM W.S.G'S PLOTBOOK OF A FORGOTTEN OPERA

Utopia Limited

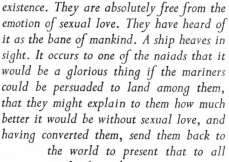

Some of the figures with which Gilbert's imagination peopled the Utopian island. His original idea was that the sea-coast of the isle should be peopled with 'Naiads' [the ladies with harps], who would be visited by the Englishmen in uniforms. 'The naiads dwell', says the plot-book, 'in a peaceful but rather monotonous existence. They are absolutely free from the emotion of sexual love. They have heard of it as the bane of mankind. A ship heaves in sight. It occurs to one of the naiads that it would be a glorious thing if the mariners could be persuaded to land among them, that they might explain to them how much better it would be without sexual love, and having converted them, send them back to the world to present that to all mankind . . .'

Phalarion the First is the first King of Utopia under its reformed Constitution. After many unhappy experiments in the direction of an ideally perfect Commonwealth, involving absolute freedom of opinion on all points, —all of which experiments having resulted in disastrous failure— the Constitution of Utopia has been finally settled as a Despotism on the following basis

1892-3

A GILBERTIAN UTOPIA

England—the powerful, happy, and blameless country
which the consensus of European civilization
has declared it to be.
—Princess Zara in *Utopia Limited*

IN THE GROUNDS of Grim's Dyke the guests parade while a band plays on the sunken lawn and tea is served in the marquee. Sunshine. Parasols. Toppers. Rich, elaborate dresses. The scrunch of metal-shod wheels on the long drive, the distant 'Whoa!' of a coachman. No poop-poop of motor-horn, no growl of aircraft to challenge the tootle of the band and the trill of the birds.

It is a picture of late-Victorian elegance. At the Gilberts' garden party you meet bishops and judges, statesmen, actors and actresses. But not royalty. Ellaline Terriss comes: 'I had always understood Mr Gilbert to be a very frightening person, and expected to be eaten up, but to my surprise I was met by one of the most kindly of men.'[1] Of course W.S.G. is expected to scatter quips among the teacups. Someone has been to a first night and remarks that a well-known actor was for a wonder singing in tune. Gilbert barks: 'Oh, I know that first-night nervousness; it soon wears off.'

They are discussing Beerbohm Tree's 1892 Hamlet. 'I never saw anything so funny in my life,' he says, 'and yet it was not in the least vulgar.'

'Staying in his house was like living in a literary firework factory,' said Rutland Barrington.

George Grossmith was invited to the new house. 'All the great charm of this great genius—this great man—lay in his home,' wrote Grossmith Senior afterwards. 'He was a marvellous host, supported always by his loyal and devoted wife. No matter whether it were a lunch, a dinner, tea, reception, or a juvenile party, he was in his element, and so were his guests. When he retired into the country, he always amused me. When people dropped in to tea, he looked so severe. He would not in a namby-pamby way say to a gentleman, "Oh, DOOOO let me tempt you to have a cup of tea," but he would walk up to him with the semblance of a colonel in command, and with a scowl say "If you don't take tea and prefer a whisky and soda—there it is." '[2]

Clever young Seymour Hicks came and was given an autographed photograph of the great man. The inscription was:

> W. S. Gilbert, born 1836, died ——,
> deeply regretted by all who didn't know him.

The same outlook may be seen at work in his next opera *Utopia Limited; or, The Flowers of Progress*. The literary fireworks factory is in full blast, blowing up the Institutions of Mr Gilbert's own elegant Victorian world. British business methods. The Party System. The Services. The Law. Even the Royal Household. Gilbert was not a rebel or a republican like Shaw or Wells, but he loved to play the gay Guy Fawkes. Into *Utopia Limited* he introduced a Court official called the Public Exploder who, 'on the first lapse of the King from political or social propriety', had to blow up His Majesty with dynamite. But Gilbert himself is really the Public Exploder in this play. He throws a squib at the English mentality: 'England has made herself what she is because in that favoured land every one has to think for himself.' And again: 'They say that in England the conversation of the very meanest is a coruscation of impromptu epigram.'

---

[1] *Ellaline Terriss*, by Herself (Cassell).

[2] 'Recollections of Sir W. S. Gilbert', by George Grossmith Senior, the *Bookman*, July, 1911. This Grossmith is not to be confused with George Grossmith Junior, his son, better known to a later generation as 'G.G. of the Gaiety'. At the time of which we are writing this young man was just coming to the fore. During the Gilbert-Sullivan split described in the last chapter Gilbert dug up the bare bones of an old farce (*The Wedding March*, 1873) and asked Grossmith Senior to doll them up with music. It was retitled *Haste to the Wedding*, but survived at the Criterion only three weeks. Grossmith Junior made his stage début in this piece, under Gilbert's direction—another example of the latter's readiness to encourage young talent.

The theme of this now-little-known opera is almost Shavian. A glamorous South Sea Island, peopled by the lazy and exotic subjects of King Paramount, is reformed into a Utopia, taking England as its model. Zara, the King's daughter, who has been educated at Girton, returns to her island home with six Englishmen—the six 'Flowers of Progress'—representing the highest achievements of British culture, as examples for the islanders to live up to. Gilbert as a dramatist had had several disputes with the censor of plays, who by a quaint British custom happens to be the official in charge of the royal household, so he naturally made this gentleman the first of the six paragons to visit King Paramount:

> This is a Lord High Chamberlain,
> Of purity the gauge—
> He'll cleanse our Court from moral stain
> And purify our stage.

Then there is a company promoter (Mr Goldbury); a County Councillor ('Great Britain's latest toy', Gilbert called him, a reference to the County Councils Act of 1888); and of course a lawyer—

> A marvellous Philologist who'll undertake to show
> That 'yes' is but another and a neater form of 'no' . . .

and the Navy ('Great Britain's proudest boast') is represented by our old friend Captain Corcoran, K.C.B., of *H.M.S. Pinafore*, who has now abandoned sail for steam—

> Though we're no longer hearts of oak,
> Yet we can steer and we can stoke,
> And, thanks to coal, and thanks to coke,
> We never run a ship ashore!
> ALL: What never?
> CAPTAIN: No, never!
> ALL: What *never*? . . . (*etc.*)

The sixth of the 'Flowers of Progress' is Captain Fitzbattleaxe, 1st Life Guards, who comes out from England with troopers in full uniform as escort to the entire party and rather especially to Zara—

> When the tempest rose,
> And the ship went *so*—
> Do you suppose
> We were ill? No, no!
> Though a qualmish lot
> In a tunic tight,
> And a helmet hot,
> And a breastplate bright
> (Which a well-drilled trooper ne'er discards),
> We stood as her escort—First Life Guards!

This plot obviously gives opportunities for a colourful stage, and for fun—especially when it is added that the native Utopian maidens, ravishing in appearance and uninhibited by nature, vamp the Lifeguardsmen as soon as they land. The island King has to apologize to Fitzbattleaxe:

KING: Your Troopers appear to be receiving a troublesome amount of attention from those young ladies. I know how strict your English soldiers are, and I should be extremely distressed if anything occurred to shock their puritanical British sensitiveness.

These were the ideas revolving in the head of Mr W. S. Gilbert, Justice of the Peace and Public Exploder, as he mixed among his guests at his garden parties. In *Utopia* he took this prosperous and complacent England of the nineties and made of it a fireworks display. Even the modest-looking ladies drinking tea on Gilbert's lawn were exploded:

English girls of well-bred notions
Shun all unrehearsed emotions.

One week-end a Dean was his guest. 'How well I remember,' says the Dean of Durham, 'a Sunday evening when Miss Nancy McIntosh was staying at Grim's Dyke and I listened with eager interest to Gilbert's perhaps over-sanguine conversation with her upon the approaching production of *Utopia Limited* in which she was to take the part of Princess Zara. But thinking of my pleasant visits to Grim's Dyke, it occurs to me that more than once Gilbert was unable to occupy his place at the head of his own table as he was suffering from gout.'[1]

Scale model made for W. S. Gilbert, here shown at his house, Grim's Dyke. After his death it was removed to the Science Museum, South Kensington. It was damaged by enemy action in the second World War

Gilbert to Carte:

I have been laid up with a most violent attack of gout in both feet and in the right hand, so I have not been able to do anything but swear for the last eighteen days.

Gout aside, he was a happy man. He was writing again for the old firm. And his life's labours had won him Grim's Dyke. A journalist who called upon him wrote: 'Comic opera does not prevent him from watching the interests of his thoroughbred Jerseys. The roofs of the vineries are heavy with great bunches, and the bee-hives are pointed out by their owner as looking very much like small country theatres doing a "tremendous booking".' The visitor found Gilbert

[1] Article by the Rt. Rev. J. E. C. Welldon, Dean of Durham, in the *Gilbert and Sullivan Journal*.

writing the new opera surrounded by reminders of past triumphs: 'By the window in the entrance hall is a model of a man-of-war, sixteen feet in length. It is perfect in every detail, and a portion of it was specially constructed as a model of the set of the scene in *H.M.S. Pinafore*.'[1] In the billiard room was the headsman's block used in *The Yeomen*. On the walls were framed drawings from *The Bab Ballads*. And on the lawn was a sundial inscribed with a reminder, from *Broken Hearts*, that 'even Time is hastening to its end'.

In the spring of 1892 report came from Cannes that Sir Arthur Sullivan was dying. He was just under fifty. The old kidney trouble had him on the rack: daily and nightly anguish, only endured through morphia. He lay in bed, thin and wan, and gave his last instructions. They read him a telegram from Queen Victoria. The Prince of Wales's surgeon called. Then D'Oyly Carte hurried from England and sat by the bedside and talked of old times, the Savoy, new plans, Gilbert, *Utopia*. A ghost of the old animation returned; but Carte came back to London wondering whether Sullivan would ever compose again. His light opera *Haddon Hall* was half-written . . . and Sullivan still had dreams of another grand opera; his rather grand incidental music for Lord Tennyson's play *The Foresters* was praised in America (it was produced at Daly's Theatre, New York, in March while Sullivan was lying in torture at Cannes). Presently he rallied, and they carried him on to the boat at Calais and brought him home to London.

To Sir Arthur Sullivan, Lambeth-born,

THE PUBLIC EXPLODER
*W.S.G. at Grim's Dyke—
with one of Bab's bees*

[1] *Illustrated Interviews*, by Harry How, *Strand Magazine*, 1893.

RUTLAND BARRINGTON AS KING
PARAMOUNT IN 'UTOPIA'
*'I am waiting until a punishment is dis-
covered that will exactly meet the enormity of
the case. I am in constant communication with
the Mikado of Japan, who is a leading
authority on such points'*

the sounds of traffic, Big Ben, Cockney street cries, always meant home. He craved no country estate. A visitor to his bachelor rooms, Queen's Mansions, Victoria Street, gives us a glimpse of exotic comfort: 'During his vast travels abroad he has amassed a large collection of rare antiquities, his taste apparently inclining him towards those curios hailing from the far East. In his entrance hall Arabian lamps hang, giving out their mysterious quaint lights in softly sombre rays, while you peep through a lovely screen of old Cairo wood-work before reaching the dwelling rooms. The doors are artistically draped with elaborate Persian and Greek hangings and, nestling beneath the spreading leaves of rare palms, you meet with large restful divans upon which Oriental silks of great beauty and price are carelessly thrown. Sir Arthur's material surroundings convey to the casual visitor an impression of artistic calm and physical comfort'.[1]

Convalescing, he stayed with the Prince and Princess of Wales at Sandringham. He sat in the sun watching cricket at Lords. He tried to get on with *Haddon Hall*, and slowly it was finished, and great was the delight of Londoners when Sir Arthur appeared again at the Savoy, to conduct the opening performance in September, 1892. Mr Gilbert was there, and went round to see him. The tunes of *Haddon Hall* were soon on everyone's lips but the critics severely handled the words by Mr Grundy—unfairly so, Sullivan thought. It was simply that Grundy wasn't Gilbert.

As soon as *Haddon Hall* was launched Gilbert presented Sullivan with the synopsis of *Utopia Limited*. This was written on thirty-seven pages of an exercise book.

The synopsis was popped into Sullivan's bag as he left once more for the Riviera. In December he wrote from Cabbé-Roquebrune, Alpes Maritimes, to Sir George Grove, his lifelong and greatest friend: 'I have a lovely villa with a very

[1] M. A. von Zedlitz, in the *Strand Musical Magazine*, 1895.

large garden right down to the sea . . . It is divine here—such sea, sky, sunshine.'[1]

And on the last day of the year, in his diary: 'Saw New Year in; hoped and prayed that it might be a happier one for me than this last, half of which was lost through my illness. Health is the secret of happiness.'

In January, 1893, Gilbert travelled out to Sullivan, and for some days they were by the southern sea together, planning their new opera of a South Sea Isle. Act 1 was to be set in a 'Utopian Palm Grove in the gardens of King Paramount's Palace, showing a picturesque and luxuriant tropical landscape, with the sea in the distance', with Utopian maidens lying lazily about the stage and thoroughly enjoying themselves in lotus-eating fashion . . .

> In lazy languor—motionless,
> We lie and dream of nothingness—

Then Gilbert travelled back to Grim's Dyke, leaving Sullivan to dream in the sunshine.

Gilbert to Sullivan:

I arrived here all right last night after a beastly passage, and three tiresome days in Paris. I send you Cook on Billiards—the study of that work has made me what I am in Billiards, and if you devote six or eight hours a day at it regularly, you may hope to play up to my form when you return.

Sullivan returned in March. Gilbert to Sullivan:

I will come on Thursday as you suggest. I assume that you are not averse to standing a bit of bread and cheese and a drop of beer to a pore working man wots bin out of work for some years? I'm going to have a shot at the duet (Act 2) this morning.

D'Oyly Carte was urging them to have *Utopia Limited* ready for October. Neither *Haddon Hall* nor *Jane Annie* had brought back former glories to the Savoy, and Carte was eager to see the old magic spell at work again—not the artificial magic of Gilbert's lozenges and potions (none of which W.S.G. attempted to put into the new opera), but the real magic of the combined Gilbert-and-Sullivan genius.

Gilbert to Sullivan, 22 June, 1893:

I have altered the finale in a manner which I hope you will like. Today for the first time I have managed to cram my foot into a boot—a stretched boot, but a boot for all that.

Gilbert went to Homburg for treatment for his gout, and wrote from there in great detail about the work, concluding:

I shall be back by the 10th, and we can talk over the matter when we meet. So far, I am worse rather than better. My right foot, which I call Labouchère, is very troublesome, and I take a pleasure (not unalloyed with pain) in cramming him into a boot which is much too small for him. My left foot (known in Homburg as

[1] *Life of Sir George Grove*, by Charles L. Graves (Macmillan).

Clement Scott)[1] is a milder nuisance, but still tiresome, and would hurt me a good deal if he could . . .

The waters have so far done me very little good. I can only walk with difficulty, even now, and have to go to and from the waters in a bath chair every morning. Mrs G—— is here heading a shoal of Americans.

Yours sincerely,

W. S. GILBERT

PS. Mrs G—— lives *entirely* on *nuts* and says she was never so well since she was fifteen.

Fitting a finale to *Utopia Limited* was as painful as cramming Gilbert's foot into a boot. At last, in desperation, he told Sullivan to write the music first. Then he got up at seven o'clock one morning at Grim's Dyke, fitted some words before breakfast, and wrote to the composer: 'It is mere doggerel—but words written to an existing tune are nearly sure to be that.'

When Mrs Carte asked Gilbert for a donation for an orchestral charity, he replied:

I hate the orchestra. They take up a lot of paying stalls—they are the most cantankerous and independent set in the theatre—and they play so loud that my words can't be heard. Moreover, like many other high-souled and independent specimens of Nature's nobility, they are the first to come begging cap in hand when they are in difficulties. Having thus blown off steam, I have much pleasure in sending five guineas for the fund.

Sullivan was summering at Weybridge, and it was an extremely hot summer. Boating, cycling, and tennis distracted him. Sullivan's diary:

August 17—Terrible heat, 90°. Impossible to work owing to regatta and fair being held. Two large musical steam roundabouts outside house. So gave myself up to the regatta and sports. Frank Cellier arrived at 5.30. Worked at opera with him at night.

August 18. Working with Cellier till Gilbert arrived 12.30. After lunch G and I worked at new opera, suggestions, alterations, etc. Real good day's work. At seven rowed him to Halliford and back. Heat awful, 93° in shade.

The scene of Act 2 which they were now threshing out is the throne room of King Paramount's Palace. Here the consequences of reorganizing South Sea Island society on an English basis are unfolded. The Flowers of Progress have done their work so well that all laws are now perfect, all lawyers are out of work, all doctors are starving, all neighbouring nations have disarmed and war is impossible, and the jails are let as model lodgings for the working classes—the reader will recognize this as a remnant of material which Gilbert had saved up in his plot-book from *Iolanthe*, eleven years previously.[2] The islanders rebel against such a Utopia, but then Princess Zara remembers that in her zeal to reform her people on English lines she has forgotten something:

[1] Clement Scott was editor of the *Theatre*, Henry Labouchère editor of *Truth*.
[2] See p. 227.

ZARA: Government by Party! Introduce that great and glorious element—at once the bulwark and foundation of England's greatness—and all will be well! No political measures will endure, because one Party will assuredly undo all that the other Party has done; and while grouse is to be shot, and foxes worried to death, the legislative action of the country will be at a standstill. Then there will be sickness in plenty, endless lawsuits, crowded jails, interminable confusion in the Army and Navy, and, in short, general and unexampled prosperity!

To the Conservative and Liberal upper and middle classes, who were the backbone of Gilbert and Sullivan audiences, this seemed rather like an anarchic bomb, and though Gilbert exploded it just for fun some people thought his sense of humour was going a bit too far. *Utopia* audiences did not know how far to take Gilbert seriously. Mr Goldbury, for instance, sings a ballad in praise of the English girl, 'the most beautiful, the bravest, and the brightest creature that Heaven has conferred upon this world'; it is set to quite serious music—but can it really be taken seriously?—

A wonderful joy our eyes to bless,
In her magnificent comeliness,
Is an English girl of eleven stone two,
And five foot ten in her dancing shoe!
She follows the hounds, and on she pounds—
    The 'field' tails off and the muffs diminish—
Over the hedges and brooks she bounds
    Straight as a crow, from find to finish.
At cricket, her kin will lose or win—
    She and her maids, on grass and clover,
Eleven maids out—eleven maids in—
    And perhaps an occasional 'maiden' over!
Go search the world and search the sea,
Then come you home and sing with me
There's no such gold and no such pearl
As a bright and beautiful English girl!

—*Bab*

For the part of Princess Zara, the Girton girl who wore the latest Parisian costumes on her return to her island home, Mr Gilbert cast his latest 'discovery', a beautiful young American who had never been on the stage before. Miss Nancy McIntosh had recently arrived in England from Cleveland, Ohio. She was the daughter of Minerva and William Alexander McIntosh. Her forefathers were pioneers and settlers in the U.S.A. Her grandfather helped to build the Pittsburgh and Cleveland Railway; her father was President of the New York and Cleveland Gas Coal Company. She came to England with no idea of going behind footlights, or of staying here, but swiftly became leading lady

Nancy McIntosh

at the Savoy, was adopted by the Gilberts as their daughter, and was still living in London in 1951 when she gave an interview to the author.

'My ambition was to be a concert singer,' she said, 'I came to London to finish my musical studies under Mr Henschel (later Sir George) and I made my public début at the "Saturday Pops" at St James's Hall, singing a Wagnerian aria with Mr Henschel's orchestra there. A fortnight later the Henschels asked me to sing after dinner at a party at their house, and it proved a fateful night for me. Many great swells came to these parties, and of course I was much impressed by it all. It happened that when Mr W. S. Gilbert entered the room I was sitting under a standard lamp, and the light was falling on my fair hair. He was always attracted to women with fair hair—his wife had the most beautiful fair hair and complexion— and he immediately turned to a neighbour and asked who I was. After I had sung he came over and told me he was looking for a soprano for his next opera. Within a few days he asked me to go round to the Savoy Theatre and sing to Sir Arthur Sullivan, and they offered me the part.'

Utopia Limited was the most lavishly staged of all the Gilbert and Sullivan operas, and the most costly. The gorgeous throne-room scene in Act 2, in which Gilbert aimed to reproduce in detail the ceremony of one of Queen Victoria's 'drawing room' receptions, thinly disguised, made an alarming estimate when Helen D'Oyly Carte worked out the figures. Mrs Carte's estimates, which may still be seen at the Savoy, included £1,500 for scenery and £3,500 for dresses. Shoes cost only 10s. a pair in 1893, but one costume (for Fitzbattleaxe) cost one hundred guineas. Court uniforms for eighteen chorus gentlemen cost £720; twenty-eight sets of jewellery, bouquets, gloves, stockings, shoes and underskirts, £420; sketches by the artist, Percy Anderson, £50. The total estimate was £6,750—but this time it was Sullivan who took fright and protested, not Gilbert.

Gilbert to Sullivan:

I quite agree with you that it is desirable that the enormous estimated expense of production should be curtailed if this can be done without cramping the piece. I confess I should be sorry to lose the Gents at Arms—who always stand two at the entrance and two at the exit of the Presence Chamber, to regulate the admission and exit of ladies presented—and I am afraid that without them the ladies will have the appearance of loafing on to the stage without any 'circumstance'. Besides, you must remember that these four people must be dressed somehow. They can't go naked (unless you insist on it), and if they are put into good uniforms they will cost at least £50 apiece. I think a little economy might be effected by cutting out two or three of the costly hussar and lancer uniforms . . .

In the end the production cost even more than the estimate. It came out at £7,200, a very large figure in those days. Another slight blow-back to old controversies occurred when Sullivan suspected the presence of yet another of Gilbert's love-stricken elderly ladies in the plot: Lady Sophy, governess to King Paramount's children, aged forty-five, and in love with the King; but Gilbert assured Sullivan that 'It is not necessary that she should be so very old, ugly, raddled, and grotesque . . . Nor do I propose that she should be "seething with love and passion".'

Rosina Brandram took the part, and Walter Passmore recollects that during rehearsals she had to pay a visit to the dentist. 'This affected for a short time her clearness of speech. I noticed Gilbert becoming fidgety and when the actor with her fluffed a line it was too much for him. "I wish," he remarked, "those two would change teeth and try again."'[1] Passmore, who was by now assuming the comedy leadership at the Savoy formerly occupied by George Grossmith, Snr, took the part of the Public Exploder, Tarara (Tarara-BOOM-de-ay was the popular song, and errand boy's catchword, of the moment).

Gilbert's audacity in mocking Court etiquette caused a raised eyebrow or so in 1893, but there is no evidence to support a widespread legend that in consequence *Utopia Limited* was ostracized by the Royal Family. What actually happened is indicated by this letter, written after the production of the opera:

Grim's Dyke, Harrow Weald, 5 Nov. '93.

Dear S.

I hear that the Prince of Wales took some exception to Barrington wearing the Order of the Garter. He doesn't seem to have *pressed* the objection, so I think we should be doing a graceful thing in removing his ground of complaint. If you agree, will you wire Carte to this effect?

Several of the noblemen in *Iolanthe* wore the Garter and no objection was made—so I concluded, reasonably I think, that it might be permitted in *Utopia*. But I suppose the Field-Marshal's Uniform makes it rather more personal to H.R.H.

Yours very truly,
W. S. GILBERT

The point of the Prince of Wales's objection was that Rutland Barrington, as King Paramount, was dressed in Act 2 as a British Field-Marshal, with Order of the Garter, to take the chair at a Utopian Cabinet Council; only one man, at that time, was entitled to this double distinction—and that man was Albert Edward, Prince of Wales. And so Paramount lost his Garter.

[1] Reminiscences of Walter Passmore, *Evening News*, London, 1930.

This scene was the wildest burlesque of Downing Street procedure, the Ministers ranging their chairs across the stage in the manner familiarized to Victorian audiences by the Christy Minstrels at the St James's Hall, Piccadilly.

'You are not making fun of us?' asks the King, sitting in the middle of the row. 'This is in accordance with the practice at the Court of St James's?'

The Lord Chamberlain replies: 'Well, it is in accordance with the practice at the Court of St James's Hall.' And then King Paramount reports progress, with minstrel chorus by the six Englishmen:

KING: Society has quite forsaken all her wicked courses,
              Which empties our police courts, and abolishes divorces.
CHORUS: Divorce is nearly obsolete in England . . .
KING: Our city we have beautified—we've done it willy-nilly—
              And all that isn't Belgrave Square is Strand and Piccadilly!
CHORUS: We haven't any slummeries in England!
KING: We have solved the labour question with discrimination polished,
              So poverty is obsolete and hunger is abolished—
CHORUS: We are going to abolish it in England!

During his very distinguished literary career Gilbert had never been honoured by State or royalty, like Sullivan; now he could not resist a self-conscious comment, where this song refers to the reform of the hereditary peerage 'on an intellectual basis'—

KING: The Brewers and the Cotton Lords no longer seek admission,
              And Literary Merit meets with proper recognition—
CHORUS: As Literary Merit does in England!

Sullivan fitted this minstrel burlesque with an orchestration imitating banjos and bones very cleverly. The music of *Utopia Limited* drew a remarkable tribute from Bernard Shaw, now writing for the *Saturday Review*. Shaw's own first play, *Widowers' Houses*, had just been produced. He was more conscious than most people of the stage revolution wrought by Gilbert and Sullivan opera, and especially of the debt owed to Richard D'Oyly Carte:[1]

Those who are old enough to compare the Savoy performances with those of the dark ages, taking into account the pictorial treatment of the fabrics and colours on the stage, the cultivation and intelligence of the choristers, the quality of the orchestra, and the degree of artistic good breeding, so to speak, expected from the

[1] This notice appears in *Music in London, 1890–94*, by George Bernard Shaw (Constable). It appeared originally in the *Saturday Review*, 19 October, 1893.

principals, best know how great an advance has been made by Mr D'Oyly Carte in organizing and harmonizing that complex co-operation of artists of all kinds which goes to make up a satisfactory operatic performance. Long before the run of a successful Savoy opera is over Sir Arthur's melodies are dinned into our ears by every promenade band and street piano, and Mr Gilbert's sallies are quoted threadbare by conversationalists and journalists; but the whole work as presented to eye and ear on the Savoy stage remains unhackneyed.

Further, no theatre in London is more independent of those executants whose personal popularity enables them to demand ruinous salaries; and this is not the least advantageous of the differences between opera as the work of a combination of manager, poet, and musician, all three making the most of one another in their concerted striving for the common object of a completely successful representation, and opera as the result of a speculator picking up a libretto, getting somebody with a name to set it to music, ordering a few tradesmen to 'mount' it, and then, with a stage manager hired here, an acting manager hired there, and a popular prima donna, comedian, and serpentine dancer stuck in at reckless salaries like almonds into an under-done dumpling, engaging some empty theatre on the chance of the affair 'catching on'.

The reader who has now followed the progress of the Carte-Gilbert-Sullivan revolution from those 'dark ages' when young Mr Richard D'Oyly Carte, dreaming of an English School of comic opera, sought the aid of Mr Sullivan and Mr Gilbert to rescue popular theatrical entertainment from the vulgar fooleries of burlesque and 'the smell of orange peel and lamp oil', will appreciate how well merited was this tribute of Bernard Shaw's. And although the music of *Utopia* has not stood the test of time, Shaw went on to discuss it in 1893 in terms which, again, marked how very far our musical theatre had progressed since the corniest of music-hall tunes were commonly strung together by illiterate musical hacks to accompany the burlesques of the sixties. Shaw warned readers of the *Saturday Review* 'not to infer that *Utopia* is full of buffooneries with the bassoon and piccolo':

Whoever can listen to such caressing wind parts—zephyr parts, in fact—as those in the trio for the King and the two Judges in the first act, without being coaxed to feel pleased and amused, is not fit even for treasons, stratagems, and spoils; whilst anyone whose ears are capable of taking in more than one thing at a time must be tickled by the sudden busyness of the orchestra as the city man takes up the parable. I also confidently recommend those who go into solemn academic raptures over themes 'in diminution' to go and hear how prettily the chorus of the Christy Minstrel song (borrowed from the plantation dance 'Johnnie, get a gun') is used, very much in diminution, to make an exquisite mock-banjo accompaniment. In these examples we are on the plane, not of the bones and tambourine, but of Mozart's accompaniments to 'Soave sia il vento' in *Cosi fan tutte* and the entry of the gardener in *Le Nozze di Figaro*. Of course these things are as much thrown away on people who are not musicians as a copy of *Fliegende Blätter* on people who do not read German, whereas anyone can understand mere horseplay with the instruments.

But people who are not musicians should not intrude into opera-houses: indeed, it is to me an open question whether they ought to be allowed to exist at all.

* * *

When Mr Carte announced that the new opera would appear on 7 October, 1893, the excitement of Press and public was unbounded—Gilbert and Sullivan again after a lapse of close on four years! The curtain came down that night and Sir Arthur Sullivan and Mr Gilbert took their bows behind the footlights. It was just like the grand old days, the wonderful first nights gone by, except that Sullivan, once so debonair, looked frail; and Gilbert, once so erect, hobbled on a stick. They stood there smiling into the auditorium which had seen so many of their triumphs, then they turned and shook hands, to a deafening roar of applause.

Next day the *Morning Standard* declared: 'A more complete success has never been achieved in comic opera even at the Savoy.' *Utopia Limited* ran 245 performances in London. It was a failure in America. It has never been seen since, except at a few amateur presentations. Why? Did the Public Exploder go too far, over-reaching his old Gilbertian tricks? Was Sullivan's music, as some critics have said, patchy? *Punch* thought it hardly ever rose above the commonplace.[1] Mr Shaw and others disagreed: 'The score is Sullivan at his brightest,' says Mr Walbrook,[2] who saw the production in 1893, and who puts his finger on the main cause for this opera's disappearance from the repertoire when he says that *Utopia Limited* is not easy to produce: 'It requires at least five first-rate comedians, all of them good comic actors, really good singers, and accomplished dancers. It demands a brilliant soprano and a fine tenor and baritone. Even the smaller parts are more than usually exacting.'[3] This was confirmed by Mr Rupert D'Oyly Carte, when he said[4] that in the 1920's he considered reviving the opera, and attended a performance by an amateur company in the North of England to study its presentation; new dress designs were prepared by Percy Anderson, but the project was abandoned because of production difficulties and costs. So, in a way, Gilbert and Sullivan *did* over-reach themselves. In their anxiety to make a successful come-back, they over-elaborated their tricks, forgetful that the beauty of their magic in the past had been its simplicity.

[1] See *Punch*, 28 October, 1893, which also accuses Gilbert of plagiarism.
[2] See *Gilbert and Sullivan Opera*, by H. M. Walbrook (F. V. White & Co.)
[3] Lecture to the Gilbert and Sullivan Society.
[4] This important statement was made to the author by the late Mr Carte in 1947.

'The grand old days, the wonderful first nights gone by' as represented in the film 'The Story of Gilbert and Sullivan' in 1953. ABOVE: Sullivan conducting the first performance of 'Trial by Jury' at the Opéra Comique. BELOW: 'Iolanthe' at the old Savoy Theatre with Gilbert (Robert Morley) and Sullivan (Maurice Evans) taking their bows

Tunbridge Wells.

Weather changed. Very cold — damp & dull.
Cellier & I indoors all day (except for half an hour's stroll)
working at accomp.ts &c. new opera.

Wrote to Princess Christian, & Clot: to say I was coming home
tomorrow.

Have been here just a fortnight, and what have I done? Little
more than nothing, first from illness and physical incapability,
secondly from brooding, and nervous terror about myself. Dr
Mauser examined me very carefully this morning — chest, heart,
lungs &c. — says I am sound enough, but my throat still
in a bad state. But practically I have done nothing
for a month. Have   **15 MONDAY** [288-77] ☽ 9h 51m   now finished & formed
Quarter Sessions Week.
1st Act, & they are rehearsing it.   A.M. (Greenwich)

Lovely day. Fr: Cellier left at 11.10. I am sorry to
leave such a lovely day.

The last entries in the diary of Sir Arthur Sullivan. The new opera, of which he
had 'finished and formed' Act I on 14 October, was 'The Emerald Isle', later
completed by Sir Edward German. Sullivan died on 22 November, but wrote
nothing in his diary after this 'lovely day'

1894-1900

FIN DE SIÈCLE

THE OLD CENTURY DIED, and the old Queen died with it. In the dwindling twilight of its final years many of the characteristic features of the nineteenth century crumbled, and many of the great Victorians passed away. There was a sense of the curtain coming down after a long pageant, the aged actors taking their last bows, reluctant to reappear again in the next bright new scene, the Brave New World that was to follow. The spell of Victorianism was broken, it was the end of a cycle; there was a curious, widespread finality about it. William Morris, Pater, Gladstone, R. L. Stevenson, Oscar Wilde, du Maurier, Lewis Carroll—they all died with these last few years of the old century, with the gaslight and the horse-cabs. The motor car's oncoming snort was heard in the wings, and so were the infant voices of Irving Berlin and George Gershwin, harbingers of jazz; and the natal cry of Noel Coward in 1899 signalled a new species of theatrical wit advancing to take over from Gilbert. Shaw and Wells were bursting with the electric spirit of the New Age, while in the fading lamplight of the old one Aubrey Beardsley was illustrating *The Yellow Book* with those hot-house drawings about which hangs the odour of decadence.

After *Utopia Limited* 'Gilbert and Sullivan' as a partnership withered away. Early in 1894 the box-office registered the fact that Gilbert was wrong in expecting this opera to be another *Mikado*.

D'Oyly Carte to Gilbert:

The piece, in its third month, is not drawing to any extent, and is obviously not going to have a long run. There is no doubt in my mind that what the people want now is simply 'fun', and little else.

He urged Sullivan and Gilbert to write a 'frankly comic piece' for the Savoy. How right he was in his estimate was soon proved by the musical comedy boom at other London theatres—*An Artist's Model* (392 performances), *The Geisha* (760), *San Toy* (768), *The Belle of New York* (697), all came between 1895 and the end of the century. George Edwardes had left D'Oyly Carte and, taking over the Gaiety Theatre, led the new vogue with tremendous gusto. Behind the imposing, over-elaborate façade of *Utopia Limited* at the Savoy Theatre decay had set in. Since the carpet quarrel the Savoy Trinity had not been quite at ease, privately. And professionally too the old, sure—and simple—touch was faltering. Four days after *Utopia's* opening performance its much-disputed finale was again scrapped and a new one introduced overnight.

Gilbert seems to have realized he was a 'played-out humorist'; after toying with

Sullivan over an idea for a new opera,[1] his thoughts wandered to a partnership with Henschel (Miss McIntosh's singing teacher),[2] and finally he produced *His Excellency* to music by F. Osmond Carr at the Lyric Theatre. He put in it some self-conscious lines, which he afterwards inserted as the final item in his collected *Bab Ballads* under the title—

THE PLAYED-OUT HUMORIST

Quixotic is his enterprise, and hopeless his adventure is,
 Who seeks for jocularities that haven't yet been said.
The world has joked incessantly for over fifty centuries,
 And every joke that's possible has long ago been made.
I started as a humorist with lots of mental fizziness,
 But humour is a drug which it's the fashion to abuse;
For my stock-in-trade, my fixtures, and the goodwill of the business
 No reasonable offer I am likely to refuse . . .

* * * *

. . . I've come to the conclusion that my mine of jocularity,
In present Anno Domini, is worked completely out!
 Though the notion you may scout,
 I can prove beyond a doubt
That my mine of jocularity is utterly worked out!

At first Gilbert thought *His Excellency* was in for a long run. 'The piece', he wrote to Mrs Carte, 'is doing admirably. If it had had the advantage of your expensive friend Sullivan's music it would have been a second *Mikado*'. But *His Excellency* was no great success. In the same year Gilbert wrote to Muriel Barnby, daughter of the composer: 'I am a crumbling man—a magnificent ruin, no doubt, but still a ruin—and like all ruins I look best by moonlight. Give me a sprig of ivy and an owl under my arm and Tintern Abbey would not be in it with me.' But even in this humour Gilbert was borrowing from the past. Many years before, in *Foggerty's Fairy*, he had written: 'You are a splendid ruin. With a sprig or two of ivy and an owl under your arm you would be complete!'[3]

He kept a stern paternal eye on the Savoy and its company so long as *Utopia Limited* was still there. One day he wrote to D'Oyly Carte:

Miss —— was away from the theatre on Tuesday night—ill.
Miss —— was dancing at a fancy ball at the Albert Hall on Tuesday night—well. I met her there.
I believe this is not the first time that Miss —— has been too ill to come to the Theatre but not too ill to go to a ball.
I think we must get rid of Miss —— .

[1] January, 1894: correspondence in the Savoy archives.
[2] Letter from Gilbert in possession of Group-Captain F. G. Brockman.
[3] Quoted in article by Miss Muriel Barnby, *Strand Magazine*, 1927.

THE OPERA THAT FAILED
*Walter Passmore in 'The Grand Duke', and
two of Gilbert's sketches of other characters*

When *Utopia* came off in the summer of
1894 Sullivan and Gilbert had nothing to
take its place. Sullivan had been over to
Berlin to conduct *Ivanhoe* and to have a look
at the native German production of *The
Gondoliers* (he reported: 'The tempo is all
too slow. There is no go in it.') A £20,000-
a-year man, he was racing his own horses
now, and was seen more often than ever at
fashionable race meetings with the Prince of Wales, at the Garrick Club, at theatres and
salons. He composed some incidental music for a Lyceum play, *King Arthur* by J.
Comyns Carr, and then, like Gilbert, he borrowed from the past: he took down from
the shelves the score of his first full comic opera *The Contrabandista*, and with his old
friend Burnand to doctor the words, he doctored the music, and they re-hashed it as
The Chieftain at the Savoy. This warmed-up dish was rejected by the public, but when
Carte brought back *The Mikado* to fill the gap, the universal delight was shown in
crowded houses. The moral was very obvious. As Francis Toye has so neatly put it, the
vinegar of Gilbert was indispensable to the oil of Sullivan for the musical dressing to be
wholly satisfactory.[1]

Jessie Bond was still in the Savoy Company, and in October 1895 she asked Gilbert
if she could be given a new song in *The Mikado* revival. He replied: 'Even if we could
find a place for it (very difficult), there is Sullivan to be reckoned with and I doubt
very much if he would care to put aside the new piece upon which he is working night
and day, in order to write a song for *Mikado*. He is like me in one respect (only in one)

[1] 'The Charm of Music—some thoughts on Gilbert and Sullivan', by Francis Toye, *Illustrated London
News*, 28 January, 1939.

[387]

—when he is in full swing of his work, as he is now, he won't stand interruption.'[1]

This 'new piece' was a new opera by Gilbert and Sullivan: their fourteenth and last. Of *The Grand Duke; or, The Statutory Duel* the least said the better. There was, of course, the usual brilliant first night in March, 1896, and Gilbert and Carte had staged the opera spectacularly in a sort of Gilbertian Ruritania, the Grand Duchy of Pfennig Halbpfennig, date 1750; and had given the Press a 'story' by importing a Hungarian beauty, Mlle Ilka von Palmay, to play 'Julia Jellicoe, an English comedienne'. In the German production of *The Mikado* this lady had played the male part of Nanki-Poo, which travesty was enough to have given Gilbert apoplexy, but he had a good artistic reason for engaging her in *The Grand Duke*. Julia Jellicoe is shown to

Ilka von Palmay

be an English girl alone among a group of Germans, all of whom are presumed to be speaking and singing in German. Julia, on the other hand, is supposed to be speaking in a strange tongue (as she exclaims, 'Ach! what a crack-jaw language this German is'). By engaging a foreign singer, the illusion was created, by inversion, that Julia spoke German with an English accent. But such ingenious Gilbertian devices were insufficient to save *The Grand Duke*.

The Times newspaper saw through it all: '*The Grand Duke* is not by any means another *Mikado*, and, though it is far from being the least attractive of the series, signs are not wanting that the rich vein which the collaborators and their various followers have worked for so many years is at last dangerously near exhaustion.'

The Grand Duke collapsed at 123 performances, the shortest run of any Gilbert and Sullivan opera since *Thespis*, their first, twenty-five years before. Back came *The Mikado*, up soared the takings at the Savoy, and this wonderful opera raced on to its one thousandth performance. . . . But what to do with Ilka von Palmay?—she had done well in *The Grand Duke*. 'She achieved at one bound a great London reputation,' said the *Illustrated London News*—but now Carte had her on his hands, on a three-year contract. A female Nanki-Poo in London was unthinkable! The dilemma was solved when a revival of *The Yeomen of the Guard* followed. The Hungarian beauty played Elsie Maynard, that 'humble merrymaid, peerly proud', with her 'song to sing, O'—as English a character as Gilbert ever created.

For this revival (1897) Gilbert himself designed a new setting for Act 2, a view of the wharf without the Tower of London background. Henry Lytton was promoted to

[1] Letter in the collection of Mr Reginald Allen, of New York.

Performed in Gilbert and Sullivan Operas at the Old Savoy or earlier

Signature	First Appearance	Signature	First Appearance
Julia Gwynne (Mrs George Edwardes)	(Opera Comique) 1878	Nelly Bromley (Mrs Archibald Stuart Wortley)	1875
Leonora Braham	1881	W R Shirley	1888
Durward Lely	1881 (Opera Comique)	J. M. Gordon (on Tour 1888)	1884
Jessie Bond	1878	Louie René	1894
Nancy McIntosh	1893	Scott Russell	1893
Henry A. Lytton	1885	Lillian Carr	1882
Elsie Henri	1885	Louie Pounds	1901
Geraldine Ulmar	1887	Cissie Saumarez (Mrs Arthur Whitby)	1889
M. Foster ???	1881	Walter Passmore	1893
Sibyl Grey	(Opera Comique) 1878	Agnes Fraser	1900
Les Stuffield	1907	???	1884
Bertha Lewis	1909	Decima Moore	1889
Sydney Granville	1907	Neva Bond	1880
Georgie Sinclair	1887	John Coates	1893
Ella S. Nelson	1892	Jennie Sullivan	1877
Evie MacPhail	1893	Madeleine Gaeton	1891
Frank H. Crimp	1894	Geoffry T. Snelson	1893
E. A. Fleming	Opera Comique 1877	Charles Stuart	1891
Annie Bernard	1883	Allen Morris	1881
Clara Dow	1907	H R Blake Johnston	1889
Blanche Gaston-Murray	1877	Tiny Murray	1882
Harry Grattan	1878	Strafford Moss	1897
Ethel Jeffreys	1889	Jessie Curtice Pounds	1882
Richard ???	1906	Kate Chard	1883

Nelly Bromley, the original plaintiff in 'Trial by Jury', is the earliest Gilbert
& Sullivan star in this remarkable collection of autographs. Miss Bromley died
in 1939 aged eighty-nine

[389]

the London company. *The Yeomen* ran over six months. Sullivan was present on the last night and filled his diary with detailed criticisms of all the artists: 'Lytton admirable, an acquisition in every way, style refined . . . Dear old Rosie (Brandram) first rate as always . . . I like little Vincent—her upper notes are of pretty quality although not strong, and she is pretty and refined.' This refers to Ruth Vincent.[1] But there is no diary reference to Gilbert; they had taken no thrilling curtain call together. New estrangements had arisen. The old partners never met now. Sullivan knew he would never collaborate again with Gilbert, and though he still dreamt of a grand opera he was a tired and saddened man, and somehow he never got to grips with it.

1896: AUTUMNAL INTERLUDE

The Alps are glittering under the morning sun, the sky is cloudless, the sweet grass of the ravine is fresh and green. No music but the cowbells and the mountain rivulet. No sign of human life but a prematurely grey-haired man and a young woman sitting by the stream. They are eating peaches, and talking . . . gaily. Premature age is forgotten. In the autumn of his life Sir Arthur Sullivan has made up his mind to propose marriage.

How did he come to care for Miss Violet in this way? Many times in these last weeks at and around Lucerne he has asked himself the question. Of course, he'd known her family for years. A truly musical family ('Anton Rubinstein introduced me to your home, remember?—that day when you were only a child, and I first sat at your piano and played my songs.') . . . Now, only yesterday, he had written out one of those songs again, a love song, and sent it up to her room at the hotel for a twentieth birthday present. Yes, a musical family, but a different social circle from that of Mrs Ronalds. Looking down at the gushing water at their feet, he tries to tell Miss Violet the difference. He goes back over his life.

Years of success. The joy of it, and the bitterness of it. And the inevitable social round. Mrs Ronalds' salon. Cowes and Cannes. Ascot. Monte. Mayfair. 'At homes.'

Queer how these attachments get hold of one. 'The unofficial ambassadress of the United States at the Court of St James's' . . . Twenty years ago she'd dazzled him with her glitter, her social eminence. Oh yes, he'd loved her, or thought he did. A magnificent figure of a woman. Queen of the *beau monde*. And she sang his songs divinely. But some of the links in the chain had worn thin. Illness came. Frustration. Now a solitary old man ('old'?—at fifty-four?) is pushed around in an invalid chair in an hotel at Lucerne . . . until one evening someone murmurs the introductions— 'Miss Violet' . . . 'Sir Arthur'.

And so these last days. Days by the lakeside talking of music, and art, and books. The day when the hotel band struck up a selection from *The Yeomen*, and he turned

[1] Another Savoy 'discovery'. Ruth Vincent, operatic, concert, and oratorio soprano, had made her stage début at the Savoy in 1896 as Gretchen in *The Grand Duke*.

Dear Miss Violet

What do you and your propose doing? Shall we sit under the trees, or lie on the grass, or saunter on the Promenade? Or shall we ... a joint letter to your sister? What time do you wish to see me today. I will, of course obey any orders you may give.

yours sincerely

A. S

Saturday

Written on the notepaper of a Lucerne hotel, the letter on the left is the first of a series from Sullivan to Violet. The fragment below is from the last

Good morning I am off in half an hour. ... last night. I ... stand it any longer so I left. Yesterday was the most miserable day I have spent.

irritably upon her and snapped: 'I suppose you hate my music. We've been together for days and you've never even mentioned it.'

'I love your music. I love every one of your operas.'

'That's Gilbert's success. The wittiest man in the world, Gilbert.'

'The wittiest music in the world, yours.'

And then they turned together and laughed. After that the years seemed to fall from him. It was the old high-spirited Sullivan. Everyone was charmed by him, men as well as women. One night in the hotel they met Puccini. The two composers bowed and conversed breezily. She stood by, cool and gentle, taking it in: the Englishman who had made his name in all but the thing he most desired, grand opera; the Italian, up-and-coming, who had just written *La Bohème*, who was going to be all in grand opera that Sullivan longed to be.

The day came when he awoke and his manservant Louis pulled back the blinds, and as the sun streamed in he knew he was in love. From his bed he gazed across the lake at the mountain tops. He thought of what might have been, had she been born twenty years earlier. Violet. Lady Sullivan.

Might have been? . . . fifty-four and twenty . . . was it yet impossible? What is age? Those mountain peaks yonder, white, ageless, beautiful. What do they say?

And now the stream, the cowbells, the peaches.

'Everything is beautiful. I am in love.'

The girl looks up at the great mountains, high, eternal, lovely. He is saying: 'I believe in the here and now. No looking backwards any more. Eyes front! Violet . . . To what are you looking forward?'

'Only to being this day with you . . . to having a perfect day with you.'

*   *   *   *

'He was very frank with me,' said the grey-haired and still beautiful old lady. She paused, and looked out of her window at the London street. A jet-plane screamed overhead. Somewhere in the neighbourhood a radio was playing boogie-woogie. 'He said he had two years to live. Could I not give him two years of my life? Could I find the love that would renew him? After that—I should still have my own life before me. He would leave me all he possessed. He said it would have to be a secret wedding—"In London. Round the corner, Hyde Park Square. Registry Office."'

'But I thought it over, and I knew it wouldn't do.'[1]

THE DAILY ROUND OF W. S. GILBERT, J.P.

At Grim's Dyke Mr Gilbert was sitting at breakfast with Mrs Gilbert and Miss McIntosh. He opened a letter from a journalist who announced that he was starting a new publication, Who's Who, and asked for details of Gilbert's career. 'Douglas Sladen,' muttered Gilbert, reading the signature, 'never heard of him.' After breakfast W.S.G. went to his study and wrote a brief reply. Says Mr Sladen: 'He replied curtly that he had never heard of me. So in went the entry in that first number of the new Who's Who in 1897—"Gilbert, W. S., journalist, wrote libretti for Sir Arthur Sullivan." Gilbert was furious! He pointed out just who he was—and the next year sent me several foolscap pages about himself to make sure.'[2]

On certain days he sat on the Uxbridge bench. 'Gilbert was very interesting in a rather abrupt way, and his fellow magistrates were a little in awe of him,' says one of the solicitors who often pleaded before him.[3] One day a woman told the magistrates 'My husband's a nasty old man, he beats me, and he's got an abscess in his back.' Mr Gilbert commented from the bench: 'Not a case of abscess makes the heart grow

[1] These recollections, and the letters, were given to the author by the lady concerned in 1947.
[2] Interview in Evening News, London, 1936.
[3] Mr Charles E. Brady, of Harrow.

fonder.' He made copious notes of evidence, but the solicitors and the culprits brought before him little realized that when Gilbert's pen appeared to be most energetic it was drawing caricatures of them! Pages of magisterial notes now in the museum of the Gilbert and Sullivan Society are thus doodled and decorated.

One day Gilbert was having his hair cut. 'And when are we to expect anything further, Mr Gilbert, from your fluent pen?' gossiped the barber.

'What d'you mean, sir, by a fluent pen?' was the reply. 'There is no such thing as a fluent pen. A pen is an insensible object. At any rate, I don't presume to inquire into your private affairs; you will please observe the same reticence in regard to mine.'

From now on he wrote nothing that has proved of lasting value. But the pen never lost its Gilbertian fluency; he became rather fond of sending letters to newspapers, and on one occasion complained of the weekend crush on the Metropolitan line at Baker Street: 'Saturday afternoon, although occurring at regular and well-foreseen intervals, always takes this railway by surprise.'

He frequently travelled up to London, and haunted the theatres. One first night he went round to the dressing-rooms and joined a crowd of flatterers who were complimenting a leading man on his portrayal of an Irishman, complete with accent.

'Excellent, my dear fellow,' boomed Gilbert, 'but why on earth did you make him talk like that?'

'Well, he's an Irishman . . . so I thought he'd talk with a brogue.'

'Then why didn't you give him one?'

Behind the bark was a kind heart. Many are the stories of Gilbert's very private generosities and benefactions (the same is true of Sullivan). And if Gilbert's wisecracks sometimes caused embarrassment, at other times he could avoid giving embarrassment by an adroit play upon words. A friend of his tells of attending a play with Gilbert who sat muttering his opinions about an atrocious performance by the principal actor—at the end Gilbert insisted on going back-stage, and his friend followed, fearing the worst, but Gilbert walked into the star's dressing-room, clapped him on the back, and said blithely: 'My dear chap!—*Good* isn't the word!'

To the Savoy when *The Gondoliers* was revived in 1898, Gilbert wrote a formal note to Mrs Carte:

I am much obliged to you for the box but I never sit in front when a piece with which I am concerned is being played, and my ladies are going to Daly's.

A few weeks later, however, he stood inconspicuously at the back of the pit during a performance of *Trial by Jury*, and then came another note to Mrs Carte:

There is a man in the chorus—a 'funny' man who is the bane of true comic opera. He has over-acted right through rehearsals and although I told the Jurymen not to make up with wigs, etc, he nevertheless took upon himself to appear last night in a grotesque flaxen wig. He occupies a place in the Jury box close to the footlights and so is extremely conspicuous. I suggest that he be put in the back row at the end furthest from the stage, then his exaggerations will not be important.

One day Sullivan called at the Savoy Theatre and stood at the back of the crowded pit. Presently a stranger touched him on the arm and said: 'Excuse me, sir, but I paid my money to hear Sullivan's charming opera, not your confounded humming!'

The exciting fact was now realized that the gold-mine of the Savoy operas was by no means exhausted; it was not even fully tapped. D'Oyly Carte staked out a new claim by sending a company to the land of gold mines. Ex-chorus-girl Jessie Vince (Mrs Swinhoe), whose recollections of touring in Germany have previously been noted, says: 'We stayed in South Africa nearly four months in 1897, including six weeks in Cape Town. We gave over a hundred performances of *The Yeomen of the Guard*; George Thorne was our Jack Point. We also played *The Mikado*, and *The Gondoliers*, *Utopia*, and *The Grand Duke*. Personally, I rather liked *The Grand Duke*, but I suppose it was a bit feeble compared to the others. *Utopia* I liked very much. We had wonderful audiences out there. Johannesburg was only a small mining town then, and we played in a very small theatre. It was always crowded. Those colonials may have been tough but they were so sentimental about England and anything English! Barny Barnato and all that lot were frequently in the audience. We girls didn't like the hotels much—they were too rough—so we got private rooms, and kept ourselves much to ourselves.'

Even in distant Argentina it was *H.M.S. Pinafore* which ran up the Union Jack at Buenos Aires in 1897 to celebrate the Diamond Jubilee of Queen Victoria, and one who was there[1] recalls the splendid scene at the Politeana Theatre when a detachment of Royal Marines from a British cruiser not only formed a guard of honour in the foyer for the arrival of distinguished guests but also appeared on the stage, on the poop of *H.M.S. Pinafore!*

[1] Mr Alfred Salinger, of Hampstead.

[394]

The Jubilee was the apotheosis of the Victorian Age, the final climax before the fade-out. How appropriate it was that Sir Arthur Sullivan's star should suddenly blaze up again now, beside his Queen's, before their eclipse. During the last three years of his life, in sudden bursts of energy between spells of sickness—'Most people suffer and get well again, I suffer and I don't,' he said—he composed three operas without Gilbert, *The Beauty Stone*, *The Rose of Persia* and *The Emerald Isle* (unfinished), all produced at the Savoy Theatre. *The Beauty Stone* was a disappointment—Sullivan found the libretto by Comyns Carr and A. W. Pinero 'heart breaking', and the opera ran only seven weeks—but in these last operas there is music of genuine Sullivan calibre; indeed, some of his contemporaries such as Sir Alexander MacKenzie thought *The Rose of Persia* 'his masterpiece in comic opera'. And at the theatre Sullivan appeared always to be his old genial self. Ellaline Terriss (Lady Seymour Hicks) was appearing in a musical comedy, *The Circus Girl*, at the Gaiety, when he called there one evening. 'There was no captious criticism from this master of melody', says Lady Hicks.[1] And yet there might well have been. It was at the Gaiety twenty-five years previously that his first opera with Gilbert, *Thespis*, had been an astonishing innovation: what bitter-sweet thoughts the 'master' must have had as he sat in the old theatre again and watched *The Circus Girl*, and heard its music by two rising young rivals, Lionel Monckton and Ivan Caryll.

In this Jubilee year Sullivan revelled in his duty to write music to mark the Sixty Glorious Years. *Victoria and Merrie England*, his ballet at the Alhambra, was a winner. He was paid the huge sum of £2,000 down, plus a share of the takings. The ballet had an innovation—'a little daring', Sullivan called it—a comic dance in waltz time written as a fugue. He also produced the official hymn 'Oh, King of Kings' for Jubilee Sunday, to be sung throughout the Empire.

Sullivan to the Prince of Wales:

> My career, Sir, is nearer its end than its commencement. I have done my State and official commissions, but nothing in my career, and no State commission could make me work with heart and soul as the forthcoming glorious occasion would impel me to do. May I hope for your Royal Highness' help in the matter?

His dream was to leave behind him a second national anthem; as he said in a letter to Alfred Austin, something to be sung 'by solo, by chorus, played by military bands—at theatres, at music halls, meetings of every description, and on the march . . . simple words and simple tune.' But Austin, though Poet Laureate, could not provide Sullivan with the right words, and it was left to A. C. Benson and Edward Elgar to score a bull's-eye on this popular target three or four years later with 'Land of Hope and Glory'.

Queen Victoria described Sullivan's hymn merely as 'pretty and appropriate'. At any rate it brought him into even closer association with Her Majesty: 'I have spent most of my time lately at Windsor and have had three long and pleasant chats with the Queen (bless her, she is so kind and gracious)', he wrote to Carte.

[1] *Ellaline Terriss*, by Herself (Cassell).

In the following year, 1898, his twenty years of work for Leeds Musical Festival was rewarded with ovations such as even he had never experienced, though his diary records a near-calamity on the opening day:

God Save the Queen and *Elijah*. Clara Butt was to sing the whole contralto part but not having thought it necessary to ascertain what time it began was not there. I saw Ada Crossley sitting below me—beckoned to her and got her up to sing the part. At the end of the 1st Part I found Clara Butt in my room crying her heart out at her folly. I didn't say much to her but told her she could sing the 2nd Part.

After the last performance the Chorus cheered me so tremendously that I suddenly broke down, and ran off the orchestra crying like a child. When I came out of my room again, all the Chorus was waiting for me, and I shook hands with them all!

It was the last time he ever saw them. Plunket Greene, who sang at the 1898 Festival, records that Sullivan was suffering all the time and had to have a deputy-conductor standing by. Among the new works performed was Elgar's 'Caractacus'.

Elgar to Sullivan:

I could not let the last night of the rehearsals go by without sending my thanks to you for making my 'chance' possible. This is, of course, only what one knows you would do but it contrasts very much with what some people do to a person unconnected with the Schools, friendless and alone.

At the end of the year Elgar wrote again from Malvern. He said that of the year's happier events 'the chief and most pleasant was meeting you'. At this period Elgar was writing the *Enigma Variations*, musical pictures of the composer's friends. 'It was my wish,' said Elgar, 'that each variation should illustrate some characteristic of a friend . . .' and two of the friends originally pictured within this orchestral work were Sullivan and Parry. After sketching out these two movements, Elgar dropped them because their musical styles seemed incompatible with the rest of the *Variations*.

Another little-known composer was encouraged when Sullivan attended a performance in London of Coleridge-Taylor's *Hiawatha*, and noted in his diary: 'Much impressed by the lad's genius. He is a composer, not a music-maker.'

When *The Sorcerer* was revived at the Savoy twenty-one years to the exact day from its first production at the Opéra Comique, Sullivan conducted, and Gilbert was in the audience. The entry in his diary shows how far apart the old partners had now drifted:

Tremendous house—ditto reception. Opera went very well. Passmore inimitable. Call for Gilbert and self—we went on together but did not speak to each other. He is mortally offended about *The Beauty Stone*, insisting that I left him out of the theatre on the first night. As he will not allow me to explain that I had nothing whatsoever to do with it, of course there is nothing to be done.

In his box were Mrs Gilbert, Mrs Merton, and Miss McIntosh like three villas, attached, detached and semi-detached!'

Rosina Brandram as Lady Sangazure in 'The Sorcerer', 1898. Speaking in 1906, Gilbert referred to 'Rosina Brandram—Rosina of the glorious voice that rolled out as full-bodied Burgundy rolls down—Rosina whose dismal doom it was to represent undesirable old ladies of sixty-five but who, with all the resources of the perruquier and the make-up box, could never succeed in looking more than an attractive eight-and-twenty [it was her only failure]'

It was the last time they met. The 'offence' had been due to a misunderstanding about invitations to the first night of *The Beauty Stone*. By a specially cruel irony, on this *Sorcerer* night (17 November, 1898) when the Great Savoyards cut one another in public, the programme contained a notice that 'It is also the twenty-first anniversary of the commencement of the successful continuous Series of Operas by W. S. Gilbert and Arthur Sullivan produced under the management of R. D'Oyly Carte, of which operas over six thousand performances have since been given in London and probably between twenty thousand and thirty thousand, under Mr Carte's direction, in the provinces; besides the many thousands of performances, authorized and unauthorized, in all parts of the world.'

What an enigma Gilbert could be! Many of his oldest admirers were staggered in this same year, 1898, when he published a collected edition of *The Bab Ballads* with two hundred new drawings, and wrote in the preface that he had long felt that many of the original illustrations to *The Bab Ballads* erred gravely in the direction of

[397]

The old 'Bab' . . . and the new

unnecessary extravagance. 'So did *The Bab Ballads*,' commented Max Beerbohm, review-ing the volume.[1] 'That is why the first drawings were so exactly right for them. To make these new drawings equally right, Mr Gilbert ought to have rewritten the poems. I am glad that his innate love for logic did not drive him to this double vandalism.' This curiously insipid whim—a 'genteel' Gilbert seems an anachronism—was followed by a violent swing in the opposite direction when a far-from-insipid Gilbert sued a newspaper for libel, made an extravagant appearance in the witness box, and told Helen D'Oyly Carte that 'The Judge summed up like a drunken monkey—he is in the last stage of senile decay and knew absolutely nothing about the case. It is a frightful scandal that such men should be allowed to sit in judgment.' After that came another appearance in a court of law, this time more to Gilbert's taste; frisking in wig

From Gilbert's sketch-book: preliminary pencil sketches for the new illustrations to the 'Bab Ballads'.

[1] The *Saturday Review*, 27 May, 1905.

and gown, he took part in a performance of *Trial by Jury* for Nellie Farren's Benefit at Drury Lane in 1898. Nellie Farren, once the agile star of Gilbert and Sullivan's first opera *Thespis*, was now a cripple.

In 1899 they were doing *H.M.S. Pinafore* again at the Savoy, with Walter Passmore as Sir Joseph Porter.

Meanwhile, Sullivan had found a new collaborator in Basil Hood, the only librettist since the break with Gilbert in whom Sullivan had complete confidence. The Eastern theme of their opera *The Rose of Persia* pleased Sullivan, too, and the opera pleased the public; and yet at rehearsals Sullivan was depressed, dissatisfied, and expected a failure. His illness was—at long last—affecting his spirits. He was shaken by the death of his two lifelong men friends, Sir George Grove and the Duke of Edinburgh. England, too, was overwhelmed by gloom induced by the first bitter reverses in the South African War. Something was needed to cheer people up, and Sullivan gave them it in *The Rose of Persia*. His diary:

Three shining stars in the 1899 'Pinafore': From left, Henry Lytton, Walter Passmore, and Robert Evett

'Hideously nervous as usual—great reception as usual—great house as usual—excellent performance as usual—everything as usual—except that the piece is really a great success I think, which is *unusual* lately.'

He had lately tried to set to music the poem 'Recessional' by Kipling, who wrote to Sullivan: 'If a layman may speak in the presence of a master, I quite recognize the difficulty you find about Recessional.' But the setting was never completed.

The outbreak of war induced in Sullivan the old feeling that he must write some 'great' music to mark the occasion. He started composing a solemn *Te Deum* to be performed when Victory came, but he never heard it performed—Victory was so long in coming. No, it was no *Te Deum* of Sullivan's that stirred England, it was Sullivan's jingling setting of Kipling's 'The Absent-minded Beggar' that became a popular war-song ('a tune guaranteed to pull teeth out of barrel organs', Kipling called it), and it was *The Rose of Persia* that gladdened London for many months.

An autographed menu[1] of Sullivan's last birthday party, 13 May, 1900, bears the

---

[1] Now in the collection of Mr Reginald Allen, of New York.

Sketches by Gilbert for 'His Excellency' to music by F. Osmond Carr. Revivals of the Sullivan operas were mounted at the Savoy as the century ended, notably 'H.M.S. Pinafore', with Ruth Vincent in a characteristically 1899 costume, as Josephine

signatures of Richard and Helen D'Oyly Carte, Herbert Sullivan (his nephew), Wilfred Bendall (his secretary), and—Fanny Ronalds.

Tortured in body, Sullivan wandered restlessly from spa to spa on the Continent. According to Sir Newman Flower's biography, he was now in constant communication with Mrs Ronalds again, writing her two letters a day. In Switzerland he started setting a new opera by Basil Hood, *The Emerald Isle*, for production at the Savoy, and when Helen D'Oyly Carte chided him for delays he replied in October, 1900:

> My Dear Helen,—I cannot help smiling at the little dig about the *Te Deum*. It was so thoroughly womanly. But my dear you are mistaken. The 'mistake' of writing the *Te Deum* had no more to do with the backward state of the opera than conducting the Leeds Festival in 1898 or writing *The Golden Legend* in 1886. The *Te Deum* was finished . . . If I hadn't been ill the opera would be ready now, but I haven't been able to write a note. Physical pain and nervous terror combined are not conducive to good mental work.

He found that morphine brought him little relief now, and bronchitis was added to his burden. He wrote again, from Switzerland: 'The first Act is done. I can hardly see the paper I am writing on, my head is so bad. I am taking quinine, that is all I can do. Is there any other remedy?'

Sullivan came back to England weak and dejected. He was in terror of his worsening condition. In his bag were fragments of the new opera; the scene was Ireland, his forefathers' Emerald Isle, and this music with its haunting croon of the 'fairy voices of Carrig-Cleena'' is his lovely swan-song. He paused awhile at Tunbridge Wells but could not work; his return to London was darkened by the news that D'Oyly Carte was seriously ill. But Mrs Carte, good business woman that she was, herself staged the 1900 revival of *Patience*; and she, good woman that she was, suggested a reconciliation with Gilbert.

Sullivan to Mrs Carte:

> I thought that if three such frightful wrecks as Gilbert, D'Oyly, and myself were to appear on the stage at the same time it would create something more than a sensation. It wasn't my intention to come to the first night of *Patience* but if it would really please Gilbert to have me there and go on with him I will come. Let us bury the hatchet and smoke the pipe of peace. I have no doubt we can get both from the property room and if the result is to relieve Gilbert of some of that awful gout I shall be well pleased.

While he was waiting for a reply Sullivan went out on a bitter winter's day and caught cold—a friend says 'It was during a visit to his mother's grave, paid, as always, on her birthday, the second of November. He went alone, and spent a long time arranging the flowers he had taken. He was weak from illness and hard work, but refused to recognize this, and struggled on for a few days longer, when his doctor found him suffering from pneumonia.'[1]

Helen Carte to Sullivan:

I am really glad to hear you will come in on Wednesday night—I know it will *truly* please Mr Gilbert much—I could see how *very much* he wished it. I suggested to D'Oyly last night that he should have an original effect of *three bath chairs* discovered —or a procession of bath chairs! Or you standing and they two in a bath chair each at the sides.

But only D'Oyly Carte and Gilbert went on the stage when the curtain fell on *Patience*. Gilbert wrote to Sullivan: 'The old opera woke up splendidly.'

The next letter from Sullivan is a pathetic note to Helen Carte, shakily written in pencil, headed 'In bed', in which he doubts whether he will ever get out again: 'Pray tell Gilbert how very much I feel the disappointment. Good luck to you all. Three invalid chairs would have looked very well from the front. Ever yours, A.S.'

All differences were forgotten by both Gilbert and Sullivan in these last weeks of 1900, the last weeks of the Old Century; but they did not meet because Gilbert's gout was worse than ever and he contracted rheumatic fever through helping to make a lake in the grounds at Grim's Dyke (the lake in which he was to meet his end); now, late in 1900, he was just off on a health cruise to Egypt. 'I sincerely hope to find you all right again on my return, and the new opera running merrily,' says his last letter to 'My dear Sullivan'.

Ten days later, on 22 November, Mrs Ronalds rushed in a cab to Victoria Street, but she was too late. Arthur Sullivan was dead, aged fifty-eight.

The Queen required that the first part of the funeral should be at the Chapel Royal, St James's Palace, where Sullivan once sang as a choirboy. Then the cortège went to St Paul's Cathedral, the Band of the Scots Guards playing the Dead March from *Saul*. The cathedral was crowded; among the flowers was a wreath from the Queen; another from *The Rose of Persia* touring company in Belfast, with the lines—

> Dear Master, since thy magic harp is broken
> Where shall we find new melodies to sing?

and the choir was the full company from the Savoy Theatre. One of them recalls it: 'We sang the unaccompanied anthem "Brother, thou art gone before us" from *The Martyr of Antioch*. The baton was in the hands of François Cellier. At the end of the service we were permitted to go down to the crypt to bid adieu to the mortal remains of our beloved friend and chief.'[2]

On that dull November day the cortège had passed the Savoy on its way along the Thames Embankment. Nearby, in a bedroom in Adelphi Terrace, overlooking the

---

[1] From an article, 'Sir Arthur Seymour Sullivan as an Old Friend Knew Him', *Argosy*, February, 1901.
[2] Letter from Mr Sidney Herbert, a member of the chorus.

river, Richard D'Oyly Carte was found prostrate by the window: 'I have just seen the last of my old friend Sullivan,' he said. They helped him back to bed. Within a few months he also was dead.

Within a few weeks of Sullivan's death the Old Century slipped away, and before the twentieth century was three weeks old came the death of Queen Victoria.

Fin de siècle.

For what shall Sullivan be chiefly honoured, half a century later?

'Sullivan led me to Beethoven.'

This phrase occurs in the writings of the English critic, Horace Thorogood.[1] He describes how, as a musically uncultivated boy, he first visited the Savoy pit during a revival of *The Mikado*:

> There I became immediately infatuated with Sullivan and for the next few years I haunted the theatre so long as the operas remained there. My head was full of Sullivan melodies. They gave me complete content. But as these visits went on, I became aware of a new and distressing doubt arising in my mind about Sullivan. For I was now perforce hearing Wagner, Tchaikovsky, Mozart, and Beethoven practically for the first time. For long I fought loyally against the conviction that these men were giants beside Sullivan, but the time came when I could deny it no longer. In the fierce glow of the great masters, my idol shivered and cracked, and finally crashed. That phase, of course, passed long since. Gradually I restored Sullivan to his true place in the galaxy of composers—no longer among the gods, yet definitely with the great. Above all, I came to realize with gratitude that it was he who prepared my mind to receive the master musicians. And this, I suggest, was one of Sullivan's greatest gifts to his countrymen. He did more than any other man to accustom the ear of ordinary Englishmen to music of pure quality—to enable them to recognize and rejoice in the finest music when they heard it. He brought the English out of the dunce's class in music.

[1] In the *Nation and Athenaeum*, London, 1927.

SIR W. S. GILBERT

'Some who knew him superficially have pictured him as a martinet, but while this may have been true of him under the stress of theatrical work, it fails to do justice to the innate gentleness and courtesy which were his great and distinguishing qualities.'

—Sir Henry Lytton, 'The Secrets of a Savoyard'

20th Century

THE SHOW GOES ON

'The Pirates of Penzance' as seen by two generations. Nineteenth Century: Walter Passmore and Rosina Brandram; Twentieth Century: Dorothy Gill and Sydney Granville

IN 1937 THE AMERICAN MAGAZINE *Fortune*, in an elaborate feature on a visit of the D'Oyly Carte Opera Company to the U.S.A., remarked that there is no joint memorial in stone or bronze on either side of the Atlantic to the two great Savoyards, but that 'a more meaningful memorial' was written in the theatres of the U.S.A., in the shape of a placard:

> ### GILBERT & SULLIVAN
> **Standing Room Only**

It is indeed a unique phenomenon that during the twentieth century, which has seen a high-pressure global exportation *from* America not only of refrigerators and autos but of popular entertainment of every kind, the importation *into* America of these English nineteenth-century operas has continued with undiminished vigour.

[405]

In the nineteenth century these works were a Revolution, in the twentieth they have become an Institution; and not a fossilized relic or an artsy-folksy custom left over from Victorian times, but a warm, living part of British and American life. The first half of the twentieth century has brought more changes, catastrophes, discoveries, revolutions, reforms, than all the years of the nineteenth; many things that Messrs Gilbert and Sullivan and their contemporaries thought eternal have been thrown into the dustcart with the discarded monarchies, the rejected moral codes, the faded old sweet songs, the exploded scientific and social beliefs, the antimacassars and bustles and whatnots of Victoriana, and yet through this cataclysm a dozen wildly nonsensical, disrespectfully satirical, and occasionally sentimental operas have persisted. It must be that their nonsense, their disrespect, and their sentiment express something basic and permanent in the Anglo-Saxon character. 'I know of no more English artistic expression than the Gilbert and Sullivan operas,' said Sir Adrian Boult when BBC Director of Music.

Another modern verdict—'Sullivan set our language to music with a skill and sensitiveness that have never been surpassed and very rarely equalled'[1]—indicates another reason for the evergreen quality of the operas. Many of Sullivan's songs have become, in the true sense of the term, English folk songs. So, too, many of Gilbert's gags have been nationalized; absorbed into our very character.

In 1900 tributes to Sullivan from Press and pulpit after his death tended to emphasize his work as a 'serious' musician. When Henry Wood conducted a memorial concert at Queen's Hall, London, on the first anniversary of his death the programme comprised the overture *In Memoriam*, *The Golden Legend*, and selections from *Ivanhoe*. But as the years passed, it was realized that Sullivan's most enduring achievement was to have established an English 'school' of light music. His brightest follower in that line, Edward German, was called upon to complete the half-finished music of *The Emerald Isle*, produced successfully at the Savoy Theatre in 1901, six months after Sullivan's death. It was not 'Gilbert and Sullivan', but it was very much in the tradition—and when it ended back came *Iolanthe*. Gilbert wrote to Mrs Carte suggesting that the stage Big Ben in this revival should be a real clock, telling the time during Act 2: 'I think people would talk about it, and it would become a good advertisement.'

Gilbert had written to Herbert Sullivan, Sir Arthur's nephew:

It is a satisfaction to me to feel that I was impelled, shortly before his death, to write to him to propose to shake hands over our recent differences and even a greater satisfaction to learn, through you, that my offer of reconciliation was cordially accepted. I wish I had been in England that I might have had an opportunity of joining the mourners at his funeral.

[1] 'The Charm of Music—some thoughts on Gilbert and Sullivan', by Francis Toye, *Illustrated London News*, 28 January, 1939.

Under his will Sir Arthur Sullivan left 'to my old friend and colleague W. S. Gilbert the autographed score of *Ruddigore* and four small silver ornaments.' Other scores were given to the Royal College of Music (*The Yeomen of the Guard* and *The Golden Legend*), the Royal Academy of Music (*The Mikado* and *The Martyr of Antioch*), François Cellier (*Patience* and *The Pirates of Penzance*), and Richard D'Oyly Carte (*Iolanthe*); to the Prince of Wales Sullivan left a tortoiseshell and silver-mounted card-box, and 'to my old and dear friend Mary Frances Ronalds' a dinner service, silver candlesticks, a Louis XIV writing-table, and the manuscript of 'The Lost Chord'.

Holiday cruise sketch by Gilbert: 'Mr and Mrs Montenegro earning their living.'

Mr Gilbert returned from abroad 'more of a cripple than ever', as he wrote after being involved in a railway accident in Egypt. Several people were killed and W.S.G. was trapped in an upturned carriage:

> We expected the carriage to roll on to the engine, when I should certainly have been boiled alive in the steam. However, the carriage remained on the slope, and Nancy, by a tremendous effort, managed to get me on to my legs (my wife and she having got out in safety) . . . I shall never forget the shrieks of the wounded and dying . . . We are none of us materially the worse for our adventure. Both ladies behaved with extraordinary pluck and self-possession.[1]

For the Gilberts of Grim's Dyke there now came the most pleasant period of their lives. In leisure and comfort they lived through those early years of the twentieth century, the Edwardian era, which retained so much of the dignity and richness of the previous Victorian age whilst quickening to the swiftly-changing pace of the new one. Mr Gilbert always looked a Victorian when you saw him in his garden; though he still played tennis, his favourite game was croquet, and 'Croquet avec Nancy' is a frequent entry in his diary (which he now had the habit of writing in French); but he was not insensitive to the spirit of the new age. A cloud of dust over the country roads north of London showed that Mr Gilbert was out on one of his snorting dragon-like motor cars, with Mrs Gilbert and Miss Nancy McIntosh, swathed in veils, clutching on by his side. 'Le motor très bien sur le top speed, beaucoup de bruit au middle speed', comments the diary.

[1] Letter to a friend quoted in *W. S. Gilbert* by Sidney Dark and Rowland Grey (Methuen), 1923.

Mrs Gilbert and Miss Nancy McIntosh [LEFT *and* RIGHT] *in the Darracq at Grim's Dyke. Mr Gilbert kept four motor cars and two chauffeurs. When this photograph was taken he was over seventy years of age*

Methodically, in a terse combination of English and French he noted the events of a well-ordered household. On 11 April: 'Diner chez nous. Billiards. Premier cuckoo.'

On a Sunday: 'Promenade "Church Parade" avec Kitty' (Mrs Gilbert). Gilbert went to church, but refused to be a patron of a local Allotment Society because one of its rules forbade allotment-digging on Sundays.

The Gilberts' neighbours were the Blackwells (of Crosse and Blackwell's jams) and when Mr Blackwell gently indicated that the Grim's Dyke gardener had intruded on the Blackwell property, W.S.G. replied that he much regretted any trespass on 'Mr Blackwell's preserves', if he might be excused the expression. (Another version of this anecdote says that it was Blackwell's dog which intruded on Gilbert's estate and provoked a request to 'keep your pickles off my preserves').

Dinner parties were frequently given for theatrical and literary friends—Maxine Elliot, Marion Terry, Barry Pain, the Bourchiers, the Cyril Maudes, the Gielguds, Herbert Sullivan—and parties on the lawns in the summer gave W.S.G. the opportunity to show off his pets. His great-niece, Mrs Parker, who lived at Grim's Dyke during her childhood, recalls: 'At a grown-up party he came to me and said, "You must be bored with this. Come and see the kittens." He once gave a £5 cheque to a small child and said, "There, don't go and get drunk on it." He loved children, and animals.'

'He had a varied collection of lemurs, pigeons, cats, cranes, dogs,' writes Nancy McIntosh, 'but they had one characteristic in common—a great love of being in the library. It was a big sunny room with walls covered from floor to ceiling with books and a dozen valuable drawings by Rubens, Andrea del Sarto, Annibale Caracci, Watteau, Permegrano and others. A wide French window opened to the south through which the animals could come and go as they liked. The pigeons came in search of cigar ash, the lemurs wandered in at teatime to beg fruit, and on one occasion when a family of a dozen half-grown turkeys made their escape from the farmyard even they came straight to the library, where Mr Gilbert found them, one on his blotting pad on the writing-table with several others grouped about it, others on chairs and tables, all holding a most animated discussion apparently about the manuscript on the desk.'

There was a pet fawn, a lovely fallow deer, which was very fond of Gilbert and used to haunt the library when she was not out in the fields with Adelina, the donkey. These two animals got into the habit of wandering off together into the surrounding country-side, telegrams would come in from distant police stations, and the fawn cost W.S.G. a small fortune in tips and fines. But the lemurs, the most charming, clean and child-like of all monkeys, were his greatest joy; one of them, Paul, invariably sat on his shoulders when he was dressing for dinner: 'Mr Gilbert was immensely delighted with this feat, and often gave an exhibition of so much of the process as was fit for presentation, taking off coat and waistcoat and putting them on again as quickly as possible, while Paul by a peculiar trick of shifting his hands and feet, managed to remain standing on Mr Gilbert's shoulders as the clothes were assumed or discarded.'

One day William Archer, the famous dramatic critic, drove up through the sur-rounding woods and called on Mr Gilbert, and remarked: 'You are fond of animals?'—and added that there must be very good shooting in the neighbourhood, to which Gilbert made this remarkable reply: 'It is a little strange—isn't it?—that "fondness for animals" should instantly call up the association of "good shooting". No, I keep that little stretch of woodland unreclaimed because I think it makes an effective con-trast to the trimness of the garden. As for shooting, I have a constitutional objection to taking life in any form. I don't think I ever wittingly killed a black-beetle. It is not humanity on my part. I am perfectly willing that other people should kill things for my comfort and advantage. But the mechanism of life is so wonderful that I shrink from stopping its action. To tread on a black-beetle would be to me like crushing a watch of complex and exquisite workmanship . . . The time will no doubt come when the "sport" of the present day will be regarded very much as we regard the Spanish bull-fight or the bear-baiting of our ancestors.'[1]

Archer and Gilbert discussed the 'dramatic revival' which was now being led by Shaw, Pinero, Barrie, Granville-Barker, and Co., and Archer remarked: 'I shall always

[1] *Real Conversations*, by William Archer (Heinemann), 1904.

feel that, as regards serious drama, you were in advance of your time.' But Gilbert himself had not written a straight play for years, and since the death of Sullivan he had had no desire to write comic opera—with one exception: The Lozenge Plot. This he could not forget. Elgar, Massenet, Liza Lehmann, Sir Alexander Mackenzie, Messager, all turned it down, as Sullivan had done in the past.

Gilbert to Cellier, 1903:

> Many thanks for your good wishes. Personally I'm rather sick of birthdays—I've had so many of them. A Gilbert is of no use without a Sullivan—and I can't find one![1]

That year he started writing a new play. 'It seems quite odd after so many years idleness,' he said, 'but I must make an effort to keep the little home together.' The Fairy's Dilemma was produced at the Garrick by Arthur Bourchier in 1904. In it the up-to-date Gilbert referred to motoring in rather out-of-date doggerel:

THE DEMON ALCOHOL: A thousand pardons! Driving here from town
      My brand-new Demon motor-car broke down;
      A puncture long delayed me—This fatality
      Affects one's character for puncture-ality.

This play did not survive long. And then at last Gilbert found a composer for the Lozenge. Edward German, fresh from his great success with Merrie England, agreed to set it; but several years were to elapse before it reached the footlights. Meanwhile, Gilbert and Sullivan Opera appeared to be fading away. After Iolanthe's revival in 1901 Mrs D'Oyly Carte had let the Savoy, and the famous theatre had quite lost its character under the changing sway of other managements; for five years there was no Gilbert and Sullivan opera in London. Knowing critics marked this as the end of an art-form. Edwardian musical comedy was flourishing; at Daly's and the Gaiety the chief impresario of this slighter, frillier, art-form was George Edwardes, whose wife, Julia Gwynne, had long ago been one of Gilbert's 'discoveries'. Now (1905) Gilbert occasionally visited these West End musical shows and noted his opinions in his diary.

Of Lady Madcap: 'Pauvre piece et pauvre musique mais les comediens amusant.'

Of Veronique: 'Assez joli musique—pauvre piece, trop long.'

Of Mr Popple of Ippleton: 'Atroce.'

And the new whimsy-style of Barrie, in Peter Pan, the old whimsicalist found rather feeble and lacking in purpose. He relished these occasional visits to London, lunching at the Garrick or the Beefsteak Club, but the diary records many easy days spent quietly in his garden, reading in a boat on his lake, pottering about with developers and printing frames now that he had taken up photography. Dame Irene Vanbrugh recalls: 'I frequently went for weekends to Grim's Dyke with my sister Violet and her husband, Arthur Bourchier. Mrs Gilbert would welcome us—she was charming, pretty, and a very dainty personality. When I was about to retire to bed she said to me: "We have breakfast at 8.30 tomorrow morning, and in this house we are most tiresomely

[1] Quoted in Gilbert, Sullivan and D'Oyly Carte, by Cellier and Bridgman (Pitman), 1927.

punctual.'' I remember we were once discussing a well-known actress who had been cast for a certain part, and Mr Gilbert who was a keen photographer, said: ''The mistake she has made in playing that part is that she's under-developed and over-exposed.'' '

Gilbert to Herbert Sullivan:

Grim's Dyke, Harrow Weald.
19 April, 1903.

My dear Sullivan,
    Marshall tells me that you want a quotation from me from one of the libretti, to inscribe on your uncle's bust. What do you say to this (from the *Yeomen*):

> Is life a boon?
> If so, it must befall
> That Death, when e'er he call
> Must call too soon.

It is difficult to find anything quite suited to so sad an occasion, but I think this might do.

Yours very truly,
W. S. GILBERT

A memorial by Sir W. Goscombe John, bearing this inscription, was erected in the Embankment Gardens, London, within a stone's-throw of the Savoy Theatre. It was unveiled by Princess Louise.

1926: Bertha Lewis places a wreath on the Sullivan Memorial on the anniversary of the composer's death

In ease and quietude at Grim's Dyke, W. S. Gilbert had slipped out of the public mind and the public Press. Like his operas, he was quietly fading away. Then in 1906 came a cable from Melbourne announcing that *Utopia Limited* had at last had its première in Australia. And suddenly in that year, when Gilbert was seventy years of age, the Grand Old Man of the English Stage popped up, like the Quicksilver Young Man who shot up through a stage-trap in the days of long ago; in his last years came a new lease of the old vigour. The gout was less troublesome. From the end of March he swam almost daily in his lake. His motor cars sped faster. His operas returned to London. The *Quarterly Review* bestowed on him that much-used label 'the English Aristophanes'. An astonishing day is recorded on 12 June, 1906, when he started the morning with a bathe, went to London, appeared at Drury Lane as the Associate in *Trial by Jury*, visited the cinematograph ('tres bien'), returned home, noted in his diary that the escaped lemurs had been recaptured, and spent the evening at 'photographie—pas de success'.

This *Trial by Jury*, a part of the Ellen Terry Jubilee Commemoration, was astonishing, too, for its galaxy of celebrities:

The learned Judge - - - -	Rutland Barrington
The Defendant - - - - -	Courtice Pounds
Counsel for the plaintiff - - -	Henry A. Lytton
Usher - - - - - -	Walter Passmore
The Associate - - - - -	W. S. Gilbert
The Associate's wife - - - -	Fanny Brough
The Plaintiff - - - - -	Ruth Vincent

The bridesmaids included Billie Burke, Zena Dare, Gertie Millar, Decima Moore, Gabrielle Ray, Louie Pounds. Among the Jury were Sir Francis Burnand, Sir Arthur Conan Doyle, Cosmo Hamilton, Anthony Hope, Brandon Thomas.

In December, 1906, Mrs D'Oyly Carte took over the Savoy Theatre again, and the old glories returned with *The Yeomen of the Guard*. One day when they were rehearsing the new Jack Point, C. H. Workman, was standing between Elsie Maynard and Phoebe, and as he kissed the cheek of first one and then the other, quickly and repeatedly, a voice came up from the stalls, incisively, as in the days of old:

GILBERT: There is too much kissing for a Savoy audience.

WORKMAN: Oh!—you would cut the kissing then, Mr Gilbert?

GILBERT: I would not, but I must ask you to.

'I was once lunching at Grim's Dyke,' says Mr Workman, 'and told over the lunch-table the story of the old German trombone-player, who, closing his music, squashed a fly across the clef, and, when he came to that particular passage the next evening, ran down the scale, remarking, "I don't know vot dot big note vas, but I blayed it." Gilbert struck in quietly from the end of the table, "Are you sure it was a fly, Workman?—it might have been a bee flat!" ' [1]

[1] Article in the *Bookman*, July, 1911.

New stars arise: Jessie Rose, C. H. Workman, and Henry Lytton, in 'Iolanthe';
RIGHT, *Lytton as Strephon with Clara Dow as Phyllis*

The return of the Savoy operas was greeted with much joy ('Première de *Patience*, grande réception', says the diary). A new generation of playgoers was as delighted as the old—and there was now a new generation of Savoy stars who became as popular as the old: Clara Dow, Elsie Spain, and C. H. Workman whose performances in the 'Grossmith' roles made him one of the truly great Savoyards, and Leo Sheffield, who writes: 'My first part was as the Second Yeoman in *The Yeomen of the Guard*; I had only two lines to say but I thought "I'm going to show them what I can do", so I supplied heaps of gestures with every word. I looked at Gilbert, who watched from the stalls, and I saw the people around him were laughing. Then he turned to François Cellier and said "There's really no need to see a man play Macbeth to prove he's an actor!" '

Mr Sheffield adds: 'But Gilbert went on to be extremely kind to me. He gave me a lot of very good advice. He came up on the stage and took me carefully over the lines, not only of my part but of other roles in the operas, for, as he said, "You *may* play the part some day." '[1]

A future star who joined the Company in 1906—a year which was truly a turning-point in its history—was Bertha Lewis, who first appeared as Kate in *The Pirates of Penzance* on tour at Southampton. For twenty-five years her portrayal of the contralto roles was to win her unbounded affection and regard on both sides of the Atlantic.

[1] Shortly after sending these recollections Leo Sheffield died, in 1951.

To celebrate the return of the operas in 1906, the O.P. Club invited Mr Gilbert to be their guest of honour at dinner; four hundred and fifty guests applauded the lively old man as he rose to speak. He spoke affectionately of 'my old friend and invaluable co-worker, Arthur Sullivan, a composer of the rarest genius, who, because he was a composer of the rarest genius, was as modest and as unassuming as a neophyte should be, but seldom is. Gentlemen, I am not at my merriest when I remember all that he has done for me in allowing his genius to shed some of its lustre upon my humble name . . .

'When Sullivan and I began to collaborate, English comic opera had practically ceased to exist. Such musical entertainments as held the stage were adaptations of the crapulous plots of the operas of Offenbach, Audran and Lecocq. The plots had generally been bowdlerized out of intelligibility, and when they had not been subjected to this treatment they were frankly improper; whereas the ladies' dresses suggested that the management had gone on the principle of doing a little and doing it well. We set out with the determination to prove that these elements were not essential to the success of humorous opera. We resolved that our plots, however ridiculous, should be coherent, that our dialogue should be void of offence, that, on artistic principles, no man should play a woman's part and no woman a man's. Finally, we agreed that no lady of the company should be required to wear a dress that she could not wear with absolute propriety at a private fancy ball; and I believe I may say that we proved our case.

'We are credited—or discredited—with one conspicuous failure, *Ruddigore; or, the Witch's Curse*. Well, it ran eight months, and, with the sale of the libretto, put £7,000 into my pocket. In the blackness of my heart the worst I wish to my rival dramatists is that they may each have a dozen such failures, and retire upon the profits . . . And while I am dealing with Savoy opera, I am anxious to avow my indebtedness to the author of *The Bab Ballads*—who, I am told, is present this evening, and from whom I have so unblushingly cribbed. I can only hope that, like Shakespeare, I may be held to have so far improved upon the original stories as to have justified the thefts that I committed.' (Cheers).

That night Mr Gilbert whirled home in his Rolls-Royce, and before he went to bed he wrote in his diary: 'Mon "speech" très bien reçu—tout a progressé avec enthousiasme.' But although he, and his operas, had staged an emphatic come-back in the reign of King Edward VII and had proved they were not Victorian relics, there was one thing that riled Gilbert—his serious plays were rapidly being forgotten. When Miss Edith A. Browne wrote a biography of Gilbert and submitted it in 1907 for his approval he returned her proofs with his own reproof:

I say nothing about the lukewarm opinion you seem to entertain as to the literary quality of these plays (especially those in verse) except to express a wonder that the author of such a series of banalities should have been thought to deserve a biographer. I can hardly believe that I owe the compliment to the easy trivialities of the Savoy libretti.

But a few days later he acknowledges a reply from Miss Browne:

Your very kind letter heaps coals of fire on my head. I hope I did not express myself too bluntly—at all events if I did, it is clear that I am forgiven. Rightly or wrongly, in the pre-Savoy days I held the foremost position among dramatic authors (there were not many of them then) and it hurt me not a little to find that work which was so well esteemed when it was produced appealed so feebly to so keen an intellect as your own.[1]

In 1908 Gilbert told a *Daily Chronicle* interviewer that one and a half million copies of his various libretti had been sold. He had received £25,000 or £30,000 in royalties for sales of the printed 'books', let alone the performing royalties.

He received so many letters begging his permission for performances of his plays without payment of royalties, that he printed what he called 'a circular reply':

In reply to your letter of the . . . I have to inform you that whenever the gross receipts of an amateur performance are handed over intact to charity, I invariably allow my pieces to be played without fee. But when the Committee deduct the cost of rent, dresses, lighting, advertisements, printing, and (possibly) refreshments and travelling expenses from the gross receipts, and then hand over the balance (if any) to a charity, I always require to be paid with the other tradespeople. It appears to me to be unreasonable that the only person concerned who is not interested in the particular charity for which the performance is given should be the only person concerned who is to be out of pocket by the performance.

* * * *

A Letter to a Schoolgirl

Dear Miss Brice,

It seems absurd to address a young lady still at school as 'Dear Madam'.

It is my practice to decline to give my autograph to applications; yet on the other hand one ought never to refuse anything to a young lady home for the holidays—so you see I am the victim of conflicting emotions. I know—we'll toss for it.

Heads, I send you my autograph: Tails I write to tell you nothing will induce me to do anything of the kind. Now for it.

It's Tails, so I won't send it to you!

Yours very truly,

W. S. GILBERT

[1] These letters are in the British Museum.

"MIKADO" BAN ENFORCED.

HOME OFFICE ACTION.

PROSECUTION TO BE ORDERED.

JAPANESE CRITICISM.

"The Mikado," an unlicensed play, having been performed at the Lyceum Theatre, Sheffield, on Thursday, the Lord Chamberlain, who, acting on his own responsibility, as Sir E. Grey explained in Parliament, withdrew the license, has reported to the Home Office, whose business it is to report to the police, who become the prosecutors.

The official attitude is that Mrs. D'Oyly Carte had been informed of the withdrawal, despite any statement by her to the contrary, and that it was unnecessary to give individual notice to persons or companies performing the opera. The performance of an unlicensed play in a licensed building cancels the license and renders the person producing the play liable to a penalty not exceeding £50.

1907: THE BANNING OF THE MIKADO

In 1907 all Gilbertians all over the world had the biggest and sourest laugh in all this history. Japan, having recently beaten Russia at war, was a rising power to whom the Western nations behaved with cautious apprehension, like cat encircling cat; and when her Prince Fushimi approached the shores of Britain on an official visit the Lord Chamberlain withdrew the licence for stage presentations of *The Mikado*. Penalty: fine up to £50. Gilbert's thinly-veiled parody of things-English was banned for fear of offending the Japanese!—the whole world laughed when it realized that Gilbertian absurdity had been outdone in real life, but it was a serious matter for Mrs Carte who had sunk £5,000 in preparations for a forthcoming revival of the opera at the Savoy. And the Middlesbrough Amateur Operatic Society, which happened to be putting on *The Mikado* within a few days, had sold £700 worth of seats; their secretary sped to London and, interviewing the Lord Chamberlain, offered to change the name of the opera and of the characters. The Lord Chamberlain was obdurate. Mr Gilbert then went to see him. The Lord Chamberlain was immovable. Mrs Carte drew up a petition to the King and presented it at Buckingham Palace. This was equally unsuccessful.

'It is one of the happiest characteristics of this glorious country that official utterances are invariably regarded as unanswerable.' (*H.M.S. Pinafore*).

But in this case they got an answer, in a letter to the *Daily Telegraph*:

Sir,—I read in your issue of today that the Lord Chamberlain informed the secretary of the Middlesbrough Amateur Operatic Society that the performance of *The Mikado* was prohibited 'owing to buffoonery in certain parts'. The piece has been leased for some years past to Mrs D'Oyly Carte, who is under contract with me not to permit any deviation whatever from the dialogue and 'business', as settled by me on the occasion of its original production at the Savoy Theatre. If any 'buffoonery' has crept into the piece during its long career in the provinces (which I have no reason to suppose to be the case), I submit that the Lord Chamberlain's obvious course would have been to suppress such buffoonery, instead of slaughtering the play outright, and by so doing depriving the public of a very popular entertainment and the proprietors of a property valued at £10,000.

Admitting the alleged 'buffoonery' for the sake of argument, why is the highly-popular music (which has certainly not been buffooned) forbidden to be played by regimental bands and on ships of war?—Your obedient servant, W. S. GILBERT.

In the House of Commons the Foreign Secretary said that he approved the action of the Lord Chamberlain; and it could not be reconsidered. The Gilbertianism of the situation mounted day by day, as the following Press extracts show.[1]

MR FABER, M.P.: Is it not a fact that the playing of music of *The Mikado* on board ships of war and by regimental bands has been forbidden? (Laughter). Is the right hon. gentleman aware that the action of the Lord Chamberlain in this matter has made this country ridiculous in the eyes of the civilized world?

THE HOME SECRETARY: I strongly protest against the last remark of the hon. member, and as regards the first question, it has nothing to do with my department.

*　　　*　　　*　　　*

Mr Vincent Kennedy, M.P., has given notice that he will ask the Prime Minister whether his attention has been called to the fact that in the play of *Hamlet* the King of Denmark is portrayed as a murderer; and whether, in view of the fact that Denmark is a friendly power, and this reference to the King is liable to cause offence in Denmark, he will ask the Lord Chamberlain to prohibit the production of this play; and whether he intends to bring in legislation to define and limit the powers of the Lord Chamberlain.

*　　　*　　　*　　　*

[1] Material taken from press-cutting collection of Mr C. W. Wordsworth, of Bognor Regis.

Verses in the *Globe* newspaper:

> In a house by the River the stalls and the pit
>   Wanted 'Willow, tit-willow, tit-willow.'
> But were told they'd no right to hear even a bit
>   Of 'Willow, tit-willow, tit-willow.'
> 'Why this utter inanity?' every one cried,
> As they asked the Lord Chamberlain why he had shied
> At the musical play which alone can provide
>   Us with 'Willow, tit-willow, tit-willow.'
>
> Is it true that Japan doesn't like us to sing
>   'Oh willow, tit-willow, tit-willow'?
> For we're cutting 'The Flowers that Bloom in the Spring'
>   Besides 'Willow, tit-willow, tit-willow.'
> We've lost the Mikado; the scenes we all know,
> Pooh-Bah and Yum-Yum and the schoolgirls must go,
> With Katisha and also the cheerful Ko-Ko
>   Who sang 'Willow, tit-willow, tit-willow.'
>
> Now, the light-hearted natives of distant Japan
>   Hearing 'Willow, tit-willow, tit-willow'
> Could scarcely do aught but respond, to a man,
>   And 'Willow, tit-willow, tit-willow'
> Might quickly become (I see no reason why
> Not) a joy to Japan; Japanese passers-by
> I can picture delightedly shouting 'Banzai!
>   That's Willow, tit-willow, tit-willow.'

*   *   *   *

Letter to the same newspaper:

Is the Lord Chamberlain aware that *The Mikado* has been played many times in Japan itself? It is only seven years since I was last in that country, and just before that *The Mikado* was given by a travelling troupe, although it was called *Three Little Maids* probably at the suggestion of some European . . .

*   *   *   *

Mrs D'Oyly Carte decided, despite the ban, to proceed with a performance by her company at the Lyceum, Sheffield, and the *Daily Mail* requested Mr K. Sugimura, 'the distinguished special correspondent of the Tokio *Asahi*, who is now in England in connection with Prince Fushimi's visit', to attend the performance and criticize as frankly as possible. Mr Sugimura reported:

I am deeply and pleasingly disappointed. I came to Sheffield expecting to discover real insults to my countrymen. I find bright music and much fun, but I could not find the insults. I laughed, and laughed very heartily. I enjoyed the music; I envy the nation possessing such music. The only part of the play to which objection might be taken by some is the presentation of the Mikado on the stage as a comic character. This would be impossible in Japan, where my countrymen regard the person of the Emperor as too high for such treatment. Yet, even with us, one of our most famous novelists, Saikaku, of the Genroku period, did treat the figure of the Emperor humorously, describing one of his characters as the Emperor Doll. That novel is still circulated in Japan. It has not been prohibited there.

Apart from the figure of the Emperor there is nothing else to criticize from the national point of view, but there are other things which a Japanese would say. I cannot understand from what part of Japan the author got the names of his characters. Yum-Yum I thought at first to be Num-Num, an incantation to Buddha. Real Japanese girls would not be called Yum-Yum or Peep-Bo. The name of the man Pooh-bah is not a Japanese name. Of course, the play shows quite an imaginary world, not in the least like Japan. The characters embrace and kiss quite publicly. In my country this would be quite shocking. No properly brought-up young lady like Yum-Yum would ever dream of doing this. The character who appealed to me most was Nankipoo. In Japan we would say he is a fine fellow. I had a pleasant evening, and I consider that the English people, in withdrawing this play lest Japan should be offended, are crediting my country with needless readiness to take offence.

Nevertheless, Gilbert himself wrote of learning 'from a friend, who had it from the King, that the Japs made the objection to *The Mikado* and that it was on their instance that it was suppressed.'[1]

Six weeks later in the House of Commons the Home Secretary announced that the prohibition of *The Mikado* was unconditionally withdrawn.

MR LEA: Will any compensation be paid by the Lord Chamberlain to the companies which have been affected by the prohibition of this play?

THE HOME SECRETARY: No, sir.

MR H. P. PEASE: Is it not a fact that the music of *The Mikado* has been played regularly by the bands of the Japanese warships lately?

No answer was returned.

Mr Gilbert's comment: 'In three years we shall probably be at war with Japan about India, and they will offer me a high price to permit *The Mikado* to be played.'

Thirty years later:

Letter from a reader, *Manchester Evening News*, 1938: 'The playing of *The Mikado* ought to be banned by the recognized authorities. This burlesque is not only adding fuel to the flame of hate but causing misunderstanding and barring the way to peace.'

[1]*W. S. Gilbert*, by Sidney Dark and Rowland Grey (Methuen), 1923.

[419]

SIR W. S. GILBERT, KT.

On 21 June, 1907, Mr Gilbert recorded in his diary that he had received a letter from the Prime Minister offering him a knighthood: 'J'accepte'.

He was the first British writer ever to receive a knighthood for his plays alone. Earlier dramatist-knights, such as Sir William Davenant and Sir John Vanbrugh, were knighted for political and other services outside their plays.

On 15 July Mr Gilbert took his forty-second bathe of the year 'avec Herbert Sullivan', noted in his meticulous way that the temperature of the water was 63 degrees, motored to Buckingham Palace, 'was duly tapped on both shoulders by Edward VII and then kissed hands,' returned to Grim's Dyke, and enjoyed his '43rd bain (70°)'.

He called the knighthood 'a tin-pot two-penny-halfpenny sort of distinction', and wrote to his fellow-dramatist Henry Arthur Jones:

> It is, I think, a good thing that the King should at last have turned his attention towards dramatic authorship as a profession worthy of recognition. The honour is conferred upon me by the melancholy virtue of my seniority—a kind of commuted old-age pension of an economical kind. Other dramatists may hope to receive it for reasons of a more complimentary description.[1]

When he spoke at Harrow School on Speech Day Mrs Alec-Tweedie asked him: ' "What on earth are we to call you? W. S. Gilbert has been heard of for so long that it seems impossible to think of you by any other name. In fact, I hardly know what the 'W' stands for."

' "Neither do I," he replied. "I believe I once heard my parents say that they christened me William."

' "Does anybody call you that?" I asked.

' "Not a soul; not even my wife."

' "Then what am I to do?"

' "Call me Bill."

' "All right, I shall," I rejoined, "and as we are now standing in 'Bill Yard' (Roll Call) nothing could be more appropriate. So herewith let me christen you 'Sir Bill'."

' "I will do the billing if you will do the cooing?" he laughed.'[2]

Gilbert, who had so often mocked at 'small titles and orders for Mayors and Recorders', regarded this tardy recognition (twenty-four years after Arthur Sullivan's knighthood) as only acceptable as an honour to his profession, and even so the attitude of Authority to his profession annoyed him, for he said: 'I found myself politely described in the official list as Mr William Gilbert, *playwright*, suggesting that my work was analogical to that of a wheelwright, or a millwright, or a wainwright, or a

[1] Letter in the collection of Mr Reginald Allen, of New York.
[2] Quoted from *Me and Mine*, by Mrs Alec-Tweedie (Hutchinson).

'*Patience*' *in 1907 :* '*Another newcomer is Miss Clara Dow, who made a pretty milkmaid, acted with spirit, and has a powerful voice of ringing quality*', *said the* '*Pall Mall Gazette*'. *Here is Miss Dow with C. H. Workman as Bunthorne and Louie Réné as Lady Jane*

shipwright, as regards the mechanical character of the process by which our respective results are achieved. There is an excellent word "dramatist" which seems to fit the situation, but it is not applied until we are dead, and then we become dramatists as oxen, sheep, and pigs are transfigured into beef, mutton and pork after their demise. You never hear of a novel-wright or a picture-wright, or a poem-wright; and why a playwright? When *The Gondoliers* was commanded at Windsor by her late Majesty, the piece was described as "by Sir Arthur Sullivan", the librettist being too insignificant an insect to be worth mentioning on a programme which contained the name of the wig-maker in bold type![1] And I had to pay £87 10s. as my share of sending the piece down to Windsor, besides forfeiting my share of the night's profits at the Savoy!'

This irascible fit soon passed, and when a complimentary banquet on his knighthood was given at the Savoy Hotel Gilbert was in his most mellow mood.

'In the course of my career I have seen many stage changes. I am old enough to remember the days (it is true I had only entered my fourth year at the time) when the Haymarket Theatre—always the most conservative theatre in London—was still lighted by candles, when its manager receiving Royalty in a Court suit walked backwards (and on one occasion fell backwards) with a pair of silver candlesticks in his hand, when the author received four double dress circles, four double upper boxes, four double pits, and four double galleries as his perquisite on the first night of the new piece, when there were no stalls, and the pit came right up to the orchestra, when the manager on a first night announced from the stage that "with your kind permission, the piece would be repeated every night until further notice," when authors were paid £50 an act for original comedies, when £20 a week was the highest salary of a leading actor, when to bring a newspaper into the green room involved a heavy fine (liquidated damages to be paid in rum punch), when there was half-price at nine o'clock, and when oysters after the play were 6d. a dozen.

'My first piece—a burlesque on the *Elixir of Love* called *Dulcamara, or the Little Duck and the Great Quack*—was produced at the St James's in those cheap and easy days. The piece was written in a week, and produced in another week; there had been no time to discuss terms, and a week after its successful production, Mr Emden, Miss Herbert's treasurer, asked me how much I expected to be paid. Blindly ignorant of the value of such things I modestly suggested thirty guineas. "Oh dear no," said Emden, "we never pay in guineas; you must make it pounds." Accordingly I made it pounds, and Emden said, as he handed me the cheque: "Now take an old stager's advice—never sell as good a piece as this for thirty pounds again." And I never have.'[2]

Lord Onslow, presiding at the Savoy banquet, said that 'throughout the whole of Sir William Gilbert's writings there is not one single word that might not be enjoyed by the most innocent member of society'. Perhaps we should find this an over-emphasis if we were to examine line-by-line *The Bab Ballads* and even the operas, but ordinary people who seek simply to enjoy themselves do not analyse line-by-line, and Lord Onslow was probably correct when he added:

'Sir William has never brought the flush of shame to the cheek of innocence.'

One of the most interesting—and amusing—characteristics of Gilbert is that he drew a sharp line between what is fit in public and what is merely frivolous in private. The puritan of the Savoy had in private conversation 'a Rabelaisian quality which has kept some of his best *mots* from printed record'.[3] It would be unseemly to go further in

---

[1] Gilbert's memory was not quite accurate. His name appears on the Windsor programme but was omitted from the announcement in the Court Circular. See colour plate facing page 360.

[2] Report in the *Daily Telegraph*, 3 February, 1908.

[3] H. G. Hibbert: *A Playgoer's Memories* (Richards), 1920.

print than the story of his asking the box-office clerk at the Savoy where Lady Gilbert was.

'She's round behind, sir.'

'Yes, I know she is, but *where* is she?'

On the stage Gilbert made clean fun pay. Virtue brought its own reward. His principles were based on firm Victorian ideas of what was proper for the good of Society. He expressed this when he gave evidence in 1909 before the Joint Parliamentary Committee on the censorship of stage plays, which had been set up after Gilbert, Pinero, Barrie, Granville-Barker, and others had called in deputation at the Home Office to protest against the 'humiliation of the censorship'. Gilbert, to the surprise of many people—remembering the banning of *The Mikado*—came out as a believer in censorship.

THE CHAIRMAN (Mr Herbert Samuel): Why do you think a censorship of some kind is desirable?

SIR WILLIAM GILBERT: Because I think that the stage is not a proper pulpit from which to disseminate doctrines of anarchism, socialism, and agnosticism. It is not the proper platform upon which to discuss questions of adultery and free love before a mixed audience.

When pressed, Gilbert qualified this by agreeing that 'the manner in which such subjects are dealt with is a very important question', and said that he did not think the *Cenci* of Shelley was fit and proper, whereas he would pass *Othello* 'because the question of adultery is treated very delicately'. His suggestion was that the censorship should not rest exclusively on one man (the Lord Chamberlain), but that there should be an appeal court of three arbiters, one of whom should be appointed by the author. He remarked feelingly that the banning of *The Mikado* was 'unwarrantable and illegal', especially as he, the author, had not been consulted.

During the twentieth century the *double entendre* has become an increasingly hard-worn form of joke on stage, film, and radio. Gilbert's operas are singularly free from it. Yet off the stage he was the first to see the chance: once when invited to a concert at the Soldiers' Daughters' Home he replied that he was unable to attend but would be delighted to see one of the soldiers' daughters home after the concert. His attitude towards women was one of Victorian gallantry spiced with skittish frivolity:

I caught a nasty chill at the Waterlows' from sitting on a damp lawn with distinctly the loveliest copper-haired lady I have ever met—at least it was that, or eating the greater part of a large melon on Sunday night. These two causes tend to the same effect . . .[1]

When Mrs Alec-Tweedie was admiring the bloom on his peaches at Grim's Dyke she likened its paint-like effect to an actress's complexion. 'They often paint,' said Sir William in a flash, 'but they do not often draw.'

Whilst he kept abreast of the advancing spirit of the twentieth century in some

[1] Letter to Miss Gordon Scott, quoted in *W. S. Gilbert, his Life and Letters*, by Sidney Dark and Rowland Grey (Methuen).

[423]

'*Tarantara!*'—*the Sergeant* [*Rutland Barrington*] *and his* '*undaunted men in blue*' *in* '*The Pirates of Penzance*', 1909. *Dorothy Court* (*Mrs Haydn Wood*) *plays Mabel*

things, there were others which his Victorianism could not abide, and when he read of suffragettes chaining themselves to the railings in Downing Street to publicize their efforts to get Votes for Women, Gilbert said: 'I shall chain myself to the railing of Queen Charlotte's Maternity Hospital and shout "Babes for Men".' This seemed to him as logical. It is not generally known that he pilloried the suffragettes in *The Mikado* among those people who 'never would be missed': when the opera was revived in 1908 he wrote a new verse for the Lord High Executioner (this is not now used):

> That well intentioned lady who's too bulky for her boots,
> The lovely suffragist—I've got her on the list.
> That single-minded patriot, who doesn't bank with Coutt's,
> The redhot Socialist. I don't think he'll be missed.
> All those who hold that publicans it's virtuous to fleece,
> And impose a heavy war tax in these piping days of peace,
> And preach the code that moralists like Robin Hood held true
> That to benefit the pauper you must rob the well-to-do—
> That peculiar variety of sham philanthropist,
> I don't think he'd be missed—I'm sure he'd not be missed.

SIR W. S. GILBERT READING HIS NEW OPERA

'The long anticipated new comic opera is in rehearsal,' says the 1909 newspaper caption to this picture, taken at the first read-through at the Savoy Theatre. On the dais are [LEFT to RIGHT] *C. H. Workman (manager of the theatre), Edward German, and Sir W. S. Gilbert. The entire cast of 'Fallen Fairies' is assembled in the stalls*

THE LAST CURTAIN

The last Gilbertian comic opera was *Fallen Fairies*. What remained of the so-often-rejected Lozenge Plot had gone through many transformations and at last, with music by Edward German, it opened at the Savoy in 1909. The scene: Fairyland, on the upper side of a cloud. 'It is doubtful whether of late years any theatrical event has been more eagerly looked forward to than this,' said the *Birmingham Post*, only to add that 'the new piece is a disappointment'.

The London *Evening News* lamented : 'Only once or twice did the old Savoy atmosphere assert itself.' Most of the critics thought that Mr German had made a brave attempt to rescue from failure an anaemic and fitful libretto (one of its strange fits was to limit the chorus to women's voices). But the opera failed. Arthur Sullivan had been right about the Lozenge.

[425]

The failure of *Fallen Fairies* was not because the twentieth-century public had lost a taste for Gilbertianism; it was rather because Gilbert had done so. In his eagerness to do something new, he offered an opera which (as he told the *Observer*) 'begins as light comedy, becomes in the 2nd Act broad comedy, and eventually merges into very strong drama, almost tragic. It thus differs from other operas. If it succeeds I hope to follow it with other pieces of the same class.'

Gilbert to Mrs Carte, a few weeks later: 'I certainly do not intend to write any more libretti.' But for a children's production of *The Mikado* he wrote a new version of Ko-Ko's 'little list' song. It added to those who never would be missed—

> All people who maintain (in solemn earnest—not in joke)
> That quantities of sugar-plums are bad for little folk,
> And those who hold the principle, unalterably fixed
> That instruction with amusement should most carefully be mixed.

The Gilberts went away in 1910 on a cruise to Constantinople. W.S.G. wrote home: 'I have been strongly advised to ally myself with the Young Turkish Party, but unfortunately I was not furnished with her address.'[1]

On his return he wrote his last play, a grim little sketch *The Hooligan*, which went into the variety bill at the London Coliseum in 1911. It was a return to the original and the deepest Gilbert, for it was a serious piece of writing on a serious social topic: 'Its scene was a condemned cell,' wrote H. M. Walbrook in the *Observer*, 'and its leading character was a physically feeble, totally illiterate, almost brainless wastrel under sentence of death. After the first performance some of the spectators, who had doubtless come to be amused, expressed their disappointment by hissing. In its succeeding performances, however, the dead silence amid which the curtain fell broke into prolonged applause . . . Every word of it was brave, and timely, and absolutely sincere.'[2]

The final line in the sketch was: 'Dead—heart failure.'

On 29 May, 1911, Sir William Gilbert called at the Junior Carlton Club and pointedly invited W. H. Kendal to lunch with him. He had not for years been on good terms with the Kendals, but Dame Madge Kendal has related how on this day her husband came home and told her that Gilbert 'ate an enormous lunch, he flattered you and he flattered me—which astonished me so much that I could not eat mine. Then he looked at his watch and said: "I must be off, as I have an appointment to teach a young lady to swim." He went away but came back and shook hands with me in the most cordial manner.'[3]

[1] Letter to Mrs Talbot, quoted in *W. S. Gilbert, his Life and Letters*, by Sidney Dark and Rowland Grey (Methuen).
[2] Article on the Centenary of Gilbert's birth, the *Observer*, 15 November, 1936.
[3] Article by Dame Madge Kendal, the *Cornhill Magazine*, September, 1933.

Dame Madge told her husband how glad she was that W.S.G. had made friends again. She adds: 'Imagine my despair on the following morning when, on coming down to breakfast, I saw on opening the daily paper—'

11

sufficiently plain. They cannot be cured by purely one-sided reforms.

Sir W. S. Gilbert.

The whole English-speaking world will hear with deep regret of the death of SIR W. S. GILBERT. He was one of the very few really original figures in our recent dramatic history; and partly through his own genius, and partly through the fortunate accident of his finding a perfect musical collaborator and exponent in SIR ARTHUR SULLIVAN, he long ago secured a position in the public consciousness which has been obtained by no other dramatist for many a long year. We do not forget the constructive power of SIR ARTHUR PINERO, or the satirical paradoxes of MR. BERNARD SHAW, or the varied gifts of the authors of *The Little Minister* and *Lady Frederick* and *The Man from Blankney's*. Clever and successful as all these have been, none of them had quite the charm of the best things of GILBERT, when those best things were sung to SULLIVAN's music. The partners produced at least four works which instantly became and have remained classics—*Pinafore*, *The Pirates of Penzance*, *Patience*, and *The Mikado*. If the successors of these did not ... success it ...

DEATH OF SIR W. S. GILBERT.

We record with much regret that Sir William Schwenck Gilbert, the poet and dramatic author, died suddenly yesterday afternoon of a heart affection while bathing at his home at Harrow Weald.

He was in London in the morning, and returned home about 4 o'clock, accompanied by two lady friends. On arrival at his residence, Grimsdyke, he said he should take his customary bath in an ornamental lake in the grounds. He subsequently dived into the water, and as it was some time before he reappeared on the surface his friends, who were on the bank, became alarmed. Going closer they saw that he was in some difficulty. One of the ladies tried to give him some assistance, while the other rushed off for help. By this time Sir William sank again. Ultimately some menservants arrived, and succeeded in recovering the body. It was examined by a doctor, who pronounced life to be extinct.

It is believed that death was caused by syncope, brought about by undue exertion in diving into the water. The lake is about 6ft. deep.

MEMOIR.

Sir Wi... ...lbert was ... 17. So...

—'*The Times*', 30 May 1911

It transpired at the inquest that Sir William was swimming with Miss Winifred Emery (niece of Mrs Cyril Maude, a great friend of the Gilberts) and Miss Preece when the latter got into difficulties. Sir William went to her aid but the sudden exertion overcame him. When they pulled him out he was dead—heart failure.

On his way from London to Grim's Dyke that day, after taking leave of Kendal, Gilbert stopped to visit a friend who, after an accident, had to lie in darkness. The nurse ushered him into the murky room, remarking, 'I won't ask what you think of her appearance, Sir William, for you can scarcely see her.'

'Her appearance matters nothing,' said Gilbert. 'It is her disappearance we couldn't stand.'

[427]

Modern Times: 'The Mikado' *redesigned by Charles Ricketts, 1926. Darrell Fancourt sings* To let the punishment fit the crime'; *Ella Halman as Katisha*

In America again: Chicago welcomes the English opera company

A DIARY

OF

MODERN TIMES

COLLAPSE AND REBIRTH OF THE GILBERT & SULLIVAN TRADITION

Fun, as a rule, has a short life. To make fun that lasts
for three generations—each of them with a different
outlook on the world, and different tastes and interests
even in things artistic—is the mark of a very high talent.
               —Robert Lynd, on the Centenary of Gilbert's birth.[1]

AFTER THE DEATH of Gilbert it looked like the collapse of the operas. From 1910 to 1919 no 'Gilbert and Sullivan' posters appeared on the hoardings in the West End. A single touring company roamed quietly around the British provinces, and none went voyaging overseas as in the brave old days. Helen D'Oyly Carte, that woman of extraordinary enthusiasm and charm, had retired in 1909, and she died in 1913. 'A more wonderful woman it has not been my lot to know,' said George Edwardes. 'The whole foundations of the Savoy business rested on her.' The foundations were removed, and it seemed that the entire edifice was toppling; or rather fading away, like Shakespeare's 'cloud-capped towers'. This towering achievement of humour and music was, it seemed, a mere hang-over from the Victorian era, incapable of outliving its own generation. It seemed so—especially when the war of 1914 broke out with its convulsive effect on morals and modes, its speeding-up of life, and the coincidental and overwhelming spread of jazz, of movies, and of a new form of stage entertainment, the revue, which came in with a blast of ragtime and swept even George Edwardesian musical comedy into the gutter. The British Foreign Secretary had said on the outbreak of war that 'The lamps are going out all over Europe'. It looked as though these would include the fantastic fairy-lamps of Gilbert and Sullivan.

And yet *The Times* had predicted in a leading article on the day after Gilbert's death: 'His best works will live perhaps longer than any other plays of the Victorian era.'

[1] Article in *News Chronicle*, 21 November, 1936.

[429]

Gilbert himself had said: 'Posterity will know as little of me as I shall know of posterity.'

We know today that of these two *The Times* was the true prophet. How Gilbert and Sullivan Opera has passed from decline into renaissance is the story of this chapter. On Mrs Carte's death her stepson Rupert (b. 1876) took over the business interests which had been founded by his famous father, Richard. As a young man Rupert had apprenticed himself to the luxury hotel enterprises of the family (he was chairman of the Savoy Hotel Company at twenty-seven), but he was his father's son in having not only shrewd business instincts but an artistic temperament, and he soon began looking closely at the touring opera company—and what he saw he didn't like. Old age and the 1914 war had decimated its ranks, fusty tradition had begun to spin cobwebs around the once-bright fairy-lamps.

'When I first took over in 1913,' said Mr Carte,[1] 'I went and watched the Company playing at a rather dreary theatre down in the suburbs of London. I thought the dresses looked dowdy—it was *Iolanthe*—and I had a talk with the Wardrobe Mistress about it. I said the dresses needed perking up. She was a bit shocked. "Oh, Mr Carte!" she declared, "they look so well!"—but she had been with the Company so many years that I began to suspect that her ideas were out-of-date, especially when she told me that the chorus ladies were still being issued by her with red-flannel knickers. I found that with constant renewal of the wardrobe the original character of the costumes had been lost and much of the colour scheme was now poorly developed. With the passing of the years changes occur in our ideas of good colour and design. Many of the settings seemed to me unattractive and without character by modern standards. There were, of course, many costumes that should be retained, such as the uniforms, the Peers, Tower Warders, etc., but I formed the view that new productions should be prepared, with scenery and dresses to the design of first-class artists who understood the operas but who would produce a décor attractive to the new generation. In any case, I did not consider it practicable to reproduce accurately the original costumes. For one thing, it is hardly possible to get people

Rupert D'Oyly Carte in 1919

[1] In a statement made to the author for this book in 1947.

(especially women) to look like those of sixty or seventy years ago—figures seem to change, so does the way of walking and movement.'

Here was a man, and a D'Oyly Carte into the bargain, who was prepared to challenge the whole question of Savoy Opera Tradition. On this he said: 'I have always kept a strict watch on any suggested changes to the words and music, but décor is a different thing. As years pass the public's sense of *style* changes remarkably. Appreciation of colour changes. Even the very shape of our women has changed! Dresses and shapes and colours which were once thought beautiful are now thought dowdy. It is this subtle change in public taste which necessitates periodic redressing of the operas.'

Mr Carte was not proposing to go to the length of the mammoth production of *H.M.S. Pinafore* 'with a real ship on real water' at New York in 1914 (like his father, he had no control over performances in America). In England the war prevented any great progress with refurbishing the operas, but a start was quietly made in 1915 when Attilo Comelli designed new dresses for the fairies in *Iolanthe*. Since then scenery and dresses have been redesigned by the following artists:

1917	The Gondoliers	Percy Anderson
1918	Patience	Hugo Rumbold
1919	The Pirates of Penzance	
1919	The Yeomen of the Guard	
1920	Trial by Jury	Percy Anderson
1920	Ruddigore	
1922	Princess Ida	
1924	Iolanthe	Norman Wilkinson
1926	The Mikado	Charles Ricketts
1929	Patience	
1929	H.M.S. Pinafore	George Sheringham
1929	The Pirates of Penzance	
1929	The Gondoliers	Charles Ricketts
1932	Iolanthe	George Sheringham
1939	The Yeomen of the Guard	Peter Goffin
1948	Ruddigore	
1953	The Mikado	Peter Goffin (scenery)
1954	Princess Ida	James Wade
1957	Patience	Peter Goffin

During the 1914–18 war Mr D'Oyly Carte was on special duties in the Navy; he would be sent off on secret journeys to distant parts of the world, and he would as mysteriously reappear in London for a few weeks, and when he did so he would put in a few touches to the preparatory work for the rebirth of the D'Oyly Carte Opera Company. It is entirely due to D'Oyly Carte-the-2nd that the Operas were not only

Leo Sheffield as Grosvenor in 'Patience', 1916, and in his later world-famed portrayal of Pooh-Bah in 'The Mikado'.

saved from decrepitude but restored to an artistic level which lent an exciting new flavour to the British theatre after the 1914–18 war. 'Young Mr Carte' as he was called, though he was now in his forties, came back from the war and with tremendous energy and sensitivity organized this renaissance; but he was that rare type of showman who is content to pull the strings of his puppets and remain himself unseen. His face was unknown in the clubs and restaurants haunted by theatrical folk, who were soon talking about this daring young man who announced that he was renting the Prince's Theatre in the West End for a season commencing 29 September, 1919, and who was not only redressing the operas but was capable of dressing-down old performers who had become lax, and of ruthlessly sacking the hopeless, and engaging new talent.

Tommy Handley was among the new artists to whom Carte gave auditions. The man who was to become radio's greatest comedian had previously played in amateur Gilbert and Sullivan productions; he now impressed Mr Carte by his singing of the Major-General's song from *The Pirates of Penzance*. He was told to leave his name, but went

'His Foe was Folly and his Weapon Wit'

In 1914 a group of Gilbert's friends subscribed to erect this memorial, by Sir George Frampton, R.A., on the Thames Embankment. Tragedy is represented on one side, Comedy on the other, holding the figure of the Mikado and other characters from the operas

on tour in a musical comedy and forgot all about it. Some weeks later he was invited to join the Number Two Gilbert and Sullivan Company. 'He had to explain that he was already signed up with the *Shanghai* Company and so the chance of becoming a Savoyard was lost. It is strange to ponder on the different career he would have had if that invitation had been just a few days earlier,' writes Ted Kavanagh.[1]

Carte-the-2nd chose so well that most of the new young artists to whom he entrusted the great adventure of bringing the Operas back into the limelight became stars, enormously popular on both sides of the Atlantic during the next decade.

1919: Rebirth

First-night notice in the London *Sunday Times:* 'The admirable company is distinguished by the inclusion of a new tenor, Mr Derek Oldham, whose pleasing presence and manner, acting capabilities, and exquisite voice delighted as much as those of any Marco I have seen and heard. The Duke of Mr Henry Lytton, the Don

[1] *Tommy Handley*, by Ted Kavanagh (Hodder & Stoughton), 1949.

Alhambra of Mr Leo Sheffield, and the Duchess of Miss Bertha Lewis are all in accord with the traditions of the parts, whilst Miss Elsie Griffin and Miss Nellie Briercliffe made a satisfactory pair of brides. The enthusiasm of the audience knew no bounds.'

So, opening with *The Gondoliers*, the D'Oyly Carte Company made a triumphant return to the West End.

Londoners who had thought the Gilbert and Sullivan operas were ten years dead were astonished to see queues waiting at the Prince's Theatre not merely all day but all night, and even the phlegmatic Mr Carte must have been surprised to learn that one result of his enterprise was that the Holborn Borough Council was requested to keep the public lavatories in the vicinity open all night.

The *Daily Telegraph*: 'After four years of war and its attendant miseries, what does the British public care about an inconvenience so comparatively trifling as a mere railway strike? Certainly not enough to permit itself to be kept away from an event of such prime importance as the Gilbert and Sullivan revival at the Prince's Theatre, whither an enormous audience gravitated to welcome Mr D'Oyly Carte's excellent company on its first visit to Central London. It was a brilliant audience and it included not only many of the chief social, theatrical, and musical notabilities of the day, but also a number of those old Savoyards with whose names the Gilbert and Sullivan operas must always be irrevocably associated. Miss Jessie Bond, Miss Geraldine Ulmar, and Mr Rutland Barrington all were there, and it surely must have been with a sense of the keenest gratification that they heard the lines that they used to speak and the tunes that they used to sing still setting an audience rocking with laughter and still receiving rapturous encores.'

The Gilbert and Sullivan revival was in competition with such still-going-strong wartime favourites as *Chu Chin Chow*, *Kissing Time*, *As You Were*, and *The Maid of the Mountains*. But the season proved that the basic appeal of the Gilbertian operas had lost none of its power. The new productions proved as glamorous as the old. Lord Fisher sat in the stalls chuckling at the First Lord in *Pinafore*, just as other real Lords of the Admiralty had done at the Savoy in Sullivan's time—but now it was Henry Lytton who 'polished up the handle of the big front door'. One after the other the operas came back in their new guise. In 1920 *Ruddigore* was revived after an absence of thirty-three years, with Henry Lytton as Robin Oakapple, the selfsame part that had given him his first chance when George Grossmith fell ill in the original production. *Princess Ida* returned from provincial exile. These long-neglected operas were received with delight —and so was Sullivan's earliest work for the stage, *Cox and Box*, with a splendid new baritone, Darrell Fancourt, as Bouncer, Sydney Granville as Cox, and Leo Darnton as Box. It was a triumphant renaissance in every way. Says Derek Oldham: 'The season of 1919–20 was indeed epic. It was sensational.'[1]

[1] In a letter to the author.

'A wandering minstrel I . . .' Derek Oldham in the Ricketts costume for Nanki-Poo, compared
with the original dress [RIGHT] worn by Charles Kenyon in 1885

GILBERT AND SULLIVAN SEASON, 1921—1922

MR. RUPERT D'OYLY CARTE proposes that the Opera to
be performed on the last night of the present season,
April 8th, 1922, shall be selected by the Public. He would be
glad, therefore, if you would record your vote below, and hand
this card to one of the District Messengers waiting at the exits
at the end of the performance, or post it in the usual way.

*Here put Opera to be
performed (only one
Opera to be given)* ......*Patience*......

*Here insert your
name and address* ......

NOTE.—Please write your name and address, also the name of the Opera chosen, in Block Letters.

Mr Oldham's début was epic in itself. He jumped into enormous popularity. No one who saw him as Mabel's 'Poor wandering one', the Apprentice in *The Pirates of Penzance* (his favourite part), will forget it, though he considers the only 'real' tenor part in the operas to be Colonel Fairfax in *The Yeomen*.

But after three years Mr Oldham left the Company to join the musical comedy *Whirled Into Happiness* at a lavish salary. 'This,' he says, 'was of course very modern and rag-timey after G. and S., and in one number I had to do a somersault of which I was inordinately proud. At this moment on my first night, a lady in the front row of the stalls put her hands over her face and was heard by our conductor to moan "Oh . . . Colonel Fairfax!" A few days later I received this letter:

Dear Mr Oldham,
    Two ardent Gilbert and Sullivanites came to see you last night. All we can say is 'Poor wandering one, why hast thou so sadly strayed?'

Yours,
Disappointed.

A New Musical Standard

Mr D'Oyly Carte had the vision to secure the services of Geoffrey Toye, the conductor and composer, and a first-rate musician, as musical director for the 1919–24 seasons. Mr Toye restored the operas to their proper musical standard and did not hesitate to rewrite the rather inadequate overture to *Ruddigore*.

When *Princess Ida* was revived the problem of casting the name part came up, as it always will—for the role of the Princess demands a voice of quality and range unusual in the Sullivan comic operas—the consequence of his ambition when he wrote *Princess Ida* 'to intensify the emotional element in the music' as he put it in the letter to Gilbert which led to their first quarrel. For the presentation in 1922 Mr Carte engaged a leading concert artist, Winifred Lawson, who made so great a success that she remained as principal soprano to the D'Oyly Carte Company for ten years, and later (1934–7) returned to the operas in Australia. The lovely quality of her voice is preserved on the gramophone recordings made in the twenties.

The First Gramophone Records

After the First World War two new instruments brought their magic power to bear on extending the spell of Gilbert and Sullivan opera to new audiences, especially in remote parts of the world unvisited by theatrical companies, first the gramophone and later the radio. The first complete gramophone recording of an opera was that of *The Mikado*, made in the London studio of HMV under Mr Carte's supervision in

1917—an acoustical recording, for this was ten years before the electrical method was introduced. The artists sang into a large horn. Among them was George Baker who subsequently took part in all the HMV recordings (both acoustic and electronic) of all the operas except one, and who thus made a remarkable world-wide reputation as a Gilbert and Sullivan singer, although he never appeared on the stage. He has followed up this success with lecture tours, both in Britain and the U.S.A. More recently, the D'Oyly Carte Opera Company has recorded the operas for Decca.

After its London triumphs the 1920 company went on tour, and at the Lyceum, Sheffield, on 25 March, 1925, gave the Jubilee Performance of *Trial by Jury*, with Leo Sheffield as the Judge, exactly fifty years after the first performance at the Royalty, Soho. A second touring company had now been put on the road, and in this Martyn Green made his first appearance in 1922 at Crewe in the humble part of Luiz in *The Gondoliers*. Others who made their mark with D'Oyly Carte in the twenties included Dorothy Gill, Marjorie Eyre, Leslie Rands, Richard Walker, Charles Goulding, Elsie Griffin, Sydney Granville, and Ivan Menzies (better known in Australia).

'*And a good judge too*'—Leo Sheffield

1926: Ricketts Redresses 'The Mikado'

Everywhere the operas were received with open arms. Rupert D'Oyly Carte's faith in Gilbert and Sullivan was richly vindicated. Now, like his father before him, he sought wider conquests. By arrangement with J. C. Williamson Ltd. he sent a company out from Australia to Japan in 1923, for a season at the Yuraku-za Theatre, Tokyo. C. H. Workman played the comedy leads, such as the Duke in *The Gondoliers*. Programmes were printed in English and Japanese.

Of all Rupert D'Oyly Carte's reforms the most spectacular, most artistic, and most heatedly-debated (by the traditionalists) was Ricketts's redressing of *The Mikado*. Charles Ricketts, R.A., was a front-rank English artist who had lived in Japan, he had a fine collection of Japanese prints and was an authority on Japanese costume and art—but it was *Utopia Limited* that Carte was thinking of reviving when he first approached Ricketts with photographs of the 1893 production.

Ricketts to Carte:

I have given the photographs of *Utopia Limited* to your man this morning. I regret that the subject is quite outside my line; there is, in fact, hardly anything to do and I should be charging you for nothing if I undertook it. Should you ever contemplate the renovation of *The Gondoliers* in, shall we say Louis XIV costume, or, better still *The Mikado* in exquisite eighteenth-century Japanese dresses—including the fantastic court dresses—I should be pleased to collaborate. *The Geisha, Madame Butterfly,* and *The Mikado* have created a dreary pink dressing gown style quite unlike anything Japanese and I believe the public would be startled by the novelty of an entirely different presentment.

Carte seized the idea with enthusiasm. They agreed to give the opera 'an entirely new aspect', and Ricketts set to work on the designs (many of which have since been acquired by the National Arts Collection Fund and are now on public exhibition). Whilst closely following true Japanese tradition, he allowed himself some liberties such as the comic suggestion of a 'big, black block' in the shape of the Lord High Executioner's hat, and the badge of crossed axes on the sleeve of that industrious mechanic. Remembering Japanese susceptibilities, Ricketts dressed the Mikado rather as a Shogun or principal representative of the Emperor than as the Emperor himself.

Ricketts to Carte:

To be frank, I should not care to undertake this task unless it were viewed as a new work requiring beauty, humour, and an element of surprise in its appearance.

The element of surprise provoked a storm of mingled praise and condemnation. Ricketts said: 'I have been severely criticized for redressing *The Mikado*. But the original setting of *The Mikado* contains nothing which it is essential to preserve. The piece was staged in a great hurry at its first appearance, and the dressing of it was given into the hands of a costumier who was told to do the best he could. Little was known at the time about Japanese dress, and the result was a production in which the costumes looked like kimonos. The new dresses I have chosen belong to a period—about 1720—when the national costume was especially beautiful. The girls' dresses, in particular, were very bright and gay. Therefore, there is nothing to lose by making the costumes conform to that period. Indeed the increased artistic effect alone justifies the heavy expense.'[1]

Compare *Punch's* opinion about the original costumes, in the issue of 1 April, 1885: 'They are singularly adverse to the display of feminine charm . . . they obliterate the natural distinctions between the sexes, importing to the prettiest girl's figure the seeming of a bolster loosely wrapped up in a dressing gown.'

Showman that he was, Mr Carte proceeded in 1926 to hit the drum with a big bang. He decided to open a London season at the Prince's Theatre with *The Mikado,* and he engaged Dr (now Sir) Malcolm Sargent as conductor. This caused almost as much fuss

[1] Interview given to the Press, 18 September, 1926.

The original Mikado costume of 1885 [LEFT] *worn by Darrell Fancourt, and Ricketts' design for the new dress*

as the new décor. Sir Malcolm tells us[1] that in his home-town of Stamford, Lincolnshire, he had taken part in amateur Gilbert and Sullivan productions at the tender age of ten:

Later I became the conductor of the society, and from that moment I have not ceased to be intensely fond of the Gilbert and Sullivan productions. In 1926 suddenly Mr Rupert D'Oyly Carte sent for me and said that he wanted to put on a big season at the Prince's Theatre, and would I take charge of the music. I could really hardly believe my ears, because it was to me the most fascinating prospect, and he said 'I want you to take complete charge of the music, and to do it as you feel it should be done.' He let me have the original manuscript scores of Sullivan, and you can judge the excitement of the young person finding himself face to face with these manuscripts, and the thrill of looking at the original orchestrations and seeing exactly how Sullivan worked. The first night was a very exciting one. I was given a perfect orchestra, larger than the Gilbert productions usually had, and I worked things up to a pitch that was pretty good musically, but to my horror some newspapers the next day gave wonderful notices of the performance and music and everything—but they said 'We must stop this young man from re-orchestrating Sullivan. We have had re-orchestrations of Handel and Bach, but this is the limit when our beautiful Sullivan's music is touched.' To my great joy, Mr D'Oyly Carte was able the next day to put a letter in saying that not one note had been touched. We were simply playing the stuff as Sullivan had written it.

[1] In a talk broadcast by the BBC in connection with the *Gilbert and Sullivan* radio-biography, 1947.

The cast was a fine one, and the new décor caused a sensation. The *Daily Telegraph* critic said: 'Is there anything in all the annals of the light lyric stage, in this or any other country, that could be compared with the unending triumphs of Gilbert and Sullivan? . . . There is, indeed, no parallel to this in all theatrical (or operatic) history —nothing to match such unfailing zest and enjoyment in the performances of works that most of those who come time and again to hear them must have known by heart almost from early youth.'

Ko-Ko: (*Mr Henry Lytton*):
 'Now what do you really think of these new costumes?'
Pooh-Bah (*Mr Leo Sheffield*):
 'Come over here, where the Lord High Costumier can't hear us'

Katisha: (*Miss Bertha Lewis*):
 'Are you Old Japanese or Early Victorian?'
Yum-Yum (*Miss Elsie Griffin*):
 'What does it matter as long as I'm charming?'

'*Punch*', 29 September, 1926

1931: Pinafore in the Caribbean

'An open-air performance of *Pinafore* was given recently by the Virgin Islanders in the harbour of the old town of Christiansted on the island of St Croix. The performers were all people of colour, natives of the islands, a nearly "practical" ship was constructed on a float, and Little Buttercup came rowing up on real sea-water in her bum-boat. The performance was the idea of Mr Ralph M. Dunbar, director of music and entertainment. Mr Dunbar is now coaching a cast of some 150 Cruzians for a performance of *The Pirates of Penzance*, which will be given on a wooded and rocky part of the shores of St Croix. There have been all sorts of Gilbert and Sullivan revivals, but *Pinafore* under a tropic moon, on real ocean water, sung by Caribbean natives, is probably the first novelty of its kind.'[1]

[1] *New York Herald*, 26 July, 1931.

[440]

1927–34: America Reconquered

Some forty years had passed since a D'Oyly Carte Company was in America. Could Rupert now repeat the famous conquest of his father's day, when Richard D'Oyly Carte 'carried the war into the pirates' camp'? When Carte-the-2nd broached the idea of an American tour he was strongly advised against it by U.S. business men, who pointed out that America had her own well-established Gilbert and Sullivan companies, with some exceedingly beautiful productions, such as those of Winthrop Ames in 1926–9; so Carte decided that the English company should make its first raid on the American Continent, not to the U.S.A., but to Canada, in a twenty-weeks' tour right across to Vancouver in 1927. A Canadian paper described them as 'the best ambassadors of Empire', and a year later they went back to Canada, this time invading United States territory at Seattle, Portland, San Francisco, Los Angeles, Denver, Chicago, and Detroit—but not New York. Broadway theatre managers were still lukewarm.

It remained for Mr Martin Beck, in the words of American magazine *Fortune*: 'to introduce the really genuine Gilbert and Sullivan to New York. In 1934 Producer Gilbert Miller told him that the D'Oyly Carte players would be a wonderful bet for his theatre. Martin Beck knew his Gilbert and Sullivan with a knowledge that went back to a performance of *The Mikado* by a Hungarian company in Budapest years ago. So impressed was he with the wisdom of Gilbert Miller's idea that he was on his way to England that same day. He and D'Oyly Carte did business quickly. Not until after the contracts for a U.S. tour were signed did Martin Beck remember he had not yet seen the company act. But he went to Manchester, where it was playing that week, to see it and approve the principals. As a result, on 31 August, 1934, a scared group of players, none of whom, not even Company Manager Frederick Hobbs, had ever been in New York before, landed at Pier Fifty-four with 105 hampers filled with costumes, 51 cases of props, and 245 pieces of scenery. It all weighed some thirty tons and it represented the biggest touring gamble that anyone had taken in the theatre since God knows when—maybe since the first time that Barnum and Bailey packed up the whole blooming circus and took it on a European tour. But after the curtain had been up for five minutes on the opening night of *The Gondoliers* it was apparent that New York was going to back up the sly good judgment of Martin Beck, and with a great deal to spare. It was a riot.'[1] *Fortune* says the bookings in fifteen weeks amounted to 350,000 dollars.

Two years later the English company was rounding off another American tour at Philadelphia when the nicest thing ever said in Anglo-American relations was voiced by the *Philadelphia Public Ledger*:

The D'Oyly Carte Savoyards have given Philadelphia the finest presentation of the most civilized form of light entertainment the theatre can offer. If there were only

[1] *Fortune* magazine, New York, 1937.

Gilbert and Sullivan: As Welcome as Ever

The Savoy Season, 1932, seen by Tom-Tit, cartoonist of the Tatler:
Leslie Rands, Charles Goulding, Muriel Dickson, Marjorie Eyre, Sydney Granville, Henry Lytton, Dorothy Gill,
Rowena Ronald

some way of keeping them on this side permanently I humbly suggest to the New Deal that it cancel England's war debt in exchange for the D'Oyly Cartians. We should be much the gainer.

Instead, the D'Oyly Carte Company has done the next best thing by frequent return visits to the U.S.A. Derek Oldham says that President Roosevelt was 'an ardent G. and S. fan'. On the eve of his Inauguration in 1937, 'Sylvia Cecil and I were kept out of the cast (we were playing at the National Theatre, Washington) so that we could go to the White House and sing "Prithee, Pretty Maiden" at the President's Party.'

1929: Back to the Savoy

In 1881 Richard D'Oyly Carte had built the Savoy as a theatre of innovations, as the home of Gilbert and Sullivan opera; in 1929 Rupert D'Oyly Carte rebuilt it with all the latest modern ideas (oddly enough, whereas the father had introduced the queue, the son abolished it—by making every seat bookable), and the operas came back to their old home. A famous critic, Ernest Newman, wrote: 'I can imagine no gayer or more exhilarating frame for the Gilbert and Sullivan operas than the Savoy as it is now. It was a subtle stroke to open with *The Gondoliers*; there is a peculiar richness of blood in the music of this work that makes the new theatre and the new designs and dresses by Mr Charles Ricketts particularly appropriate. In this opulent setting the opera acquires a new vitality.'

[442]

Dorothy Gill, John Dean, Muriel Dickson, Sydney Granville, Darrell Fancourt, Martyn Green

A Socialist government was now in power, and it was no longer necessary for every boy and every gal alive to be a little Liberal or else a little Conservat-*ive*, but many people remarked that whatever the vagaries of our constitution, these Gilbertian entertainments are ageless. For example, while the poses ridiculed in *Patience* have changed, *poseurs* remain.

But though the plays are ageless, the players are not.

In 1933, on the final night of a Savoy season, Sir Henry Lytton bade farewell[1]—it was an emotional occasion when that little man was seen for the last time in the role of Ko-Ko; but the real significance of his long career, and of the grip the Savoy Operas had achieved on all classes, had been registered three years previously when Mr Lloyd George, Britain's ex-Premier, presided over a celebrity-packed luncheon in Lytton's honour at the Savoy Hotel. The Lord Chancellor (Lord Sankey) sent a telegram: 'Sir Henry is the most celebrated Lord Chancellor of our time' and Ll.-G. said that both he and Lytton had been forty years on the stage, but he feared *he* had not given the same satisfaction. 'The first time Sir Henry heard of me was when I put up his income tax twenty-one years ago and then he put me on the list.'

In his reply Sir Henry Lytton admitted that there was a New York critic who had written: 'If Henry Lytton, the comedian from England, is funny then a funeral is a scream.' He also told of a porter on a train in Canada, when they were touring there, who was asked what the average tip was he received. He replied three dollars. On receiving this sum he went into raptures of thanks. 'But why are you so pleased?' asked Lytton. 'Because, sah, you is the only gen'l'man yet who has ever come up to the average.'

Charles Goulding, Sydney Granville

[1] To London audiences. He continued to tour for some while. His last performance of all was at the Gaiety Theatre, Dublin, in 1934, as Jack Point.

A New Life for Grim's Dyke

In 1936 Lady Gilbert and Sir Henry Lytton both passed away. Lady Gilbert was eighty-six. After her death Grim's Dyke was sold. It is now used as a rehabilitation centre for male tuberculosis patients. The extensive rooms and gardens have proved to be a delightful—and highly efficient—centre for a valuable experiment in adapting these men physically and mentally for a return to normal life. During the summer months the lawns, once the setting for Gilbert's lavish garden parties, are constantly occupied by patients playing bowls, croquet, or clock-golf, and at all times of the year the large Music Room is now the scene of darts, table-tennis, billiards, and snooker. Sir William Gilbert's study is a common room, and his bedroom a surgery. Other rooms are now workshops for woodwork, weaving, rug-making, etc.

To preserve old associations the five 'houses' of the Centre have been named Pinafore, Gondoliers, Utopia, Yeomen, and Pirates. Performances of some of the operas have been given by patients and by visiting amateur companies in the Music Room.

OLD SAVOYARDS   *February 8th, 1934.*

L.G. (*after presentation ceremony*): " Well, my dear Lytton, in our time we've both played many parts—for you it's the loving cup—for me it's the bird, look you! "

—*by permission of the 'Daily Express'*

[444]

SIR H. LYTTON PLAYS HIS 'HARDEST PART'

From Our Theatre Correspondent

'GENTLEMEN, I am much touched by this reception."

These, the first lines of Ko-Ko in " The Mikado," were given a deeper meaning on Saturday by Sir Henry Lytton, who, walking on to the historic Savoy stage for the last time, was given a tumultuous welcome.

It was a great occasion. More than 4,000 people had failed to get seats for the final night of the best town season the D'Oyly Carte company has had for years.

LONDON'S FAREWELL

And it was London's farewell to the great little man, who has done so much for Gilbert and Sullivan—and for us.

"This is my most difficult part," said Sir Henry at the end of this memorable evening. "On February 4 next year I complete 50 years on the stage. It has

CENTRE: *Mr Lloyd George presides at a luncheon to Henry Lytton on his knighthood. The toast-master is dressed as Jack Point*

LEFT: *Sir Henry on the day of his farewell performance at the Savoy in 1933, with his successor in the leading roles, Martyn Green*

G.B.S. on Gilbert

Bernard Shaw once described himself as a dramatist who had taken Gilbert's paradoxes seriously. The *Times Literary Supplement*, on the centenary of Gilbert's birth, 1936, commented: 'He meant that while he had seen the absurdity in current institutions, codes, and ideals, as piercingly as Gilbert, and had pilloried it as wittily, he had also had his remedies to propose. After scarifying poor humanity he has always been ready to redirect it on the path to Utopia Unlimited. But in the depths of Gilbert's soul there was only pessimism and the sentimentality that is the pessimist's quicksalve. The sentimentalism is rank in *Broken Hearts*, *Pygmalion and Galatea* and the other forgotten blank-verse plays; the pessimism comes out again and again with a startling cry through the mouth of the most fantastic of his operatic homunculi. 'Submit !' says the mock-inquisitor, Don Alhambra del Bolero, most unexpectedly to Casilda lamenting her unique matrimonial entanglement with the gondoliers—

> Submit to Fate without unseemly wrangle:
> Such complications frequently occur—
> Life is one closely complicated tangle:
> Death is the only true unraveller!

Yet we have only thus to quote a few lines from any of Gilbert's songs to be reminded that if he cannot join the Pantheon where the tragic and grave dramatists are enthroned he may at any rate go to Parnassus with the poets.'

1938: Mikado Film and 'Swing' Mikado

A *Mikado* film was made in colour, with Martyn Green as Ko-Ko, Jean Colin as Yum-Yum, and Kenny Baker as Nanki-Poo. 'With the best will in the world it is difficult to regard the film of *The Mikado* with other than modified rapture,' commented D. Graham Davis in the *Gilbert and Sullivan Journal*.

The film was in the main a 'traditional' presentation of the opera. We have discussed at the beginning of this book whether conventional Gilbert and Sullivan methods can succeed in modern media such as films, radio, and television, and whether in the theatre the stylized presentation conceived by Mr Gilbert in the Hansom Cab Era can continue to appeal to fresh generations of young people attuned to new rhythms of life in the Electronic Era. There was no doubt on this point among the uninhibited producers of two modernized versions of *The Mikado* which appeared in the U.S.A. While the Pinewood film studio in England was turning out its decorous version of the opera with the approval and association of Mr D'Oyly Carte, the Americans threw decorum to the winds and (without his approval or association, this being America) presented the world with *The Swing Mikado*, followed by *The Hot Mikado* in 1939. The latter was jiving merrily in the Hall of Music at the New York World Fair while war was breaking out in Europe.

In *The Hot Mikado* the modernized lyrics to a jazzed-up Sullivan score included this addition to Ko-Ko's little list of Society offenders:

> There's the candid camera addict who takes pictures while you snore,
> All debutantes whose photos get in public prints galore,
> All subway guards who crush your ribs and curse you for your pains,
> And film producers who are sure the public has no brains . . .

These modernized lyrics were by Dave Greggory and William Tracy. Later—

> There's the radio comedian whose jokes are thick with mould,
> And the glamour girl of sixty who refuses to grow old,
> All waiters so superior they make you want to crawl,
> And the guy who when the check arrives will stall, and stall, and stall.
> All men who start each statement with 'Now I'm not prejudiced'—
> I got them on my list, they'll none of 'em be missed.

of the bridegroom, who is a son of Mr. and Mrs. L. McEvoy of Sheridan rd. [TRIBUNE Photo]

Tho 'Swing Mikado' Is Rowdy, You Can Take Aunt Prudence

BY EDWARD BARRY

Imagine Queen Victoria a little tipsy and with her hat askew and have some idea of what this "The Mikado" is lik

"THE SWING MIKADO"

Revival of Negro version of Gilbert Sullivan operetta with swing arrangements by Gentry Warden and choruses by Sammy Dyer. Directed by Harry turn. Presented ... Tuesday even

Frederic Comes of Age

In 1940 that unhappy hero Frederic, apprenticed in infancy to the pirates of Penzance, came of age. Having been so unfortunate as to be born on Leap Year Day, Frederic had for many years been troubled about his age:

> How quaint the ways of paradox!
> At common sense she gaily mocks!
> Though in the usual way,
> Years twenty-one I've been alive,
> Yet reckoning by my natal day,
> I am a little boy of five!

—so he sang when *The Pirates of Penzance* was first produced in 1880. Though Gilbert does not state explicitly the date of Frederic's birth, he does make Frederic sing 'In 1940 I of age shall be.' Frederic's coming of age was therefore celebrated by a performance of this opera by the D'Oyly Carte Company at Streatham Hill Theatre, London, on 29 February, 1940, when his reference to his birthday was widely cheered by an audience that had braved the black-out to attend from far and wide. This paradoxical twenty-first birthday was duly recognized by the BBC which thus showed in wartime a nice sense of British values.

1942 : Sullivan Centenary

In a blacked-out London the centenary of Sullivan's birth was celebrated by a broadcast performance of *The Golden Legend* from the Albert Hall, Sir Henry Wood conducting. It is interesting to read the modern view on this work as expressed by the music critic of *The Times*: 'The cantata starts effectively, but its mood is too consistently vespertinal and its text too prone to bathos to appeal as more than a curiosity to an audience of today.' The BBC celebrations included a performance of *The Gondoliers* and a talk by Dr Thomas F. Dunhill, in which he said: 'This week we are celebrating with mingled gratitude and pride the centenary of the birth of the most popular of all British composers—Arthur Sullivan . . . The truth, as we know now, is that Sullivan was a curious and rather tantalizing mixture of talent and genius. His talent has faded; his genius is for all time. His talent concerned itself with the making of serious music; his genius took wing, and lightly skimmed on the surface of the waters into which his talent plunged.'

Redesigning the Albert Memorial

Mr Peter Goffin's new scenery and dresses for *The Yeomen of the Guard* had made their début at Edinburgh at Christmas 1939, but owing to the war it was not until the late forties that the public generally realized what a transformation had taken place. Not only were the designs quite different from The Tradition, they were significant of the completely new approach which has been outlined in the first chapter of this book. It was applied again to Mr Goffin's new sets for *The Mikado* (1952) and to Mr James Wade's designs for *Princess Ida* (1954): the idea that the designer's job is not merely to add a pretty decoration to the play (as it was in Victorian times) but to share and develop its mood and plot.

Mr Peter Goffin had designed the London productions of many plays, from Shakespeare to Shaw and T. S. Eliot, when he was invited by Mr Rupert D'Oyly Carte to redesign *The Yeomen of the Guard*. He says he felt as if he had been asked to redesign the Albert Memorial: 'Having previously regarded the unique world of the Gilbert and Sullivan opera as a fixed star in a changing theatrical firmament, the possibility of altering any of its features had hardly occurred to me. In common with many others, I had supposed that its continuing life depended on the perfect preservation of the physical form in which it had been realized three-quarters of a century ago. Here was something already shaped and determined, always on view, to be revered, ridiculed, or merely ignored.'[1] On the contrary, Mr Goffin found that in the twenty years between the wars there had been fourteen new productions with fresh costumes and scenery, but he makes the point that it was not until Charles Ricketts audaciously redressed *The Mikado* that the costumes were regarded as anything more than a piece of decoration.

[1] 'Designing for Gilbert and Sullivan', by Peter Goffin, *The Studio*, June, 1955.

Peter Goffin who
redesigned 'The Yeomen' and 'The Mikado'

Isidore Godfrey
musical director, D'Oyly Carte Company

New scenery for 'The Mikado' in 1953 by Peter Goffin

In Gilbert's original 1888 production of *The Yeomen of the Guard* both acts were set on Tower Green, with the great square block of the White Tower painted on the backcloth. In the new Goffin design this direct representation of the Tower dominating the opera has disappeared (the old and the new are illustrated on pages 18 and 19). Goffin has a pictorial drop curtain on view during the playing of the overture (*see* colour plate facing page 304). 'By this,' he writes, 'I suggested something of the shape and colour of things to come, and opened the correspondence between sight and sound. Moreover, having thus established the physical nature of the entire scene in advance, I freed myself from the restriction of actual representation in the form of the stage setting itself.'

The Press gave Mr Goffin's revolution a mixed reception. Some of the popular papers were hostile. Typical of their comments was the *Daily Herald*'s reference to 'a Picasso tree and a cement suggestion of the Mersey Tunnel'. The critic hoped that 'the characterless décor' might be scrapped. *The Scotsman* declared that the designer had introduced 'almost another dimension' into Gilbert and Sullivan opera: 'There is less of the superficial tinkle and make-believe of the other plays, and certainly a closer approach to artistic reality.' *The Times*, the *Observer*, and the *Daily Telegraph* hailed the innovation with modified rapture, and the critic of *Punch* wrote a notice (14 February, 1940) which has stood the test of time as a piece of good judgment:

'Vandalism!' hissed an old lady down the back of my neck.

'How dare they!' came a growl on my left in the tone you or I would use if we heard someone had bombed the Uffizi or put on a can-can show in the crypt of St Paul's.

Such fevered resentment was aroused because the D'Oyly Carte Company have scrapped their old sets. Personally I think they have done very well. I have always felt there has been far too little arson in the storerooms of opera companies. Light or heavy, opera is the bastard of the arts, and if its parentage is to be forgotten it needs all the help it can get from an attractive appearance; to go on clothing it according to the conventions of the past is only to emphasize its theatrical awkwardness and suggest it is too out of date to be capable of expression in current terms.

The 1940's: Renaissance Again

After World War II, Rupert D'Oyly Carte had to set about building up the operas again, though they had not sunk into quite such a decline as that during the first war. Even in the dark hour of 1941 there was a season at the Savoy—'to show Hitler', as *The Times* remarked, 'that London is still itself'. When one of Hitler's bombs found a home among the scenery and costumes it was *Ruddigore, or The Witch's Curse* that suffered most and consequently the unlucky opera did not reappear until 1948.

Darrell Fancourt, O.B.E.
died 1953

The long war years had taken a span out of our lives, and when peace came a new generation had arisen who knew next to nothing of the Gilbert and Sullivan operas, but very soon there were all the signs of a new renaissance, and when the BBC broadcast its *Gilbert and Sullivan* radio-biography over a period of six weeks in 1947 (repeated in 1949 and in 1956) there was no mistake that the wonderful spell still held its magic over millions of people, for the BBC had one of the most enthusiastic mails on record. Letters came in from all over the world. Such a comment as this was typical:

'Listening to the broadcasts in these anxious and humiliating days was like warming oneself at a fire on a cold night—these recollections of a period when Britain really did set the world ablaze.'

Puck put a girdle round the world in Shakespeare's imagination. Gilbert and Sullivan have beaten all imagination by doing so in reality, and by holding the globe girdled in their bond of fun through all these changing years. In 1947 the D'Oyly Carte company made its first post-war visit to the U.S.A. 'My outstanding recollection,' says Martyn Green, 'is of my first entrance as Ko-Ko on our opening night in New York after nine years absence—to be greeted with a reception that left me breathless with its enthusiasm and sincerity.'

The English company has visited America several times since. The winter tour of 1955–6 marked the seventy-fifth anniversary of the first Gilbert and Sullivan visit to North America in 1880—an outstanding record, surely, in all theatrical history.

In England, on the rising post-war tide of the operas, came the sad and sudden news of the death at the Savoy Hotel of Rupert D'Oyly Carte, aged seventy-one, in 1948. The control of his opera interests succeeded to his daughter, Bridget. Thus, for the second time in this history it fell to a woman member of the Carte dynasty— in 1901 Helen, in 1948 Bridget—to take full control over the operas which have become so phenomenal a piece of show business.

What They Left

In 1948 Mr Rupert D'Oyly Carte left	£288,436
1913 Mrs Richard D'Oyly Carte (Helen Lenoir)..	£117,670
1911 Sir W. S. Gilbert	£111,971
1901 Mr Richard D'Oyly Carte	£240,817
1900 Sir Arthur Sullivan	£54,527

It will be realized that not all of this money was made from the operas. Considerable sums were earned by Sullivan and Gilbert independently, and the D'Oyly Cartes have developed around the Savoy Hotel a wealthy array of hotels and other properties; nevertheless, these figures make an astounding contrast with the modest circumstances of Gilbert, Sullivan, and Carte when they were first working together—when in 1877 Carte paid the other two a fee of six guineas a performance for *The Sorcerer*.

Darrell Fancourt

The D'Oyly Carte Company was appearing at Sadler's Wells Theatre, London, for the Coronation Season, 1953, when it was announced that Darrell Fancourt (who had received the O.B.E. in the Coronation Honours) would give his farewell performance. He was sixty-five years of age; he had joined the Company in 1920, coming to it from the concert stage (his only previous stage experience had been in Sir Thomas Beecham's Covent Garden production of *Prince Igor* in 1919). Fancourt stayed with D'Oyly Carte thirty-three years. He had a magnificent voice and a magnetic stage presence and it was in his macabre interpretation of the role of the Mikado that he intended to leave the stage on 1 August. He fell ill a few days before the promised last appearance and died on 29 August. It was said that he had played the part of the Mikado more than 3,000 times.

A New Comedian and a New Spirit

In 1951 Martyn Green left the D'Oyly Carte Company, seeking new pastures in America. Together with Ella Halman and Radley Flynn, he joined S. M. Chartock's newly-formed Gilbert and Sullivan Company in the U.S.A. That excellent tenor Thomas Round had also left the company, so Miss D'Oyly Carte had to set about rebuilding it. She found in Peter Pratt a leading comedian who is a worthy successor to Grossmith and Lytton. Others who made their mark in the fifties included Ann Drummond-Grant, Leonard Osborn, Neville Griffiths, Muriel Harding, Joan Gillingham, Joyce Wright, Fisher Morgan, and Donald Adams.

The London *Sunday Times* detected in 1953 signs of a new spirit blowing through the operas, 'so that these bizarre and charming entertainments may now be seen with pleasure, which has certainly not been the case for some years. . . . Standards of singing have improved, comic business has been mercifully simplified.' That year *The Mikado* was given new sets by Peter Goffin.

Another sign of a new spirit was the appointment of Robert Gibson as Director of Production. Mr Gibson started his musical career as a Manchester Cathedral choirboy and his acting career in repertory companies. For a time he was in America as stage manager at Radio City Music Hall, New York, and later as Professor of Drama at Oberlin College. His first newly-realized Gilbert and Sullivan opera appeared in 1954—*Princess Ida*.

At Shepperton film studios during the making of 'The Story of Gilbert and Sullivan'. RIGHT: *Miss Bridget D'Oyly Carte. Facing her: Miss Eileen Herlie in the role of Mrs Richard D'Oyly Carte. From the left: Mr Sidney Gilliat, director; Mr Peter Finch as Richard D'Oyly Carte; Mr Leslie Baily who collaborated with Mr Gilliat in the film script*

And now in Technicolor

In 1953 Sir Alexander Korda, head of London Film Productions, sponsored a large scale *Story of Gilbert and Sullivan*, produced by Launder and Gilliat at Shepperton Studios, and directed by one of England's leading comedy-film experts, Sidney Gilliat. It was a lavish picture in Technicolor, with Robert Morley as Gilbert and Maurice Evans as Sullivan. It did not purport to be a true documentary: excerpts from the operas were threaded on a light-hearted story by Sidney Gilliat and Leslie Baily which was based (but only based) on fact. The script writers were scolded by the purists but there are many respectable precedents for such artistic licence, from Laurence Housman's dramatizations based on the life of Queen Victoria to the historical plays of Shakespeare.

The Gilbert Estate

Sir William Gilbert's heiress, Miss Nancy McIntosh, died in 1954, aged eighty, leaving the bulk of her estate to the Royal General Theatrical Fund Association. A portrait of Sir William by Sir Hubert Herkomer she bequeathed, as W.S.G. wished, to the Garrick Club. His desk, chair, and piano are now in the London Museum. His surviving diaries, letters and plot books were purchased by the British Museum.

The above theatrical charity, which provides annuities for stage people in their old age and in time of unemployment, does *not* benefit from performances of the Gilbert and Sullivan operas. This is because on the death of Lady Gilbert in 1936 Mr Rupert D'Oyly Carte exercised an option to purchase outright the exclusive *performing rights* of the operas. This right will belong to the D'Oyly Carte Opera Company until the copyright expires in 1961.

Miss McIntosh derived income from other licences granted by Sir William Gilbert to various firms who publish his opera libretti, and to the publishers of his *Bab Ballads* and his plays, and from broadcasting, television, and cinema rights: this income now goes to the Royal General Theatrical Fund Association.

The last close personal link with Gilbert has thus been broken. But the stories about him seem to be inexhaustible. Since *The Gilbert & Sullivan Book* was first published in 1952 the author has had the privilege of meeting a number of people whose memories of him bear on the history that has been told in these pages. One of these is Mrs Gielgud, daughter of Kate Terry and mother of Val and Sir John Gielgud. She was born in 1868 at Moray Lodge, the house of her father Arthur James Lewis where in the previous year, 1867, the first of young Arthur Sullivan's comic operettas, *Cox and Box*, had been performed by the Moray Minstrels.[1]

Mrs Gielgud recalls the children's parties at Mr and Mrs Gilbert's house: 'Mr Gilbert was always the life and soul of the party. I remember one Christmas when he was most excited about a new toy of his. It was just after the Savoy Theatre had been opened with its wonderful new electric light and at the party instead of candles the Christmas tree was covered with electric lamps. How excited we were, clamouring to switch the new illumination on and off at the wall switch. I remember, too, going behind the scenes at the Savoy and seeing how the fairies carried batteries under their dresses for the electric stars on their wands. This was a great innovation and very pretty.'

And then there is Julia Neilson (Mrs Julia Neilson-Terry). We have already told how Gilbert introduced Miss Neilson to the stage as his own protégée when she was twenty years of age and how he lambasted the critics for their ungenerous attitude to a beginner.[2] In 1955, when she was eighty-seven years of age, the author called upon her at her London home.

'Gilbert as a producer could be quite ruthless,' she said. 'He did not suffer fools gladly. But he could also be most generous and was particularly helpful to beginners

[1] *See* p. 88.   [2] *See* p. 318.

like me, putting one at one's ease with a kind remark or a joke. At rehearsal of one of his plays I had to say "Stay, stay" but in my excitement I said "Stay, stay! Stay, stay!"'

' "No, my dear," Gilbert cut in, "one pair of stays, not two".'

The Mikado as a Ballet

The Ballet Russe de Monte Carlo presented *The Mikado* as a ballet in 1955, choreography by Antonia Cobos, orchestration by Vittorio Rieti. The *New York Herald Tribune* was one of several journals which were severely critical: 'The company's new production is set to some of Sullivan's most engaging airs, but the wit of Gilbert is wholly absent.'

Mr Louis Weissman, who was present at the first New York performance at the Lewishon Stadium, tells us that the re-orchestrated music seemed too coarse in style for Sullivan's delicate tunes, and he queries how successfully such jokes as Gilbert's can ever be conveyed by miming, but he adds this reflection: 'An interesting point is that *Gaîté Parisienne*, arranged from Offenbach's music by Manuel Rosenthal, shared the same programme and proved what could be done with the music if the arranger is a musician of talent. *Gaîté Parisienne* has been a strong favourite since it was written and there is no reason why *The Mikado* couldn't be a hit ballet if it were approached by someone who knew Sullivan's musical style well enough to make him sparkle, as Mackerras did in *Pineapple Poll*. There is room for specula-

*Three little maids from school in the
Monte Carlo Ballet*

tion here about the ballet possibilities of other Gilbert and Sullivan operas. What might an imaginative choreographer and a gifted arranger make of *Iolanthe* or *Ruddigore*?'

In Concert Hall and on TV

In 1955 a Danish version of *H.M.S. Pinafore* was introduced into the repertory of the Royal Theatre, Copenhagen. In 1956–7, in London, Mr Peter Goffin made new stage and costume designs for *Patience*.

As time goes on the boundaries of Gilbert and Sullivan widen with recreative energy, rather than shrivel with age. The D'Oyly Carte Company, perhaps to entrench itself even more thoroughly in public favour before the expiry of the Gilbert copyright in 1961, has been tending to loosen its monopolistic hold on the operas.

Rather more broadcasting and television has been permitted; in the 1955 BBC Promenade Concert Season half of one evening's programme was devoted to items from the operas, conducted by Sir Malcolm Sargent. Apart from a sprinkling of new works, the Proms are devoted to the classics of music; the implied compliment to Sullivan is handsome, if overdue. We have earlier referred to the remarkable notice of this concert written by Mr Neville Cardus in the *Manchester Guardian*.[1] Some further quotation is worth making now, as illustrating the increasing rather than diminishing stature of Sullivan. After referring to the 'vile abuse of Sullivan's orchestration' in theatre productions, which has too often degraded his name, and to the revelation of its true quality when the music is in the hands of such musicians as Sir Malcolm and the BBC Symphony Orchestra, Mr Cardus writes:

> The astonishing fact about Sullivan's tunes is that no matter how long one has lived with them, they are constantly coming fresh to the ear with a distinction one has not altogether expected. Sir Malcolm's conducting missed not a point. It revealed those qualities of Sullivan which place him in the front of all composers of comic opera. He is superior in orchestration to Johann Strauss and also in range of comic characterization. He lacks the sauciness and raciness of Offenbach, the sensuous allurements of Lehar and Strauss; but he is ahead of all three in craftsmanship, variety of invention, graciousness, and the gentle touch of pathos. His occasional rum-ti-tum rhythms and echoes of the pew and the Victorian hymn-book are forgotten as we listen to the best of him perfectly performed.

Amateur Productions

One of the most remarkable aspects of the Gilbert and Sullivan operas is their unflagging appeal to amateur operatic societies. In recent years American 'musicals' with big box-office reputations have attracted the attention of amateurs but in spite of this competition something like 500 amateur companies in Britain produce one or more of the Gilbert and Sullivan works every year—truly a phenomenal figure.

Because all such performances must (until 1961) be licensed by the D'Oyly Carte Opera Company it is possible to keep a check on the number of amateur performances. It would be interesting to compare the 'G. & S.' 500-a-year with the number of amateur productions of Shakespeare, but of course the Bard is out of copyright and no statistics are kept.

Additionally there are many amateur performances in other parts of the English-speaking world. During the unrest in Cyprus (1956) an army unit on service there staged *The Pirates of Penzance*, and the officer-producer afterwards wrote to Miss Bridget D'Oyly Carte: 'In spite of all difficulties we confounded the pessimists by staging three performances in a lucky clear week. A number of people told me they had come through "a sense of duty" but had been thoroughly captivated by the opera. A Scots

[1] See p. 22.

[456]

D'Oyly Carte principals in the nineteen fifties: Fisher Morgan as the Sergeant of Police (Pirates of Penzance); Donald Adams as the Mikado; Peter Pratt as the Lord Chancellor (Iolanthe)

lady who "loathed Gilbert and Sullivan" (never having seen any of the operas) came on all three nights and is now in the process of booking to see all the operas on her return to Britain. I should, on behalf of our whole company, like to thank you most sincerely for the personal interest you have shown in our efforts, and the encouragement, assistance and kindness you have extended to us. We have all been given an ever-fresh interest and occupation for five months, at a time when diversion from the eternal round of duty was otherwise only too lacking, and judging from their comments our audience enjoyed thoroughly a form of entertainment unique in Cyprus at any time.'

During the occupation of the Channel Islands by the Germans in the late war the amateurs in Jersey managed to produce *The Pirates*, with the Major-General in a Jersey militia officer's ancient uniform without a sword (verboten). Many 'G. & S.' operas were played by Britishers in enemy prisoner-of-war camps.

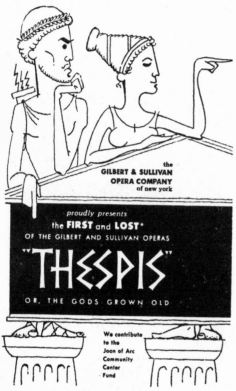

*Programme cover, 'Thespis'
revival, 1953*

Thespis Revived

The first and least known of the operas, *Thespis*, was revived in 1953 through the enterprise of The Gilbert and Sullivan Opera Company of New York, a lively amateur organization, directed by Mrs Ada Birenbaum. Sullivan's music for *Thespis* having disappeared (apart from two numbers),[1] the New York Company provided new music for Gilbert's libretto; it was composed by Frank Miller, then the first 'cello of the NBC Symphony Orchestra, and an experienced conductor of Gilbert and Sullivan productions. The *New York Times* critic described it as a 'very clever attempt' to recreate the lost opera.

So, on amateur and professional stage, in concert hall, ballet, radio, films, and television the works of W. S. Gilbert and Arthur Sullivan take on new forms. They have become not merely what is called 'show business', not only a tradition, but a part of the culture of the English-speaking peoples. It is a bumper harvest from the seed that was sown with *Thespis* in 1871.

[1] See p. 109.

When, in 1951, the operas came back to their old home, the Savoy Theatre, for the Festival of Britain, Sir Malcolm Sargent returned to his old love as their director of music, sharing the conductorship with the permanent conductor, Isidore Godfrey. That a symphonic conductor of front rank like Sir Malcolm should lend his baton to these too-often disparaged works was a healthy reminder of their true quality. 'The finest operas Britain has produced,' wrote Stephen Williams in the London *Evening News*. 'Any Festival of Britain would be ridiculously incomplete without them.'

The place that Sir William Gilbert and Sir Arthur Sullivan have found in history lies in the fact that the entire English-speaking world would be ridiculously incomplete without them.

It is a happy bondage in which Gilbert and Sullivan hold the world, and, apparently, it is everlasting.

ACKNOWLEDGEMENTS

Sir Newman Flower was the godfather of this book, and to him I owe a great deal. After my BBC biography of Gilbert and Sullivan he suggested that it should be expanded and published in more permanent form than the radio offers. As co-author of the official biography of Sir Arthur Sullivan,[1] he facilitated my access to the Sullivan diaries. Nor could I have written anything as comprehensive as this book aims to be without the collaboration of Mrs Elena Bashford, Miss Bridget D'Oyly Carte, the late Miss McIntosh, Mr Louis Weissman and Mr Reginald Allen, of New York, and Mr D. Graham Davis, the editor of *The Gilbert and Sullivan Journal*, who has been most helpful in the checking of innumerable facts. A number of quotations have been taken from documents in Mr Reginald Allen's Gilbert and Sullivan collection, now in the Pierpont Morgan Library, New York.

For illustrations I thank particularly the Raymond Mander and Joe Mitchenson Theatre Collection, the Enthoven Collection at the Victoria and Albert Museum, the City Libraries of Leeds and Birmingham, the Gilbert and Sullivan Society (of London), and the D'Oyly Carte Opera Company.

To Sir Malcolm Sargent, Mr Stanley Parker, Mr Frederick Lloyd, Mr Howard G. Dunkley, Mr F. B. Cockburn, and Mrs Mary Carter (niece of Sir William Gilbert) I am especially indebted for help and advice.

So far as possible I have given in the text the sources of quotations, but I should like to acknowledge here my general debt of gratitude to the publishers, authors, and authors' representatives who have given permission for the use of passages from copyright works.

[1] *Sir Arthur Sullivan*, by Herbert Sullivan and Newman Flower (Cassell), 1927.

INDEX

NOTE: *In this index G = Gilbert and S = Sullivan; italic figures refer to illustrations*

Edinburgh, 448

Edinburgh, Alfred Duke of, 99, 117, 118, 134, 160, 183, 196, 208, 221 and n., 244, 271, 312, 358, 399

Edinburgh, Alexandrovna Duchess of, 117, 118 and n., 271

Edward VII, 420. *See also* Wales, Prince of

Edwardes, George, 283, 385, 410, 429

Egypt, 222, 402, 407

Ehrlich, Professor, 346

Elburn, Beatrice, *282*

Eldon Road, Kensington, 71

Electric light, first used in theatre, 214–15, 216, 219, 231, 235, 236.

Electrical Times, 216

Elgar, Sir Edward, 94, 292, 396, 410

Elgar-Blake, Carice, 292

Elliott, Maxine, 408

Elliott, L., *102*

Emerald Isle, The (Sullivan), *384*, 395, *401*, 406

Emery, Winifred (Mrs Cyril Maude), 408

Engaged (Gilbert), 134

Erlanger Theatre, Chicago, *428*

Ervine, St John, 142

Essex Villas, Kensington, 71

Eugénie, Empress, 38, 39, 104, 107

Evans, Maurice, *383, 453*

Everard, Miss, 161

Everett, C. R., 29

Evett, Robert, *399*

Exeter, 231

Eyes and No Eyes (Gilbert), 116

Eyre, Marjorie, *131, 168, 282, 286, 437, 442*

Fairy's Dilemma, The (Gilbert), 410

Fallen Fairies (Gilbert), 113, 425–6

Fancourt, Darrell, *96, 180, 222, 260, 428, 434, 439, 443, 451, 452*

Farren, Nellie, 111, *399*

Far West, The (Russell), 30

Feast of Roses overture (Sullivan), 48

Festival of Britain (1951), 25, *40, 459*

Fifth Avenue Theatre, New York, 9, 176, 181, 184, 280–1

Film versions, 5, 7, 446, 454

Finch, Peter, *214, 453*

Fine, Sylvia, 14–16

Fisher, Lord, 434

Fledermaus, Die (Strauss), 119

Fleet, 314

Flower, Sir Newman, 86 and n., 401

Flynn, Radley, *168, 260, 452*

Foggerty's Fairy (Gilbert), 386

Forbes-Robertson, Sir Johnston, 211

Ford, Ernest, 134, 363

Foresters, The (Tennyson), S's music to, 373

Fortescue, Miss, *103*, 228

Fortune, 405, 441

Forty Thieves (pantomime), 164, *166*

Foster, Stephen, 30

Frampton, Sir George, *433*

Francillon, F. E., 52

Francillon, R. E., 52, 202

Fry, C. B., 56

Fulham, 145, 230

Fun, G's work in, 39, 53, 54, 55, 67, 76, 77, 89, 101, 110, *120*, 125, 226

Fushimi, Prince Sadanaru, 416, 418

Gaîte Parisienne (Rosenthal), 455

Gaiety Theatre, 104 and n., 106, 107, 110–11, 119, 160n., 164, 213, 214, 283, 305, 309–10, 385, 395

Gaiety Theatre, Dublin, 443n.

Ganz, William, 93–4

Gardiner, Evelyn, *217, 225*

Garrick Club, 454

Garrick Theatre, 334, 410

Gaskell, Mrs, 62

Gast, Peter, 278

Gast, William, 311

Gay, John, 64

Gelsthorpe, Blossom, *282*

George V, 222

German, Sir Edward, 251, *384*, 406, 410, 425

Germany, 5, 47–52, 119, 278–80, 346, 387

Gibson, Robert, 20, 452

Gielgud, Sir John, 88, 454

Gielgud, Kate Terry, 88, 408, 454

Gielgud, Val, 88, 454

Gilbert family, 29, 37

Gilbert, Anne (mother), 27, 44

Gilbert, Sir William S., 2, 38, 61, 68, 139, 220, 364, 373, 404; on 'gagging' and stage business, 11–14; birth and ancestry, 27–9; education, 29–30, 36–7; first literary effort, 38–9; at King's College, 41–2; in Education Dept. of Privy Council, 44, 46; first appearance in print, 44; joins volunteers, 46; becomes barrister, 46; contributes to *Fun*, 53, 55, 67, 76, 101, 110, *120*, 125, 226; scores success with *Bab Ballads*, 56–7; writes first burlesque, 60, 67; his 'doodles', 69–71, 134; marries Lucy Turner, 71; attracts attention as dramatist, 72 *et seq.*; illustrates father's book, 78, 92; reviews *Cox and Box*, 89; meets S, 98, 100;